Winchester Bibliographies of 20th Century Writers

W. H. DAVIES
a bibliography

Sylvia Harlow is the proprietor of Tiger Books. An antiquarian bookseller she specialises in literature published from the 17th–20th century. She combines this with publishing her own bibliographic checklists on 19th-century authors. Sylvia Harlow lives in East Kent with her husband and two cats.

Mr and Mrs W. H. Davies
at Nailsworth, Gloucestershire, in 1935

W.H. DAVIES
a bibliography

by Sylvia Harlow

ST PAUL'S BIBLIOGRAPHIES · WINCHESTER

OAK KNOLL BOOKS · NEW CASTLE · DELAWARE
1993

First published in 1993 by St Paul's Bibliographies,
West End House, 1 Step Terrace, Winchester, UK
as part of the *Winchester Bibliographies of 20th Century Writers*

Published in North and South America by
Oak Knoll Books, 414 Delaware Street,
New Castle, DE 19720, USA

British Library Cataloguing in Publication Data

A catalogue record for this book is available from the British Library

Library of Congress Cataloging-in-Publication Data

Harlow, Sylvia, 1940–
    A bibliography of W.H. Davies / by Sylvia Harlow.
       p.   cm.—(Winchester bibliographies of 20th century writers)
    Includes index.
    ISBN 0-938768-43-3 (USA)
       1. Davies, W. H. (William Henry), 1871–1940—Bibliography.
I. Title. II. Series.
Z8218.8.H37   1993
[PR6007.A8]
016.821'912—dc20 93–8210

ISBN (UK) 1-873040-00-8—ISBN (USA) 0-938768-43-3

Printed in Great Britain by The Alden Press Ltd, Oxford

FOR MY
FATHER

Contents

Illustrations

With the exception of the frontispiece and the dust-jacket of
A Poet's Pilgrimage, all illustrations are reproduced by courtesy of
the British Library

Introduction

To those familiar with the work of W. H. Davies it will not come as a surprise to learn that *The Autobiography of a Super-Tramp (A3)*, first published in 1908, is still in print. In fact, to June 1992 54,727 copies of the latest paperback edition *(A3yy)* – the 55th edition/ impression, had been sold.

The resurgence of interest in this poet began in 1980 when *Young Emma (A52)* was published – forty years after his death (26 September 1940). The long-lost manuscript had been rediscovered by Jonathan Cape and, as both the primary actors in the story were deceased (Mrs Helen Matilda Davies died in 1979 and there were no children from the marriage) they decided to publish. WHD had had misgivings about publication from the beginning and eventually asked Jonathan Cape to destroy their copy of the manuscript (see notes A52). The manuscript had first been offered for publication in 1924 but, acting on the advice of George Bernard Shaw, Jonathan Cape decided not to publish as this clearly autobiographical work cast an unfavourable light on its two major characters, WHD and his wife Helen. In 1980 and 1981 *Young Emma (A52)* was reviewed world-wide and generated new interest in its author. Then, in 1985, Oxford University Press published *Selected Poems: W. H. Davies* chosen by Jonathan Barker *(A53)* which included poems from *The Soul's Destroyer and Other Poems (A1)* reprinted for the first time in eighty years, and at the same time they published new editions of *The Autobiography of a Super-Tramp (A3yy)* and *Later Days (A26h)*.

A self-educated man, WHD left school in 1885 at the age of fourteen and tramped in the USA in his early years. He only became a serious writer at the age of twenty-eight. From a bibliographical point of view he is extremely interesting for at the height of his popularity he was very good at maximising the publication of his work. Many of his poems were reprinted again and again, on occasions with minor (or sometimes major) textual changes, including the re-arrangement of verses and frequently, under different titles. This is reflected in the title/ first line index.

WHD's usual practice was to publish his poems in periodicals and later in book form; textual changes were often made between editions. I have identified many of these in Section A. In the course of my research I was privileged to be allowed to study the private collection of books and manuscripts known as the Helen Davies Bequest (HDB). This is WHD's own collection of his books and manuscripts. I have included details of the textual changes I found in these manuscripts because they reveal WHD's creative process; changes made between editions are essential bibliographical reading for librarians and collectors.

In this bibliography I have tried to trace the publishing history of his works, WHD's original contributions to periodicals (section C); the inclusion of his works in anthologies (section D) and by the BBC in broadcasting (section E); in addition to articles and books about him (section F). In order to avoid confusion in Section A I have not standardised terminology but have used the publishers' own terms when listing editions and impressions. The title-pages are described in quasi-facsimile and are, as far as possible, accurately represented using upper and lower case, italics and underline where originally used. WHD's inscriptions in his presentation copies are faithfully transcribed. It is interesting to note that he always added his full signature in brackets even in copies presented to his wife, Helen. This shows a powerful ego in someone who preferred to be considered 'reflective' in his attitude to life.

WHD enjoyed broadcasting and was involved in the early days of the BBC's Daventry Experimental Broadcasting Station. Although, currently, the BBC's written archives do not extend beyond 1980 it is interesting to note that the work of this poet, both poetry and prose, has been used extensively in broadcasting programmes spanning 53 years.

Although he was nowhere as prolific as his peers I am sure that WHD would prefer to be remembered for the quality rather than the quantity of his work. From my point of view I have very much enjoyed working with both his written and recorded work and hope that others will be as fascinated as I have been. Unfortunately, from reviews and other sources, I am aware of editions of his works that I have been unable to trace. This applies particularly to American publications. Any further information concerning these, in addition to corrections and additions, would be most welcome.

It is important to note that the Helen to whom the books in the HDB collection are inscribed was his wife, Helen Matilda Davies and not Helen Thomas the wife of Edward Thomas, who was a good friend of WHD.

Finally, in the course of my research I discovered a book of poems by William Henry Davies entitled *Autumn Leaves*, published by E A Vidler, Melbourne, Australia in 1926 (in the holding of New York Public Library, USA) and listed in the National Union Catalogue under WHD. Close examination of the contents of this book, in addition to discussion and correspondence, in particular with Jane La Scala, Director Executive Services, the State Library of Victoria, Melbourne, Victoria, reveal that this work is that of another William Henry Davies.

Sylvia Harlow
March 1993

Acknowledgements

No bibliography is possible without the support of others and this is no exception. I am indebted to so many that this list may not be exhaustive but I will try.

My special thanks are due to Peter Flavell in whose keeping is W. H. Davies' own collection of books and manuscripts (Helen Davies Bequest (HDB)). They were cared for until her death in 1979 by his wife, Mrs Helen Matilda Davies. And to Michael Perkin and Robert Cross without whose guidance and support this book would definitely not have been published.

Inevitably most of my time has been spent in the many libraries with W. H. Davies collections and these include:

1 British Library, London where the staff were particularly patient
2 Harry Ransom Humanities Research Centre, University of Texas, Austin, Texas, USA (HRHRC) – my special thanks to Cathy Henderson, Research Librarian, for her advice and guidance
3 Newport Central Library, Newport, Gwent (NL) – special thanks to Susan Pugh whose enthusiastic support was very much appreciated
4 University of Reading Library, Reading, Berks – grateful thanks to David Nott, Special Collections Librarian, for his help with the Finzi collection (RUL, Finzi)

Other libraries from whom I have had much appreciated support include the University of Cambridge Library, the University of Kent Library, Canterbury, Colindale Newspaper Library, Edinburgh City Library, the National Library of Scotland, Edinburgh, Sevenoaks Public Library, Kent and the State Library of Victoria, Melbourne, Australia.

For information on W. H. Davies' broadcasting activities and the use of his work in broadcasting programmes my thanks are due to the BBC Written Archives Centre, Caversham, Berks, in particular Neil Somerville for his patience and endurance.

For W. H. Davies' publishing history my thanks to his publishers and in particular to Messrs Jonathan Cape who allowed me access to their archives at Reading University Library (here special thanks to Michael Bott, Keeper of Archives and Manuscripts). W. H. Davies' other publishers include Duckworth & Co, the Medici Society, Faber, Oxford University Press and Methuen, all of whom helped.

My grateful thanks are also due to Zoe Powell and Norman Phillips, relatives of W. H. Davies, for their help and advice.

And finally, my thanks and appreciation to all my long-suffering colleagues and helpers, especially Brian Butler, Monica Galton, Chris Hodgkinson, Janet Lamb, Stephanie Main, Ian Rennie and Richard Valentine whose help has sustained me and kept me sane.

Abbreviations

BBC	British Broadcasting Corporation
BFEBS	British Forces Educational Broadcasting Service
BL	British Library, London
CH	Chris Hodgkinson
GMT	Greenwich Mean Time
HDB	Helen Davies Bequest
HRHRC	Harry Ransom Humanities Research Center, University of Texas at Austin, Texas, USA
JG	John Galton
NL	Newport Central Library, John Frost Square, Kingsway, Newport, Gwent, NP9 1PA
OUP	Oxford University Press
RNIB	Royal National Institute for the Blind
RUL	University of Reading Library, Whiteknights, Reading, RG6 2AE
RUL, Finzi	Finzi Collection, University of Reading Library
RV	Richard Valentine
SH	Sylvia Harlow
SL	Sevenoaks Library, Sevenoaks, Kent
TLS	*The Times Literary Supplement*
WHD	W. H. Davies

A chronology of events
in the life and work of W. H. Davies

(The reference sources for the majority of this information are *W. H. Davies: A Critical Biography (F324)* by Richard Stonesifer, *Writers of Wales: W. H. Davies (F345)* by Lawrence W. Hockey and *W. H. Davies: Selected Poems (A53)* chosen by Jonathan Barker to all of whom acknowledgement is due.)

1871 20 April: WHD born at Church House Inn, 14 Portland Street, Newport (3 July 1871 at 6 Portland Street according to Lawrence W. Hockey)

1874 Matilda Davies (sister) born
      November: Francis Davies (father) dies aged 31 leaving three children under the age of five years: Francis Gomer Boase, William Henry and Matilda

1875 September: Mary Ann Davies (mother) remarries and becomes Mrs Joseph Hill (the three children are adopted by their inn-keeping grandparents, Captain and Lydia Davies, and live with them)

1879 Captain Davies surrenders his publican's licence and retires with his 'family' to 38 Raglan Street and later to Upper Lewis Street, Newport
      attends Temple Street School

1883 moves to Alexandra Road School and joins a gang of juvenile delinquents

1884 25 January: report in *Monmouthshire Merlin and South Wales Advertiser (F1)* about five boys (including WHD) charged with stealing handbags

1885 writes his first poem, 'Death'
      leaves Alexandra Road School and works for an ironmonger

1886 May: Captain Davies (paternal grandfather) dies
      25 November: signs 5-year apprenticeship papers for picture-framing
      recites poem 'A Stormscape' at 'Mutual Improvement Class'

1887 27 February: 'A Stormscape' (C1) printed in *Monmouthshire Merlin and South Wales Advertiser*
      presents paper entitled 'In Defence of the Stage' to 'Mutual Improvement Class'

1891 completes apprenticeship
      first experience of doss-houses in London

1892 now a drunkard, experiences taverns and brothels of Bristol

1893 March: Mrs Lydia Davies (paternal grandmother) dies and leaves him small weekly income
      returns to Newport (from Bristol) to live with his mother (Mary Ann Hill) and her second family
      June: sets sail for America (from Liverpool), arrives in New York and commences his tramping days

1

meets Brum (a professional tramp) in the Long Island Sound and
learns about 'beating one's way' (stealing rides on trains)
serves 30-day jail sentence for vagrancy in New Haven
'beats' his way to Michigan with Brum planning to spend winter
voluntarily in jails

1894   April: WHD and Brum are released from jail; they then pick fruit on a
farm near St Joseph, Michigan
meets Australian Red (another professional tramp) in Chicago and
'beats' his way to Baltimore with him
returns to Liverpool, and after a few days sets out for Baltimore again,
arriving in October
returns to Glasgow; spends some time in London, staying in
Southwark

1895
1897 } tramping in the USA

1898   spends summer picking fruit in Illinois
October: leaves Chicago for Baltimore in order to return to England
but then meets Australian Red again
works his way back to Liverpool on a boat and returns to Newport

1899   wanders in London and reads about fortunes to be made in Klondike
gold rush
travels to Canada intending to dig gold in the Klondike
20 March: suffers accident whilst stealing ride on train in Renfrew,
Ontario, which results in amputation of his foot
24 March: accident reported in *Renfrew Mercury (F2)*
June: back in his mother's home in Newport a cripple
submits poems to publishers but they are rejected
August: in lodgings at Blackfriars Road, London; moves to lodgings
at Rowton House, Newington Butts (and stays for two years)
'The Robber', blank verse tragedy rejected
sonnets are rejected

1900? prints 2000 copies of single sheet of poems and later burns them
1901   moves to The Ark, Southwark Street, London
1902   September: sets out to tramp around the Midlands
December: returns to Newport for Christmas
1903   moves to The Farmhouse, Marshalsea Road, London
1904   January: submits manuscript to Clement K. Shorter, publisher, which
is returned
May: submits manuscript of *The Soul's Destroyer (A1)* to Watts &
Co, printers
June: returns to Newport to negotiate lump sum from his trustees to
finance publication
1905   January: money negotiated from his trustees arrives from Newport
12 January: arranges with Watts & Co, 17 Johnston's Court, Fleet
Street, London to print 250 copies [including 30 copies for review]
of *The Soul's Destroyer (A1)*

March: collects copies of *The Soul's Destroyer (A1)* from printers
featured as tramp poet in newspaper articles
12 October: meets Edward Thomas
October: returns to his mother's house, 6 Llanwern Street, Newport,
but later moves to 1 Woodland Road, Newport, and finally arrives
at 42 Dudley Street, Newport in December

1906   23 January: moves to Edward Thomas' cottage in Kent on rent-free
basis
February: moves to Stidulph's Cottage, Egg Pie Lane, The Weald,
Sevenoaks
meets Walter de la Mare, W. H. Hudson, Norman Douglas, Hilaire
Belloc, John Galsworthy, Joseph Conrad, John Masefield and
many others
November: Elkin Mathews publish *New Poems (A2)*

1907   6 March: Alston Rivers publish second edition of *The Soul's
Destroyer (A1a)* which contains only 14 of the original 40 poems
June: George Bernard Shaw begins his preface to WHD's autobiography which is then sent to Duckworth & Co but GBS objects
to the contract

1908   April: A. C. Fifield publish *The Autobiography of a Super-Tramp
(A3)*, financed by Mrs G. B. Shaw
October: A. C. Fifield publish *Nature Poems (A4)*
December: contributes 'How It Feels To Be Out Of Work' (C7) to
English Review

1909   July: moves into lodgings in Sevenoaks, Kent
September: Duckworth & Co publish *Beggars (A5)*

1910   21 February: A. C. Fifield publish *Farewell to Poesy (A6)*

1911   17 February: Duckworth & Co publish *A Weak Woman (A7)*
receives aid from Royal Literary Fund
receives Civil List pension of £50
November: A. C. Fifield publish *Songs of Joy (A8)*

1912   March: Duckworth & Co publish *The True Traveller (A9)*
December: *Georgian Poetry 1911–1912 (D2)* published by Poetry
Bookshop

1913   January: opening of Poetry Bookshop
28 July: meets D. H. Lawrence
commences writing for *Literary Digest*
September: Elkin Mathews publish *Foliage (A10)*

1914   January: meets Rupert Brooke, Alice Meynell, and others
commences writing for *English Review*
moves from Sevenoaks to 29 Clarence Gardens, London
March: B. T. Batsford publish *Nature (A11)*
5 November: Methuen publish *The Bird of Paradise (A12)*

1915   November: *Georgian Poetry 1913–1915 (D7)* published by Poetry
Bookshop
Civil List pension increased to £100

1916   meets Jacob Epstein
        moves to 14 Great Russell Street, London
        first public readings of his poetry
        sits for the artist William Rothenstein
        1 June: A. C. Fifield publish *Child Lovers (A13)*
        November: A. C. Fifield publish *Collected Poems (A14)*; Alfred A.
            Knopf, New York, publish *Collected Poems (A14a)* with William
            Rothenstein's portrait as frontispiece
1917   commences writing for *New Statesman*
        Alfred A. Knopf publish *The Autobiography of a Super-Tramp (A3c)*
        April: Edward Thomas killed at Arras
        November: *Georgian Poetry 1916–1917 (D12)* published by Poetry
            Bookshop
1918   sits for the artist Augustus John
        meets the Sitwells, William Nicholson and Richard Church
        March: Andrew Melrose publish *A Poet's Pilgrimage (A15)*
        May: *New Paths (D13)* published by C. W. Beaumont
        25 May: Beaumont Press publish *Raptures (A16)*
        October: A. C. Fifield publish *Forty New Poems (A17)*
1919   meets Martin Armstrong and Arnold Bennett
        November: *Georgian Poetry 1918–1919 (D14)* published by Poetry
            Bookshop
1920   becomes engaged to Welsh girl and then breaks off engagement
        September: A. C. Fifield publish *The Song of Life (A18)*
1921   moves to 13 Avery Row, Brook Street, London
        Jonathan Cape take over publishing rights of WHD's books
        September: Yale University Press publish *The Captive Lion (A19)*
        October: commences to edit *Form (B1)*
1922   January: ceases to edit *Form (B1)*
        'Rheumatism' strikes
        meets Helen Matilda Payne
        September: Jonathan Cape publish *The Hour of Magic (A20)*
        October: *Shorter Lyrics of the Twentieth Century (B2)* published by
            Poetry Bookshop
        November: *Georgian Poetry 1920–1922 (D21)* published by Poetry
            Bookshop
        Jonathan Cape publish *Reflections (BI 1)* by Edmond X. Kapp with
            introductory comments by Laurence Binyon and WHD
        moves to Tor Leven, Cantelupe Road, East Grinstead, Sussex
1923   5 February: marries Helen Matilda Payne at Registry Office in East
            Grinstead with Conrad Aiken and Martin Armstrong as witnesses;
            he presents both of his witnesses with inscribed second edition of
            Foliage (A10a)
        True Travellers: A Tramp's Opera (A22) rejected for the theatre
        April: Jonathan Cape publish *Collected Poems: Second Series
            (A21)*

13 June: contributes 'What I Gained and Lost by Not Staying at School' *(C198)* to *Teachers World*

8 September: contributes 'Poets and Critics' (C206) to *New Statesman*

October: Jonathan Cape publish *True Travellers: A Tramp's Opera (A22)*

December: Jonathan Cape publish *Selected Poems (A23)*

1924　April: Jonathan Cape publish *Secrets (A24)*; Simpkin, Marshall, Hamilton & Kent publish *Moll Flanders (BI 2, 3)* with introduction by WHD

November: George Bernard Shaw advises Jonathan Cape against the publication of *Young Emma (A52)*

1925　25 October: Jonathan Cape publish *A Poet's Alphabet (A25)*

October: Jonathan Cape publish *Later Days (A26)*

November: E. Benn publish *Augustan Book of Poetry (A27)*

Collins publish *Burns' Poetical Works (BI 4)* with introduction by WHD

Jonathan Cape publish *Adventures of a Scholar Tramp* by Glen Mullin *(BI 5)* with introduction by WHD

1926　20 July: honoured with degree of 'Doctor in Litteris, Honoris Causa, University of Wales'

October: Jonathan Cape publish *The Song of Love (A28)* and *The Adventures of Johnny Walker, Tramp (A29)*

1927　October: Jonathan Cape publish *A Poet's Calendar (A30)*

November: Jonathan Cape publish *Dancing Mad (A31)*

1928　September: Faber & Gwyer publish *Moss and Feather (A32)* as an Ariel poem

October: Jonathan Cape publish *Collected Poems (A33)*

November: Jonathan Cape publish *Forty-Nine Poems (A34)*

9 November: Gregynog Press publish *Selected Poems (A35)*

1929　28 October: Jonathan Cape publish *Ambition (A36)*

1930　John Masefield awarded the laureateship, much to WHD's disgust

Newport hold civic luncheon in WHD's honour

22 September: Jonathan Cape publish *Jewels of Song (B3)*

A Greene Forest (BI 6) published by Hesperides Press with introduction by WHD

1931　moves from Malpas House, Oxted to Shenstone, Nailsworth, Gloucestershire with his wife Helen

December: Fytton Armstrong publish *In Winter (A37)*

1932　10 October: Jonathan Cape publish *Poems 1930–31 (A38)*

1933　20 March: Jonathan Cape publish *My Birds (A39)*

18 September: Jonathan Cape publish *My Garden (A40)*

1 December: Gregynog Press publish *The Lovers' Song-Book (A41)*

1934　24 September: Jonathan Cape publish *The Poems of W. H. Davies (A42)*

1935　1 April: Jonathan Cape publish *Love Poems (A43)*

1936   2 October: Jonathan Cape publish *The Birth of Song (A44)*
1937   R. H. Johns publish *The Romance of the Echoing Wood (BI 7)* with
        epilogue by WHD
1938   May: *Jewels of Song (B3)* re-issued as *An Anthology of Short Poems
        (B4)*
        21 September: Newport unveils plaque on Church House Inn: 'Wm
        Henry Davies/ poet & author/ born here/ 1871 [sic]' (WHD's last
        public appearance)
        suffers a stroke
1939   suffers heart attacks
        8 October: Jonathan Cape publish *The Loneliest Mountain (A45)*
        broadcasts in Birmingham
        November: Jonathan Cape publish *My Garden and My Birds (A46)*
1940   26 April: Jonathan Cape publish *The Poems of W. H. Davies 1940
        (A47)*
        26 September: dies at Nailsworth
1941   June: Faber & Faber publish *Common Joys (A48)*
1942   12 May: Jonathan Cape publish *Collected Poems of W. H. Davies
        (A49)* (with Harold Knight portrait)
1943   Jonathan Cape publish *Collected Poems of W. H. Davies (A49a)*
        (with Osbert Sitwell introduction)
1951   2 July: Jonathan Cape publish *The Essential W. H. Davies (A50)*
        (selected with introduction by Brian Waters)
1963   25 March: Jonathan Cape publish *The Complete Poems of W. H.
        Davies (A51)* (published simultaneously with *W. H. Davies: A
        Critical Biography (F324)* by Richard Stonesifer)
1971   *Writers of Wales: W. H. Davies (F345)* by Lawrence W. Hockey
        published by University of Wales Press on behalf of the Welsh Arts
        Council
1979   Mrs Helen Matilda Davies dies
1980   *The Super-Tramp in Monmouthshire (F363)* by Sybil Hollingdrake
        published
        10 November: Jonathan Cape publish *Young Emma (A52)*
1983   *Poetry Wales: W. H. Davies (F365)* published by Poetry Wales Press
1985   24 January: OUP publish *W. H. Davies: Selected Poems (A53)* chosen
        by Jonathan Barker

A Books and pamphlets

A1 THE SOUL'S DESTROYER   the Author (1905)

THE SOUL'S DESTROYER/ And Other Poems (in Gothic)/ BY/ WILLIAM
H. DAVIES/ at foot: OF THE AUTHOR,/ FARMHOUSE, MARSHALSEA
ROAD, S.E./ (short rule) / Two Shillings and Sixpence

8vo; (B)–D and (E)–G in eights, H in four, (I) in two; 54 leaves: (1–4) 5–7 (8) 9–107
(1)pp; 19.0 × 12.5 cms; (Ashley copy 19.6 × 12.8 cms untrimmed)

(1) half-title: THE SOUL'S DESTROYER; (2) blank; (3) title-page; (4) blank; 5–6
CONTENTS; 7 To this Book (in Gothic); (8) blank; 9–(108) text; (108) at foot:
(rule)/ PRINTED BY WATTS AND CO., 17, JOHNSON'S COURT, FLEET
STREET, LONDON E.C.; poem titles in capitals

contents: p7 To this Book; p9 The Soul's Destroyer; p21 Home; p22 Neighbours;
p23 The Rill; p24 Self's Motive; p25 The Cannibal's Lament; p26 Unholy Meat;
p27 Love's Coming; p28 The Passing of Poesy; p35 In a Lodging House; p38
Autumn; p39 Sleep; p41 Hereafter; p42 Young Poets; p43 Death; p44 False Helen;
p45 The Night Walker; p47 Absence; p48 The Moon; p49 Beauty's Light; p50 Lines
to a Sparrow; p52 The Figure in Wax; p53 A Drinking Song; p54 Her Name; p55
A Poet's Epitaph; p56 Nature; p58 The Cuckoo; p59 Old Times; p61 Love Absent;
p62 Spring; p64 Lake Superior; p65 Calumny; p66 The Prover; p67 Fortune; p68
Saints and Lodgers; p71 The Lodging-House Fire; p74 The Hill-Side Park; p76
Beauty's Quest; p92 The Devil's Guest

edges: trimmed

binding: pale grey [fading to buff] paper wrappers printed in black; front cover:
THE SOUL'S DESTROYER/ And Other Poems (in Gothic)/ BY/ WILLIAM H.
DAVIES/ at foot: OF THE AUTHOR,/ FARMHOUSE, MARSHALSEA ROAD,
S.E./ (rule) / Two Shillings and Sixpence; spine, back and inside covers: blank

date of publication: recorded as August 1905 in the English Catalogue although,
according to his biographer, Richard Stonesifer *(F324)*, WHD collected three
packages of copies from Watts & Co, printers, during the first week of March 1905
and sent the copy which was to launch his career to George Bernard Shaw in June of
that year

print run: 250 copies; *price*: 2s.6d.

copies seen: BL (shelf mark: 11658.aaa.213; accession date: 12 July 1947); Ashley
577 (undated); HRHRC (4 copies: one a presentation copy to Duncan Williams);
SH (2 copies)

reviews: A Cripple Poet: Realistic and Whimsical Word Pictures: Curious Life
History, A. St. John Adcock, *Daily Mail*, 22 July 1905, 3; A Poet of the Lodging-
House, Arthur Symons, *Outlook*, 29 July 1905, 391, XVI, 129; *Bookman*,
September 1905, XXVIII, 168, 213; *Athenaeum*, 2 September 1905, 300; The Poet

in the Doss-House, Newman Howard, *Academy*, 16 September 1905, LXIX, 942–943; A Poet at Last!, Edward Thomas, *Daily Chronicle*, 21 October 1905, 3

notes: (a) the Ashley copy has the ownership signature of A. St. John Adcock who wrote the first article about WHD in the *Daily Mail*
(b) WHD paid Watts & Co £19 for printing 250 copies (photocopies of the receipt, dated 12 July 1905, are held at NL and Jonathan Cape archives, RUL)
(c) the initial 30 copies sent for review resulted in only two disappointing notices
(d) J. B. Pinker took over as WHD's literary agent in August 1905 and sold the remaining copies for half a guinea each (*W. H. Davies: A Critical Biography* by Richard Stonesifer *(F324)*)
(e) 'To this book', 'Home', 'Neighbours', 'Self's Motive', 'The Cannibal's Lament', 'Unholy Meat', 'The Passing of Poesy', 'Hereafter', 'Young Poets', 'False Helen', 'The Night Walker', 'Absence', 'The Moon' ('The Moon' in *Complete Poems (A51)* is not this one), 'The Figure in Wax', 'Her Name', 'Nature', 'Old Times', 'Spring', 'Lake Superior', 'Calumny', 'Fortune', 'Beauty's Quest' and 'The Devil's Guest' are not known to have been reprinted
(f) 'The Rill', 'The Poet's Epitaph' and 'The Cuckoo' were reprinted for the first time in *W. H. Davies, Selected Poems* chosen by Jonathan Barker (*A53*)
(g) A. C. Fifield advertised editions of this book which I have been unable to trace (1906 4th edition, 1s.; price increased to 1s.4d.)

A1a First trade edition   Alston Rivers Ltd 1907

THE SOUL'S DESTROYER/ AND OTHER POEMS BY/ WILLIAM H. DAVIES/ at foot: LONDON: ALSTON RIVERS LTD./ BROOKE ST. HOLBORN BARS/ MCMVII

8vo; (A)–C in eights; the first pages of gatherings B and C signed VOL.-B. and VOL.-C. respectively on inner margins; 24 leaves: (i–vi) vii–xlv (3)pp; 19.5 × 14.5 cms

(i) half-title: THE SOUL'S DESTROYER AND OTHER POEMS; (ii) blank; (iii) title-page; (iv) BRADBURY, AGNEW, & CO. LD [sic]., PRINTERS/ LONDON AND TONBRIDGE; (v) CONTENTS; (vi) blank; vii–(xlvi) text; (xlvi) at foot: (rule)/ BRADBURY, AGNEW, & CO. LD [sic]., PRINTERS, LONDON AND TONBRIDGE.; (xlvii–xlviii) blank; poem titles in capitals

contents: pvii The Soul's Destroyer; pxxi Love's Coming; pxxiii In a Lodging House; pxxvi Autumn; pxxvii Sleep; pxxix Death; pxxx Beauty's Light; pxxxii Lines to a Sparrow; pxxxv A Drinking Song; pxxxvii Love Absent; pxxxviii The Prover; pxxxix Saints and Lodgers; pxlii The Lodging House Fire; pxlv The Hill-side Park

edges: trimmed

binding: sage-green paper wrappers printed in blue; front cover: THE SOUL'S DESTROYER/ AND OTHER POEMS BY/ WILLIAM H. DAVIES/ at foot: LONDON: ALSTON RIVERS LTD./ BROOKE ST. HOLBORN BARS/ MCMVII; inside front cover, in a panel: starts: The/ ends: 1s. NET PER VOL.; spine, back and inside back cover: blank

date of publication: 6 March 1907; *price*: 1s.

THE SOUL'S DESTROYER

And Other Poems

BY

WILLIAM H. DAVIES

OF THE AUTHOR,

FARMHOUSE, MARSHALSEA ROAD, S.E.

Two Shillings and Sixpence

A1

copies seen: BL (shelf mark: 11604.ee.28/3; accession date: 23 February 1907); HRHRC; HDB; SH

review: Democratic Sonnets, Edward Thomas, *Bookman*, April 1907, XXXII, 187, 27

text changes from A1:
The Soul's Destroyer: 1st stanza line 33: 'to' to 'with', line 45: 'Sweet daffodils, that plead with their smiles' to 'As daffodils, that plead with their sweet smiles'; 2nd stanza line 28: 'Though' to 'As'; 3rd stanza line 12: "o th" to 'of the', line 28 up: 'heavens' to 'heaven'; 4th stanza line 5: 'silence never' to 'never silence'; 5th stanza lines 25/26: 'though I/ Had retribution as' to 'as if/ Some retribution was'; line 28: 'Though' to 'As'
Love's Coming: 2nd stanza lines 1/2: 'Now, when she entered there,/ He tilted head, for sure' to 'When she had entered,/ He tilted then his head,'
In a Lodging House: line 24: 'me to' to 'to me'
Lines to a Sparrow: line 41: 'one' to 'a'
Love Absent: 1st stanza line 2 and 3rd stanza line 1: 'Alterreen' to 'Alteryn'
The Hill-side Park: line 24: 'Though gold his rocks' to 'As gold his locks'

note: according to Lawrence W. Hockey *(F345)* the printing of this edition was arranged by Edward Thomas who became a close friend of WHD after their first meeting on 12 October 1905. He also chose the fourteen poems from the original forty

A1b   Second impression   Alston Rivers Ltd 1908

as *A1a* apart from: (ii) *First Edition, March 6,* 1907/ *New Edition, August* 19, 1908; (iii) MCMVIII; (iv) in a panel: starts: The/ Contemporary/ Poets Series./ ends: 1s. NET PER VOL.; *binding*: orange-brown card wrappers printed in blue; front cover: MCMVIII; inside front cover: blank

date of publication: 19 August 1908; *price*: 1s.

copy seen: NL

A1c   Third impression   Alston Rivers Ltd 1910

as *A1b* apart from: (ii) *Reprinted, August* 1908/ *Reprinted, August* 1910; (iii) MCMX; *binding*: tan card wrappers printed in black; front cover: MCMX

date of publication: August 1910; *price*: 1s.

copies seen: HRHRC; NL

text corrections in HRHRC's copy:
The Soul's Destroyer: 1st stanza line 17 up: 16 lines deleted, therefore: 'Oft had I mourned those days forever gone' to 'One morning I awoke with lips gone dry'
Love's Coming: 2nd stanza lines 7/8: 'When she had entered,/ He tilted then his head,' to: 'When she had entered there/ He cocked his head with care,'
The Lodging-House Fire: 2nd stanza line 1: 'I woke eight chimes and rose' to: 'Eight bells and then I woke'

note: HRHRC copy: head of front cover in possibly Jonathan Cape's hand: 'File Copy: Bought the entire remainder from Alston Rivers [illegible] March 25, 1916. Sent 24 to author in lieu of royalties on the 40 I bought. I have the right to reprint when these are sold, subject to royalty.'

A1d *Re-issue of third impression* Jonathan Cape 1921

The Souls [sic] Destroyer/ and other Poems by/ William H. Davies/ (publisher's device)/ at foot: Jonathan Cape/ Eleven Gower Street, London

as *A1c* apart from: 19.3 × 14.0 cms; (ii) *Third Impression. Reissued/ by Jonathan Cape* 1921; the title-page is a cancel; *endpapers*: cream; *binding*: bright blue calico grain cloth; front cover: blank; spine, on a white paper label 3.7 cms deep, in blue: (double rule)/ The/ Soul's/ Dest-/ royer/ (fleuron)/ W. H./ Davies/ (double rule); back cover: blank; *dust-jacket*: not seen

date of publication: February 1922; *price*: 5s.

print run: made up from third impression sheets with a cancel title-page

copy seen: RUL, Finzi

A2 NEW POEMS Elkin Mathews 1907

NEW POEMS/ BY/ WILLIAM H. DAVIES/ AUTHOR OF/ "The Soul's Destroyer"/ at foot: LONDON/ ELKIN MATHEWS, VIGO STREET/ 1907

8vo; (A)–E in eights; 40 leaves: (1–6) 7–74 (6)pp; 16.0 × 10.7 cms variable

(1) half-title: NEW POEMS; (2) blank; (3) title-page; (4) blank; (5) dedication: TO/ HELEN AND EDWARD THOMAS; (6) NOTE signed W. H. D.; 7–8 CONTENTS; 9–(75) text; (75) at foot: THE END; (76) LONDON:/ PRINTED BY GILBERT AND RIVINGTON LTD.,/ ST. JOHN'S HOUSE, CLERKENWELL, E.C.; (77–78) starts: BY THE SAME WRITER/ ends: THOMAS in *The Daily Chronicle*.; (79–80) blank

contents: p9 Margery; p10 The Ways of Time; p11 A Safe Estate; p12 The Likeness; p13 Ale; p15 The Distinction; p16 "Scotty" Bill; p17 The Lament of Age; p18 The Ox; p19 Catharine; p21 The City's Ways; p23 The Forsaken Dead; p26 The Dying; p27 Time's Rule; p28 A Familiar Face; p29 A Blind Child; p30 The Calm; p32 Strange People; p33 The Happiest Life; p35 The Primrose; p37 The Homeless Man; p39 Violet to the Bee; p41 In June; p42 Wondering Brown; p44 Music; p46 Facts; p47 New-Comers; p49 Parted; p50 The End of Summer; p52 The Jolly Tramp; p54 One We Love; p55 Saturday Night in the Slums; p57 The Toothache; p58 April; p61 Whiskey; p62 Hope Abandoned

paper: chain lines 2.5 cms apart and vertical

endpapers: cream; *edges*: uncut, top edge trimmed

binding: sage-green cloth, horizontally or vertically shot with lighter green, lettered in gilt; front cover: NEW POEMS/ at foot: W. H. DAVIES; spine, vertically upwards: at head: WILLIAM H./ DAVIES/ centred: NEW POEMS/ horizontally at foot: ELKIN/ MATHEWS; back cover: blank; *dust-jacket*: not seen

date of publication: 3 December 1906 according to Elkin Mathews *(F372)* with the title-page dated 1907; recorded by the English Catalogue as January 1907 but actually November 1906 according to Lawrence W. Hockey *(F345)*

print run: 1000 copies; *price*: 1s.6d.

copies seen: BL (shelf mark: 011651. g. 34; accession date: 5 December 1906); HDB; SH

reviews: The Bookman's Table, *Bookman*, January 1907, XXXI, 184, 193; A Welsh Poet, *Morning Post*, 3 January 1907, 2; Verse and Poetry, *Academy*, 19 January 1907, LXXII, 1811, 58; A Poet of the People, Edward Thomas, *Daily Chronicle*, 24 January 1907, 3; *Athenaeum*, 16 March 1907, 319

mss: HRHRC hold an undated mss in WHD's hand of 'Catharine' with the title 'Going to School' on notepaper headed 14 Great Russell St, W.C. which incorporates the corrections identified in the HDB second impression (the address and corrections indicate that this mss is not the earliest)

note: dedicated to Helen and Edward Thomas who had befriended WHD in 1905

A2a Second impression   Elkin Mathews 1913

NEW POEMS/ BY/ WILLIAM H. DAVIES/ (publisher's device)/ at foot: LONDON/ ELKIN MATHEWS, CORK STREET/ 1913

as *A2* apart from: (2) starts: *By the Same Writer*/ ends: 2s.6d.; (3) title-page; (4) *First Printed January* 1907/ *Reprinted (2nd Thousand) October* 1913; (75) at foot: (rule)/ LONDON: PRINTED BY WILLIAM CLOWES AND SONS, LIMITED; (76) blank; (77–80) two stubs; *dust-jacket*: not seen

paper: watermarked: (crown)/ Abbey Mills/ Greenfield, chain lines 2.4 cms apart and vertical

date of publication: October 1913

print run: 1000 copies; *price*: 1s.6d.

copy seen: HDB

WHD's corrections (the HDB copy has the following corrections in WHD's hand which are reflected in *A2b* indicating final text):
Ale: omit first 2 stanzas
The Ox: 6th stanza last line: 'Robin cometh there no more' to 'Robin Redbreast comes no more'
Catharine: line 4: 'melted' to 'would melt'; line 7: 'morn we two did wait' to 'summer's morn we wait'; line 18: 'beside' to 'and near'; last line: ' "Alone, for Catharine is dead." ' to ' "And tell the master Catharine's dead." '
New-Comers: omit last 10 lines; line 11 up: 'as' to 'like'

notes: (a) the HDB copy is inscribed: 'To Dinah/ with love/ from the author/ W. H. Davies.'

(b) Elkin Mathews advertised a 2nd edition 1907, 1s.6d., which I have been unable
to trace

A2b   Life & Colour Series No 15   Jonathan Cape 1922

New Poems/ W. H. Davies/ (publisher's device)/ at foot: Jonathan Cape/ Eleven
Gower Street, London

8vo; (A)–D in eights, E in two; 34 leaves: (i–vi) vii–viii 9–67 (1)pp; 17.0 × 11.0 cms
variable

(i) half-title: New Poems; (ii) blank; (iii) title-page; (iv) *First Published January
1907/ Second Impression October 1913/ New Edition, revised, November 1922/ All
rights reserved/* at foot: PRINTED IN GREAT BRITAIN BY RICHARD CLAY &
SONS, LIMITED,/ BUNGAY, SUFFOLK.; (v) dedication as *A2*; (vi) Note signed
W. H. D.; vii–viii contents as *A2*; 9–(68) text

endpapers: cream; *edges*: uncut, top edge trimmed

binding: cream paper-covered boards with a decorative vertical linear design in
black and two shades of mustard, mustard cloth spine; front cover: blank; spine, on
a white paper label 3.7 cms deep, in black and mustard: (mustard rule)/ New/
Poems/ (mustard fleuron)/ W. H./ Davies/ (mustard rule); back cover: blank

dust-jacket: pinkish-beige printed in black; front, within a decorative border: New
Poems/ by/ W. H. Davies/ (publisher's device)/ *The Life & Colour Series, No. 15/* at
foot: Jonathan Cape/ Eleven Gower Street, London; spine: New/ Poems/ (fleuron)/
W. H./ Davies/ at foot: Jonathan/ Cape; back: starts: *The Life & Colour Series/*
ends: *Jonathan Cape, Eleven Gower Street, London* (16 titles listed); front flap:
starts: *The Complete Works of/* ends: *By W. H. Davies :: 2s.6d. net*; back flap:
blank

date of publication: December 1922; *price*: 2s.6d.

copies seen: BL (shelf mark: 011645.de.43; accession date: 7 December 1922);
RUL, Finzi; HDB; SH

text changes from A2:
Ale: completely revised being two stanzas shorter with re-arrangement of remaining
    four stanzas
"Scotty" Bill: 1st stanza line 2: 'arise' to 'rise'
The Ox: 6th stanza last line: 'Robin cometh there.' to 'Robin Redbreast comes.'
Catharine: line 4: 'melted' to 'would melt', line 7: 'one morn we two did wait' to
    'one summer's morn we wait', line 18: 'beside' to 'and near', last line: ' "Alone, for
    Catharine is dead." ' to ' "And tell the master Catharine's dead." '
The Forsaken Dead: line 40: 'dreamer who might have remained' to 'dreamer here
    who might remain'
The Calm: line 9: 'Of' to 'For'
New-Comers: ten lines shorter; last line: 'as' to 'like'
The Toothache: 1st stanza line 2: 'before' to 'ere'

notes: (a) the HDB copy is inscribed: 'To Dinah/ from Billy./ (W. H. Davies.)'
(b) also seen with double mustard rules on the spine

(c) the National Union Catalogue records an edition published by B. Humphries, Boston with an undated title-page in the holding of New York Public Library, New York, USA

A3 THE AUTOBIOGRAPHY OF A
SUPER-TRAMP   A C Fifield 1908

The Autobiography of/ a Super-Tramp. By W./ H. Davies. With a Pre-/ face by Bernard Shaw./ at foot: London. A. C. Fifield,/ 44 Fleet Street, E.C./ 1908

8vo; (A)–I and K–U in eights; 160 leaves: (1–2) (i–iv) v–xiv (1) 2–295 (9)pp; 19.0 × 12.0 cms variable

(1–2) blank; (i) half-title: The Autobiography of/ a Super-Tramp.; (ii) BY THE SAME AUTHOR:/ THE SOUL'S DESTROYER, AND OTHER POEMS./ NEW POEMS.; (iii) title-page; (iv) starts: *All Rights reserved*./ ends: PLYMOUTH; v–vi Contents; vii–xiv Preface by G. Bernard Shaw signed G. B. S./ Ayot St. Lawrence. 1907; (1)–295 text; 295 below text: The End; (296) blank; (297–304) starts: The Poems of W. H. Davies./ ends: LONDON: A. C. FIFIELD, 44 FLEET STREET, E.C.; running headlines throughout the text: The Autobiography of/ A Super-Tramp

contents: pvii preface by G. Bernard Shaw; I p1 Childhood; II p11 Youth; III p20 Manhood; IV p28 Brum; V p34 A Tramp's Summer Vacation; VI p40 A Night's Ride; VII p49 Law in America; VIII p57 A Prisoner his own Judge; IX p66 Berry Picking; X p75 The Cattleman's Office; XI p87 A Strange Cattleman; XII p96 Thieves; XIII p102 The Canal; XIV p108 The House-Boat; XV p118 A Lynching; XVI p125 The Camp; XVII p134 Home; XVIII p143 Off Again; XIX p152 A Voice in the Dark; XX p164 Hospitality; XXI p169 London; XXII p183 The Ark; XXIII p195 Gridling; XXIV p208 On the Downright; XXV p218 The Farmhouse; XXVI p229 Rain and Poverty; XXVII p235 False Hopes; XXVIII p242 On Tramp Again; XXIX p253 A Day's Companion; XXX p259 The Fortune; XXXI p266 Some Ways of Making a Living; XXXII p272 At Last; XXXIII p282 Success; XXXIV p289 A House to Let

endpapers: cream; *edges*: top and fore edge trimmed

binding: buff calico grain textured cloth, lettered in red; front cover: The Auto-biography/ of a Super-Tramp./ W. H. Davies.; spine: THE/ AUTOBIOGRAPHY/OF A/ SUPER-TRAMP/ W. H. DAVIES./ at foot: FIFIELD; back cover: blank; *dust-jacket*: not seen

date of publication: April 1908; *price*: 6s.

copies seen: BL (shelf mark: 012331.i.56; accession date: 9 June 1908); HRHRC; HDB; SH

reviews: A Poet and Mr Shaw, Edward Thomas, *Daily Chronicle*, 23 April 1908, 3; The Poet-Tramp: "The Autobiography of a Super-Tramp", *Westminster Gazette*, 2 May 1908, 4; "Duke and Tramp", *TLS*, 14 May 1908, 156; A Book of the Open Road, *Morning Post*, 14 May 1908, 2; *Punch*, 20 May 1908, 134, 378; Shorter

Reviews, *Academy*, 30 May 1908, LXXIV, 1882, 836; *Athenaeum,* 13 June 1908, 728; by Jacob Tonson (Arnold Bennett), *New Age*, 1 August 1908, III, 14, 274; Vagrants, Beggars and Tramps, John Cooke, *Quarterly Review*, October 1908, 209, 417, 388–408

mss: in WHD's hand; originally titled My Life; 364pp on lined paper addressed The Weald, Kent and dated 1908; wrapped in brown paper and loose in a box file (HDB); title-page: My Life/ by/ William H. Davies./ The Weald, Kent./ 1908./ at foot: Published as "The Autobiography of/ a Super-Tramp",/ the title being suggested by G. Bernard Shaw./ W. H. D.

WHD's manuscript corrections:

II	p14 line 4: 'pier edge' to 'edge of the pier'
VI	p47 line 19: 'very well have' to 'have very well'
X	p85 line 10: 'glad of' to 'thankful'
XV	p119 line 10: 'of' to 'in'; p120 line 13 up: 'low buzz of' to 'buzz of low'
XVII	p136 line 18: 'and' to 'or'
XIX	p157 line 12: 'seemed' to 'seems'
XXII	p191 line 8 up: 'unless' to 'except'
XXV	p227 line 14: 'before' to 'after'
XXVII	p235 lines 11/12: 'sympathy' to 'sympathetic ears'
XXVIII	p252 line 2: 'that had' to 'having'
XXXII	p272 line 2 up: 'pleased' to 'well satisfied'
XXXIV	p294 line 17: 'would' to 'might'

text changes from manuscript to first printing (A3) (references are to *A3* not mss):

III	p22 line 9: 'aggravated, especially under the consideration' to 'aggravated, for life is is a serious subject to him. That man is not to be aggravated, especially under the consideration'
IV	p32 line 9: 'out-of-the-way' to 'out of the way', line 10: 'they are' to 'are'
VII	p53 line 18: 'the' to 'was'
IX	p66 line 7: 'hay-ricks' to 'hayricks'; p67 line 1: 'would' to 'would always', line 12: 'son' to 'own son'; p69 line 9 up: 'real, but more quiet laughter' to 'a real, but more quiet delight'; p73 line 7 up: 'me' to 'us'
X	p76 line 11 up: 'always being' to 'being always'; p78 line 12: 'succeeded' to 'succeeding', line 8 up: 'be' to 'soon be'
XI	p89 line 15: 'of a' to 'for a'
XII	p97 line 14: 'remember' to 'remembered'
XIII	p102 line 6 up: 'could' to 'was to'; p103 line 3: 'month's pay or more' to 'month or more's pay'; p107 line 15: 'previous round' to 'round previous'
XIV	p109 line 9: 'all day gathering' to 'gathering all day'
XV	p118 line 5: 'so' to 'this'
XVI	p128 line 14: 'than' to 'but'
XVIII	p145 line 5 up: 'projects' to 'prospects'; p147 line 15: 'sea table' to 'table'
XIX	p152 line 13: 'or' to 'of'
XX	p164 line 7 up: 'be' to 'give'; p165 line 7: 'to be certain' to 'so certain'; p166 line 3: 'weeks' to 'days'
XXI	p171 line 3: 'and' to 'and the'; line 6: 'others' to 'other', line 11 up: 'boats' to 'ships'; p173 line 1: 'morning' to 'mornin''; line 3: 'set arter your body' to 'set about yer at once'; p176 line 4 up: 'chance' to 'prospect'
XXII	p184 line 2: 'nothing' to 'nothing at all'
XXIII	p203 line 18: 'dirty as' to 'as dirty as'

XXIV   p210 line 2 up: 'snips' to 'sniffs'; p213 line 16: 'saying that he' to 'saying he'; p215 line 20: 'out-of-the-way' to 'out of the way'; p216 line 5 up: 'home' to 'home; sleeping there that night I rose early the following morning and started for home'

XXV   p221 line 10 up: 'not what or what' to 'not or what not'; p222 line 12: 'the' to 'a'; p224 last line: 'at' to 'to'

XXVIII   p251 line 3: 'food, bed' to 'bed, food'

XXIX   p255 line 8 up: 'Waited' to 'Waiting'

XXX   p262 line 6 up: 'At this moment, the landlord entered, and, though he had not heard the question, he too, would like to know when Macquire intended seeing his lawyer' added; p263 line 14: 'you' to 'you'

XXXIII   p282 line 5: 'has been' to 'were'; p283 line 15: 'in writing' to 'by writing', line 19: 'step' to 'other step'; p284 line 13: 'interview' to 'review'

notes: (a) copies bound in pale grey cloth rather than buff but with identical lettering have been identified

(b) the agreement between Mrs Bernard Shaw, who was to finance the publication, and Fifield is dated 10 February 1908 (320pp to be published in 1908 at approximately 6/-, Jonathan Cape archives, RUL)

(c) according to Lawrence Hockey *(F345)* Mrs Shaw gave WHD £60 to finance the book

(d) WHD was encouraged by Edward Thomas to write this book; he helped with the proof corrections and then reviewed it glowingly in the *Daily Chronicle*

(e) the HRHRC copy is a signed presentation copy to Sir Thornley Stoker (Sir Thornley and Lady Stoker had written to WHD in appreciation of the book)

(f) translated into Swedish in 1924

(g) permission was given to the RNIB to issue the book in Moon type for the sole benefit and use of the blind (letter dated 27 July 1937, Jonathan Cape archives, RUL)

A3a Second edition   A C Fifield 1908

as *A3* apart from: (1) starts: *Crown 8vo. Canvas. 320 pages. 6s./* ends: London: A. C. Fifield, 44 Fleet Street, E.C.; (2) starts: JUST PUBLISHED/ ends: LONDON: A. C. FIFIELD; (ii) starts: BY THE SAME AUTHOR:/ ends: NATURE POEMS, AND OTHERS.; (iii) Second Edition; (297–304) starts: The Poems of W. H. Davies./ ends: LONDON: A. C. FIFIELD, 44 FLEET STREET, E.C.; *edges*: trimmed

copy seen: BL (shelf mark: 12330.r.44; accession date: 4 September 1931)

note: A. C. Fifield advertised editions that I have been unable to trace (3rd impression 1907/ 3rd edition 1907, 6s.; 4th impression 1907)

A3b Third edition   A C Fifield 1911

A3c First American edition   Alfred A Knopf 1917

within decorative panel: THE AUTOBIOGRAPHY/ OF A SUPER-TRAMP/ BY WILLIAM H. DAVIES/ PREFACE BY BERNARD SHAW/ NEW YORK (publisher's device) MCMXVII/ ALFRED A. KNOPF

8vo; 23 unsigned gatherings of eight; 184 leaves: (i–vi) vii–xvii (xviii) xix–xx (xxi–xxii) 1–345 (1)pp; 20.7 × 14.0 cms variable

(i) half-title: The Autobiography/ of a Super-Tramp/ at foot: (decoration incorporating publisher's monogram); (ii) in a triple-ruled panel: starts: THE NEWEST BORZOI BOOKS/ ends: WILLIAM H. DAVIES; (iii) title-page; (iv) starts: COPYRIGHT, 1917, BY/ ends: PRINTED IN THE UNITED STATES OF AMERICA; (v) fly-title: Preface by/ Bernard Shaw; (vi) blank; vii–xvii PREFACE signed G. B. S./Ayot St. Lawrence. 1907; (xviii) blank; xix–xx Contents; (xxi) fly-title: The Autobiography/ of a Super-Tramp; (xxii) blank; 1–345 text; 345 below text: THE END; (346) blank

endpapers: cream; *edges*: uncut, top edge blue-grey

binding: red calico grain cloth, ruled in green, lettered in blue; front cover, within a triple border: THE/ AUTOBIOGRAPHY/ OF A/ SUPER-TRAMP/ BY/ WILLIAM H DAVIES/ WITH A PREFACE/ BY BERNARD SHAW (the whole within an outer border with decorative corners); spine: (decorative rule)/ THE/ AUTO-/ BIOGRAPHY/ OF A/ SUPER-/ TRAMP/ BY/ WM H DAVIES/ (deep decorative rule)/ ALFRED A KNOPF; back cover, at foot: blind-blocked publisher's device; *dust-jacket*: not seen

price: $2.50

copies seen: BL (shelf mark: 12316.v.20; accession date: 5 April 1917); HRHRC; HDB

reviews: by EFE, *Boston Transcript*, 18 April 1917, 6; Notable Books in Brief, *New York Times (Book Review)*, 22 April 1917, 159; Underworld Decorum, George Bernard Donlin, *The Dial*, 3 May 1917, LXII, 741, 398; *St Louis*, May 1917, 15, 153; *ALA Booklist*, June 1917, 13, 399; *Cleveland*, June 1917, 83; by Irwin Granish, *Masses*, October 1917, 9, 29; *Pittsburgh*, October 1917, 22, 670; Panhandler and Poet, Louis Untermeyer, *Yale Review* (new series), October 1917, VII, 1, 199–202

notes: (a) the HRHRC copy is a presentation copy to Alfred A. Knopf; the BL copy was presented by A. C. Fifield
(b) the HDB copy is inscribed: 'To Helen,/ from/ Billy Davies. (W. H. Davies.)'

A3d   Fourth English edition   A C Fifield 1917

The Autobiography of/ a Super-Tramp. By W./ H. Davies. With a Pre-/ face by Bernard Shaw./ Fourth Edition/ at foot: London: A. C. Fifield, 13,/ Clifford's Inn, E.C. 1917

as *A3* apart from: (1) starts: *The Works of William H. Davies*/ ends: *A Pilgrim in Wales. 1917. Melrose.*; (2) starts: Some Press Notices of/ ends: London: A. C. Fifield, 13 Clifford's Inn, E.C.; (ii) blank; (297–304) starts: Mr. Fifield's New List./ ends: London: A. C. Fifield, 13 Clifford's Inn, E.C.; *binding*: dark rose calico grain cloth; front cover: blind-blocked border and decorative wreath; spine, within a black panel: (rule)/ THE AUTO-/ BIOGRAPHY/ OF A SUPER-/ TRAMP/ W. H. DAVIES/ PREFACE BY/ BERNARD SHAW/ (rule)/ at foot, within a black panel: FIFIELD; back cover: blank; *dust-jacket*: not seen *price*: 6s.

copies seen: HRHRC; RUL, Finzi

note: p(298) 'Fifield's' misprinted 'Fifiela's'

A3e　Fifth English edition　　　　　　　　　　A C Fifield 1920

The Autobiography of/ a Super-Tramp. By W./ H. Davies. With a Pre-/ face by Bernard Shaw./ Fifth edition, with a note by the author/ and five poems, and a frontispiece from/ a photograph of 1908/ at foot: London: A. C. Fifield, 13,/ Clifford's Inn, E.C.4. 1920

8vo; (A) in eight plus tipped-in frontispiece, B–I and K–U in eights; 160 leaves: (1–2) (i–v) vi–xiv (1) 2–304pp plus frontispiece not included in the pagination; 19.2 × 12.5 cms

(1) starts: The Complete Samuel Butler/ ends: London: A. C. Fifield, 13 Clifford's Inn, E.C.4; (2) starts: *Some Press Notices of*/ ends: London: A. C. Fifield, 13 Clifford's Inn, E.C.4.; (i) half-title: The Autobiography of/ a Super-Tramp.; (ii) starts: *The Works of William H. Davies*/ ends: *A Pilgrim in Wales. 1917. Melrose.*; portrait frontispiece captioned: W. H. DAVIES AND THE COTTAGE IN THE WEALD/ Where the "Autobiography" was written/ From a copyright photograph by Holbrook Jackson in 1908; (iii) title-page; (iv) *First published April* 1908, *reprinted/ September* 1908, 1911, 1917, 1920/ *All Rights reserved./ Copyright in U.S.A./* at foot: *The Mayflower Press, Plymouth, England.* William Brendon & Son, Ltd.; (v)-vi Contents; vii–xiv Preface by G. Bernard Shaw. signed G. B. S./ Ayot St. Lawrence. 1907.; (1)–295 text; 296 Author's Note to the Fifth Edition signed W. H. D./ CORNWALL, *August*, 1920.; 297 Autumn; 298–299 A Drinking Song; 300–301 Sleep; 302 Love's Coming; 303 The Lodging-House Fire; 304 at foot: THE END; running headlines throughout the text: The Autobiography of/ A Super-Tramp

contents: as A3 apart from: p296 Author's Note to Fifth Edition; p297 Autumn; p298 A Drinking Song; p300 Sleep; p302 Love's Coming; p303 The Lodging-House Fire

endpapers: cream; *edges*: trimmed

binding: royal blue calico textured cloth, lettered in gilt; front cover: a wreath within a single blind-blocked border; spine, within a gilt panel: (rule)/ THE AUTO-/ BIOGRAPHY/ OF A SUPER-/ TRAMP/ W. H. DAVIES/ (rule)/ at foot, within a gilt panel: FIFIELD; back cover: blank

dust-jacket: mottled grey, printed in black; front: The Autobiography of/ a Super-Tramp. By W./ H. Davies. With a Pre-/ face by Bernard Shaw./ Fifth Edition, with a Note by the/ Author and Five Poems, and Portrait./ I recommend this most remarkable/ Autobiography of a Supertramp [sic] to your special attention./ G. Bernard Shaw (in facsimile script)/ Note made by Mr. Bernard Shaw on the MS. received/ by the Publisher.; spine: THE/ AUTOBIO-/ GRAPHY/ OF A/ [text illegible on dust-jacket examined at HRHRC]/ Five Poems/ and Portrait/ at foot: FIFIELD; back: starts: *The Works of William H. Davies*/ ends: London: A. C. Fifield, 13 Clifford's Inn, E.C.4.; both flaps: blank *date of publication*: November 1920; *price*: 7s.6d.

copies seen: BL (shelf mark: 010855.cc.21; accession date: 15 November 1920); HRHRC

review: "Interesting Reprints", *New Statesman*, 11 December 1920, XVI, 400, 313–314

notes: (a) p296 (in some copies): '1920' poorly registered as '920'
(b) agreement with Fifield dated 17 September 1920 (Jonathan Cape archives, RUL)
(c) the HRHRC copy is a presentation copy to Tom and Rose Patmore from the author
(d) 'Autumn', 'A Drinking Song', 'Sleep', 'Love's Coming' and 'The Lodging-House Fire' were first published in *A1*
(e) Jonathan Cape advertised a 1921 edition which I have been unable to trace

A3f   Jonathan Cape 1923

date of publication: November 1923

print run: 500 copies printed on 5 October 1923; bound by Nevett; *price*: 7s.6d.

note: new Foreword signed W.H.D.

A3g   Jonathan Cape 1924

print run: 1000 copies printed on 5 August 1924; bound by Nevett

A3h First American Borzoi pocket book edition   Alfred A Knopf 1924

date of publication: January 1924

A3i Second American Borzoi pocket book edition   Alfred A Knopf 1925

within decorative border: THE AUTOBIOGRAPHY/ OF A SUPER-TRAMP/ *by*/ WILLIAM H. DAVIES/ *Preface by*/ BERNARD SHAW/ (publisher's device)/ *New York*/ ALFRED . A . KNOPF

as *A3c* apart from: 17.2 × 11.0 cms; (i) half-title: The Autobiography/ of a Super-Tramp; (ii) in a decorative panel: starts: THE BORZOI POCKET BOOKS/ ends: NEW YORK: ALFRED . A : KNOPF; (iii) title-page; (iv) COPYRIGHT, 1917, WILLIAM H. DAVIES/ *Pocket-Book Edition, Published, January 1924*/ *Second Printing, November, 1925*/ at foot: MANUFACTURED IN THE UNITED STATES OF AMERICA; *binding*: dark maroon ribbed cloth, blocked in black and cerise, lettered in cerise; front cover, within a double black border: foliate design in black, with, superimposed in a black oval panel with a cerise background, publisher's device; spine: THE AUTOBIOGRAPHY/ of a/ SUPER-TRAMP/ (black decoration)/ DAVIES/ at foot: ALFRED A/ KNOPF; back cover: blind-blocked publisher's device; *edges*: trimmed; *dust-jacket*: not seen *date of publication*: November 1925

copy seen: HRHRC

A3j   First Travellers' Library edition   Jonathan Cape 1926

THE AUTOBIOGRAPHY OF A/ SUPER-TRAMP/ by/ W. H. DAVIES/ (publisher's device)/ at foot: LONDON/ JONATHAN CAPE 30 BEDFORD SQUARE

as *A3e* apart from: 17.2 × 11.8 cms; (i) half-title: THE TRAVELLERS' LIBRARY/ (decorative star)/ THE AUTOBIOGRAPHY OF A SUPER-TRAMP; (ii) starts: THE TRAVELLERS' LIBRARY/ ends: Uniform with this volume (the last title listed is CAN SUCH THINGS BE by Ambrose Bierce); (iii) title-page; (iv) starts: FIRST PUBLISHED IN 1908/ ends: PRINTED IN GREAT BRITAIN; xv Author's Note to the Fifth Edition signed W. H. D./ CORNWALL, *August*, 1920.; xvi Foreword to the New Edition signed W. H. D.; (296) blank; 304 at foot: THE END/ PRINTED BY BUTLER AND TANNER LTD., FROME AND LONDON; *binding*: royal blue calico grain cloth, blocked and lettered in gilt; front cover: blank; spine: *The*/ AUTO-/ BIOGRAPHY/ OF A/ SUPER-/ TRAMP/ (decorative star)/ W.H.DAVIES/ (publisher's device)/ at foot: JONATHAN/ CAPE; back cover: blind-blocked publisher's monogram; *dust-jacket*: not seen

date of publication: April 1926

print run: 2000 copies printed on 24 February 1926; bound by Nevett; *price*: 3s.6d.

copy seen: BL (shelf mark: 012208.m.1/3; accession date: 15 April 1926)

review: *Now & Then*, Christmas 1927, 26, 36

A3k   Travellers' Library edition: second impression   Jonathan Cape 1926

THE AUTOBIOGRAPHY OF A/ SUPER-TRAMP/ by/ W. H. DAVIES/ *With a Preface by*/ G. BERNARD SHAW/ (publisher's device)/ at foot: LONDON/ JONATHAN CAPE 30 BEDFORD SQUARE

as *A3j* apart from: (ii) starts: THE TRAVELLERS' LIBRARY/ ends: Uniform with this volume (the last title listed is ROMAN PICTURES by Percy Lubbock); (iii) title-page; (iv) starts: FIRST PUBLISHED IN 1908/ ends: PRINTED IN GREAT BRITAIN; 8pp publisher's catalogue: starts: A LIST OF VOLUMES ISSUED IN/ ends: JONATHAN CAPE THIRTY BEDFORD SQUARE (22 titles listed); *binding*: decorative rule at head and base of spine; *dust-jacket*: not seen

date of publication: July 1926

print run: 2000 copies printed by Butler & Tanner on 11 June 1926; bound by Nevett

copy seen: NL

A3l Travellers' Library edition: third impression   Jonathan Cape 1926

date of publication: January 1927

print run: 1500 copies printed by Butler & Tanner on 1 October 1926; bound by Nevett

A3m Travellers' Library edition: fourth impression   Jonathan Cape 1927

print run: 4000 copies printed by Butler & Tanner on 28 January 1927; bound by Nevett

A3n Travellers' Library edition: fifth impression   Jonathan Cape 1927

date of publication: October 1927

print run: 4000 copies printed by Butler & Tanner on 2 October 1927; bound by Nevett

A3o Travellers' Library edition: sixth impression   Jonathan Cape 1928

print run: 4000 copies printed by Butler & Tanner on 4 October 1928; bound by Nevett

A3p American Travellers' Library edition
                                    Jonathan Cape & Harrison Smith 1929

A3q Travellers' Library edition: seventh impression   Jonathan Cape 1929

date of publication: February 1929

print run: 2000 copies printed by Letchworth on 27 February 1929; bound by Nevett

A3r Travellers' Library edition: eighth impression   Jonathan Cape 1929

date of publication: September 1929

print run: 4000 copies printed by Letchworth on 6 September 1929; bound by Nevett

A3s Travellers' Library edition: ninth impression   Jonathan Cape 1930

date of publication: June 1930

print run: 4000 copies, 3 June 1930 (printed and bound by Garden City Press); *price*: 4s.6d.

A3t   The Life and Letters Series   Jonathan Cape 1930

THE LIFE AND LETTERS SERIES NO. 6/ (rule)/ W. H. DAVIES/
THE AUTOBIOGRAPHY/ OF A SUPER-TRAMP/ With a Preface by/
G. BERNARD SHAW/ With four photographs of the author/ at foot: London
– JONATHAN CAPE – Toronto

16mo: (A)–K in sixteens plus an 8pp publisher's catalogue and four tipped-in
portraits not included in the pagination; 160 leaves: (1–4) 5–15 (16) 17–19 (20) 21–
307 (308) 309–318 (2)pp; 20.1 × 13.5 cms

(1) half-title: THE LIFE & LETTERS/ SERIES, VOLUME 6/ THE/ AUTO-
BIOGRAPHY/ OF A SUPER-TRAMP/ at foot: (Life and Letters monogram); (2)
starts: (fleuron) *The Life and Letters Series* is a selection/ ends: be found at the end
of this book; frontispiece captioned: WILLIAM HENRY DAVIES/ after a portrait in
oils by Augustus John/ *Frontispiece*; (3) title- page; (4) starts: First published by Mr.
A. C. Fifield in 1908/ ends: LETCHWORTH :: :: :: HERTS; 5–6 CONTENTS; 7–
15 PREFACE BY G. BERNARD SHAW signed G. B. S./ Ayot St. Lawrence. 1907.;
(16) blank; 17–18 AUTHOR'S NOTE TO THE FIFTH EDITION signed W. H. D./
Cornwall, *August*, 1920.; 19 FOREWORD TO NEW EDITION signed W. H. D.;
(20) blank; 21–307 text; (308) blank; portrait captioned: WILLIAM HENRY
DAVIES/ from a camera portrait by E. O. Hoppe; 309 Autumn; 310–311 A
Drinking Song; 312–313 Sleep; 314–315 Love's Coming; 316–318 The Lodging-
House Fire; 318 below text: THE END; (319–320) blank; (321) starts: (Life and
Letters monogram)/ ends: & SIXPENCE *net*; (322–328) starts: THE LIFE AND
LETTERS SERIES/ ends: *Manchester Guardian*; portraits also facing pp120 and
250

endpapers: cream; *edges*: trimmed

binding: grass green calico grain cloth, lettered in gilt; front cover: THE AUTO-
BIOGRAPHY/ OF A SUPER TRAMP (decorative rule)/ left-hand side, at foot: (Life
and Letters monogram); spine: THE AUTO=/ BIOGRAPHY/ OF A SU=/ PER
TRAMP/ (Life and Letters monogram)/ W. H. DAVIES/ at foot: JONATHAN
CAPE; back cover: blind-blocked publisher's device; *dust-jacket*: not seen

date of publication: 6 October 1930

print run: 4000 copies, 11 July 1930 (printed and bound by Garden City Press);
price: 4s.6d.

copies seen: BL (shelf mark: 10824.aaa.20; accession date: 2 October 1930); HDB;
SH

note: the HDB copy is inscribed: 'To Dinah (Helen)/ from/ Bunny (W. H. Davies)/
1930.'

A3u   Travellers' Library edition: tenth impression   Jonathan Cape 1931

date of publication: May 1931

print run: 4000 copies, 14 May 1931 (printed and bound by Garden City Press)

A3v   Travellers' Library edition: eleventh impression   Jonathan Cape 1932

date of publication: January 1932

print run: 4000 copies, 19 January 1932 (printed and bound by Garden City Press)

A3w   American cheap edition   Alfred A Knopf 1932

A3x   Travellers' Library edition: twelfth impression   Jonathan Cape 1933

date of publication: February 1933

print run: 4000 copies, 17 February 1933 (printed and bound by Garden City Press)

A3y   Travellers' Library edition: thirteenth impression
                                             Jonathan Cape 1936

date of publication: January 1936

print run: 2000 copies, 27 January 1936 (printed and bound by Garden City Press)

A3z Travellers' Library edition: fourteenth impression
                                             Jonathan Cape 1937

print run: 2000 copies, 30 November 1936 (printed and bound by Garden City Press)

A3aa Travellers' Library edition: fifteenth impression
                                             Jonathan Cape 1938

print run: 2000 copies printed by Garden City Press; bound by A. W. Bain

A3bb Second American cheap edition   Alfred A Knopf 1938

A3cc Gaelic edition   1938

8vo; 328pp

binding: pink calico grain cloth lettered in blue

dust-jacket: white, printed in red, black and blue with a circular panel on the front cover and a caricature of WHD showing his peg leg, complete with pipe, crutch and red spotted kerchief; lettered in white outlined in black over a red panel

copy seen: HRHRC

A3dd   Travellers' Library edition: sixteenth impression

Jonathan Cape 1939

as *A3j* apart from: (ii) starts: (fleuron) A descriptive list of some of the volumes in/ ends: publishers.; (iv) starts: FIRST PUBLISHED IN 1908/ ends: LIMITED; 16pp publisher's catalogue: starts: A LIST OF TITLES/ ends: 218. ALL THE CONSPIRATORS. Christopher Isherwood (paged (1)–16); *binding*: blocked and lettered in silver; *dust-jacket*: mainly canary yellow, printed in turquoise and black; front, top half yellow: (double turquoise rule)/ (design incorporating two ships and two castles within decorative diamond-shaped border, printed in black and turquoise)/ WITH AN INTRODUCTION BY BERNARD SHAW (in black), lower half turquoise, printed in black within yellow panels: (yellow rule)/ THE TRAVELLERS' LIBRARY/ THE AUTOBIOGRAPHY OF A/ SUPER-TRAMP/ (blank panel)/ W. H. DAVIES/ (decoration)/ at foot: (yellow rule)/ (black rule incorporating three yellow and black stars)/ signed in turquoise at foot: HAWES; spine, divided into two colours as front: (double turquoise rule)/ THE AUTO-/ BIOGRAPHY OF/ A SUPER-TRAMP (in black)/ (black decorative star)/ W. H. DAVIES (in black)/ (ship decoration in black and turquoise)/ (decorative rule)/ THE/ TRAVELLERS'/ LIBRARY/ (yellow rule)/ within a yellow panel: No.3/ (publisher's device)/ JONATHAN/ CAPE (within a yellow panel)/ (black rule incorporating one decorative star in black and turquoise); back, on a yellow background, within a turquoise border: starts: *The Travellers' Library* is the most extensive/ ends: LONDON; front flap, on a yellow background in black: starts: No. 3/ ends: net; back flap: blank

print run: 2000 copies printed by Garden City Press; bound by A. W. Bain; *price*: 3s.6d.

copy seen: RUL, Finzi

A3ee   Travellers' Library edition: seventeenth impression

Jonathan Cape 1940

print run: 2000 copies printed by Garden City Press

A3ff   New English edition   Jonathan Cape 1942

date of publication: 27 July 1942

print run: 2000 copies printed on 13 March 1942 by Butler & Tanner; *price*: 5s.

A3gg   New English edition: second impression   Jonathan Cape 1943

print run: 3000 copies printed on 6 January 1943

A3hh   New English edition: third impression   Jonathan Cape 1944

date of publication: January 1944

print run: 2000 copies printed on 18 January 1944

A3ii New English edition: fourth impression   Jonathan Cape 1944

date of publication: September 1944

print run: 5500 copies printed on 24 July 1944

A3jj New English edition: fifth impression   Jonathan Cape 1945

date of publication: August 1945

print run: 6000 copies printed on 5 April 1945

A3kk New English edition: sixth impression   Jonathan Cape 1946

print run: 5000 copies printed on 30 August 1946

A3ll New English edition: seventh impression   Jonathan Cape 1947

print run: 4600 copies printed on 19 August 1947; *price*: 3s.

A3mm New English edition: eighth impression   Jonathan Cape 1948

print run: 5000 copies printed on 30 July 1948

A3nn New English edition: ninth impression   Jonathan Cape 1950

The/ AUTOBIOGRAPHY/ *of a*/ SUPER-TRAMP/ By/ W. H. DAVIES/ (publisher's device)/ *With a preface by*/ G. BERNARD SHAW/ at foot: JONATHAN CAPE/ THIRTY BEDFORD SQUARE

16mo; (A)–K in sixteens; 160 leaves: (1–4) 5–15 (16) 17–19 (20) 21–307 (308) 309–318 (2)pp; 17.7 × 11.7 cms

(1) half-title: THE AUTOBIOGRAPHY OF A/ SUPER-TRAMP; (2) *By the same Author*/ COLLECTED POEMS OF W. H. DAVIES/ THE ADVENTURES OF JOHNNY WALKER, TRAMP/ LATER DAYS/ ETC.; (3) title-page; (4) starts: FIRST PUBLISHED IN 1908/ ends: LONDON; 5–6 CONTENTS; 7–15 PREFACE BY G. BERNARD SHAW signed G. B. S./ Ayot St. Lawrence. 1907.; (16) blank; 17–18 AUTHOR'S NOTE TO THE FIFTH EDITION signed W. H. D./ Cornwall, *August*, 1920.; 19 FOREWORD TO NEW EDITION signed W. H. D.; (20) blank; 21–307 text; (308) blank; 309 AUTUMN; 310–311 A DRINKING SONG; 312–313 SLEEP; 314–315 LOVE'S COMING; 316–318 THE LODGING-HOUSE FIRE; 318 below text: THE END; (319–320) blank

binding: grass green calico grain cloth, lettered in black; front cover: blank; spine: *The*/ AUTO- / BIOGRAPHY/ OF A/ SUPER-/TRAMP/ (decorative star)/ W. H. DAVIES/ at foot: (publisher's device); back cover: blank; *dust-jacket*: not seen *print run*: 5000 copies printed on 22 March 1950 by Butler & Tanner Ltd; bound by A. W. Bain

copy seen: SH

A3oo   *Windsor Selections Series*   Allen & Unwin 1951

date of publication: July 1951; *price*: 4s.6d.

notes: (a) School edition
(b) introduction by W. G. Bebbington

A3pp   *New English edition: tenth impression*   Jonathan Cape 1952

print run: 5000 copies printed on 30 January 1952; *price*: increased to 7s.6d. on 1 May 1952

A3qq   *New English edition*   Jonathan Cape 1955

The/ AUTOBIOGRAPHY/ *of a*/ SUPER-TRAMP/ *by*/ W. H. DAVIES/ (publisher's device)/ *With a preface by*/ G. BERNARD SHAW/ at foot: JONATHAN CAPE/ THIRTY BEDFORD SQUARE/ LONDON

8vo; (A)–I and K–Q in eights; 128 leaves: (1–4) 5–13 (14) 15 (16) 17 (18) 19–253 (3)pp; 16.7 × 12.6 cms

(1) half-title: THE AUTOBIOGRAPHY OF A/ SUPER-TRAMP; (2) starts: *by the same author*/ ends: THE ESSENTIAL W. H. DAVIES; (3) title-page; (4) starts: FIRST PUBLISHED IN 1908/ ends: BUNGAY, SUFFOLK; 5–6 CONTENTS; 7–13 PREFACE BY G. BERNARD SHAW signed G. B. S./ Ayot St. Lawrence. 1907; (14) blank; 15 AUTHOR'S NOTE TO 1920 EDITION signed W. H. D./ Cornwall, *August*, 1920.; (16) blank; 17 FOREWORD TO 1923 EDITION signed W. H. D.; (18) blank; 19–243 text; 244 AUTUMN; 245–246 A DRINKING SONG; 247–248 SLEEP; 249–250 LOVE'S COMING; 251–253 THE LODGING-HOUSE FIRE; 253 at foot: THE END; (254–256) blank

endpapers: cream; *edges*: trimmed

binding: green paper-covered boards, lettered in silver; front cover: THE AUTO-BIOGRAPHY OF A/ SUPER-TRAMP; spine: THE/ AUTO-/ BIOGRAPHY/ OF A/ SUPER-/ TRAMP/ (decorative rule)/ W. H./ DAVIES/ at foot: (publisher's device); back cover: blank; *dust-jacket*: not seen

date of publication: 14 November 1955

print run: 10,000 copies, 14 November 1955 (printed and bound by Clay); *price*: 10s.6d.

copy seen: BL (shelf mark: 12653.b.30; accession date: 31 October 1955)

note: price increases: 1 January 1960 13s.6d., 1 April 1961 15s.; 1 January 1963 16s.

A3rr First Digit Books edition   Brown, Watson 1960

The Autobiography of a/ SUPER TRAMP/ *by*/ W. H. DAVIES/ Preface by George Bernard Shaw/ at foot: (publisher's device)/ BROWN, WATSON, LTD.,/ LONDON.

paperback; (1–4) 5–316 (4)pp; 17.0 × 11.0 cms

as *A3e* (but with slightly different pagination) apart from: (2) starts: *Some Other Digit General Titles* -/ ends: by Leo Margulis; (3) title-page; (4) starts: The Autobiography of a/ ends: 25 Prince George Street, Portsmouth, Hants.; (317–320) starts: THE/ GOD OF CHANNEL ONE/ ends: ABOVE ADDRESS; frontispiece omitted; *binding*: paper wrappers

date of publication: 24 October 1960; *price*: 3s.6d.

copy seen: BL (shelf mark: WP.9655/394; accession date: 27 October 1960)

note: contains the Foreword to the 1923 edition

A3ss Second Digit Books edition   Brown, Watson 1962

as *A3rr* apart from: (2) starts: *Some Other Digit Titles* -/ ends: The Short Stories of LIAM O'FLAHERTY – 2/6; (4) First Digit Edition, October 1960/ Reprinted, February 1961/ This Edition, June 1962; (317–320) starts: DIGIT BOOKS/ The Atom Station/ ends: exciting exploits!; *binding*: paper wrappers

date of publication: 29 June 1962; *price*: 3s.6d.

copy seen: BL (shelf mark: WP.9655/507; accession date: 9 April 1963)

A3tt Third Digit Books edition   Brown, Watson 1963

date of publication: April 1963

A3uu New English edition   Jonathan Cape 1964

date of publication: 27 April 1964

print run: 1500 copies printed on 17 December 1963 by Fletcher; *price*: 16s.

A3vv New English edition: second impression   Jonathan Cape 1966

print run: 1500 copies printed on 18 August 1965 by Fletcher; *price*: 21s.

A3ww Corgi paperback   Corgi 1971

W. H. Davies/ The Autobiography of a/ Super-Tramp/ *With a Preface by*/ G. Bernard Shaw/ (publisher's device)/ CORGI BOOKS/ TRANSWORLD PUBLISHERS LTD/ A National General Company paperback; (1–4) 5–252 (3)pp; 17.3 × 11.0 cms

as *A3rr* apart from: (1) starts: In his Preface, George Bernard Shaw had/ ends: endure; (2) blank; (3) title-page; (4) starts: THE AUTOBIOGRAPHY OF A SUPER-TRAMP/ ends: Richard Clay (The Chaucer Press), Ltd., Bungay, Suffolk; (254) below text: THE END; (255–256) starts: A SELECTION OF FINE READING/ ends: (NOV. 71)....................................; *binding*: paper wrappers: printed in full-colour; front, over the silhouette of a tramp, lettered in white (outlined in black): THE/ AUTOBIOGRAPHY/ OF A/ SUPER-TRAMP/ W H DAVIES; spine: not known; back, in white, over a mirror image of the front: starts: As a very young man the poet W. H. Davies visited/ ends: classics of this century./ at foot: UK...40p/ Australia...$1.25/ New Zealand...$1.25

price: 40p.

copy seen: BL (shelf mark: X 900/9280; accession date: 29 November 1971)

A3xx   1976

paperback (not seen)

note: BL (shelf mark: X 708/ 20354)

A3yy   Oxford paperback edition   Oxford University Press 1980

W. H. DAVIES/ The Autobiography of a/ Super-Tramp/ With a Preface by/ GEORGE BERNARD SHAW/ at foot: Oxford New York Toronto Melbourne/ OXFORD UNIVERSITY PRESS/ 1980

paperback: (1–4) 5 (6) 7–13 (14) 15 (16) 17 (18) 19–253 (3)pp; 19.5 × 12.8 cms

as *3ww* apart from: (1) half-title: THE AUTOBIOGRAPHY OF A/ SUPER-TRAMP; (2) starts: *by the same author/* ends: THE COMPLETE POEMS; (3) title-page; (4) starts: *Oxford University Press, Walton Street, Oxford* OX2 6DP/ ends: ISBN 0–19–281293–9/ at foot: *Printed in Great Britain by/ Cox & Wyman Ltd., Reading*; (254) blank; (255–256) starts: *Other Paperbacks from Oxford/* ends: of a forgotten classic, originally published in 1899.; *binding*: paper wrappers: front, printed in blue-green and black over a harbour scene with a ship and a barge in the background and seamen in the foreground: (black rule)/ The Autobiography of a (in black)/ Super-tramp (in blue-green)/ (black rule)/ Preface by George Bernard Shaw (in black)/ W. H. Davies (in blue-green); spine, vertically downwards: DAVIES (in blue-green) THE AUTOBIOGRAPHY OF A/ SUPER-TRAMP (in black)/ at foot: (publisher's device in white); back, divided vertically into two with the scene from the front wrapping on to the back: starts: (black publisher's device) OXFORD PAPERBACKS (in pale blue)/ ends: £1.95 net (in black) in UK ISBN 0 192812939 (in white)

date of publication: 17 April 1980

print run: probably 10,000; *price*: £1.95

copy seen: BL (shelf mark: X 909/ 45164; accession date: 17 April 1980)

notes: (a) as at June 1992 54,727 copies had been sold (personal communication with OUP, 8 June 1992)
(b) reprinted in 1986, 1989 and 1992
(c) price increases: £2.50; £2.95 23 October 1986; £3.95 25 March 1988; £5.99 7 January 1992

A4 NATURE POEMS   A C Fifield 1908

Nature Poems/ And Others/ By/ William H. Davies/ Author of "The Soul's Destroyer," "New Poems,"/ "Autobiography of a Super-Tramp."/ at foot: London/ A. C. Fifield, 44 Fleet Street, E.C./ 1908

8vo; (A)–D in eights; 32 leaves: (1–5) 6 (7) 8–62 (2)pp; 16.8 × 11.0 cms variable

(1) half-title: Nature Poems/ And Others; (2) in a panel: starts: UNIFORM WITH THIS./ ends: LONDON: A. C. FIFIELD.; (3) title-page; (4) *All rights reserved*/ at foot: PRINTED BY/ WILLIAM BRENDON AND SON, LTD./ PLYMOUTH; (5)–6 Contents; (7)–62 text; 62 below text: THE END; (63–64) starts: *Crown 8vo. Canvas. 320 pages. 6s.*/ ends: London: A. C. Fifield, 44 Fleet Street, E.C.

contents: p7 The Muse; p8 The Rain. A Life's Love; p9 Robin Redbreast; p10 Tyrants; p11 To a Butterfly. The Milkmaid's Call; p12 The Wind; p13 Jenny; p14 Sweet Youth; p15 Nature's Friend; p16 A Maiden and Her Hair; p17 Sweet Music; p18 Early Morn; p19 The Battle. A Beggar's Life; p20 The Moth; p21 Day's Black Star; p22 Go, Angry One. Dead Born; p23 The Change; p25 A Richer Freight. School's Out; p26 A Happy Life; p27 The Sweetest Dream; p28 Love's Birth; p33 Nature's Moods; p34 Truly Great; p35 A Familiar Voice; p36 A Summer's Noon; p37 Life; p38 In Days Gone; p39 March; p40 The Laughers; p41 The Thieves; p42 Solitude; p43 Australian Bill; p44 The Boy; p45 A Swallow that flew into the Room; p46 A Lovely Woman; p47 Money; p48 The Cheat; p49 Where We Differ. When I Returned; p50 The Daisy; p51 A Vagrant's Life; p52 A Luckless Pair; p53 The Trickster. The Two Lives; p54 Beauty's Danger; p55 Childhood's Hours; p56 The Sea; p58 Vain Beauty; p59 Waiting

paper: watermarked: (crown)/ Abbey Mills/ Greenfield; chain lines 2.4 cms apart and vertical

endpapers: cream; *edges*: uncut, top edge trimmed

binding: grey mottled paper-covered boards, printed in black; front cover: Nature Poems/ and others/ William H. Davies; spine, vertically downwards: Nature Poems. William H. Davies; back cover: blank; *dust-jacket*: not seen

date of publication: October 1908; *price*: 1s.

copies seen: BL (shelf mark: 011650.de.6; accession date: 31 December 1908); HDB; SH

reviews: *TLS*, 22 October 1908, 367; A Poet by Birth, Edward Thomas, *Daily Chronicle*, 4 November 1908, 3; A Newport-Born Poet: Mr Wm H. Davies's Latest Book, *South Wales Argus*, 14 November 1908, (3); Eight Voices, *Nation*, 14 November 1908, IV, 7, 280–283; Book of the Week: Recent Verse, F. S. Flint, *New Age*, 26 November 1908, IV, 5, 95; Books and Persons (An Occasional Causerie),

Jacob Tonson (Arnold Bennett), *New Age*, 3 December 1908, IV, 6, 112; Nature Poems, *Morning Post*, 31 December 1908, 2; More Poetry, *Academy*, 9 January 1909, LXXVI, 1914, 659; *Nation*, 14 January 1909, 88, 2271, 40; The Bookman's Table, *Bookman*, February 1909, XXXV, 209, 238

previous printings:
'Nature's Moods', 'Love's Birth' and 'Joy and Pleasure', *Nation*, 2 May 1908, III, 5, 159, 11 July 1908, III, 15, 526 and 8 August 1908, III, 19, 676 respectively

text changes from first printing to A4:
Nature's Moods: line 3: 'Hills' to 'hills', line 13: 'Clouds – Cloud' to 'Clouds, Cloud'

notes: (a) the HRHRC copy is a signed presentation copy to Samuel Looker
(b) 'Life' ('Alone beneath Heaven's roof I stand;') and 'The Two Lives' ('Youth thinks green apples sweet') are not known to have been reprinted
(c) Edward Thomas introduced WHD to Frank Cazenove, a partner in The Literary Agency of London. He took over WHD's marketing affairs and arranged publication in literary periodicals. He also negotiated *Nature Poems*
(d) A. C. Fifield advertised editions of this book which I have been unable to trace (2nd impression, 3rd thousand 1908; 3rd impression 1908; 3rd edition, wrappers 1s.3d.)
(e) 'School's Out' was reprinted by the BBC in a music leaflet for use by schools listening to the schools' programmes during autumn term 1943

A4a   Second edition   A C Fifield 1910

as *A4* apart from: (2) starts: <u>Mr Davies' New Volume of Poetry</u>/ ends: London: A. C. Fifield, 13 Clifford's Inn, E.C.; (3) Author of "The Soul's Destroyer,"/ "The Autobiography of a Super-Tramp,"/ "Farewell to Poesy," etc./ *First Edition, October*, 1908/ *Reprinted, May*, 1910/ at foot: London: A. C. Fifield, 13 Clifford's Inn, E.C./ 1910; (63–64) starts: The Works of the "Super-Tramp"/ ends: London: A. C. Fifield, 13 Clifford's Inn, E.C.; *binding*: front cover, at foot: A. C. Fifield; *dust-jacket*: not seen

date of publication: recorded as May 1910 in the English Catalogue but June 1910 according to WHD's first bibliographer (George Francis Wilson *(F95)*)

copies seen: BL (shelf mark: X 989/70108; accession date: 30 June 1977); HRHRC

A4b   Third edition   A C Fifield 1916

as *A4* apart from: (2) in a panel: starts: Child Lovers & other Poems/ ends: *London: A. C. Fifield*; (3) *Reprinted, December*, 1916/ at foot: London: A. C. Fifield, 13 Clifford's Inn, E.C./ 1916; *binding*: grey card wrappers, printed in green-black; front cover: Nature/ Poems/ & others/ By W. H./ Davies/ Third edition. 1s. net/ London: A. C. Fifield; spine: Nature/ Poems/ W. H./ Davies/ 3rd/ edition/ Fifield; back cover, in a panel: starts: *Cloth extra, gilt, 6s. net; postage* 4d./ ends: *London: A. C. Fifield*

date of publication: recorded as January 1917 in the English Catalogue but December 1916 according to George Francis Wilson *(F95)*; the corrections on the second edition at HRHRC in WHD's hand give the new date as November 1916 *copies seen*: HRHRC; SH

text corrections to the second edition at HRHRC in WHD's hand:
Robin Redbreast: line 4: 'poor, dead things' to 'of withered things'
The Wind: line 4: 'very old' to 'that are old', line 10: 'Oft I hear rise' to 'Hear rising'
A Maiden and Her Hair: 6th stanza line 4: 'See' to 'They'
Day's Black Star: line 4: 'clouds' to 'cloud'
The Laughers: 2nd stanza line 2: 'shrieketh' to 'he shrieks'
The Daisy: 4th stanza line 2: 'Out of all' to 'And gone from'

A4c Life & Colour Series No 3   Jonathan Cape 1921

Nature Poems/ and others (double fleuron)/ by W. H. Davies/ (publisher's device)/ at foot: Jonathan Cape/ Eleven Gower Street, London

8vo; (A)–D in eights (the last leaf of the final gathering is a stub pasted to the endpaper); 32 leaves (one a stub): (1–5) 6 (7) 8–62pp; 16.8 × 10.8 cms; the first two leaves are cancels

as *A4* apart from: (1) half-title: Nature Poems; (2) starts: *By the Same Author/* ends: *The Life & Colour/ Series :: No. 6*; (3) title-page; (4) *First Published* 1908/ *Second Impression* 1910/ *Third Impression* 1916/ *Reissued by Jonathan Cape ::::* 1921; (5)–6 Contents; (7)–62 text; 62 below text: THE END; *binding*: as A2b; front cover: blank; spine, on a white paper label 3.4 cms deep, in black and mustard: (mustard double rule)/ Nature/ Poems/ (mustard fleuron)/ W. H./ Davies/ (mustard double rule); back cover: blank; *dust-jacket*: pinkish-beige printed in black; front, within a decorative border: Nature Poems/ and others (double fleuron)/ by W. H. Davies/ (publisher's device)/ *The Life & Colour Series, No. 3./* at foot: Jonathan Cape/ Eleven Gower Street, London; spine: Nature/ Poems/ (fleuron)/ W. H./ Davies/ at foot: Jonathan/ Cape; back: starts: *The Life & Colour Series/* ends: *Jonathan Cape, Eleven Gower Street, London* (10 titles listed); front flap: starts: *The Complete Works of/* ends: *W. H. Davies :: 2s.6d. net*; back flap: blank

date of publication: October 1921; *price*: 2s.6d.

copy seen: RUL, Finzi

note: the National Union Catalogue records an edition published by B. Humphries, Boston with an undated title-page in the holding of the Public Library of Cincinnati and Hamilton County, Cincinnati, Ohio, USA

A5 **BEGGARS**   Duckworth & Co 1909

BEGGARS/ BY/ W. H. DAVIES/ AUTHOR OF/ "THE AUTOBIOGRAPHY OF A SUPERTRAMP [sic]," "THE SOUL'S DESTROYER,"/ "NATURE POEMS," ETC./ (publisher's device)/ at foot: DUCKWORTH & CO./ 3, HENRIETTA STREET, COVENT GARDEN/ 1909

8vo; (A) in four plus tipped-in frontispiece, B–I and K–U in eights; 156 leaves: (1–2) (i–iv) v–vi (1) 2–300 (4)pp plus frontispiece not included in the pagination; 18.4 × 12.4 cms

(1–2) blank; (i) half-title: BEGGARS; (ii) *All Rights Reserved*; portrait frontispiece of WHD reclining in a meadow smoking his pipe with a walking stick by his side, protected by a tissue guard; (iii) title-page; (iv) blank; v–vi CONTENTS; (1)–300 text; 300 at foot: WILLIAM BRENDON AND SON, LTD./ PRINTERS, PLYMOUTH; (301–304) starts: (double rule)/ ends: 3 HENRIETTA STREET, COVENT GARDEN, LONDON, W.C./ (double rule)

contents: I p1 The Nationalities as Beggars; II p10 A Tramp's Camp in Texas; III p19 Daring Beggars; IV p27 Dilemmas of Travellers; V p34 Queer Places; VI p42 Stiffs; VII p49 American Prisons; VIII p58 Experiences of Others; IX p66 The American Lakes; X p74 The Happy Life; XI p82 Boy Desperadoes; XII p89 American and English Beggars; XIII p97 Beggars' Slang; XIV p105 Bony's Wits; XV p114 Favouritism; XVI p122 A Law to Suppress Vagrancy; XVII p130 Stubborn Invalids; XVIII p138 The Earnings of Beggars; XIX p146 Charity in Strange Quarters; XX p154 Enemies of Beggars; XXI p161 The Lowest State of Man; XXII p169 The Lodger Lover; XXIII p176 The Handy Man; XXIV p183 On Books; XXV p191 Narks; XXVI p199 The Scribe in a Lodging-House; XXVII p207 Licensed Beggars; XXVIII p213 Navvies and Frauds; XXIX p222 A First Night in a Lodging-House; XXX p230 Gentleman Bill; XXXI p238 Fallacies Concerning Beggars; XXXII p247 Lady Tramps; XXXIII p256 Meeting Old Friends; XXXIV p263 The Comparison; XXXV p270 The Supper; XXXVI p278 The Literary Life; XXXVII p285 The Sport of Fame; XXXVIII p293 Beggars in the Making

endpapers: cream; *edges*: trimmed

binding: grass-green ribbed morocco grain cloth, blind-blocked, lettered in dark green; front cover, in blind: a central panel surrounded by four lozenge-shaped panels, upper panel, lettered in dark green: W. H. DAVIES/ within double-bordered central panel: Beggars; spine, lettered in gilt: BEGGARS/ W. H./ DAVIES/ at foot: DUCKWORTH & CO.; back cover: blind-blocked publisher's device

date of publication: September 1909; *price*: 6s.

copies seen: BL (shelf mark: 012331.ee.79; accession date: 14 September 1909) (1st issue); HRHRC (both issues); RUL, Finzi (2nd issue); HDB (1st issue); SH (2nd issue)

reviews: A Book of the Week, X, *Country Life: The Journal for all interested in Country Life and Country Pursuits*, 18 September 1909, XXVI, 663, 397–398; The World of Books, *Nation*, 18 September 1909, V, 25, 889; *Athenaeum*, 16 October 1909, 455; The Life of a Tramp, *Morning Post*, 21 October 1909, 2; Beggars, Arthur Ransome, *Bookman*, October 1909, XXXVII, 217, 47–48 (portrait – the frontispiece from the first issue of the book); *New Age*, 18 November 1909, VI, 3, supplement 3

notes: (a) second issue: mid-blue calico grain cloth, blocked and lettered in navy; front cover as A5; spine: BEGGARS/ W. H./ DAVIES/ at foot: DUCKWORTH; back cover: (navy publisher's device); *dust-jacket*: cream, printed in blue as the cloth binding; both flaps: blank; frontispiece omitted
(b) the HDB copy is stamped 'PRESENTATION COPY' on the title-page

A6   FAREWELL TO POESY   A C Fifield 1910

Farewell to Poesy/ And Other Pieces/ By/ William H. Davies/ at foot:
London/ A. C. Fifield, 13 Clifford's Inn, E.C./ 1910

8vo; (A)–D in eights; 32 leaves: (1–7) 8 (9) 10–60 (4)pp; 17.0 × 11.0 cms variable

(1) half-title: Farewell to Poesy/ And Other Pieces; (2) in a panel: starts: BY THE
SAME AUTHOR./ ends: Mathews, Vigo Street, W.; (3) title-page; (4) *All rights
reserved*/ at foot: PRINTED BY/ WILLIAM BRENDON AND SON, LTD./
PLYMOUTH; (5) Some of these poems have appeared in *The Nation*, and the/
author thanks the editor for permission to reprint them.; (6) blank; (7)–8 Contents;
(9)–60 text; 60 below text: THE END; (61–64) starts: Nature Poems/ ends:
London: A. C. Fifield, 13 Clifford's Inn, E.C.

contents: p9 Farewell to Poesy. The Dark Hour; p10 Jenny Wren; p11 The
Milkmaid's Song; p12 The Idiot and the Child; p13 A Month Ago. The Trusting
Young; p14 Now; p15 Rose; p16 The Green Tent; p17 Selfish Hearts; p18 To the
Wind at Morn; p19 No Master. The Dumb World; p20 On the Death of a Little
Child; p21 The Poppy; p22 Knitting; p23 Clouds; p24 In the Country; p25 The
Kingfisher. An Old House in London; p27 Scotty's Luck. Happy Wind; p28 The
Sluggard. The House Builder; p29 Old Ragan; p30 To a Flirt; p31 On Expecting
Some Books; p33 The Sailor to His Parrot; p34 Time's Justice; p35 Angry; p36 The
Call of the Sea; p37 Come, Honest Boys; p38 Death's Game; p39 To the New Year;
p40 The Philosophical Beggar; p47 Fancy

paper: watermarked: (crown)/ Abbey Mills/ Greenfield; chain lines 2.4 cms apart
and vertical

endpapers: cream; *edges*: uncut, top edge trimmed

binding: grey mottled paper-covered boards printed in black; front cover: Farewell
to Poesy/ and other Poems/ William H. Davies; spine, vertically downwards:
Farewell to Poesy. William H. Davies; back cover: starts: 13 Clifford's Inn, E.C.
February 21, 1910./ ends: London: A. C. Fifield, 13 Clifford's Inn, E.C.

dust-jacket: pale grey, printed in black; front: Farewell to Poesy/ and other Poems/
William H. Davies/ One Shilling nett/ at foot: London: A. C. Fifield; spine, vertically
downwards: Farewell to Poesy. William H. Davies; back: starts: 13 Clifford's Inn,
E.C. *February* 21, 1910./ ends: London: A. C. Fifield, 13 Clifford's Inn, E.C.; both
flaps: blank

date of publication: 21 February 1910 according to A. C. Fifield but recorded as
March 1910 in the English Catalogue

price: 1s.

copies seen: BL (shelf mark 011650.eee.31; accession date: 13 July 1910); HDB; SH

reviews: Blake's Muse, ET, *Daily Chronicle*, 28 March 1910, 6; Farewell to Poesy,
Morning Post, 7 April 1910, 2; *Athenaeum*, 16 April 1910, 456; Mr W. H. Davies'
"Farewell", Austin H. Johnson, *The Thrush*, May 1910, II, 2, 158–159; Some
Recent Verse, *TLS*, 19 May 1910, 177; Singing Birds, *Academy*, 21 May 1910,
LXXVIII, 1985, 492; The Natural Poet, Edward Thomas, *Bookman*, May 1910,
XXXVIII, 224, 80–81; Recent Verse, *The Spectator*, 30 July 1910, 105, 4283, 174;
My Study Table, Rev T. A. Seed, *Great Thoughts*, 1910, 53 (LIII), 227

previous printings:
'The Dark Hour', 'The Milkmaid's Song', 'On Expecting Some Books', 'Clouds', 'Knitting', 'Now' and 'An Old House in London' (as 'An Old House'), 'Angry' and 'The Kingfisher', *Nation*, 9 January 1909, IV, 15, 580, 6 February 1909, IV, 19, 717, 6 March 1909, IV, 23, 862, 22 May 1909, V, 8, 284, 19 June 1909, V, 12, 426, 14 August 1909, V, 20, 720, 18 September 1909, V, 25, 888 and 8 January 1910, VI, 15, 612
'In the Country' and 'Jenny Wren', *Country Life*, 29 May 1909, XXV, 647, 766 and 31 July 1909, XXVI, 656, 147
'Rose', *Westminster Gazette*, 4 January 1910, 2

text changes from first printings to A6:
The Milkmaid's Song: 3rd stanza line 2: 'Cows' to 'cows'; 6th stanza line 1: 'Cow' to 'cow';
7th stanza (omitted in *Farewell to Poesy*): 'Now what gave I, to hear her song,/ As home she went, and I along?'; 8th stanza (7th in *Farewell to Poesy*) line 1: 'maid' to 'Maid'
On Expecting Some Books: line 11: 'Snowdrops' to 'snowdrops', line 16: 'books' to 'Books'; 14 additional lines added between 'They will not disappoint, like these.' and 'O may their coming never cease!' in *Farewell to Poesy*
Clouds: 1st stanza line 1: 'clouds' to 'Clouds'; 5th stanza line 1: 'cloudlets' to 'Cloudlets'; line 2: 'clouds' to 'Clouds', line 3: 'ants' to Ants', line 4: 'moths' to 'Moths'; 6th stanza line 1: from 'clouds' to 'Clouds'
An Old House in London: title to: 'An Old House'; 4 additional lines added between 'Stood happy horses, sheep and cows.' and 'From thy back windows thou couldst see,', line 21 up: 'State' to 'state'
Rose: 2nd stanza line 1: 'do' to 'can'
Knitting: line 3: 'When barks a saucy pup at him' to 'When saucy pup doth bark at him -', line 3 up: 'Sun' to 'sun', line 2 up: 'Tide' to 'tide'
Jenny Wren: line 20: 'Scold' to 'scold'
Now: 1st stanza line 2: 'around' to 'round'
Angry: 1st stanza line 1 and 4th stanza line 1: 'See' to 'see'

notes: (a) 'The Kingfisher' was included in *The Jupiter Anthology of Twentieth Century Poetry* recorded on disc
(b) A. C. Fifield were not entirely happy with 'The House Builder' and suggested alternative wording for lines 9/10 ('As though a passing butterfly,/ Did try to move a stuggy bull') which was not incorporated into the final printing (letter dated 12 November 1909, Jonathan Cape archives, RUL)
(c) A. C. Fifield advertised a 2nd thousand 1910, 1s. which I have been unable to trace

A6a Life & Colour Series No 4   Jonathan Cape 1921

Farewell to Poesy/ and other pieces (double fleuron)/ by W. H. Davies/ (publisher's device)/ at foot: Jonathan Cape/ Eleven Gower Street, London

8vo; four unsigned gatherings of eight; 32 leaves: (i–ii) (1–7) 8 (9) 10–60 (2)pp; 17.0 × 11.0 cms variable

as *A6* apart from: (i–ii) blank; (2) starts: *By the Same Author*/ ends: The Life &

Colour/ Series : : No. 4; (3) title-page; (4) starts: *First Published* 1910/ ends: William Brendon & Son, Ltd.; (61–62) blank; *binding*: as A2b; front cover: blank; spine, on a white paper label 3.3 cms deep, in black and mustard: (double mustard rule)/ Fare-/ well/ to/ Poesy/ (mustard fleuron)/ W. H./ Davies/ (double mustard rule); back cover: blank; *dust-jacket*: mottled pinkish-beige printed in black; front, within a black decorative border: Farewell to Poesy/ by W. H. Davies (fleuron)/ (publisher's device)/ *The Life & Colour Series, No. 4./* at foot: Jonathan Cape/ Eleven Gower Street, London; spine: Fare-/ well to/ Poesy/ (fleuron)/ W. H./ Davies/ at foot: Jonathan/ Cape; back: starts: *The Life & Colour Series/* ends: *Jonathan Cape, Eleven Gower Street, London* (10 titles listed); front flap: starts: *The Complete Works of/* ends: *W. H. Davies :: 2s.6d. net*; back flap: blank

date of publication: September 1921; *price*: 2s.6d.

copies seen: BL (shelf mark: 011645.de.35; accession date: 24 January 1922); RUL, Finzi

reviews: Poetry, JCS, *London Mercury*, February 1922, V, 28, 428–430; A Group of Poems by W. H. Davies, *Harper's Magazine*, March 1922, CXLIV, DCCCLXII, 488

notes: (a) printed by The Mayflower Press
(b) the National Union Catalogue records an edition published by B. Humphries, Boston with an undated title-page in the holding of Yale University, New Haven, USA

A7 A WEAK WOMAN   Duckworth & Co 1911

A WEAK WOMAN/ A Novel (in Gothic)/ BY/ W. H. DAVIES/ AUTHOR OF/ "THE AUTOBIOGRAPHY OF A SUPER-TRAMP," "BEGGARS," ETC./ (publisher's device)/ DUCKWORTH & CO./ 3 HENRIETTA STREET, COVENT GARDEN/ 1911

8vo; (A) in four, B–I and K–U in eights, X in four; 160 leaves: (i–vi) vii–viii (1) 2–305 (7)pp; 18.6 × 12.3 cms

(i–ii) blank; (iii) half-title: A WEAK WOMAN; (iv) starts: BY THE SAME AUTHOR/ ends: A. C. FIFIELD, 13 Clifford's Inn, E.C.; (v) title-page; (vi) *All rights reserved*; vii–viii CONTENTS; (1)–305 text; 305 at foot: THE END; (306) PRINTED BY/ WILLIAM BRENDON AND SON, LTD./ PLYMOUTH; (307–312) starts: BEGGARS/ ends: 3 HENRIETTA ST., COVENT GARDEN, LONDON, W.C.

contents: I p1 My Family; II p9 A Marriage; III p16 More Trouble; IV p24 My Plans; V p31 Leaving Home; VI p39 Kind Strangers; VII p48 Mrs Figgs and Her Lodgers; VIII p57 The Major; IX p66 Enlightened; X p75 A New Acquaintance; XI p83 A Dreamer; XII p92 A Surprise; XIII p102 The One Thing Lacking; XIV p111 Selling a Manuscript; XV p121 Vagabonds; XVI p130 Petticoat Alley; XVII p140 Punch; XVIII p149 Relations; XIX p158 An Evening Out; XX p167 Helping the Poor; XXI p177 Death at Home; XXII p186 Hampstead; XXIII p194 The Song; XXIV p203 Love; XXV p212 Three Years After; XXVI p221 Old Acquaintance; XXVII p230 The World's Mockery; XXVIII p239 A Poet's Revenge; XXIX p249 The Absent One; XXX p259 The Arrival; XXXI p269 A Painful Experience; XXXII p279 Murder; XXXIII p288 The Murderer; XXXIV p298 The End *endpapers*: cream; *edges*: trimmed

binding: grass-green embossed calico grain cloth, blind-blocked, lettered in black and gilt; front cover blocked as *A5*, lettered in black, upper panel: W. H. DAVIES/ central panel: A/ Weak/ Woman; spine, lettered in gilt: A/ WEAK/ WOMAN/ W. H./ DAVIES/ at foot: DUCKWORTH & Co.; back cover: black publisher's device

dust-jacket: fine dark green net design on a pale grey background, lettered in navy; front: A/ Weak/ Woman/ at foot: W. H. DAVIES; spine: A/ WEAK/ WOMAN/ W. H./ DAVIES/ at foot: DUCKWORTH & CO.; back, in a panel: starts: ANONYMOUS/ ends: LONDON: DUCKWORTH & CO., 3 HENRIETTA STREET, W.C.; both flaps: blank

date of publication: 17 February 1911; *price*: 6s.

copies seen: BL (shelf mark: 012618.ccc.1; accession date: 17 February 1911) (1st issue); HRHRC (1st issue, 2 copies; 2nd issue, 1 copy); CH (2nd issue); NL (1st issue, signed by WHD)

reviews: Mr W. H. Davies's Prose, *Nation*, 4 March 1911, VIII, 32, 922 (by Edward Garnett); *Athenaeum*, 25 March 1911, 329; Fiction, *Academy*, 25 March 1911, LXXX, 2029, 362; Life and the Super-Tramp, *Country Life*, 8 April 1911, XXIX, 744, 502–503

notes: (a) second issue binding: mid-blue fine-ribbed cloth, blind-blocked, lettered in navy and gilt; front, blocked as *A5*, lettered in navy as first issue; spine, lettered in gilt as first issue apart from: at foot: DUCKWORTH (& Co. omitted); back: blank (b) according to a letter from WHD to Edward Garnett dated 10 December 1910 and addressed 45 London Road, Sevenoaks it was essential to change the name 'Hansom' to 'Ransom' because if he did not he was likely to offend a family in Sevenoaks

A8   SONGS OF JOY   A C Fifield 1911

Songs of Joy/ and others/ By/ William H. Davies/ at foot: London/ A. C. Fifield, 13 Clifford's Inn, E.C./ 1911

8vo; (A)–F in eights; 48 leaves: (1–6) 7–8 (9) 10–94 (2)pp; 17.2 × 10.8 cms variable

(1) half-title: Songs of Joy/ and others; (2) in a panel: starts: BY THE SAME AUTHOR/ ends: 13 CLIFFORD'S INN, E.C.; (3) title-page; (4) *All rights reserved*/ at foot: PRINTED BY/ WILLIAM BRENDON AND SON, LTD./ PLYMOUTH; (5) Some of these poems have appeared in *The Nation,*/ *The English Review, The Westminster Gazette*, and/ *The Vineyard*. The author thanks the editors for/ permission to reprint them.; (6) blank; 7–8 Contents; (9)-94 text; 94 at foot: THE END; (95–96) starts: THE WORKS OF WILLIAM H. DAVIES/ ends: LONDON: A. C. FIFIELD, 13 CLIFFORD'S INN, E.C.

contents: p9 Songs of Joy; p11 The Example; p12 In May; p14 The Flood; p15 Leisure; p16 Love's Power; p17 Fancy's Home; p18 War; p19 Self-Love; p20 In the Wood; p21 Sheep; p22 Love and Immortality; p23 Days that have been; p25 To a Working Man; p26 Treasures; p31 Beauty's Revenge; p33 Days too Short; p34 Dreaming of Death; p35 The Stars at Work; p36 The Temper of a Maid; p37 The

Power of Music; p39 Christ the Man; p40 Ingratitude; p41 The Grey-haired Child; p42 The Posts; p43 Rich or Poor; p44 The Harvest Home; p45 The Winged Flower; p46 Seeking Beauty; p48 The Owl; p49 The Little Man; p50 Sound and Grace; p51 A Mother's Science; p52 The East in Gold; p53 Man; p55 Sadness and Joy; p57 Love's Happiness; p59 Circumstance; p60 Slum Children; p61 To a Rich Lady; p62 To Sparrows Fighting; p63 A Woman's Glory; p64 The Happy Child; p65 The Two Flocks; p66 A Dream; p68 The Elements; p70 Beauty's Bait; p71 The Heap of Rags; p73 The Quarrel; p75 O Happy Blackbird; p76 To a Bore; p77 Fairies, Take Care; p79 Captives; p80 The Doubtful One; p81 The Little Ones; p83 Shopping; p84 The Sleepers; p86 The Bed-sitting-Room; p88 The Child and the Mariner

paper: watermarked: (crown)/ Abbey Mills/ Greenfield; chain lines 2.4 cms apart and vertical

endpapers: cream; *edges*: uncut, deckle fore edge, top edge gilt

binding: lime green fine net grain cloth, blind-blocked, lettered and decorated in gilt; front cover, within a blind-blocked border: SONGS OF JOY AND OTHERS/ (fleuron)/ (fleuron) W. H. DAVIES (fleuron); spine: SONGS/ OF / JOY/ (fleuron)/ WILLIAM/ H./ DAVIES/ (fleuron)/ at foot: FIFIELD; back cover: blank; dark green ribbon marker; *dust-jacket*: not seen

date of publication: November 1911; *price*: 2s.6d.

copies seen: BL (shelf mark: 011650.e.104; accession date: 22 November 1922); HDB; RUL, Finzi; SH

reviews: *Athenaeum*, 30 December 1911, 816; In the Minor Key, *Country Life*, 13 January 1912, XXXI, 783, 47; Recent Verse, *The Spectator*, 27 January 1912, 108, 4361, 123; by AJH, *Poetry Review*, February 1912, I, 2, 84–85; "In Divers Tones", *Academy and Literature*, 10 February 1912, LXXXII, 2075, 167–168; Songs and Singers, Edward Thomas, *Bookman*, February 1912, XLI, 245, 265–266; *Literary Digest*, 4 May 1912, 44, 18 (1150), 952 (includes 'Days That have Been', 'The East in Gold', 'Days Too Short', 'The Temper of a Maid' and 'Shopping'); The English Lyric, *Westminster Gazette*, 18 May 1912, 5

mss: in WHD's hand; on unlined paper watermarked (apart from the last 12 leaves): Audrey Note/ FR, chain lines 2.5 cm apart and vertical; addressed 45 London Road, Sevenoaks, Kent and dated 1911; clipped into brown paper wrappers (HDB); there is also an undated but earlier mss at the British Museum (mss no 54168D) of 'The Sleepers' on 45 London Road, Sevenoaks notepaper, which accurately reflects the first printing of the poem in *Nation*

WHD's manuscript corrections:
Songs of Joy: 4th stanza line 2: 'state' to 'store'
War: 1st stanza line 2: 'pace' to 'lives'
The Little Man: 2nd stanza line 2: 'I said' to 'said I'
The Child and the Mariner: line 39 up: 'set in fire' to 'set in a sea of fire', line 8 up: 'hands' to 'hand'

text change from manuscript to A8:
Treasures: 15th stanza line 3: 'who' to 'that'

previous printings:
'Songs of Joy', 'Sadness and Joy', 'Leisure' and 'The East in Gold', *Vineyard*,

November 1910, I, 2, 123, January 1911, I, 4, 313, May 1911, I, 8, 541 and August 1911, I, 11, 741 respectively
'The Example' and 'The Temper of a Maid', *Open Window*, July 1911, II, 201–202
'In May' and 'O Happy Blackbird', 'Fairies, Take Care' and 'Days too Short', *English Review*, June 1910, V, 385–386, May 1911, VIII, 186 and September 1911, IX, 186 respectively
'Love's Power', 'Shopping', 'The Flood', 'Seeking Beauty', 'Beauty's Revenge', 'The Quarrel', 'The Winged Flower' and 'Fancy's Home', *Westminster Gazette*, 13 June 1910, 2, 16 June 1910, 2, 16 November 1910, 2, 28 November 1910, 2, 6 January 1911, 2, 27 June 1911, 2, 4 July 1911, 2 and 8 September 1911, 2 respectively
'Man', 'The Power of Music', 'The Sleepers', 'Days that have been', 'The Heap of Rags' and 'The Elements', *Nation*, 8 January 1910, VI, 15, 612, 22 October 1910, VIII, 4, 163, 28 January 1911, VIII, 18, 723, 11 March 1911, VIII, 24, 969, 20 May 1911, IX, 8, 294 and 16 September 1911, IX, 25, 878 respectively
'To Sparrows Fighting', *Odd Volume*, 1910, 14

text changes from first printings to A8:
Shopping: 3rd stanza line 3: 'or they will' to 'lest they should'
The Power of Music: 1st stanza line 2: 'thick-walled' to 'thick walled', line 4: 'wide open' to 'wide-open'; 6th stanza line 2: 'sleep' to 'Sleep'
The Sleepers: 1st stanza line 1: 'Thames's stony side' to 'waterside', line 5: 'four' to 'five'; 3rd stanza line 3: 'and lo!' to 'and saw'; 4th stanza line 5: 'said' to 'thought'
Days that have been: title from: Days That Have Been; 2nd stanza line 2: 'Butterfly' to 'butterfly'
The Heap of Rags: line 17: 'It sighed and moaned, would roar' to 'Would sigh, and moan and roar'; 4 additional lines between: 'Yet that poor thing' and 'the thing that showed no face'
The Elements: 1st stanza line 3: 'sun' to 'Sun'; 2nd stanza line 2: 'rain' to 'Rain'; 3rd stanz line 1: 'winds' to 'Winds'; 4th stanza line 1: 'lightning' to 'Lightning'; 5th stanza line 2: 'thunder's' to 'Thunder's', line 3: 'nightingale' to 'Nightingale'
Man: line 20: 'Man is no more' to 'And is Man more'; 4 lines omitted: 'Who knows what Life is for?/ Some hold it still with awe;/ Some rattle it for noise -/ But no man knows its use.'
Songs of Joy: 4th stanza line 2: 'small' to 'low'
Love's Power: 1st stanza: 'I ask no time when sunrise is,/ It's up or not, Sweetheart, with thee;/ And when I first behold thy face,/ That is the break of day to me.' omitted; 2nd stanza (1st in *A8*), line 1: 'full tide, or when' to 'high tide or low', line 2: 'Low water is, that ships may' to 'That ships may out of port or', line 3: 'Or out of port; when thou dost come' to 'When thou dost come, and not before,'; 2nd stanza (3rd in *A8*), line 3: 'does begin' to 'opens, Love'
Days too Short: title from: Days Too Short

notes: (a) HRHRC hold a mss of 'Beauty's Revenge' in the hand of Herbert E. Palmer with a note to the effect that he had wanted to quote it in his anthology *Post Victorian Poetry* (Dent 1938) but that WHD denied all knowledge of it at that time
(b) 'Leisure' was included in *The Jupiter Anthology of Twentieth Century Poetry* recorded on disc
(c) 'Leisure' was included in the 'Rhyme Sheet' series published by Poetry Bookshop
(d) 'Sheep' was set to music by Cramers
(e) price increased to 3s.6d.

A8a   Life & Colour Series No 7   Jonathan Cape 1921

Songs of Joy/ and Others, by/ William H. Davies/ (publisher's device)/ at foot: Jonathan Cape/ Eleven Gower Street, London

8vo; (1)–6 in eights; 48 leaves: (i–ii) (1–6) 7–8 (9) 10–94pp; 17.0 × 10.5 cms variable

as *A8* apart from: (i–ii) blank; (1) half-title: Songs of Joy/ and Others; (2) starts: *By the Same Author*/ ends: *The Life & Colour*/ *Series* :: :: *No.* 7; (3) title-page; (4) *First Published* 1911/ *Second Edition* 1921/ *All rights reserved; binding*: as *A2b*; front cover: blank; spine, on a white paper label 3.8 cms deep, in black and mustard: (double mustard rule)/ Songs/ of/ Joy/ (mustard fleuron)/ W. H./ Davies/ (double mustard rule); back cover: blank; *edges*: top and fore edge trimmed; *dust-jacket*: mottled pinkish-beige printed in black; front, within a decorative panel: Songs of Joy/ by W. H. Davies/ (publisher's device)/ *The Life & Colour Series, No. 7*/ at foot: Jonathan Cape/ Eleven Gower Street, London; spine: Songs/ of/ Joy/ (fleuron)/ W. H./ Davies/ at foot: Jonathan/ Cape; back: starts: *The Life & Colour Series*/ ends: *Jonathan Cape, Eleven Gower Street, London* (12 titles listed); front flap: starts: *The Complete Works of*/ ends: *W. H. Davies :: 2s.6d. net*; back flap: blank

price: 2s.6d.

copy seen: RUL, Finzi

text changes from A8:
A Dream: one stanza shorter – lacks that commencing: 'Into my mouth it goes with mine'
Days that have been: title to: Days that have Been

note: the National Union Catalogue records an edition published by B. Humphries, Boston with an undated title-page in the holding of Harvard University, Cambridge, USA (subsequently reviewed by William Rose Benet, *Saturday Review of Literature*, 31 July 1937, XVI, 14, 17 so probably 1937)

A9   **THE TRUE TRAVELLER**   Duckworth & Co 1912

THE/ TRUE TRAVELLER/ By/ W. H. DAVIES/ Author of "The Auto-biography of a Super-Tramp"/ (publisher's device)/ at foot: LONDON/ DUCKWORTH & CO./ 3 HENRIETTA STREET, COVENT GARDEN/ 1912

8vo; (A) in four, B–I and K–T in eights, U in four plus a 20pp publisher's catalogue; 152 leaves: (i–vii) viii (1) 2–291 (5)pp plus a 20pp publisher's catalogue ((1–2) 3–19 (1)pp); 18.4 × 12.2 cms

(i–ii) blank; (iii) half-title: THE TRUE TRAVELLER; (iv) in a panel: starts: BY THE SAME AUTHOR/ ends: SONGS OF JOY, AND OTHERS; (v) title-page; (vi) blank; (vii)–viii CONTENTS; (1)–291 text; (292) PRINTED BY/ WILLIAM BRENDON AND SON LTD./ PLYMOUTH; (293–296) starts: SOME PRESS OPINIONS./ ends: 3 HENRIETTA STREET, COVENT GARDEN; 20pp publisher's catalogue: starts: A SELECTION FROM/ ends: T. & S.

contents: I p1 First Adventures; II p8 Bourbon and the Duke; III p17 The Soup-Kitchen; IV p26 The Woman in the Woods; V p45 The Nurse; VI p56 Back in Baltimore; VII p80 In Glasgow; VIII p90 A Night Out; IX p100 A Strong Woman; X p111 Blackmail; XI p125 The Religious Beggar; XII p146 My Disgrace; XIII p171 Yank; XIV p182 House-Calling; XV p192 Spring Cleaning; XVI p205 Jack the Giant-Killer; XVII p212 The Simple Life; XVIII p224 A Shock; XIX p229 Back in London; XX p243 Thieves in a Lodging-House; XXI p260 Mad Kitty; XXII p275 The Finder; XXIII p286 The End

paper: chain lines 2.8 cms apart and vertical

endpapers: cream; *edges*: trimmed

binding: lime green calico grain cloth, blind-blocked, lettered in gilt; front cover: (blind-blocked double rule head and base); spine: (double gilt rule)/ THE TRUE/ TRAVELLER/ W. H. DAVIES/ at foot: DUCKWORTH/ (double gilt rule); back cover: blind-blocked publisher's device; *dust-jacket*: not seen

date of publication: March 1912; *price*: 6s.

copies seen: BL (shelf mark: 12635.de.13; accession date: 19 March 1912) (1st issue); HRHRC (2 copies: both issues); HDB (1st issue); RUL, Finzi (2nd issue); SH (2nd issue)

reviews: The World of Books, *Nation*, 30 March 1912, X, 26, 1062; *Athenaeum*, 13 April 1912, 408; The True Traveller, Edward Thomas, *Bookman*, May 1912, XLII, 248, 84; The Science of the Sea, *Academy and Literature*, 14 September 1912, LXXXIII, 2106, 339–340

notes: (a) second issue: bound in lime green calico grain cloth and lettered in black; front cover within a double black panel: THE/ TRUE TRAVELLER/ W. H. DAVIES; spine: (double black rule)/ THE TRUE/ TRAVELLER/ W. H. DAVIES/ at foot: DUCKWORTH/ (double rule); back cover: black publisher's device; 20pp publisher's catalogue omitted
(b) one of the HRHRC copies has a single rule at head and base of spine; back cover: blank

A10   FOLIAGE   Elkin Mathews 1913

FOLIAGE/ VARIOUS POEMS/ BY/ WILLIAM H. DAVIES/ (publisher's device)/ at foot: LONDON/ ELKIN MATHEWS, CORK STREET/ 1913

8vo; (B)–E in eights; 32 leaves: (1–7) 8–63 (1)pp; 15.5 × 10.5 cms variable

(1) half-title: FOLIAGE; (2) starts: *By the Same Writer*/ ends: *2s. 6d.*; (3) title-page; (4) blank; (5) *The Author thanks the editors of the following magazines*/ *for permission to reprint these poems*: THE ENGLISH/ REVIEW, NATION, WESTMINSTER GAZETTE, NEW/ STATESMAN, NASH'S, VINEYARD *and the* ODD/ VOLUME.; (6) blank; (7)–8 CONTENTS; 9–(64) text; (64) at foot: (rule)/ LONDON: PRINTED BY WILLIAM CLOWES AND SONS, LIMITED.

contents: p9 Thunderstorms; p10 Strong Moments; p11 A Greeting; p12 Sweet Stay-at-Home; p14 The Starved; p15 A May Morning; p16 The Lonely Dreamer;

p17 Christmas; p19 Laughing Rose; p20 Seeking Joy; p21 The Old Oak Tree; p23 Poor Kings; p24 Love and the Muse; p25 My Youth; p26 Smiles; p27 Mad Poll; p28 Joy Supreme; p29 Francis Thompson; p31 The Bird-Man; p32 Winter's Beauty; p33 The Church Organ. Heigh Ho, the Rain; p34 Love's Inspiration; p35 Night Wanderers; p36 Young Beauty; p37 Who I Know; p38 Sweet Birds, I Come; p39 The Two Lives; p40 Hidden Love; p41 Life is Jolly; p42 The Fog; p43 A Woman's Charms; p44 Dreams of the Sea; p46 The Wonder-Maker; p47 The Helpless; p48 An Early Love; p49 Dream Tragedies; p50 Children at Play; p51 When the Cuckoo Sings; p52 Return to Nature; p59 A Strange City

paper: watermarked: (crown)/ Abbey Mills/ Greenfield; chain lines 2.4 cms apart and vertical

endpapers: cream; *edges*: uncut, top edge trimmed

binding: sage green cloth, horizontally or vertically embossed with lighter green, lettered in gilt; front cover: FOLIAGE/ at foot: W. H. DAVIES; spine, vertically upwards: WILLIAM H./ DAVIES/ centred: FOLIAGE/ horizontally at foot: ELKIN/ MATHEWS; back cover: blank; *dust-jacket*: not seen

date of publication: September 1913; *price*: 1s.6d.

copies seen: BL (shelf mark: 011651.g.147; accession date: 13 September 1913); RUL, Finzi; HDB; SH

reviews: *Athenaeum*, 11 October 1913, 376; New Lamps for Old, *TLS*, 6 November 1913, 506 (by Walter de la Mare); Poets New and Old, *Academy and Literature*, 29 November, 1913, LXXXV, 2169, 683; *Poetry Review*, November 1913, III, 5, 267; Foliage, Edward Thomas, *Bookman*, November 1913, XLV, 266, 120–121; Recent Verse, *The Spectator*, 20 December 1913, 111, 4460, 1085; Some Recent Poetry, Darrell Figgis, *Nineteenth Century and After: A Monthly Review*, January 1914, 75, 473, 186–196; The Younger Poets, *Poetry and Drama*, March 1914, II, 5, 59–60; Foliage, *Canadian Magazine*, October 1914, XLIII, 6, 631

mss: in WHD's hand on paper watermarked: Audrey Note/ FR; addressed 45 London Rd, Sevenoaks, Kent and dated 1913; clipped into brown paper wrappers (HDB); there are also mss in WHD's hand at HRHRC of 'Joy Supreme', 'Young Beauty', 'The Wonder Maker', 'My Youth' and 'Laughing Rose' on notepaper headed 14, Great Russell St, W.C. signed with his stamp (as WHD's earlier address was 45 London Road, Sevenoaks the HDB mss must be earlier)

WHD's manuscript corrections:
Christmas: line 14: 'eat and drink' to 'drink and eat'
The Old Oak Tree: 2nd stanza line 6: 'break my bones' to 'come to blows'; last stanza lengthened by 2 lines
Joy Supreme: line 5: 'charm' to 'shame'
Who I Know: title: to 'Whom I Know'
The Two Lives: 4th stanza last line: 'the' to 'a'
Return to Nature: line 85: 'squirrels' to 'furious squirrels'
A Strange City: line 31 up: 'a place' to 'a town'

text change from manuscript to A10:
A Woman's Charms: line 2: 'near' to 'close'

previous printings:
'Children at Play', *Vineyard*, November 1911, 2nd year, 2, 131
'When the Cuckoo Sings', 'Hidden Love', 'Dream Tragedies', 'Love's Inspiration'

and 'Laughing Rose', *Nash's Magazine*, October 1911, V, 1, 125, November 1911, V, 2, 231, January 1912, V, 4, 491, March 1913, VII, 6, 803 and April 1913, VIII, 1, 84 respectively

'Joy Supreme' and 'A Woman's Charms', 'Christmas' and 'The Strange City' (as 'A Strange City'), *English Review*, January 1912, XI, 204–205, August 1912, XII, 204, December 1912, XIII, 1 and April 1913, XIV, 1–12 respectively

'Young Beauty', 'The Two Lives' and 'Smiles', *Rhythm*, June 1912, II, V, 20, August 1912, II, VII, 84 and September 1912, II, VIII, 135 respectively

'Strong Moments', 'Mad Poll', 'Dreams of the Sea', 'Night Wanderers', 'Love and the Muse' and 'Francis Thompson', *Nation*, 17 February 1912, X, 20, 819, 29 June 1912, XI, 13, 477, 19 October 1912, XII, 3, 142, 28 December 1912, XII, 13, 571, 1 February 1913, XII, 18, 748 and 8 March 1913, XII, 23, 928 respectively

'Winter's Beauty', 'The Wonder-Maker', 'A Greeting' and 'The Lonely Dreamer', *Westminster Gazette*, 23 February 1912, 2, 25 June 1912, 2, 2 July 1912, 2 and 9 October 1912, 2 respectively

'Thunderstorms', *New Statesman*, 12 April 1913, I, 1, 17

text changes from first printings to A10:
Dreams of the Sea: 3rd stanza line 3: 'gusty' to 'lusty'
The Wonder-Maker: 1st stanza line 8: 'end' to 'cost'
Sweet Stay-at-Home: 16 lines longer
When the Cuckoo Sings: line 9: 'I then, as Robin does in Spring' to 'Then, like red
    Robin in the spring', line 10: 'Forsake the places where men are' to 'I shun those
    haunts where men are found', line 12: 'The birds are dumb and trees are bare' to
    'Leaves fall and birds can make no sound'

notes: (a) the HRHRC mss of 'Joy Supreme' is one stanza shorter, commencing with: 'When I set eyes on red, ripe plums' reversing 'ripe, red'
(b) HRHRC mss of 'Young Beauty': 2nd stanza line 2: 'Young Beauty, full of love that's sweet'
(c) 'The Strange City' was reprinted from the *English Review* as a separate item (12pp)
(d) NL hold a mss by Lawrence W. Hockey entitled 'The Strange City by W. H. Davies' in which he explains the differences between the version published in the *English Review* and that published in *Foliage* under the title 'A Strange City': "the blank verse commentary was re-arranged and assembled under the title of 'A Strange City'. Similarly the rhyming octosyllabic couplets of the other part of the commentary were knit together, with new material added and re-published as 'Return to Nature'". The other poems were re-published in *Foliage* as follows:

title	first line	page
Heigh Ho, the Rain	The lark that in heaven dim	2
Poor Kings	God's pity on poor kings	3
The Fog	I saw the fog grow thick	3
The Church Organ	The homeless man has heard thy voice	5
The Starved	My little Lamb, what is amiss?	6
Who I know	I do not know his grace the Duke	6
Night Wanderers	They hear the bell of midnight toil	10
The Helpless	Those poor, heartbroken wretches, doomed	8
A May Morning	The sky is clear	9
The Old Oak Tree	I sit beneath your leaves, old oak	10
My Youth	My youth was my old age	10

(page numbers relate to the reprint from the *English Review*)

A10a *Life & Colour Series No 16*   Jonathan Cape 1922

Foliage, Various/ Poems by W. H. Davies/ (publisher's device)/ at foot:
Jonathan Cape/ Eleven Gower Street, London

8vo; (A)–D in eights; 32 leaves: (i–vi) vii–viii 9–62 (2)pp; 17.0 × 11.0 cms variable

as *A10* apart from: (i) half-title: Foliage; (ii) blank; (iii) title-page; (iv) *New and
Revised Edition, 1922*/ at foot: PRINTED IN GREAT BRITAIN BY RICHARD
CLAY & SONS, LIMITED,/ BUNGAY, SUFFOLK.; (v) *The Author thanks the
Editors of the following/ magazines for permission to reprint these poems*: THE/
ENGLISH REVIEW, NATION, WESTMINSTER GAZETTE, NEW/ STATES-
MAN, NASH'S, VINEYARD *and the* ODD VOLUME.; (vi) blank; vii–viii
Contents; 9–(63) text; (64) blank; *binding*: as A2b; front cover: blank; spine, on a
white paper label 3.7 cms deep, in black and mustard: (double mustard rule)/
Foliage/ and/ other/ Poems/ (mustard fleuron)/ W. H./ Davies/ (double mustard rule);
back cover: blank; *edges*: uncut, top edge trimmed; *dust-jacket*: mottled pinkish-
beige, printed in black; front, within a decorative border: Foliage & other poems/ *by*
W. H. Davies/ (publisher's device)/ *The Life & Colour Series, No.* 16/ at foot:
Jonathan Cape/ Eleven Gower Street, London; spine: Foliage/ and/ other/ Poems/
(fleuron)/ W. H./ Davies/ at foot: Jonathan/ Cape; back: starts: *The Life & Colour
Series*/ ends: *Jonathan Cape, Eleven Gower Street, London* (16 titles listed); front
flap: starts: *The Complete Works of*/ ends: *By W. H. Davies :: 2s.6d. net*; back flap:
blank

date of publication: December 1922; *price*: 2s.6d.

copies seen: BL (shelf mark: 011645.de.44; accession date: 7 December 1922);
RUL, Finzi

text change from A10:
Who I Know: title to 'Whom I Know'

note: the National Union Catalogue records an edition published by B. Humphries,
Boston with an undated title-page in the holding of New York Public Library, New
York, USA

A11 NATURE   B T Batsford Ltd 1914

within a panel: (double rule)/ NATURE/ By/ *William H. Davies*/ (rule)/
(vignette of a tree)/ (rule)/ *Published by B. T. Batsford, Ltd., London.*/ (rule)

8vo; (A)–C in eights, D in four, E in two; 30 leaves: (i–ii) 1–53 (5)pp; 17.3 × 12.5
cms

(i) half-title: FELLOWSHIP BOOKS/ *Edited by Mary Stratton*/ NATURE; (ii) title-
page; 1–(54) text; 1 at head, within a decorative panel: "*One impulse from a vernal
wood*/ *May teach you more of man,*/ *Of moral evil and of good,*/ *than all the ages
can.*"; (54) below text: (diamond-shaped tailpiece); (55) *Printed by Morrison &
Gibb Limited*/ *Edinburgh* 1914; (56–58) blank; first page of text within a panel;
decorated catch-words throughout; decorations at beginning of paragraphs
throughout

contains: p1 One impulse from a vernal wood; p3 When I at night stand at my cottage door; p14 Of primrose boys; p32 He lived a hermit for a year; p53 When happy I

paper: watermarked: (crown)/ Abbey Mills/ Greenfield; chain lines 2.4 cms apart and vertical

endpapers: cream with a grey decorative border; *edges*: trimmed, top edge gilt

binding: royal blue textured calico grain cloth, blocked and lettered in gilt; front cover, within two concentric but different decorative panels: NATURE/ WILLIAM H. DAVIES; spine, within a panel: Nature/ (fleuron)/ W.H./ Davies/ (decoration)/ at foot: Batsford; back cover: (publisher's device); dark blue ribbon marker

dust-jacket: cream with an embossed surface, printed in navy; front, within a decorative border: FELLOWSHIP BOOKS/ A new contribution by various writers/ toward the expression of the Human/ Ideal & Artistic Faith of our own day/ NATURE/ By/ *William H. Davies/* at foot: Price 2/- net; spine, within a panel: Nature/ (fleuron)/ W. H./ Davies/ (decoration)/ at foot: Batsford; back, within a decorative border: starts: FELLOWSHIP BOOKS/ ends: B. T. BATSFORD, LTD., 94 HIGH HOLBORN; both flaps: blank

date of publication: March 1914; *price*: 2s.

copies seen: BL (shelf mark: 012202.a.2/18; accession date: 25 March 1914); HRHRC; RUL, Finzi; HDB; SH

review: *London Quarterly and Holborn Review*, 1914, 122, 175

mss: location not known although part I of 'He lived a hermit for a year' in WHD's hand on undated notepaper headed 45 London Road, Sevenoaks is held at SL; this poem was originally entitled 'The Train' but altered to 'Nature' by WHD

note: Fellowship Books were designed by James Guthrie

A12 THE BIRD OF PARADISE   Methuen & Co Ltd 1914

THE/ BIRD OF PARADISE/ AND OTHER POEMS/ BY/ W. H. DAVIES/ at foot: METHUEN & CO. LTD./ 36 ESSEX STREET W.C./ LONDON

8vo; (1)–5 in eights and 6 in four plus an 8pp publisher's catalogue; 44 leaves: (1–8) 9–11 (12–13) 14–86 (2)pp plus an 8pp publisher's catalogue ((1)-8); 17.0 × 10.7 cms variable

(1–2) blank; (3) half-title: THE BIRD OF PARADISE; (4) starts: BY THE SAME AUTHOR/ ends: Nature (1914); (5) title-page; (6) *First Published in 1914*; (7) NOTE/ For permission to reprint these poems/ the author thanks the editors of the following magazines: *The Nation, The New/ Statesman, The Westminster Gazette, The/ New Weekly,* and *Poetry and Drama.*; (8) blank; 9–11 Contents; (12) blank; (13)–86 text; (87) blank; (88) PRINTED BY/ WILLIAM BRENDON AND SON, LTD./ PLYMOUTH; 8pp publisher's catalogue paged ((1)–8) starts: A FEW OF/ MESSRS. METHUEN'S/ ends: Midshipman to Field-Marshal.

contents: p13 When I am Old; p15 Two Spring Songs; p17 The Best Friend; p19

Heaven; p20 Sweet Night; p21 Early Spring; p23 The Mind's Liberty; p24 The Two Spirits; p26 When on a Summer's Morn; p27 Again I Sing; p29 The Dumb World; p32 The Weeping Child; p34 The Den; p36 This World; p37 A Fleeting Passion; p38 Plants and Men; p40 A Midsummer Night's Storm; p41 The Dreaming Boy; p44 The Hawk; p45 The Signs; p46 The Long Sleep; p48 The Moon; p49 A Great Time; p50 Her Absence; p52 The Wanderer; p55 The Child and the Man; p57 The Black Cloud; p58 When I in Praise; p59 Sweet Child; p60 In a Garden; p63 The Life Divine; p65 Love's Youth; p66 Rich Days; p67 Near a Quiet Stream; p68 The Child Chatters; p70 The Hermit; p72 In the End; p73 The Emigrant; p75 The Collier's Wife; p76 Stars; p78 Come, Let Me Close; p79 On the Mountain; p80 Infancy; p81 In Silent Groves; p82 The Rev Ebenezer Paul; p83 Nell Barnes; p85 The Bird of Paradise

paper: watermarked: (crown)/ Abbey Mills/ Greenfield; chain lines 2.4 cms apart and vertical

endpapers: cream; *edges*: deckle fore edge, top edge trimmed

binding: grey mottled paper-covered boards, printed in black; front cover: The Bird of Paradise/ and other Poems/ William H. Davies; spine, vertically downwards: The Bird of Paradise. William H. Davies; back cover: blank

dust-jacket: pale grey, printed in black; front: The Bird of Paradise/ and other Poems/ William H. Davies/ [?1s.] net [the dust-jacket examined had a sticker with 1/6/ NET partially obscuring the price]/ at foot: London: Methuen & Co. Ltd.; spine, vertically downwards: The Bird of Paradise. William H. Davies.; back, within a double panel: starts: The/ Poems of Rudyard Kipling/ ends: (rule)/ METHUEN & CO. LTD. LONDON; both flaps: blank

date of publication: 5 November 1914; *price*: 1s.

copies seen: BL (shelf mark: 011649.f.30; accession date: 5 November 1914); RUL, Finzi; HDB; CH; SH

reviews: Two Poets, *TLS*, 3 December 1914, 538; Recent English Poetry, M. D. Armstrong, *Fortnightly Review*, 1914, 101; Mr Davies and Others, *Nation*, 12 December 1914, XVI, 11, 344–345; Recent Verse, *New Statesman*, 16 January 1915, IV, 93, 371; Recent Verse, *The Spectator*, 27 March 1915, 114, 4526, 444–446; *Welsh Outlook*, April 1915, II, 16, 159

mss: in WHD's hand addressed 14 Great Russell St, W.C.1 on paper watermarked: Audrey Note/ FR; clipped into brown paper wrappers (HDB); NL also hold an unsigned mss of 'The Wanderer' in WHD's hand on 45 London Rd, Sevenoaks notepaper with the address changed to 29 Clarence Gardens, N. W. (this is the earlier mss as the address on the notepaper accurately reflects the chronology of WHD's movements)

WHD's manuscript corrections:
Again I Sing: 3rd stanza last line: 'his' to 'art his'
Her Absence: line 6: 'dirt' to 'ash'
Rich Days: 2nd stanza line 3: 'damsons red, and blue-black plums' to 'blue-black damsons, yellow plums', last line: 'loveliest' to 'loneliest'

text changes from manuscript to A12:
The Dreaming Boy: line 10: 'see' to 'trace'
Rich Days: 2nd stanza line 3: 'blue-black damsons, yellow plums' to 'cherries red, and blue-black plums', last line: 'loneliest' to 'loveliest'

previous printings:
'The Best Friend', *Odd Volume*, 1913, 40
'The Bird of Paradise', *Poetry and Drama*, December 1913, I, 4, 421
'Early Spring' and 'Her Absence', *New Weekly*, 28 March 1914, I, 2, 44
'Love's Youth', *Blue Review*, July 1913, 1, 3, 151
'The Signs', 'A Great Time', 'This World', 'The Mind's Liberty', 'The Dumb World', 'Heaven' and 'The Wanderer' , *New Statesman*, 28 June 1913, I, 12, 370, 23 August 1913, I, 20, 626, 4 October 1913, I, 26, 819, 1 November 1913, II, 30, 115, 20 December 1913, II, 37, 338, 17 January 1914, II, 41, 467 and 28 March 1914, II, 51, 787 respectively
'In a Garden', 'The Hawk', 'The Hermit', 'In Silent Groves', 'The Collier's Wife' and 'A Midsummer Night's Storm', *Nation*, 19 July 1913, XIII, 16, 608, 30 August 1913, XIII, 22, 814, 8 November 1913, XIV, 6, 256, 22 November 1913, XIV, 8, 361, 10 January 1914, XIV, 15, 642 and 30 May 1914, XV, 9, 341 respectively
'Infancy', 'Near a Quiet Stream' and 'Two Spring Songs' ('From France' and 'Starers'), *Westminster Gazette*, 28 November 1913, 2, 5 February 1914, 2 and 8 April 1914, 2 respectively

text changes from first printings to A12:
The Mind's Liberty: 2nd stanza line 2: 'day and night the porters work' to 'porters work both day and night', line 3: 'oft-times' to 'ofttimes', line 4: 'Thrice fifty miles from where I walk' to 'That flows thrice fifty miles away'
The Bird of Paradise: 4th stanza line 4: 'bed-post' to 'bedpost'
The Dumb World: line 14: 'toenails' to 'toe-nails'
The Wanderer: line 17: 'beg' to 'begs', line 29: 'and happy for it' to 'for days and days', line 30: 'him for it' to 'his ways'
The Hawk: 1st and last stanzas *only* printed; 2nd stanza: 'I cannot keep my eyes from thee,/ That neither moves nor stings;/ That in clear air and motionless,/ Can stand with silent wings;/ Supported by thy force of mind,/ As thou, with eyes that glow,/ Art watching birds and harvest mice/ In the green fields below.'
Early Spring: originally printed in 3 stanzas; 2nd stanza line 1: 'Nature seen on every side' to 'with green Nature all around'; 3rd stanza (not in *Collected Poems (A14)*): 'These watery swamps and thickets wild -/ Called Nature's slums – to me are more/ Than any courts where fountains play,/ And men-at-arms guard every door;/ For I could sit down here alone,/ And count the oak trees one by one.'

note: reprinted 1915 (George Francis Wilson *(F95)* records a 2nd edition 1919)

A12a New edition   Jonathan Cape 1926

The/ Bird of Paradise/ and other poems/ by/ W. H. Davies/ (publisher's device)/ at foot: Jonathan Cape/ Thirty Bedford Square, London

8vo; (1)–5 in eights, 6 in four; 44 leaves: (1–8) 9–11 (12–13) 14–86 (2)pp; 17.2 × 11.0 cm variable; the title-page is a cancel

as *A12* apart from: (5) title-page; (6) *Reprinted* 1915/ *Re-issued by Jonathan Cape*, 1926; (7) NOTE; *binding*: pale blue mottled paper-covered boards, royal blue cloth spine; front cover: blank; spine, on a white paper label 2.8 cms deep, in blue: THE/ BIRD/ OF/ PARADISE/ W. H./ DAVIES; back cover: blank; *edges*: trimmed; *dust-jacket*: mottled cream with an embossed surface, printed in bright blue; front, within a decorative border: THE/ BIRD OF PARADISE/ AND OTHER POEMS/ by/ W. H. DAVIES/ at foot: JONATHAN CAPE 30 BEDFORD SQUARE; spine, vertically downwards: W. H. DAVIES (decorative bird) THE BIRD OF PARADISE; back: starts: *Books by W. H. Davies*/ ends: *Jonathan Cape Thirty Bedford Square London*; front flap: starts: THE BIRD OF PARADISE/ ends: *3s.6d. net*; back flap: blank

date of publication: April 1926

print run: 500 copies printed on 15 September 1925 by William Brendon & Son; bound by Burn, Nevett and Methuen; *price*: 3s.6d.

copies seen: BL (shelf mark: 011645.de.161; accession date: 8 April 1926); HDB

text changes from A12:
Early Spring: one stanza shorter
Sweet Child: 1st stanza line 1: 'that' to 'thou'
Rich Days: 2nd stanza line 3: 'cherries red, and blue-black plums' to 'blue-black damsons, yellow plums'; last line: 'loveliest' to 'loneliest'

A13 CHILD LOVERS A C Fifield 1916

Child Lovers/ And other Poems/ By William H. Davies/ Author of "Songs of Joy," etc. etc./ at foot: London: A. C. Fifield, 13,/ Clifford's Inn, E.C. 1916.

8vo; (A)–B in eights; 16 leaves: (1–6) 7–28 (4)pp; 19.6 × 13.0 cms

(1) half-title: Child Lovers, and other Poems; (2) starts: By the same Author/ ends: Shaw. 1907. 3rd edition. 6s. Fifield.; (3) title-page; (4) *All rights reserved*/ at foot: WILLIAM BRENDON AND SON, LIMITED, PRINTERS/ PLYMOUTH, ENGLAND; (5) Contents; (6) The Author thanks the editors of the/ following magazines for permission to reprint/ these poems: *Nation, English Review, New/ Statesman, Poetry and Drama, Forum, Book of/ Homage* and *Country Life.*; 7-(29) text; (29) below text: THE END; (30) blank; (31–32) starts: The Works of "The Super-Tramp."/ ends: London: A. C. Fifield, 13 Clifford's Inn, E.C.

contents: p7 The Inexpressible; p8 This Night; p9 The Visitor; p10 April's Charms; p11 Kitty and I; p12 Thou Comest, May; p13 The Hospital Waiting-Room; p14 The White Cascade; p15 The One Singer; p16 The Inquest; p18 The Two Children; p19 Come, Thou Sweet Wonder; p20 Charms; p21 Friends; p22 The Power of Silence; p23 A Mother to Her Sick Child; p24 The White Monster; p25 Child Lovers; p27 My Lady Comes; p28. Body and Spirit

edges: trimmed

binding: ginger paper wrappers, printed in black; front cover: Child Lovers/ and other Poems/ By William H. Davies/ Author of "Songs of Joy," etc. etc./ at foot: London: A. C. Fifield. 1916. 1s. net.; spine, vertically downwards: Child Lovers, and other Poems. W. H. Davies.; back cover: blank

date of publication: 1 June 1916; *price*: 1s.

copies seen: BL (shelf mark: 011649.h.68; accession date: 1 June 1916); RUL, Finzi; HDB; SH *reviews*: Under Two Poets, *TLS*, 8 June 1916, 269 (by Walter de la Mare); Child Lovers and Other Poems, Edward Thomas, *Bookman*, August 1916, L, 299, 136–137

previous printings:
'The Power of Silence', 'Kitty and I' and 'The Inquest', *English Review*, October 1915, XXI, 233–235
'The Inexpressible' (as 'Shakespeare Works'), *A Book of Homage to Shakespeare*, 1916, 105
'This Night', 'April's Charms', 'Thou Comest, May', 'Friends', 'The Hospital Waiting-Room', 'The White Monster', 'Child Lovers', 'The Two Children', 'Come, Thou Sweet Wonder' and 'The White Cascade', *Nation*, 26 December 1914, XVI, 13, 416, 17 April 1915, XVII, 3, 85, 29 May 1915, XVII, 9, 289, 19 June 1915, XVII, 12, 388, 17 July 1915, XVII, 16, 513, 18 September 1915, XVII, 25, 804, 9 October 1915, XVIII, 2, 53, 27 November 1915, XVIII, 9, 328, 29 January 1916, XVIII, 18, 641 and 4 March 1916, XVIII, 23, 793 respectively
'The Visitor' and 'Charms', *Form*, April 1916, I, 1, 45 and 48
'Body and Spirit', *Poetry and Drama*, December 1914, II, 8, 350

text changes from first printings to A13:
The Two Children: 2nd stanza line 4: 'their' to 'his'
Come, Thou Sweet Wonder: 1st stanza line 1: 'wonder' to 'Wonder', line 4: 'driest' to 'dri'st'
April's Charms: 4th stanza last line: 'fills' to 'fill'

note: agreement with Fifield dated 3 May 1916 (32pp at approximately 1/-, Jonathan Cape archives, RUL)

A13a Second edition   A C Fifield 1916

as *A13* apart from: (4) *First published June 1*, 1916/ *Reprinted June 25*, 1916; *binding*: mottled grey paper wrappers, printed in brown; front cover: Child Lovers/ And other Poems/ By William H. Davies/ Author of "Songs of Joy," etc. etc./ at foot: London: A. C. Fifield. 1916. 1s. net./ Second edition; spine, vertically downwards: Child Lovers and other Poems W. H. Davies.; back cover, in a panel: starts: *Uniform in style and price*/ ends: LONDON: A. C. FIFIELD

date of publication: July 1916; *price*: 1s.

copy seen: HRHRC

A13b New edition   Jonathan Cape 1921

Child Lovers/ And other Poems/ William H. Davies/ (publisher's device)/ Jonathan Cape/ Eleven Gower Street, London.

8vo; (A)–B in eights; 16 leaves including two stubs (the second pasted to the rear endpaper): (1–4) 5 (6) 7–28 (4)pp; 19.7 × 13.0 cms; the title-page is a cancel

as *A13* apart from: (1) title-page; (2) *First published by/ A. C. Fifield*, 1916/ *Second Impression*, 1916/ *Re-issued by Jonathan/ Cape* :: 1921/ at foot: *All Rights Reserved*; (3–4) a stub; (31–32) a stub pasted to the rear endpaper; *endpapers*:

cream; *binding*: mid-blue calico grain cloth; front cover: blank; spine, on a white paper label 3.5 cms deep, in black: (double blue rule)/ Child/ Lovers/ (blue fleuron)/ W. H./ Davies/ (double blue rule); back cover: blank; *dust-jacket*: not seen

date of publication: February 1922; *price*: 3s.6d.

copy seen: RUL, Finzi

A14   **COLLECTED POEMS**   A C Fifield 1916

Collected Poems/ by/ William H. Davies/ *With a portrait in collotype/ from a pencil sketch by/ WILL ROTHENSTEIN,/ and facsimile of author's script/* at foot: London/ A. C. Fifield, 13 Clifford's Inn, E.C./ 1916

8vo; (A) in eight plus tipped-in frontispiece, B–I and K in eights; 80 leaves: (i–vi) vii (viii) 9–160pp; 18.7 × 12.6 cms variable

(i) blank; (ii) starts: *The separate works of William H. Davies/* ends: *A Pilgrim in Wales. 1916. Melrose.*; (iii) half-title: Collected Poems/ by/ William H. Davies. (in facsimile of the author's script); (iv) blank; frontispiece: collotype portrait of the author from a sketch by Will Rothenstein protected by a tissue guard and signed W. R. 1916; (v) title-page; (vi) *Copyright in England and U.S.A./ All rights reserved*; vii Note: This single volume/ collection of what I believe to/ be my best pieces is published in/ response to a frequently expressed/ wish from the press and public./ For permission to do this, my thanks/ are due to the publishers of my/ separate volumes of poems -/ Mr A. C. Fifield, Mr Elkin Mathews,/and Messrs Methuen & Co./ W. H. D. (in facsimile of author's script); (viii) blank; 9–12 Contents; 13–160 text; 160 below text: (fleuron)/ PRINTED BY WILLIAM BRENDON AND SON, LTD./ PLYMOUTH, ENGLAND

contents: 1 Thunderstorms; 2 Songs of Joy; 3 The Moon; 4 The Rain; 5 Infancy; 6 Leisure; 7 The Visitor; 8 The Kingfisher; 9 The Inexpressible; 10 Charms; 11 Autumn; 12 This Night; 13 In May; 14 Days too Short; 15 The Sleepers; 16 Child Lovers; 17 Sweet Stay-at-Home; 18 The Elements; 19 Come, thou sweet Wonder; 20 A Maiden and her Hair; 21 Day's Black Star; 22 The Example; 23 The Likeness; 24 The Two Children; 25 The Mind's Liberty; 26 The Battle; 27 The Lonely Dreamer; 28 The East in Gold; 29 A Mother to her sick Child; 30 The Happy Child; 31 To Sparrows Fighting; 32 The White Cascade; 33 Nell Barnes; 34 In the Country; 35 Nature's Friend; 36 The Flood; 37 Christ the Man; 38 Dreams of the Sea; 39 A Great Time; 40 Man; 41 Truly Great; 42 The Sluggard; 43 When on a Summer's Morn; 44 Farewell to Poesy; 45 Early Morn; 46 Robin Redbreast; 47 A Lovely Woman; 48 Friends; 49 The Laughers; 50 The Boy; 51 The Dark Hour; 52 Jenny Wren; 53 Kitty and I; 54 A Drinking Song; 55 Money; 56 Sadness and Joy; 57 Fancy's Home; 58 Happy Wind; 59 Sleep; 60 When I am Old; 61 Joy and Pleasure; 62 The Heap of Rags; 63 The Hawk; 64 The Weeping Child; 65 Seeking Beauty; 66 The Hermit; 67 Sheep; 68 The Idiot and the Child; 69 Starers; 70 Plants and Men; 71 The One Singer; 72 Lines from "The Soul's Destroyer"; 73 April's Charms; 74 The Call of the Sea; 75 Her Absence; 76 The Dreaming Boy; 77 The Power of Music; 78 The Muse; 79 The Owl; 80 My Lady Comes; 81 The Daisy; 82 Fairies, take Care; 83 A Blind Child; 84 Thou comest, May; 85 The Best Friend; 86 Rich Days; 87 The Bird of Paradise; 88 This World; 89 The Lodging House Fire; 90 Body and Spirit; 91 Love's Coming; 92 The Little Ones; 93 Where we Differ; 94 Parted; 95 The Blind Boxer; 96 Now; 97 Clouds; 98 The Posts; 99 No Master; 100 Rich or Poor; 101 The Sea; 102 A Life's Love; 103 April's Boys and Girls; 104 Sweet Child; 105 Death's Game; 106 Sweet Youth; 107 A Plain Life; 108 Heaven; 109 Ale; 110 A Fleeting Passion; 111 The Child and the Mariner

paper: watermarked: ANTIQUE DE LUXE

endpapers: cream; *edges*: deckle fore edge, top edge trimmed

binding: dark turquoise diagonal fine-ribbed cloth, blind-blocked and lettered in gilt; front cover, within a blind single border: Collected Poems/ by/ William H. Davies. (in facsimile of the author's script); spine: Collected/ Poems/ W. H./ Davies. (in facsimile of the author's script)/ at foot: FIFIELD; back cover: blank; grey ribbon marker

dust-jacket: mottled grey, printed in black; front: Collected Poems/ By/ William H. Davies/ Author of "Nature Poems," "Songs of Joy,"/ "Child Lovers," "The Bird of Paradise,"/ etc., etc./ *With a Portrait in Collotype from a/ pencil sketch by William Rothenstein,/ and facsimile of author's script/* at foot: Author's Note/ "This single volume collection of what I/ believe to be my best pieces is published in/ response to a frequently expressed wish/ from the press and public."/ *Six Shillings net/ London: A. C. Fifield*; spine: Collected/ Poems/ William/ H./ Davies/ With/ Portrait/ by/ William/ Rothenstein/ 6s. net/ at foot: Fifield; back: starts: Mr. Fifield's Recent List/ ends: London: A. C. Fifield, 13 Clifford's Inn, E.C.; both flaps: blank

date of publication: November 1916; *price*: 6s.

copies seen: BL (shelf mark: 011649.h.105; accession date: 15 November 1916); HRHRC; HDB; RUL, Finzi; SH

reviews: Athenaeum, December 1916, 592; The Poet of Joy, *Nation*, 2 December 1916, XX, 9, 327–328; W. H. Davies, J. C. Squire, *New Statesman*, 16 December 1916, VIII, 193, 254–256; *TLS*, 4 January 1917, 7; W. H. Davies' Collected Poems, *Bookman*, June 1917, LII, 309, 99 (portrait by E. O. Hoppe)

previous printings:
1, 17, 27 and 38, *Foliage (A10)*
2, 6, 13, 14, 15, 18, 22, 28, 30, 31, 36, 37, 40, 56, 57, 62, 65, 67, 77, 79, 82, 92, 98, 100 and 111, *Songs of Joy (A8)*
3, 5, 25, 33, 39, 43, 60, 63, 64, 66, 69, 70, 75, 76, 85, 86, 87, 88, 104, 108 and 110, *The Bird of Paradise (A12)*
4, 20, 21, 26, 35, 41, 45, 46, 47, 49, 50, 55, 61, 78, 81, 93, 101, 102 and 106, *Nature Poems (A4)*
7, 9, 10, 12, 16, 19, 24, 29, 32, 48, 53, 71, 73, 80, 84 and 90, *Child Lovers (A13)*
8, 34, 42, 44, 51, 52, 58, 68, 74, 96, 97, 99 and 105, *Farewell to Poesy (A6)*
11, 54, 59, 72, 89 and 91, *The Soul's Destroyer (A1)*
23, 83, 94 and 109, *New Poems (A2)*
103 and 107 not previously printed were re-titled 'Following a Bee' and 'No Idle Gold' respectively in *Complete Poems (A51)*
95, *Nation*, 24 May 1913, XIII, 8, 314

text changes from previous printings to A14:
The Blind Boxer: line 5: 'Aye' to 'For' and 'boxer' to 'Boxer', line 6: 'Leap full' to 'Have leapt'
The Owl: 1st stanza line 3: 'prophecy' to 'prophesy'
Ale: 1st two stanzas omitted, commences: 'Now do I hear thee weep and groan,'

notes: (a) the RUL, Finzi copy has a fleuron in place of the printers' imprint on p160
(b) the HDB copy is inscribed: 'My book,/ W. H. Davies./ Nov. 1916'
(c) agreement with Fifield dated 13 September 1916 (price to be 5/- or 6/- net, Jonathan Cape archives, RUL)
(d) 'Leisure': 4th stanza line 2: 'skies' misprinted 'stars'

A14a   *First American Edition*   Alfred A Knopf 1916

The Collected Poems of/ WILLIAM H. DAVIES/ *With a portrait by/ Willliam Rothenstein/* at foot: (publisher's device)/ New York . Alfred A. Knopf . Mcmxvi

8vo; one gathering of eight with tipped-in frontispiece and tipped-in errata slip, eleven gatherings of eight; 96 leaves: (1–6) 7–190 (2)pp plus frontispiece and errata slip not included in the pagination; 19.0 × 13.0 cms variable

(1) half-title: The Collected Poems of/ WILLIAM H. DAVIES; (2) in a panel: starts: SOME NEW BORZOI BOOKS/ ends: *By Nicolay Gogol*; tinted portrait frontispiece signed at foot: (c) WILLIAM ROTHSTEIN [sic] W. R. 1916; (3) title-page; (4) COPYRIGHT, 1916, BY/ WILLIAM H. DAVIES/ at foot: PRINTED IN THE UNITED STATES OF AMERICA; (5) as *A14* vii; (6) blank; 7–10 CONTENTS; tipped-in errata leaf: starts: ERRATA/ POEMS/ ends: " " " 60th line, "Rose" should read "grown."; verso of errata leaf: blank; 11–190 text; 190 below text: FINIS; (191–192) within a panel: starts: (publisher's device)/ ends: 220 WEST FORTY-SECOND STREET, NEW YORK

contents: p11 Thunderstorms; p12 Songs of Joy; p14 The Moon; p15 The Rain; p16 Laughing Rose; p17 Infancy; p18 Leisure; p19 The Visitor; p20 The Kingfisher; p21 The Inexpressible; p22 Charms; p24 Autumn; p25 This Night; p26 In May; p28 Days too Short; p29 The Sleepers; p31 Child Lovers; p33 Sweet Stay-at-Home; p35 The Elements; p37 Come, thou sweet Wonder; p38 A Maiden and her Hair; p40 Day's Black Star; p41 The Example; p42 The Ox; p44 The Two Children; p45 The Mind's Liberty; p46 The Battle; p47 The Lonely Dreamer; p48 The East in Gold; p49 A Mother to her sick Child; p50 The Happy Child; p51 To Sparrows fighting; p52 The White Cascade; p53 Nell Barnes; p55 In the Country; p57 Nature's Friend; p59 The Flood; p60 Christ the Man; p61 Dreams of the Sea; p63 A Great Time; p64 Man; p66 Truly Great; p68 The Sluggard; p69 When on a Summer's Morn; p70 Farewell to Poesy; p71 Early Morn; p72 Robin Redbreast; p73 A Lovely Woman; p75 Friends; p77 The Laughers; p79 The Boy; p81 The Dark Hour; p83 Jenny Wren; p85 Kitty and I; p87 A Drinking Song; p89 Money; p91 Sadness and Joy; p93 Fancy's Home; p94 Happy Wind; p95 Sleep; p97 When I am old; p98 Joy and Pleasure; p100 The Heap of Rags; p102 The Hawk; p103 The Weeping Child; p104 Seeking Beauty; p106 Margery; p107 A Greeting; p108 The Hermit; p109 The Bird-Man; p110 Sheep; p112 The Idiot and the Child; p113 Starers; p114 Plants and Men; p115 The One Singer; p116 lines from "The Soul's Destroyer"; p117 April's Charms; p118 The Call of the Sea; p120 Her Absence; p121 The Dreaming Boy; p123 Whom I know; p124 The Power of Music; p126 The Muse; p127 The Owl; p128 My Lady Comes; p129 The Daisy; p131 Fairies, take Care; p133 A Blind Child; p135 Thou comest, May; p136 The Best Friend; p137 Rich Days; p138 "The Ways of Time"; p139 The Bird of Paradise; p141 This World; p142 A Woman's Charms; p144 The Lodging-house fire; p148 Body and Spirit; p150 Catharine; p152

Strong Moments; p153 The Little Ones; p155 Night Wanderers; p156 Love's Coming; p158 Where we differ; p159 Parted; p160 The Blind Boxer; p162 Now; p164 Clouds; p166 The Posts; p167 No Master; p168 Rich or Poor; p169 The Sea; p171 A Life's Love; p172 Sweet Child; p173 Death's Game; p174 April Boys and Girls; p175 Newcomers; p177 Sweet Youth; p178 A Plain Life; p179 Heaven; p180 Ale; p182 The Likeness; p183 A Fleeting Passion; p184 The Child and the Mariner

paper: watermarked: OLDE STYLE

endpapers: cream; *edges*: uncut, top edge trimmed and greyish-brown in colour

binding: orange paper-covered boards with an embossed surface, lettered in black; front cover, within a black border: Collected Poems/ by/ William H. Davies. (in facsimile of author's script); spine: THE/ COLLECTED/ POEMS OF/ WILLIAM H./ DAVIES/ at foot: ALFRED A./ KNOPF; back cover: publisher's monogram; *dust-jacket*: not seen

date of publication: November 1916; *price*: $1.25

copies seen: BL (shelf mark: 011649.ee.83; accession date: 5 April 1917); HRHRC; HDB; SH

reviews: *Literary Digest*, 20 January 1917, 54, 134–135; by Clement Wood, *New York Call*, 4 February 1917, 12; *Springfield Republican*, 5 February 1917, 6; *ALA Booklist*, March 1917, 13, 256; *The Independent*, 26 March 1917, 89, 556; *American Review of Reviews*, April 1917, 55, 438; by William Stanley Braithwaite, *Bookman*, June 1917, 45, 436; Panhandler and Poet, Louis Untermeyer, *Yale Review* (new series), October 1917, VII, 1, 201; William H. Davies: Poet, Ezra Pound, *Poetry*, November 1917, XI, 2, 99–102; Latest Books of English Poets, Jessie Rittenhouse, *Bookman*, June 1918, XLVII, 4, 444–451

note: contains the 111 poems collected in *A14* plus an additional twelve poems: 'Laughing Rose', 'A Greeting', 'The Bird-Man', 'Whom I know', 'A Woman's Charms', 'Strong Moments' and 'Night Wanderers' from *Foliage (A10)*; 'The Ox', 'Margery', '"The Ways of Time"', 'Newcomers' and 'Catharine' from *New Poems (A2)*

A14b Second English edition   A C Fifield 1920

date of publication: November 1920; *price*: 7s. (in cloth) or 6s.

note: A. C. Fifield advertised a 3rd edition 1916 7s.6d. which I have been unable to trace

A14c Third English impression   Jonathan Cape 1921

Collected Poems/ By William H. Davies/ With a Frontispiece from a Pencil/ Sketch by William Rothenstein/ (publisher's device)/ Jonathan Cape/ Eleven Gower Street, London

as A14 apart from: (i–ii) a stub; (v) title-page (vi) *Third Impression. Reprinted/ by Jonathan Cape 1921/ All Rights Reserved*; 160 below text: (fleuron); the title-page is a cancel; the frontispiece is omitted; *binding*: pale grey calico grain cloth; spine, at foot: Jonathan/ Cape; *edges*: trimmed; *dust-jacket*: not seen *print run*: probably made up from second edition sheets

copy seen: RUL, Finzi

A14d Second American edition   Alfred A Knopf 1922

A14e Fourth English impression   Jonathan Cape 1924

date of publication: December 1923; *price*: 6s.

note: parchment and lambskin editions were advertised in *Current Literature of the Month*, 1924, 181, 14

A14f Fifth English impression   Jonathan Cape 1925

print run: 1000 copies printed on 19 December 1925 by Butler & Tanner; bound by Nevett

note: 22 copies remaindered to Foyles (2/-)

A14g Third American edition   Alfred A Knopf 1927

THE/ COLLECTED POEMS/ OF/ WILLIAM . H . DAVIES/ at foot: (publisher's device)/ NEW YORK/ ALFRED . A . KNOPF/ 1927

8vo; (A) in ten, (B–I) and (K–M) in eights; 98 leaves: (i–iv) (1–10) 11–190 (2)pp; 19.0 × 12.8 cms; the title-page is a cancel

(i–ii) blank; (iii) half-title: The Collected Poems of/ WILLIAM H. DAVIES; (iv) blank; (1) title-page; (2) COPYRIGHT 1916 BY WILLIAM H. DAVIES/ PUBLISHED, NOVEMBER, 1916/ SECOND PRINTING, MARCH, 1922/THIRD PRINTING, MAY, 1927/ at foot: MANUFACTURED IN THE UNITED STATES OF AMERICA; (3) as *A14* vii; (4) blank; (5–8) CONTENTS; (9) fly-title: The Collected Poems of/ WILLIAM H. DAVIES; (10) blank; 11–190 text; 190 below text: FINIS; (191) starts: A NOTE ON THE TYPE IN/ ends: NEW YORK.; (192) blank

endpapers: cream; *edges*: trimmed

binding: orange paper-covered boards, lettered in black; red cloth spine; front cover: Collected Poems/ by/ William H. Davies. (in facsimile of author's script); spine: THE/ COLLECTED/ POEMS OF/ WILLIAM H./ DAVIES/ at foot: ALFRED/ . A ./ KNOPF; back cover: blind-blocked publisher's device; *dust-jacket*: not seen

date of publication: May 1927

copy seen: HRHRC

note: frontispiece omitted

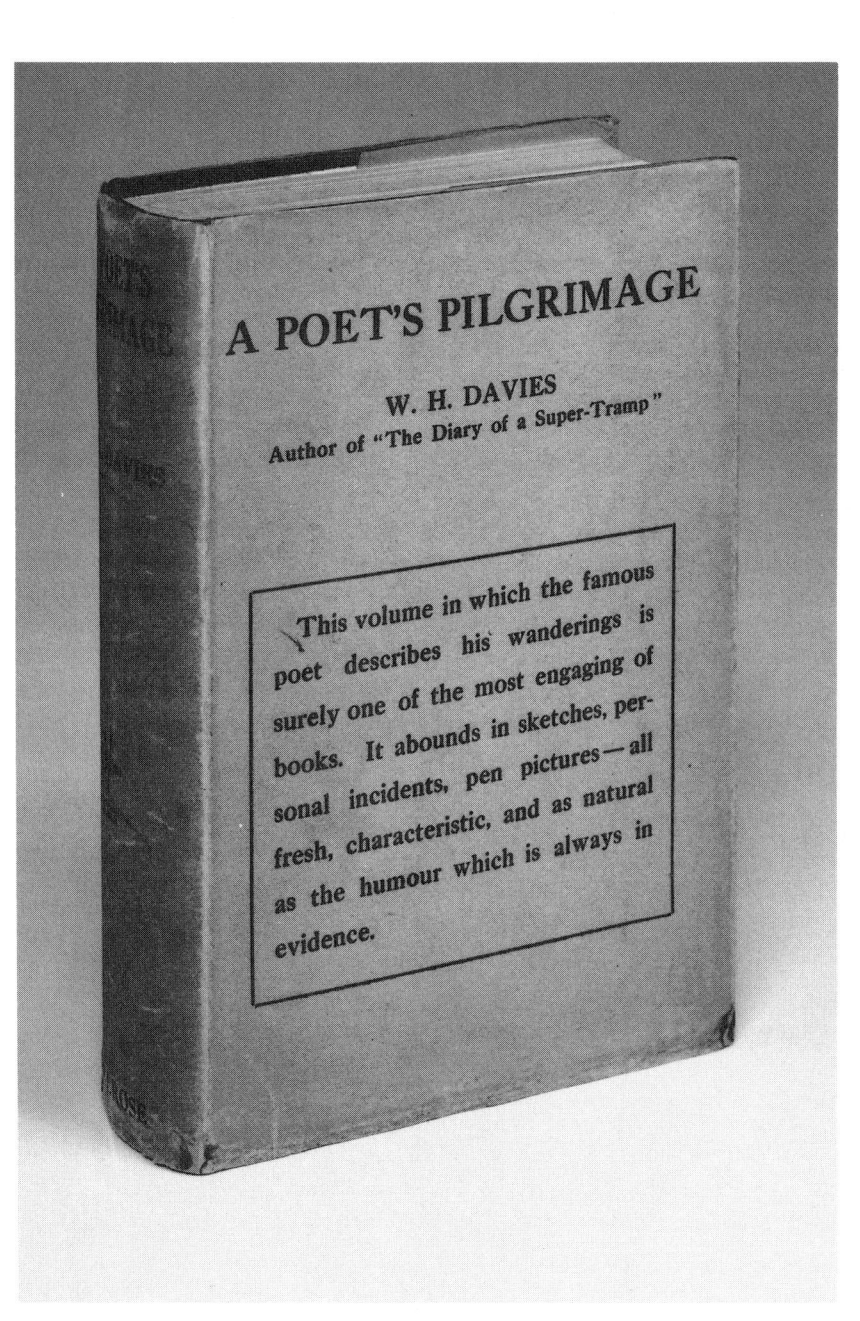

A POET'S PILGRIMAGE

W. H. DAVIES

Author of "The Diary of a Super-Tramp"

This volume in which the famous poet describes his wanderings is surely one of the most engaging of books. It abounds in sketches, personal incidents, pen pictures — all fresh, characteristic, and as natural as the humour which is always in evidence.

A15   A POET'S PILGRIMAGE   Andrew Melrose 1918

A POET'S/ PILGRIMAGE/ By/ W. H. DAVIES/ Author of "The Auto-biography of a Super-Tramp"/ at foot: LONDON: ANDREW MELROSE, LTD/ 3 YORK STREET, COVENT GARDEN, W.C/ 1918

8vo; (A)–I, K–U and X–AA in eights (the final 2pp of the last gathering are endpaper and pastedown); 190 leaves: (1–4) 5 (6–8) 9–14 (15–16) 17–25 (26–28) 29–49 (50–52) 53–61 (62–64) 65–77 (78–80) 81–89 (90–92) 93–101 (102–104) 105–117 (118–120) 121–135 (136–138) 139–151 (152–154) 155–166 (167–168) 169–178 (179–180) 181–193 (194–196) 197–204 (205–206) 207–218 (219–220) 221–229 (230–232) 233–247 (248–250) 251–270 (271–272) 273–278 (279–280) 281–288 (289–290) 291–304 (305–306) 307–322 (323–324) 325–334 (335–336) 337–346 (347–348) 349–362 (363–364) 365–378 (2)pp; 18.3 × 12.0 cms

(1) half-title: A POET'S PILGRIMAGE; (2) in a panel: starts: By the same Author/ ends: 3rd edition. 6s. Fifield.; (3) title-page; (4) blank; 5 CONTENTS; (6) blank; (7) fly-title: THE START; (8) blank; 9–14 text; (15) fly-title: CHILDREN; (16) blank; 17–25 text; (26) blank; (27) fly-title: OLD SAILORS; (28) blank; 29–49 text; (50) blank; (51) fly-title: AT SWANSEA; (52) blank; 53–61 text; (62) blank; (63) fly-title: THE LOST SEX; (64) blank; 65–77 text; (78) blank; (79) fly-title: IN NEATH VALLEY; (80) blank; 81–89 text; (90) blank; (91) fly-title: THE PROPHETESS; (92) blank; 93–101 text; (102) blank; (103) fly-title: WELSH SONG AND PRIZE-/ FIGHTING; (104) blank; 105–117 text; (118) blank; (119) fly-title: THE SIN OF MOUNTAINS; (120) blank; 121–135 text; (136) blank; (137) fly-title: PLAYING FOR COPPERS; (138) blank; 139–151 text; (152) blank; (153) fly-title: TINTERN ABBEY; (154) blank; 155–166 text; (167) fly-title: THE RAG- AND BONE MAN; (168) blank; 169–178 text; (179) fly-title: THE BLIND BOXER; (180) blank; 181–193 text; (194) blank; (195) fly-title: OLD ACQUAINTANCE; (196) blank; 197–204 text; (205) fly-title: A FAMILIAR COUNTRY; (206) blank; 207–218 text; (219) fly-title: A VALLEY OF INDUSTRY; (220) blank; 221–229 text; (230) blank; (231) fly-title: A LONG WALK; (232) blank; 233–247 text; (248) blank; (249) fly-title: WILLIAM; (250) blank; 251–270 text; (271) fly-title: THE COMMERCIAL TRAVELLERS; (272) blank; 273–278 text; (279) fly-title: WASTING TIME; (280) blank; 281–288 text; (289) fly-title: THE HUNT; (290) blank; 291–304 text; (305) fly-title: THE SAVERNAKE FOREST; (306) blank; 307–322 text; (323) fly-title: THE OTHER LODGER; (324) blank; 325–334 text; (335) fly-title: JANE'S SHADOW; (336) blank; 337–346 text; (347) fly-title: SLUG AND ANOTHER; (348) blank; 349–362 text; (363) fly-title: THE END; (364) blank; 365–378 text; 378 below text: THE END./ at foot: *Printed by* Butler & Tanner, *Frome and London.*; (379–380) blank; running title between rules at head of each page

contents: I p9 The Start; II p17 Children; III p29 Old Sailors; IV p53 At Swansea; V p65 The Lost Sex; VI p81 In Neath Valley; VII p93 The Prophetess; VIII p105 Welsh Song and Prize-Fighting; IX p121 The Sin of Mountains; X p139 Playing for Coppers; XI p155 Tintern Abbey; XII p169 The Rag and Bone Man; XIII p181 The Blind Boxer; XIV p197 Old Acquaintance; XV p207 A Familiar Country; XVI p221 A Valley of Industry; XVII p233 A Long Walk; XVIII p251 William; XIX p273 The Commercial Travellers; XX p281 Wasting Time; XXI p291 The Hunt; XXII p307 The Savernake Forest; XXIII p325 The Other Lodger; XXIV p337 Jane's Shadow; XXV p349 Slug and Another; XXVI p365 The End

contains: p9 The Start; p29 Old Sailors; p65 The Lost Sex; p81 In Neath Valley; p181 The Blind Boxer; p197 Old Acquaintance; p244 To the Woman who will read this poem to her Husband; p281 Wasting Time; p291 The Hunt; p308 How strange is this: I cannot pass this wood; p349 Slug and Another

paper: chain lines 2.5 cms apart and vertical

endpapers: cream; *edges*: trimmed

binding: royal blue calico grain cloth, blind-blocked, lettered in gilt and blind; front cover, blind, within a blind-blocked border: A POET'S/ PILGRIMAGE/ W. H. DAVIES; spine, in gilt: (rule)/ A POET'S/ PILGRIMAGE/ W. H. DAVIES/ at foot: MELROSE/ (rule); back cover: blank

dust-jacket: buff, printed in black; front: A POET'S PILGRIMAGE/ W. H. DAVIES/ Author of "The Diary [sic] of a Super-Tramp"/ within a panel: starts: This volume in which the famous/ ends: evidence.; spine: A POET'S/ PILGRIMAGE/ W. H. DAVIES/ 6/-/ NET/ MELROSE; back, within a double ruled panel: starts: *Friendly Books for Thoughtful Readers*/ ends: (rule)/ London: ANDREW MELROSE, Ltd.; both flaps: blank

date of publication: March 1918; *price*: 6s.

copies seen: BL (shelfmark: 010347.f.43; accession date: 12 April 1918); RUL, Finzi; HDB; SH

reviews: A Walk Among Men, *TLS*, 11 April 1918, 170; *Punch*, 17 April 1918, 154, 256; A Poet's Pilgrimage, *The Spectator*, 27 April 1918, 4687, 445–446; A Poet's Pilgrimage, John Freeman, *Bookman*, May 1918, 320, 69–70

previous printings:
'The Hunt' (as part of 'The Beggar's Hunt'), *Blue Review*, May 1913, I, 1, 24–27
'Slug and Another' (as 'A Plain Life'), *Collected Poems (A14)*, 1916
'The Blind Boxer', *Nation*, 24 May 1913, XIII, 8, 314

text changes from first printings to A15:
The Blind Boxer: line 5: 'Aye' to 'For', 'boxer' to 'Boxer, line 6: 'Who had big' to 'That had hard', line 14: 'Leap full' to 'Have leapt'

notes: (a) 'Wasting Time', 'Slug and Another' and 'To the Woman who will read this poem to her Husband' re-titled 'The Moon and a Cloud', 'No Idle Gold' and 'I am the Poet Davies, William' in *Collected Poems (A33)*
(b) the HDB copy is inscribed: 'W. H. Davies./ 1918.'
(c) Melrose advertised *A Pilgrim in Wales*, 1916 which I have been unable to trace

A15a Travellers' Library edition   Jonathan Cape 1927

A POET'S PILGRIMAGE/ by/ W. H. DAVIES/ AUTHOR OF 'THE AUTOBIOGRAPHY OF A SUPER-TRAMP'/ (publisher's device)/ at foot: LONDON/ JONATHAN CAPE 30 BEDFORD SQUARE

16mo; (A)–H in sixteens plus a 40pp publisher's catalogue; 128 leaves: (1–6) 7–255 (1)pp plus a 40pp publisher's catalogue (paged (1–2) 3–39 (1)); 17.0 × 11.6 cms

(1) half-title: THE TRAVELLERS' LIBRARY/ (decorative star)/ A POET'S PILGRIMAGE; (2) starts: (fleuron) A descriptive list of some of the volumes in/

ends: or to the publishers.; (3) title-page; (4) starts: FIRST ISSUED IN THE TRAVELLERS' LIBRARY 1926/ ends: LIMITED; (5) CONTENTS; (6) blank; 7–255 text; (256) blank; 40pp publisher's catalogue: starts: A LIST OF THE/ ends: THE GARDEN CITY PRESS LTD. LETCHWORTH, HERTS.

endpapers: cream; *edges*: trimmed

binding: royal blue cloth, blocked and lettered in gilt; front cover: blank; spine: (decorative rule)/ A/ POET'S/ PILGRIMAGE/ (decorative star)/ W. H. DAVIES/ (publisher's device)/ at foot: JONATHAN/ CAPE/ (decorative rule); back cover: blind-blocked publisher's monogram; *dust-jacket*: not seen

date of publication: September 1927; *price*: 3s.6d.

copy seen: SH

review: *Now & Then*, Christmas 1927, 26, 36

notes: (a) reprinted 1931
(b) printed by Garden City Press

A15b St Giles Library No 13   Jonathan Cape 1940

W. H. DAVIES/ A Poet's Pilgrimage/ (publisher's device)/ THE/ SAINT GILES/ LIBRARY/ at foot: JONATHAN CAPE/ THIRTY BEDFORD SQUARE LONDON

as *A15a* apart from: 16.7 × 11.2 cms; (1) half-title: The Saint Giles Library/ NO. 13/ A POET'S PILGRIMAGE; (2) starts: A list of the books included/ ends: this volume; (3) title-page; (4) starts: FIRST PUBLISHED 1927/ ends: BOUND BY A. W. BAIN & CO. LTD.; (5) CONTENTS; (6) blank; 7–255 text; (256) blank; 4pp publisher's catalogue: starts: A LIST OF TITLES/ ends: 40 WILLIAM BLAKE Arthur Symons; *binding*: beige calico grain cloth embossed with brown, blocked in reddish-brown; front cover: (publisher's device); spine: A POET'S/ PILGRIMAGE/ W. H./ DAVIES/ (publisher's device)/ at foot: JONATHAN/ CAPE; back cover: blank; *dust-jacket*: not seen

date of publication: 5 April 1940

print run: transferred from Travellers' Library; *price*: 1s.9d.

copy seen: SH

A16 **RAPTURES**   Beaumont Press 1918

RAPTURES (in red)/ A BOOK OF POEMS/ BY W. H. DAVIES

8vo; * in four, (a) in four, b–c in eights, d in four (the endpapers and pastedowns are part of the first and final gatherings); 24 leaves excluding endpapers: (i–iv) (1–8) 9–38 (6)pp; 23.0 × 14.5 cms variable

excluding endpapers: (i–iv) blank; (1) half-title: RAPTURES; (2) limitation: This is the third book issued by the Beaumont/ Press 22 copies (two of which are not for

sale)/ have been printed on Japanese vellum signed/ by the author and numbered 1 to 22 and 250/ copies on hand-made paper numbered 23 to 272./ This is No. ; (3) title-page; (4) blank; (5–7) CONTENTS (in red on p(5) and incorporating first lines); (8) blank; 9–38 text; (39) HERE ENDS RAPTURES A BOOK OF POEMS/ by W. H. Davies the Typography and Binding/ arranged by Cyril William Beaumont Printed/ on his Press in London and Published by/ him at 75 Charing Cross Road in the/ City of Westminster Completed/ on the first day of May/ MDCCCCXVIII/ (red publisher's device)/ at foot: The cover has been designed/ by Pickford Waller and the Binding/ executed by F. Sangorski and G. Sutcliffe; (40–44) blank; the first initial of each poem is in red

contents: p9 Raptures; p10 Confession; p11 Easter; p12 My Love Could Walk; p13 My Old Acquaintance; p14 Birds; p15 Jove Warns Us; p16 The Excuse; p17 In the Snow; p18 Molly; p19 Killed in Action (Edward Thomas); p20 Lovely Dames; p21 Cowslips and Larks; p22 When Yon Full Moon; p23 Till I Went Out; p24 To My Thoughts; p25 Rags and Bones; p26 A Strange Meeting; p27 The Bell; p28 Exalted Flower; p29 The Girl is Mad; p30 In Time of War; p31 In England; p32 The Dancer; p33 How Late; p34 Brothers; p35 Come Let Us Find; p36 What thoughts are Mine; p37 Angel and Mystery; p38 Late Singers

paper: watermarked: F J Head & Co/ Hand Made; chain lines 3.3 cms apart and vertical

endpapers: pale grey; *edges*: deckle fore edge, top edge trimmed

binding: beige paper-covered boards decorated with violet and green design representing pansies, mushroom coloured embossed buckram spine; front cover, on a pale blue paper label 4.5 × 7.2 cms, in purple, within a green decorative border: RAPTURES/ A/ (decorative pansy) BOOK OF POEMS (decorative pansy)/ BY/ W. H. DAVIES; spine, on a pale blue paper label 7.5 cms deep, in purple, vertically upwards: RAPTURES　W. H. DAVIES; back cover: blank; *dust-jacket*: not seen

date of publication: recorded as December 1918 in the English Catalogue but 25 May 1918 according to George Francis Wilson *(F95)*

print run: 272 copies; *price*: 10s.6d.

copies seen: HRHRC (no 264); HDB (no 205); SH (no 141)

reviews: *To-day*, July 1918, III, 17, 193; Philomelia, *Nation*, 6 July 1918, XXIII, 14, 369

mss: in WHD's hand on paper watermarked: Audrey Note/ FR with chain lines 2.5 cms apart and horizontal; addressed 14 Great Russell Street, W.C. and dated 1918; clipped into brown paper wrappers (HDB); HRHRC also hold a mss of 'Raptures' in the hand of A. E. Coppard

text change from manuscript to A16:
In England: line 14: 'they' to 'those earthquakes'

previous printings:
'Raptures' and 'Molly', *To-day*, March 1917, I, 1, 26 and January 1918, II, 11, 172 respectively
'Confession' and 'What Thoughts are Mine', *Form*, April 1917, 1, 2, 18
'Birds', 'Lovely Dames', 'Come, Let Us Find', 'My Love Could Walk' and 'My Old Acquaintance', 'The Dancer', 'Easter', 'Killed in Action (Edward Thomas)', 'Rags and Bones', 'When Yon Full Moon', 'Late Singers' and 'In Time of War', *Nation*,

3 June 1916, XIX, 10, 289, 23 September 1916, XIX, 26, 791, 4 November 1916, XX, 5, 179, 30 December 1916, XX, 13, 472, 10 February 1917, XX, 19, 653, 5 April 1917, XXI, 1, 14, 21 April 1917, XXI, 3, 70, 2 June 1917, XXI, 9, 223, 28 July 1917, XXI, 17, 432, 15 September 1917, XXI, 24, 612 and 17 November 1917, XXII, 7, 243 respectively

'Cowslips and Larks', 'A Strange Meeting', 'In the Snow', 'Till I Went Out' and 'To My Thoughts', *New Statesman*, 23 September 1916, VII, 181, 591, 18 November 1916, VIII, 189, 160, 9 December 1916, VIII, 192, 232, 6 January 1917, VIII, 196, 327 and 9 June 1917, IX, 218, 231 respectively

text changes from first printings to A16:
Come, Let Us Find: 1st stanza line 5: 'every' to 'many a'; 2nd stanza line 4: 'life from that can' to 'life can live and', line 5: 'every' to 'on a'
What Thoughts are Mine: 2nd stanza line 2: 'And I'm' to 'And I'; 3rd stanza line 5: ' "puss, puss, puss" ' to ' "Puss, Puss, Puss" '

notes: (a) the HDB copy is inscribed: 'My book./ W. H. Davies./ June 1918.'
(b) 'Raptures', 'Molly', 'Confession', 'Easter', 'What Thoughts are Mine', 'My Old Acquaintance', 'In England' (as 'England'), My Love Could Walk', 'Birds', 'Jove Warns Us', 'The Excuse', 'In the Snow', 'Killed in Action (Edward Thomas)', 'Lovely Dames', 'Cowslips and Larks', 'When Yon Full Moon', 'Till I Went Out', 'To My Thoughts', 'Rags and Bones', 'A Strange Meeting', 'Exalted Flower', 'In Time of War', 'The Dancer', 'Come, Let Us Find' and 'Late Singers' also appear in *Forty New Poems (A17)*
(c) WHD had greetings cards printed to send to his friends, with one stanza from 'Birds' and a tipped-in coloured illustration of a stonechat

A16a   Special edition   Beaumont Press 1918

as *A16* apart from: 22.8 × 14.7 cms variable; limitation signed: W. H. Davies.; *paper:* Japanese vellum; *endpapers:* Japanese vellum and part of the first and final gatherings; *binding:* vellum, lettered and decorated in gilt; front cover, within a decorative panel: RAPTURES/ A/ (decorative pansy) BOOK OF POEMS (decorative pansy)/ BY/ W. H. DAVIES; spine: R/ A/ P/ T/ U/ R/ E/ S/ ./ W/ ./ H/ ./ D/ A/ V/ I/ E/ S; back cover: blank; *edges:* top edge trimmed

print run: 22 copies; *price:* 42s.

copies seen: BL (shelf mark: C57.i.16; accession date: 24 September 1918) (no 17); HRHRC (no 14); HDB (no 15)

note: the HDB copy is inscribed: 'Confession/ One hour in every hundred hours./ I sing of childhood, birds and flowers;/ Who reads my Character in my song,/ Will not see much in me that's wrong./ But in my ninety hours and nine,/ I would not tell what thoughts are mine;/ They're not so pure as find their words/ In songs of childhood, flowers and birds./ W. H. Davies.'

A17   **FORTY NEW POEMS**   A C Fifield 1918

Forty New Poems/ By/ William H. Davies/ at foot: London: A. C. Fifield, 13,/ Clifford's Inn, E.C.4. 1918

8vo; (A)–C in eights, D in four; 28 leaves: (1–6) 7–53 (3)pp; 19.0 × 12.5 cms variable

(1–2) blank; (3) half-title: Forty New Poems; (4) starts: *The Works of William H. Davies*/ ends: *A Pilgrimage in Wales*. 1918. *Melrose*.; (5) title-page; (6) *All rights reserved*/ at foot: PRINTED BY WILLIAM BRENDON AND SON, LTD., PLYMOUTH, ENGLAND; 7–8 Contents (poem titles in italics); 9–53 text; (54) THE END; (55) starts: *The Works of William H. Davies*/ ends: London: A. C. Fifield, 13 Clifford's Inn, E.C.4.; (56) blank

contents: p9 Raptures; p10 The Voice; p11 Confession; p12 Easter; p13 My Love could Walk; p14 My Old Acquaintance; p15 A Winter's Night; p16 Birds; p18 Jove Warns Us; p19 The Excuse; p20 In the Snow; p21 Molly; p22 Killed in Action (Edward Thomas); p23 Lovely Dames; p24 The Shameless One; p25 Cowslips and Larks; p26 We Arm to Fight; p27 Forgiveness; p28 That Day She Seized; p29 The Bell; p30 A Strange Meeting; p31 When yon Full Moon; p32 Till I Went Out; p33 The Soul's Companions; p34 To my Thoughts; p35 The Holly on the Wall; p36 How Late; p37 Brothers; p39 Exalted Flower; p40 What Thoughts are Mine; p41 Angel and Mystery; p42 They're Taxing Ale again; p43 The Girl is Mad; p44 In Time of War; p45 England; p47 Come, let us Find; p48 The Birds of Stee [sic]; p49 Rags and Bones; p50 The Dancer; p51 On hearing Mrs Woodhouse play the Harpsichord; p52 Passion's Greed; p53 Late Singers

paper: watermarked: (crown)/ Abbey Mills/ Greenfield; chain lines 2.4 cms apart and vertical

endpapers: cream; *edges*: uncut, deckle fore edge, top edge trimmed

binding: dark turquoise net grain cloth, blind-blocked, lettered in gilt; front cover, within a blind-blocked border: FORTY NEW POEMS/ (fleuron) W.H.DAVIES (fleuron); spine: (fleuron)/ FORTY/ NEW/ POEMS/ W.H./ DAVIES/ (fleuron)/ at foot: FIFIELD; back cover: blank

dust-jacket: pale grey, printed in blue; front: FORTY NEW POEMS/ (fleuron) W.H.DAVIES (fleuron)/ at foot: *Four Shillings net*/ London: A. C. *Fifield*; spine: (fleuron)/ FORTY/ NEW/ POEMS/ W. H./ DAVIES/ (fleuron)/ 4s./ Net/ at foot: Fifield; back, within a panel: starts: A. C. Fifield's AUTUMN LIST, 1918/ ends: 13 CLIFFORD'S INN, LONDON, E.C.4; both flaps: blank

date of publication: October 1918; *price*: 4s.

copies seen: BL (shelf mark: 011648.ee.110; accession date: 30 September 1918); HRHRC (3 copies in turquoise, 1 in grey); RUL, Finzi; HDB; SH

reviews: Life and Letters: Mr W. H. Davies, J. C. Squire, *Land & Water*, 3 October 1918, LXXII, 2943, 15; The Tramp and the Citizen, *TLS*, 14 November 1918, 553; Two Books of the Week, *Country Life*, 23 November 1918, XLIV, 1142, 456–457; The Happiest of Poets, John Freeman, *Bookman*, January 1919, LV, 328, 143–144; by Oscar Lloyd, *Welsh Outlook*, February 1919, VI, 61, 48; *To-day*, February 1919, IV, 24, 232; A Medley of Verse, *The Spectator*, 10 May 1919, 122, 4741, 598–599

previous printings:
'The Holly on the Wall', 'On Hearing Mrs Woodhouse Play the Harpsichord' and 'The Birds of Steel', *Nation*, 29 December 1917, XXII, 13, 440, 18 May 1918, XXIII, 7, 171 and 10 August 1918, XXIII, 19, 499 respectively
for other first printings see *A16*

text changes from first printings to A17:
England: line 4: 'Their bleeding mouths being froze' to 'With bleeding mouths that freeze'
Come, Let Us Find: as *A16*
What Thoughts are Mine: 2nd stanza line 2: as *A16*, last line: ' "bow-wow" ' to ' "Bow-wow" '; 3rd stanza as *A16*

notes: (a) 'Raptures', 'Molly', 'Confession', 'Easter', 'What Thoughts are Mine', 'My Old Acquaintance', 'England' (as 'In England'), 'My Love Could Walk', 'Birds', 'Jove Warns Us', 'The Excuse', 'In the Snow', 'Killed in Action (Edward Thomas)', 'Lovely Dames', 'Cowslips and Larks', 'When Yon Full Moon', 'Till I Went Out', 'To My Thoughts', 'Rags and Bones', 'A Strange Meeting', 'Exalted Flower', 'In Time of War', 'The Dancer', 'Come, Let Us Find' and 'Late Singers' also appear in *Raptures (A16)*
(b) Contents: p8 line 6 up: 'Steel' misprinted 'Stee'
(c) secondary binding at HRHRC: grey fine net grain cloth, blind-blocked, lettered in gilt; front cover: a wreath within a blind-blocked border; spine: as above but with FIFIELD in deeper lettering
(d) agreement with Fifield dated 30 July 1918 (to be published during 1918 at approximately 4/- net, Jonathan Cape archives, RUL)

A17a   New edition   Jonathan Cape 1924

note: bound by Nevett

A18   **THE SONG OF LIFE**   A C Fifield 1920

The Song of Life/ and Other Poems/ By/ William H. Davies/ *With a frontispiece from a portrait/ by LAURA KNIGHT/* at foot: London: A. C. Fifield, 13/ Clifford's Inn, E.C.4. 1920

8vo; (A) in eight plus tipped-in frontispiece, B–D in eights; 32 leaves: (1–6) 7–43 (44–46) 47–61 (3)pp plus frontispiece not included in the pagination; 18.7 × 13.0 cms variable

(1–2) blank; (3) half-title: The Song of Life/ and Other Poems; (4) starts: *The Works of William H. Davies/* ends: *A Pilgrimage in Wales. 1918. Melrose.*; frontispiece captioned: W. H. DAVIES, 1920/ A Portrait by Laura Knight, lower right hand side of portrait, in script: To W H Davies/ from/ Laura Knight/ 4 April 1920; (5) title-page; (6) *All rights reserved/* at foot: *The Mayflower Press, Plymouth, England.* William Brendon & Son, Ltd.; 7–8 Contents (poem titles in italics); 9–43 text; (44) blank; (45) fly-title: The Song of Life; (46) blank; 47–61 text; 61 below text: END.; (62) blank; (63) starts: *The Works of William H. Davies/* ends: London: A. C. Fifield, 13 Clifford's Inn, E.C.4.; (64) blank

contents: p9 Oh, Sweet Content!; p10 The Villain; p11 Love Speechless; p12 The Dog; p13 The Rat; p14 The Cat; p15 To-Day; p16 How Kind is Sleep; p17 The Force of Love; p18 When Leaves Begin; p19 Passion's Hounds; p20 Love Impeached; p21 The Truth; p22 The Coming of Peace; p23 April's Lambs; p24 The

Coming of Spring; p25 A Song; p26 Love's Caution; p27 Trees; p28 What County?; p29 A Child's Pet; p30 The Flirt; p31 The Captive Lion; p32 The Clock; p33 A Bird's Anger; p34 Bird and Brook; p35 One Thing Wanting; p36 The Mint; p37 Worm-Proof; p38 Comfort; p39 Her Mouth and Mine; p40 Let Me Confess; p41 Love's Silent Hour; p42 Now That She Gives; p43 You Interfering Ladies; p45 The Song of Life

paper: chain lines 2.5 cms apart and vertical

endpapers: cream; *edges*: deckle fore edge, top edge trimmed

binding: light-blue diagonal fine-ribbed cloth, blind-blocked, lettered in gilt; front cover, within a blind-blocked border: blind-blocked wreath; spine, lettered and decorated in gilt: (fleuron)/ THE/ SONG/ OF/ LIFE/ W.H./ DAVIES/ (fleuron)/ at foot: FIFIELD; back cover: blank; *dust-jacket*: not seen

date of publication: September 1920; *price*: 5s.

copies seen: BL (shelf mark: 011649.g.131; accession date: 31 August 1920); HRHRC; HDB; SH

reviews: To-day, September 1920, VIII, 43, 34; The World of Books, *Nation*, 4 September 1920, XXVII, 23, 697; "Spontaneity in Poetry", *TLS*, 16 September 1920, 596; Nature Poets, *Nation*, 18 September 1920, XXVII, 25, 760–762; "The Song of Life" Mr W. H. Davies's New Poems, C. Kennett Burrow, *John o'London's Weekly*, 9 October 1920, IV, 79, 12 (portrait); Poetry, *London Mercury*, November 1920, III, 13, 111; A Natural Singer, S, *Bookman's Journal and Print Collector*, 12 November 1920, III, 55, 48

mss: in WHD's hand on paper addressed 14 Great Russell St, London, W.C. and dated 1920; clipped into brown paper wrappers (HDB); there are also unsigned mss in WHD's hand at HRHRC of 'Comfort' and 'Worm-proof' on unheaded undated notepaper (that of 'Comfort' must be the earlier mss as it has the correction: 2nd stanza line 5: from 'linnet there' to 'little bird'); there are also signed mss in WHD's hand at NL of 'Trees', 'Love's Caution' and 'The Cat' all undated, the last mentioned on 14 Great Russell St, W. C. headed notepaper; HRHRC also hold a signed mss in WHD's hand of 'How kind is Sleep' in an Autograph Poetical Album written for Sir Roderick Meiklejohn by Siegfried Sassoon, Robert Graves, WHD and Edith Sitwell, in Oxford 17–18 March 1919 and dated by the owner 15 April 1919 (the date indicates that this must be the earlier mss)

WHD's manuscript corrections:
A Bird's Anger: last line: 'thy' to 'your'
The Song of Life: X line 2: 'while' to 'time'; XI line 3: 'cut and costly flowers' to 'many a lovely flower', line 5: 'a few short hours' to 'their little hour'; XXVII line 3: 'to scent the world' to 'scent my soul'; XL line 3: 'again real music' to 'hear real music'

text change from manuscript to A18:
The Song of Life: XL line 3: 'real' to 'that'

previous printings:
'April's Lambs', 'The Force of Love', 'Her Mouth and Mine', 'The Flirt', 'How Kind is Sleep', 'Let Me Confess' and 'Now That She Gives', *To-day*, April 1918, III, 14, 42, December 1918, IV, 22, 144, April 1919, V, 26, 62, September 1919, VI, 34, 15, December 1919, VI, 34, 122, May 1920, VII, 39, 87 and June 1920, VII, 40,131 respectively

'Love Impeached', *The Owl*, May 1919, I, 12
'The Rat', *The Chapbook*, July 1919, 1, 1, 30
'Love's Caution', *London Mercury*, November 1919, I, 1, 13
'The Song of Life', *English Review*, January 1920, XXX, 1–9
'When Leaves Begin' and 'The Truth', 'Passion's Hounds', 'The Dog' and 'A Child's Pet', 'What County?' and 'Love's Silent Hour', *Nation*, 6 April 1918, XXIII, 1, 14, 8 March 1919, XXIV, 23, 672, 10 May 1919, XXV, 6, 170, 9 August 1919, XXV, 19, 562 and 10 April 1920, XXVII, 2, 45 respectively
'The Coming of Peace' and 'The Cat', *New Statesman*, 21 December 1918, XII, 298, 241 and 12 July 1919, XIII, 327, 371 respectively
'Worm-Proof' and 'Comfort', *Voices in Poetry and Prose*, August 1919, II, 2, 45

notes: (a) variant binding: turquoise cloth
(b) the HDB copy is inscribed: 'My book/ W. H. Davies./ Sept. 1st. 1920'
(c) agreement with Fifield dated 3 June 1920 (Jonathan Cape archives, RUL)

A19 THE CAPTIVE LION   Yale University Press 1921

The Captive Lion/ &/ Other Poems/ By William Henry Davies/ (publisher's device)/ at foot: New Haven/ Yale University Press/ Mdccccxxi

8vo; 6 unsigned gatherings of eight, 1 unsigned gathering of 6 plus 1; 55 leaves: (i–iv) v–vii (viii) 1–37 (38–40) 41–99 (3)pp; 18.7 × 12.7 cms

(i) half-title: The Captive Lion/ &/ Other Poems/ (3 dots in an inverted triangle)/ PUBLISHED ON THE/ KINGSLEY TRUST ASSOCIATION/ PUBLICATION FUND; (ii) blank; (iii) title-page; (iv) Copyright, 1921, by/ William Henry Davies./ (double rule)/ The publishers are indebted to *The New/ Republic* for permission to reprint "When/ Autumn's Fruit."; v–vii Contents; (viii) blank; 1–37 text; (38) blank; (39) half-title: The Song of Life; (40) blank; 41–99 text; (100) PRINTED IN THE UNITED STATES OF AMERICA; (101–102) blank

contents: p1 The Captive Lion; p2 Oh, Sweet Content!; p3 The Villain; p4 Love Speechless; p5 The Dog; p6 The Rat; p7 The Cat; p8 Today; p9 How Kind is Sleep; p10 The Force of Love; p11 When Leaves Begin; p12 Passion's Hounds; p13 Love Impeached; p14 The Truth; p15 The Coming of Peace; p16 April's Lambs; p17 The Coming of Spring; p18 A Song; p19 Love's Caution; p20 Trees; p21 What County?; p22 A Child's Pet; p23 The Flirt; p24 The Clock; p25 A Bird's Anger; p26 Bird and Brook; p27 When Autumn's Fruit; p28 One Thing Wanting; p29 The Mint; p30 Worm-Proof; p31 Comfort; p32 Her Mouth and Mine; p33 Let Me Confess; p34 Love's Silent Hour; p35 Now That She Gives; p36 You Interfering Ladies; p37 Ladies' Men; p41 The Song of Life; p56 Raptures; p57 Confession; p58 Easter; p59 My Love Could Walk; p60 My Old Acquaintance; p61 A Winter's Night; p62 Birds; p64 Jove Warns Us; p65 The Excuse; p66 In the Snow; p67 Molly; p68 Killed in Action (Edward Thomas); p69 Lovely Dames; p70 The Shameless One; p71 Cowslips and Larks; p72 We Arm to Fight; p73 Forgiveness; p74 That Day She Seized; p75 The Bell; p76 A Strange Meeting; p77 When yon Full Moon; p78 Till I Went Out; p79 The Soul's Companions; p80 To my Thoughts; p81 The Holly on the Wall; p82 How Late; p83 Brothers; p85 Exalted Flower; p86 What Thoughts are Mine; p87 Angel and Mystery; p88 They're Taxing Ale Again; p89 The Girl is

Mad; p90 In Time of War; p91 England; p93 Come, Let Us Find; p94 The Birds of Steel; p95 Rags and Bones; p96 The Dancer; p97 On Hearing Mrs Woodhouse Play the Harpsichord; p98 Passion's Greed; p99 Late Singers

endpapers: cream; *edges*: trimmed

binding: light tan paper-covered boards, decorated in green, lettered in black; front cover, an outer green border with an inner green border, divided horizontally into three panels: top panel, in black: THE CAPTIVE LION/ AND OTHER POEMS/ central panel, decorated with a green repeating pattern in eleven rows with alternate rows offset/ lower panel, in black: BY WILLIAM HENRY DAVIES; spine, vertically upwards, in black: THE CAPTIVE LION & OTHER POEMS . DAVIES; back cover: blank; *dust-jacket*: plain glacene

date of publication: September 1921; *price*: $1.50

copies seen: BL (shelf mark: X-908/4305; accession date: 30 October 1962); HRHRC (3 copies, one a presentation copy to Robert H. Schauffer)

reviews: The Poetry of a Super-Tramp, William Stanley Braithwaite, *Boston Evening Transcript*, 24 September 1921, 5; This Davies, Mark Van Doren, *Nation*, 12 October 1921, 113, 2936, supplement 422; *Springfield Republican*, 11 November 1921, 8; Poets in Purple and Drab, *New York Times (Book Review)*, 20 November 1921, 24; *The Dial*, December 1921, 71, 6, 716; The Captive Lion, John Gould Fletcher, *The Freeman*, 21 December 1921, IV, 93, 356–357

previous printings:
'When Autumn's Fruit', *New Republic*, 26 January 1921, XXV, 321, 251
for other first printings see *A16*, *A17* and *A18*

text change from first printing to A19:
When Autumn's Fruit: 1st stanza last line: 'blackbird' to 'chaffinch'

notes: (a) a compilation of *A17* and *A18* with the exception of two poems: 'The Voice' and 'When Autumn's Fruit'
(b) 'Ladies' Men' re-titled 'Men that have Strength' in *Collected Poems (A33)*
(c) the copy at HRHRC, which was originally presented to Robert H. Schauffer, has the following author correction: Birds: 4th stanza line 2: 'they always please' to 'how well they please'

A20 THE HOUR OF MAGIC   Jonathan Cape 1922

The/ HOUR *of* MAGIC/ *and other Poems by*/ W. H. Davies/ (publisher's device)/ *Decorated by*/ William Nicholson/ at foot: Jonathan Cape/ Eleven Gower Street, London

8vo; (A) in ten, (B–C) in eights; 26 leaves: (i–xii) 1–2 (3) 4–6 (7) 8–10 (11) 12–14 (15) 16–18 (19) 20–22 (23) 24–26 (27) 28–34 (6)pp; 19.0 × 12.5 cms variable

(i–ii) blank; (iii) half-title: *The Hour of Magic*/ at foot: (vignette of a tree); (iv) frontispiece: full-page black and white decoration of a cockerel on a sundial; (v) title-page; (vi) (decorative flower)/ at foot: *First published 1922*/ *All Rights reserved*; (vii) *Contents*; (viii) blank; (ix) (vignette of a bird on a hat above a walking stick) signed N; (x) blank; (xi) dedication: To Elizabeth Drury, with our love/ W.D.-W.N.; (xii) blank; 1–34 text; (35) full-page black and white illustration of WHD sleeping at a table, head resting on his crossed arms with patterns and signs above him; (36) blank; (37) (vignette of a candlestick); (38) blank; (39) HERE ENDS THE HOUR OF MAGIC/ AND OTHER POEMS BY W. H. DAVIES/ DECORATED BY WILLIAM NICHOLSON/ NOW PRINTED FOR THE FIRST TIME/ IN GARAMOND TYPE AT THE SIGN/ OF THE DOLPHIN & PUBLISHED/ AT ELEVEN GOWER STREET/ BY JONATHAN CAPE/ SEPTEMBER/ MDCCCC/ XX/II; (40) blank; poem titles in italics.

contents: p1 The Hour of Magic; p2 The Beautiful; p4 Impudence; p5 Wasted Hours; p6 Two Women; p8 Pastures; p9 Her Merriment; p10 Joy; p12 Lamorna Cove; p13 Wild Oats; p14 The Grief of Others; p16 The Portrait; p18 A Thought; p20 Our Sussex Downs; p21 Telling Fortunes; p22 The Collar; p24 To a Fool; p25 Strength; p26 To Bacchus; p28 A Woman's History; p30 The Trance

illustrations: full-page: frontispiece and pp(3), (7), (11), (15), (19), (23), (27) and (35); decorations: pp(iii), (vi), (ix), 1, 2, 4, 5, 6, 8, 9, 10, 12, 13, 17, 18, 20, 22, 24, 25, 26, 29, 34 and (37)

paper: chain lines 2.8 cms apart and vertical

endpapers: dark blue design on a grey-blue background visually representing a night sky with white stars and hinting at Zodiac figures; *edges*: deckle fore edge, top edge gilt

binding: cream mottled paper-covered boards with an embossed surface; front cover, on a gold paper label 4.3 × 7.0 cms, in black, within a panel: *The* HOUR *of* MAGIC/ *and other poems by/ William. h. Davies./* (decorative bird)/ *Designs by William Nicholson*; spine, on a gold paper label 3.5 cms deep, in black: *The/* HOUR/ *of/* MAGIC/. . ./ *W. H./ Davies*; back cover: blank

dust-jacket: mottled cream with an embossed surface; front, in black, within a green decorative border: *The/* Hour *of* Magic/ *and other Poems by/* W. H. Davies/ (vignette of a lamb)/ *With Designs by/* William Nicholson; spine: *The/* HOUR/ *of/* MAGIC/ W.H./ Davies/ *Designs by/* William/ Nicholson/ at foot: Jonathan/ Cape; back: starts: *The Works of W. H. Davies/* ends: *Eleven Gower Street, London*; front flap: starts: (decorative green rule)/ ends: *Magic* 7s.6d. *net*; back flap: blank

date of publication: recorded as October 1922 in the English Catalogue but actually September according to Lawrence Hockey *(F345)*

price: 7s.6d.

copies seen: BL (shelf mark: 011645.eee.6; accession date: 4 October 1922); HRHRC; RUL, Finzi; HDB; SH

reviews: The Hour of Magic, *Country Life*, 14 October 1922, LII, 1345, 481; Poets and Poetry: Mr W. H. Davies, A. Williams-Ellis, *The Spectator*, 28 October 1922, 129, 4922, 604; *Saturday Review*, 28 October 1922, 134, 638; by FLL, *New Statesman*, 28 October 1922, 20, 116; Mr Davies' "Album Verses", *TLS*, 2 November 1922, 699; Mr Drinkwater and Mr Davies, J. Middleton Murry, *Nation and Athenaeum*, 25 November 1922, 32, 4830, 321–322; *To-day*, December 1922, IX, 52, 70; Poetry, JCS, *London Mercury*, November 1922, VII, 37, 94–96; 'The Hour of Magic', John Freeman, *Bookman*, December 1922, LXIII, 375, 166 *mss*: in WHD's hand on paper watermarked: RYMANS/ HERTFORD BANK/ LONDON; addressed 13 Avery Row, W. and dated 1922 (HDB); there are also earlier typed mss, corrected in WHD's hand, of 'The Collar' and 'Strength' in the Jonathan Cape archives, RUL (the mss used for Harold Monro's February 1922 *Chapbook*); 'The Collar' has the following author correction: line 7: from 'smoke' to 'mist'; additionally there is an earlier corrected mss in WHD's hand of 'The Trance' in the Jonathan Cape archives, RUL with the following author corrections: line 15: from 'creature' to 'thing that's strange' and line 19: from 'dark' to 'half'; HRHRC hold a signed mss in WHD's hand of 'Pastures' in an Autograph Poetical Album written for Sir Roderick Meiklejohn by Siegfried Sassoon, Robert Graves, WHD and Edith Sitwell written in Oxford 17–18 March 1919 and dated by the owner 15 April 1919 (the date indicates that this is the earlier mss)

previous printings:
'A Thought' (as 'When I look into a glass') and 'Her Merriment' (as 'When I had met Fee Fie the twentieth time'), 'The Portrait' and 'A Woman's History', *Form* (new series), October 1921, 1, 1, 6, November/ December 1921, 1, 2, 42 and January 1922, 1, 3, 80 respectively
'To Bacchus' and 'Joy', *To-day*, December 1920, VIII, 44, 57 and December 1921, VIII, 48, 218 respectively
'Our Sussex Downs', *Nation and Athenaeum*, 23 September 1922, XXXI, 26, 821
'The Collar' and 'Strength', *The Chapbook*, February 1922, 25, 5
'Lamorna Cove', *Nation*, 21 August 1920, XXVII, 21, 642
'Impudence', 'Telling Fortunes', 'Two Women' and 'The Hour of Magic', *Harper's Magazine*, March 1922, CXLIV, DCCCCLXII, 488–489
'Wild Oats', *Youth*, March 1922, 1, 2, 56

text changes from first printings to A20:
Lamorna Cove: line 1: 'your' to 'our'
A Woman's History: 2nd stanza line 1: 'sixteenth' to 'fifteenth'

notes: (a) WHD obviously altered 'Her Merriment' after its first publication (as 'When I had met Fee Fie the twentieth time') in *Form (B1)* because the HDB mss reflects later changes
(b) the HDB copy is inscribed: 'To Helen/ From/ Billy Davies./ (W. H. Davies.)'

A20a   First American edition   Harper & Brothers 1922

The/ HOUR *of* MAGIC/ *and other Poems by*/ W. H. Davies/ (vignette of a bee)/ *Decorated by* William Nicholson/ at foot: Harper & Brothers, Publishers/ New York & London/ Mcmxxii

8vo; (A) in ten, (B–C) in eights; 26 leaves (the final leaf is a stub pasted to the endpaper): (i–xii) 1–34 (6)pp including a stub; 19.0 × 12.5 cms variable; the title-page is a cancel

as *A20* apart from: (v) title-page; (vi) (vignette of a flower)/ at foot: *Made and printed in Great Britain/ by George W. Jones, 12–14 Gough Square, London, E.C.4.*; *dust-jacket*: spine: at foot: Harper &/ Brothers; back and both flaps: blank

price: $1.50

copies seen: HRHRC; SH

reviews: A Modern Poet and His Hour of Magic, William Stanley Braithwaite, *Boston Transcript*, 20 January 1923, 5; Shopgirls, Fauns and Ghosts, *New York Times (Book Review)*, 28 January 1923, 2; Lyrics and Magic, Mark Van Doren, *Nation*, 31 January 1923, CXVI, 3004, 125; Recent Books in Brief Review, *Bookman*, April 1923, LVII, 215–224 (222)

note: the title-page is a cancel

A20b *Special large paper edition*   Jonathan Cape 1922

as *A20* apart from: (ii) limitation: (fleuron) *Of this large paper Edition/ of "The Hour of Magic"/ have been printed* 110 *copies./ Of these* 100 *only are for sale/* (fleuron) *Copy number*   signed W. H. Davies./ William Nicholson; spare gilt label tipped-in at end; *paper*: cream parchment; *endpapers*: cream with a yellow vertical design; *binding*: mottled pale blue paper-covered boards with an embossed surface, white buckram spine; *dust-jacket*: clear glacene

print run: 110 copies; *price*: 25s.

copies seen: HDB (presentation); SH (no 73)

A21   COLLECTED POEMS:
SECOND SERIES   Jonathan Cape 1923

Collected Poems:/ Second Series, *by*/ W. H. Davies/ (publisher's device)/ at foot: Jonathan Cape/ Eleven Gower Street, London

8vo; (A) in eight plus tipped-in frontispiece, B–I and K in eights; 80 leaves: (1–6) 7–11 (12–14) 15–157 (3)pp plus frontispiece not included in the pagination; 19.0 × 12.5 cms variable; first page of each gathering signed D.C.P. on inner margin

(1–2) blank; (3) half-title: Collected Poems: Second Series./ by/ William H. Davies. (in facsimile of author's script); (4) blank; frontispiece captioned: WILLIAM H. DAVIES/ *After a painting in oils by* Augustus John/ (frontispiece); (5) title-page; (6) *First published in 1923/ All rights reserved/* at foot: *Printed in Great Britain by* Butler & Tanner, *Frome and London*; 7–11 Contents; (12) blank; (13) fly-title: Collected Poems/ Second Series; (14) blank; 15–157 text; (158–160) blank

contents: 1 The Ways of Time; 2 Impudence; 3 Easter; 4 Raptures; 5 A Child's Pet; 6 A Thought; 7 The Hour of Magic; 8 A Bird's Anger; 9 On hearing Mrs. Woodhouse play the Harpsichord; 10 Margery; 11 The Villain; 12 How Kind is Sleep; 13 Killed in Action (Edward Thomas); 14 The Bell; 15 When yon Full Moon; 16 Catharine; 17 The Dog; 18 The Rat; 19 The Cat; 20 Birds; 21 Passion's Hounds; 22 The Coming of Peace; 23 The Coming of Spring; 24 What County?; 25 To-day; 26 A Strange Meeting; 27 Music; 28 Smiles; 29 Let Me Confess; 30 The Captive Lion; 31 Worm-proof; 32 England; 33 Bird and Brook; 34 Now That She Gives; 35 Christmas; 36 Night Wanderers; 37 Love Impeached; 38 Love's Silent Hour; 39 Winter's Beauty; 40 Facts; 41 Strong Moments; 42 Jove Warns Us; 43 A Greeting; 44 To a Fool; 45 An Early Love; 46 Dream Tragedies; 47 The Grief of Others; 48 Love and the Muse; 49 The Wonder Maker; 50 Joy; 51 Hidden Love; 52 A Winter's

Night; 53 Two Women; 54 The Excuse; 55 Her Mouth and Mine; 56 They're Taxing Ale again; 57 Cowslips and Larks; 58 My Love could Walk; 59 The Dancer; 60 Rags and Bones; 61 Lovely Dames; 62 The Voice; 63 Late Singers; 64 Molly; 65 My Old Acquaintance; 66 Passion's Greed; 67 Forgiveness; 68 Angel and Mystery; 69 How Late; 70 The Beautiful; 71 The Forsaken Dead; 72 Confession; 73 Come, let us Find; 74 Wasted Hours; 75 Till I Went Out; 76 Her Merriment; 77 Wild Oats; 78 The Soul's Companions; 79 That Day She Seized; 80 Lamorna Cove; 81 In Time of War; 82 Our Sussex Downs; 83 In the Snow; 84 The Portrait; 85 Children at Play; 86 Trees; 87 The Collar; 88 The Two Lives; 89 Strength; 90 To Bacchus; 91 What Thoughts are Mine; 92 Pastures; 93 Telling Fortunes; 94 Love's Caution; 95 Seeking Joy; 96 Laughing Rose; 97 Oh, Sweet Content; 98 My Youth; 99 When Leaves Begin; 100 Joy Supreme; 101 Young Beauty; 102 The Force of Love; 103 One Thing Wanting; 104 April's Lambs; 105 The Truth; 106 Love Speechless; 107 The Ox; 108 The Clock; 109 The Flirt; 110 A Woman's Charms; 111 The Trance; 112 The Song of Life

paper: watermarked: ANTIQUE DE LUXE; chain lines 2.7 cms apart and vertical

endpapers: cream; *edges*: uncut, deckle fore edge, top edge trimmed

binding: pale grey calico grain cloth lettered in gilt; front cover: Collected Poems Second Series./ by/ William H. Davies. (in facsimile of author's script); spine: Collected/ Poems/ (Second/ Series)/ W. H./ Davies. (in facsimile of author's script)/ at foot: JONATHAN/ CAPE; back cover: blank

dust-jacket: cream with an embossed surface, printed in black and blue-grey; front, within a blue-grey decorative panel: Collected Poems/ Second Series/ W. H. Davies/ (blue-grey publisher's device)/ with a frontispiece portrait; spine: (blue-grey decorative rule)/ Collected/ Poems/ Second Series/ (fleuron)/ W. H. Davies/ at foot: (blue-grey publisher's device)/ Jonathan / Cape/ (blue-grey decorative rule); back: starts: *Books by W. H. Davies*/ ends: *Jonathan Cape, Eleven Gower St., London*; front flap: starts: Uniform with this volume/ ends: Collected Poems 6s. net/ Second Series; back flap: blank

date of publication: April 1923

print run: 2000 copies printed on 3 March 1923; bound by Nevett; *price*: 6s.

copies seen: BL (shelf mark: 011649.h.119; accession date: 29 March 1923); HRHRC; RUL, Finzi; HDB (2 copies); SH

reviews: A Voice Apart, *TLS*, 12 April 1923, 245; Books in Brief, *Nation and Athenaeum*, 28 April 1923, XXXII, 4 (4852), 126; by Frank Lucas, *New Statesman*, 5 May 1923, 21, 114; Poets and Poetry: A Master of the Lyric, Martin Armstrong, *The Spectator*, 12 May 1923, 130, 4950, 805; *To-day*, June 1923, IX, 54, 157; Poetry, JCS, *London Mercury*, June 1923, VIII, 44, 206–207

previous printings:
1, 10, 16, 27, 40, 71 and 107, *New Poems (A2)*
2, 6, 7, 44, 47, 50, 53, 70, 74, 76, 77, 80, 82, 84, 87, 89, 90, 92, 93 and 111, *The Hour of Magic (A20)*
3, 4, 5, 9, 13, 14, 15, 20, 26, 32, 42, 52, 54, 56, 57, 58, 59, 60, 61, 62, 63, 64, 65, 66, 67, 68, 69, 72, 73, 75, 78, 79, 81, 83 and 91, *Forty New Poems (A17)*
8, 11, 12, 17, 18, 19, 21, 22, 23, 24, 25, 29, 30, 31, 33, 34, 37, 38, 55, 86, 94, 97, 99, 102, 103, 104, 105, 106, 108, 109 and 110, *The Song of Life (A18)*

28, 35, 36, 39, 41, 43, 45, 46, 48, 49, 51, 85, 88, 95, 96, 98, 100, 101 and 110, *Foliage (A10)*

text changes from previous printings to A21:
The Ways of Time: 1st two stanzas omitted, commences: 'As butterflies are but winged flowers'
Impudence: 1st stanza line 1: 'gray' to 'grey'

note: the HDB copies are inscribed: 'To my wife/ "Dinah", (Helen)/ with the author's love./ March 29th. 1923./ W. H. Davies.' and 'My book,/ W. H. Davies./ March 29th. 1923'

A21a *Special large paper edition*   Jonathan Cape 1923

as *A21* apart from: 21.0 × 16.0 cms variable; (ii) limitation: (fleuron) *Of this edition of/ "Collected Poems:/ Second Series,"/ have been printed/ 106 copies. Of/ these* 100 *only are for sale./* (fleuron) *Copy No:* signed W. H. Davies.; frontispiece protected by a tissue guard; spare paper labels tipped-in at end; *paper*: cream parchment; *endpapers*: cream; *binding*: mottled cream paper-covered boards with an embossed surface, blue cloth spine; front cover, on a white paper label 5.3 × 8.8 cms, in blue, within a decorative border: *Collected Poems/* SECOND SERIES/ *by/ William H. Davies;* spine, on a white paper label 4.2 cms deep, in blue: COLLECTED/ POEMS/ *Second Series/* (fleuron)/ W. H. DAVIES; back cover: blank; *edges*: deckle fore edge, top edge gilt, uncut; *dust-jacket*: not seen

print run: 106 copies printed on 15 March 1923; bound by Nevett; *price*: 30s.

copies seen: HRHRC (2 copies: nos 4 and 57); SH (no 4)

A21b *Limited edition*   Jonathan Cape 1923

date of publication: December 1923; *price*: 12s.6d.
note: printed on parchment in a lambskin binding

A21c *Second impression*   Jonathan Cape 1923

as *A21* apart from: (4) *Uniform with this volume/* Collected Poems: First Series/ by W. H. DAVIES; (6) *First published* 1923/ *Second Impression* 1923/ *All rights reserved/* at foot: *Printed in Great Britain by* Butler & Tanner Ltd., *Frome and London*

copy seen: SH

A21d *First American edition*   Harper & Bros 1923

price: $2

A22   TRUE TRAVELLERS   Jonathan Cape 1923

TRUE TRAVELLERS/ *A Tramps Opera* in/ Three Acts/ *by*/ WILLIAM H. DAVIES/ (rule)/ *With*/ *Decorations by*/ WILLIAM NICHOLSON/ (rule)/ (vignette of a boot)/ at foot: *London:*/ JONATHAN CAPE, ELEVEN/ GOWER STREET

8vo; (A) in four plus tipped-in frontispiece, B-D in eights plus one tipped-in illustration per gathering, E in four; 36 leaves: (i–viii) (1–2) 3–21 (22–24) 25–38 (39–40) 41–52 (4)pp plus 4 full-page illustrations not included in the pagination; 21.5 × 17.0 cms variable

(i–ii) blank; (iii) half-title: TRUE TRAVELLERS; (iv) blank; frontispiece in green and black of two tramps asleep being awakened by a crowing cockerel, overprinted: *True Travellers/ by William h. Davies.* signed in green N.; (v) title-page; (vi) FIRST PUBLISHED IN MDCCCCXXIII/ PRINTED IN GREAT BRITAIN/ AT THE DE LA MORE PRESS/ 3 & 4 BARRETT ST./ LONDON/ (decorative star); (vii) *Characters*; (viii) blank; (1) fly-title: *True Travellers/ Act One/* (vignette of a frog holding a hat); (2) blank; full-page illustration in green and black of a beetle holding a hat in the rain signed in green N.; 3–21 text; 21 below text: *Curtain/* (vignette of a boot); (22) blank; (23) fly-title: *True Travellers/ Act Two/* (vignette of a snail); (23) blank; full-page illustration in green and black of a tramp signed in green N.; 25–38 text; 38 below text: *Curtain/* (vignette of a boot); (39) fly-title: *True Travellers/ Act Three/* (vignette of two butterflies on a thistle); full-page illustration in green and black of a cricket playing a flute signed in green N.; 41–52 text; 52 below text: (vignette of a mayfly); (53) full-page illustration of a boot casting a shadow; (54–56) blank

contains: p3 This man, that came a beggar to our door; p5 I could not love him more -; p6 See how the glowworm's light is found; p11 A mother's love, a mother's love; p15 With all our mirth, I doubt if we shall be; p16 Good people keep their holy day; p17 On what sweet banks were thy pure fancies fed; p18 Thy love shall go behind no cloud; p19 Ah life, we are no sooner dressed; p21 We are so happy that we need; p25 Around that waist, scarce bigger than my neck; p26 Her body's a fine house; p28 Oh for a glass of wine! Let us enjoy a sweet content; p29 The woods and banks of England now; p32 Without contentment, what is life?; p35 When Autumn's fruit is packed and stored; p36 Now that the tears of love have reached; p38 The world may charge a man with sin; p41 Where she is now, I cannot say -; p43 Let Joy now hold you like a bride; p44 Men that have strength to rule their sex; p45 That man, too fat to see his feet; p47 Night is the only time I live; p49 When diamonds, nibbling in my ears. With thy strong tide of beauty I must go; p50 Let them be free to go their way; p51 Who bears in mind misfortunes gone

illustrations: full-page, two-tone: frontispiece, facing pp3, 25 and 41; full-page, black and white: p53; decorations on pp(v), (1), 6, 11, 21, (23), 28, 38, (39) and 52

paper: watermarked: (crown)/ Abbey Mills/ Greenfield; chain lines 2.4 cms apart and horizontal

endpapers: cream; *edges*: deckle lower edge, top edge trimmed

binding: pale green paper-covered boards with an embossed surface, blocked and printed in black; front cover: TRUE TRAVELLERS/ an OPERA/ (vignette of a beetle holding a hat)/ *by William h. Davies./ decorated by William Nicholson/* (decorative rule); spine: TRUE/ TRAVEL-/ LERS/ at foot: JONATHAN/ CAPE; back cover: (publisher's device)

dust-jacket: cream with an embossed surface, printed in green and black; front: TRUE TRAVELLERS (in black)/ *A Tramp's Opera* by (in green)/ W. H. Davies/ (vignette in black and green, within a panel, of a beetle holding a hat in the rain)/ at foot: *With/ Decorations by* (in green)/ William Nicholson; spine: TRUE/ TRAVEL-/ LERS/ *by* (in green)/ W. H./ Davies/ *With/ Decorations/ by* (in green)/ William/ Nicholson/ at foot: (green publisher's device)/ Jonathan/ Cape; back: starts: *Books by W. H. Davies/* ends: *Jonathan Cape, Eleven Gower St., London*; front flap: starts: (black rule)/ ends: *True Travellers 7s. 6d. net*; back flap: blank

date of publication: October 1923

print run: 1500 copies printed on 31 July 1923; bound by Nevett; *price*: 7s.6d.

copies seen: BL (shelf mark: 011779.i.29; accession date: 4 October 1923); HRHRC; RUL, Finzi; HDB; SH

reviews: The Tramp's Opera, *TLS*, 25 October 1923, 704; Hornpypes and Funeralles [sic], F. L. Lucas, *New Statesman*, 24 November 1923, XXII, 554, 214–216; A Poet's Opera, *The Spectator*, 24 November 1923, 131, 4978, 805; Mr Davies in Burkins, *Saturday Review*, 5 January 1924, 137, 3558, 14; True Travellers, RH, *Bookman*, January 1924, LXV, 388, 217–218 (illustration from the book); A Literary Letter: A Multitude of Poets, CKS, *The Sphere*, 26 January 1924, XCVI, 1253, 104; by Maxwell Anderson, *New York World*, 9 March 1924, b; A Parcel of Printed Plays: Tramps, Gypsies and One or Two Bores in Newly Published Drama, *New York Times (Book Review)*, 23 March 1924, 5; *Nation*, 4 June 1924, 118, 3074, 662; A Tramp's Opera, DBW, *New Republic*, 11 June 1924, XXXIX, 497, 81

mss: there is a mss of 'The Woods and Banks' in WHD's hand on paper headed 14 Great Russell Street, London, W.C. in the Jonathan Cape archives, RUL

previous printings:
'Who Bears in Mind' (as 'The Happy Man'), theatre programme for the comedy *Not So Bad as We Seem* by Bulwer Lytton, performed at Devonshire House on 30 November 1921 (32pp printed by Spottiswoode, Ballantyne & Co Ltd). At this performance the part of the newsman was played by WHD; other members of the cast included Ivor Novello, A. A. Milne, William Orpen and Compton Mackenzie (a copy of this programme is held at NL)
'When Autumn's Fruit', 'Where She is Now', 'On What Sweet Banks' and 'The Woods and Banks', *New Republic*, 26 January 1921, XXV, 321, 251, 15 June 1921, XXVII, 341, 80, 13 July 1921, XXVII, 345, 196 and 4 January 1922, XXIX, 370, 155
'Without Contentment', *To-day*, June 1921, VIII, 46, 149
'With Thy Strong Tide of Beauty' (as 'A Second Innocence'), *Nation and Athenaeum*, 26 February 1921, XXVIII, 22, 739
'Men that have Strength', *The Captive Lion* (A19)

text changes from first printings to A22:
When Autumn's Fruit: 1st stanza last line: 'blackbird' to 'chaffinch'
Where She is Now: originally printed in 2 stanzas *not* 4; 1st stanza line 3: 'Sun's' to 'sun's'
Who Bears in Mind: line 4: 'shadows' to 'shadow'

note: according to an article in *The Londoner*, week ending 8 October 1921 *(F82)* *True Travellers* was originally written by WHD for Nigel Playfair, for ultimate production at the Lyric Theatre, Hammersmith. It was intended to be an update, using his own tramping experiences, on *The Beggar's Opera* and it's sequel *Polly*, with music by Frederic Austin. Richard Stonesifer *(F324)* also tells us that WHD wanted William Nicholson to design the scenery. In the event, much to WHD's disappointment, the project was rejected for the stage

A22a Second impression   Jonathan Cape 1923

print run: 500 copies printed on 13 December 1923; bound by Nevett

A22b Special edition   Jonathan Cape 1923

as *A22* apart from: (iv) limitation: (fleuron) *Of this Special Edition of True Travellers/ have been printed* 100 *copies only for sale./* (fleuron) *Copy No.* signed W. H. Davies.; *paper*: chain lines 2.7 cms apart and horizontal; *binding*: green, brown and blue marbled paper-covered boards, green buckram spine; front cover, on a pinkish-brown paper label 8.0 × 5.5 cms, in black: TRUE/ TRAVELLERS/ An Opera *by/* William h. Davies/ (vignette of a beetle holding a hat); spine, on a pinkish-brown paper label 3.0 cms deep, in black: TRUE/ TRAVEL-/ LERS/ (fleuron)/ W. H./ Davies; back cover: blank; *dust-jacket*: not seen

print run: 100 copies printed on 31 July 1923; bound by Nevett; *price*: 21s.

copies seen: HRHRC (out of series); HDB (2 copies: 1 a presentation copy, 1 out of series); no 67 (sold at Dominic Winter Book Auctions, Swindon, 8 April 1992)

notes: (a) boxed in a pale green paper-covered box with a paper label on the upper cover identical to that on the front cover of the book
(b) the HDB copies are inscribed: 'To Dinah (Helen)/ from/ Bunny (W. H. Davies.)' and 'My book,/ W. H. D./ The Woods and Banks./ The woods and banks of England now,/ Late coppered with dead leaves and old,/ Have made the early violets grow,/ And bulge with knots of primrose gold./ Hear how the blackbird flutes away,/ Whose music scorns to sleep at night:/ Hear how the cuckoo shouts all day/ For echoes – to the world's delight:/ Hallo, you imp of wonder, you -/ Where are you now, cuckoo? Cuckoo!/ W. H. Davies.'

A22c First American edition   Harcourt, Brace & Co 1923

print run: used the sheets of the English edition; *price*: $2

A23 **SELECTED POEMS**   Jonathan Cape 1923

SELECTED POEMS (in rustic lettering)/ *by/* W. H. DAVIES/ *Decorated with woodcuts by/* STEPHEN BONE/ (publisher's device)/ at foot: JONATHAN CAPE (in rustic lettering)/ ELEVEN GOWER STREET LONDON

8vo; (A)–E in eights; 40 leaves: (i–ii) (1–4) 5–75 (3)pp; 20.2 × 14.2 cms variable

(i–ii) blank; (1) half-title: SELECTED POEMS; (2) blank; (3) title-page; (4) FIRST PUBLISHED IN MDCCCCXXIII/ MADE AND PRINTED IN GREAT BRITAIN/ BY CHAS. WHITTINGHAM AND GRIGGS/ (PRINTERS), LTD. AT THE CHISWICK/ PRESS, TOOKS COURT/ LONDON; 5–6 *Contents*; 7–(76) text; (77–78) blank; poem titles in italics throughout

contents: p7 The Moon; p8 Leisure; p9 Thunderstorms; p10 Sweet Stay-at-Home; p12 The Kingfisher; p13 Songs of Joy; p14 Truly Great; p15 In May; p16 The Elements; p17 The Rain; p18 Autumn; p19 Days too Short; p20 The Example; p21 The Mind's Liberty; p22 The White Cascade; p23 The Happy Child; p24 Dreams of the Sea; p26 A Great Time; p27 When on a Summer's Morn; p28 The Hawk; p30 Sheep; p31 Starers; p32 The Idiot and the Child; p34 Plants and Men; p35 A Blind Child; p36 Body and Spirit; p38 Easter; p39 Raptures; p40 Cowslips [sic]; p41 When yon Full Moon; p42 Birds; p44 On hearing Mrs Woodhouse play the Harpsichord; p45 Oh, Sweet Content!; p46 A Child's Pet; p47 The Bell; p48 The Villain; p49 Love's Caution; p50 Wasted Hours; p51 Impudence; p52 The Hour of Magic; p53 The Portrait; p55 A Thought; p56 The Ways of Time; p57 The Bird of Paradise; p58 A Maiden and her Hair; p60 Kitty and I; p61 Money; p62 Lovely Dames; p63 Strong Moments; p64 Happy Wind; p65 Robin Redbreast; p66 Days that have Been; p67 The Inexpressible; p68 The Sleepers; p70 The Truth; p71 The Sluggard; p72 Joy; p74 The Hermit; p75 Early Morn; p(76) Pastures

illustrations: full-page: pp11, 29, 33, 69 and 73; decorations: pp7, 8, 17, 18, 19, 22, 24, 34, 37, 38, 39, 42, 47, 51, 52, 64, 65, 67, 70, 74 and 75

paper: chain lines 2.7 cms apart and vertical

endpapers: cream; *edges*: uncut, top edge trimmed

binding: dark mustard calico grain cloth; front cover: blank; spine, on a white paper label 3.3 cms deep, in black: (green double rule)/ Selected/ Poems/ (green fleuron)/ W. H./ DAVIES/ (green double rule); back cover: blank

dust-jacket: cream background, printed in black; front: SELECTED POEMS (in rustic lettering)/ by/ W. H. DAVIES (in rustic lettering)/ (vignette identical to that on p11)/ WITH WOODCUTS BY/ STEPHEN BONE (in rustic lettering); spine: (decorative rule)/ *Selected/ Poems/ by/* W. H./ DAVIES/ *With/ woodcuts/ by/* STEPHEN/ BONE/ at foot: Jonathan/ Cape/ (decorative rule); back: starts: *Books by W. H. Davies/* ends: *Jonathan Cape, Eleven Gower St., London*; front flap, at foot: SELECTED POEMS (in rustic lettering) 7s. 6d. net; back flap: blank

date of publication: December 1923

print run: 1250 copies; bound by Nevett; *price*: 7s.6d.

copies seen: BL (shelf mark: 011645.f.18; accession date: 6 December 1923); HDB; SH; HRHRC

reviews: Poetry and Verse, A. M. Ritchie, *Nation and Athenaeum*, 19 January 1924, XXXIV, 16, 576–577; A Literary Letter: A Multitude of Poets, CKS, *The Sphere*, 26 January 1924, XCVI, 1253, 104; Poets and Poetry: Old and New Poetry, Edgell Rickword, *The Spectator*, 9 February 1924, 132, 4989, 209–210

note: contents page: 'Cowslips and Larks' misprinted 'Cowslips'

A23a   Large paper edition   Jonathan Cape 1923

A23b   First American edition   Harcourt, Brace & Co 1925

SELECTED POEMS (in rustic lettering)/ *by*/ W. H. DAVIES/ *Decorated with woodcuts by*/ STEPHEN BONE/ at foot: NEW YORK/ HARCOURT, BRACE & CO. (in rustic lettering)

8vo; (A)–E in eights; 40 leaves: (i–ii) (1–4) 5–(76) (2)pp; 20.2 × 14.0 cms; the title-page is a cancel

as *A23* apart from: (3) title-page; (4) MADE AND PRINTED IN GREAT BRITAIN/ BY CHAS. WHITTINGHAM AND GRIGGS/ (PRINTERS), LTD. AT THE CHISWICK/ PRESS, TOOKS COURT/ LONDON; *edges*: trimmed; *dust-jacket*: spine, at foot: Harcourt,/ Brace &/ Company/ (decorative rule); back: starts: THE BEST POEMS OF (in rustic lettering)/ ends: NEW YORK; front flap: starts: SECRETS/ ends: 383 MADISON AVENUE, NEW YORK; back flap: starts: True Travellers:/ ends: 383 MADISON AVENUE, NEW YORK

print run: made up from sheets of the English edition

copy seen: HRHRC

reviews: Three Poets and One Anthologist: crystalline Art of HD – Poems by Richard Aldington and W. H. Davies, Herbert S. Gorman, *New York Times (Book Review)*, 10 May 1925, 7; *The Dial*, August 1925, LXXIX, 2, 174; In Brief Review, *Bookman*, August 1925, LXI, 6, 708–716 (715); Mr Davies' Poetry, George H. Dillon, *Poetry*, October 1925, XXVI, 1, 44–47

notes: (a) the title-page is a cancel
(b) contents page: 'Cowslips and Larks' misprinted 'Cowslips'

A24 SECRETS   Jonathan Cape 1924

within a decorative border: SECRETS/ *by*/ W. H. DAVIES/ (publisher's device)/ at foot: *Jonathan Cape Ltd*/ ELEVEN GOWER STREET LONDON

8vo; (A)–C in eights (the first leaf of the first gathering is a stub); 24 leaves including a stub: (1–4) 7–48pp; 19.0 × 12.8 cms variable; first page of gatherings B and C signed S. on inner margins

(1–2) a stub; (3) half-title: *Secrets*/ (fleuron); (4) starts: *By the Same Author*/ ends: SELECTED POEMS; (5) title-page; (6) FIRST PUBLISHED IN MCMXXIV/ MADE & PRINTED IN GREAT BRITAIN/ BY BUTLER & TANNER LTD./ FROME AND/ LONDON/ (fleuron); 7–8 *Contents*; 9–48 text; poem titles in italics; poems on pp37 and 43 printed completely in italics

contents: p9 The Poet's Horse; p10 The Rainbow; p11 Love, Like a Drop of Dew; p12 The Nature Lover; p13 One Token; p14 Rogues; p15 Leaves; p16 At Night; p17 The Pond; p18 See Where Young Love; p19 A Miracle; p20 The Rivals; p21

Earth Love; p22 Love's Payment; p23 In Spring-time; p24 My Garden; p25 The Schemes of Love; p26 The Meadow; p27 Cant; p28 The Trick; p29 Breath; p30 The Cave; p31 The World Approves; p32 Down Underground; p33 The Fear; p34 The Fates; p35 The Two Stars; p36 The Rabbit; p37 To a Lady Friend; p38 The Two Heavens; p39 The Doll; p40 The Snowflake; p41 Secrets; p42 Our Longer Life; p43 When Love is Young; p44 Dust; p45 Pity; p46 The Joy of Life; p47 Violet and Oak; p48 Evil

illustrations: decorations on pp9, 10, 11, 13, 15, 16, 17, 18, 20, 21, 24, 26, 30, 31, 33, 35, 36, 38 and 46

paper: chain lines 2.6 cms apart and vertical

endpapers: cream; *edges*: deckle fore edge, top edge trimmed

binding: cream paper-covered boards mottled with mustard and an inverted fleur-de-lis and diamond design in dark green, green cloth spine; front cover: blank; spine, on a white paper label 2.5 cms deep, in green: (decorative rule)/ Secrets/ by/ W.H./ Davies/ (decorative rule); back cover: blank

dust-jacket: cream, with an embossed surface, printed in black and bordeaux; front, within a bordeaux decorative double border, in black open outline lettering: SECRETS/ (decorative dot) Poems by (decorative dot)/ W. H. DAVIES/ (publisher's device in bordeaux); spine, in black: Secrets/ by/ W. H./ Davies (bordeaux fleuron)/ at foot: Jonathan/ Cape; back, in black: starts: *Books by W. H. Davies/* ends: *Jonathan Cape Ltd, Eleven Gower Street, London*; front flap, in black: starts: SECRETS/ ends: *Secrets 3s.6d. net*; back flap: blank

date of publication: April 1924

print run: 1500 copies printed on 8 February 1924; bound by Nevett; *price*: 3s.6d.

copies seen: BL (shelf mark: 011645.ee.109; accession date: 9 April 1924); HRHRC (4 copies); RUL, Finzi; HDB (2 copies); SH (2 copies); RV

reviews: by Vita Sackville-West, *Nation and Athenaeum*, 26 April 1924, 35, 118; Poetry, JCS, *London Mercury*, May 1924, X, 55, 98–100; Mood, *The Spectator*, 17 May 1924, 132, 5003, 807–808; The Secrets of Mr Davies, HEP, *Country Life*, 24 May 1924, LV, 1429, 820; Mr Davies' New Vein, *TLS*, 5 June 1924, 353; Books to Read, *The Adelphi*, June 1924, II, 1, 86; by GHW, *Welsh Outlook*, July 1924, XII, 7, 196; Secrets, Graves and Epitaphs, F. L. Lucas, *New Statesman*, 26 July 1924, XXIII, 588, 470

mss: in WHD's hand addressed Tor Leven, East Grinstead and dated 1924; clipped into brown paper wrappers (HDB); there are also typed mss of 'Love's Payment', 'Love like a drop of dew', 'The Leaves' and 'The Fates' in the Jonathan Cape archives, RUL

text change from manuscript to A24:
Earth Love: line 2: 'butterfly or bee' to 'bee or butterfly'

previous printings:
'At Night' and 'Violet and Oak', 'See Where Young Love' and 'One Token', *The Spectator*, 10 February 1923, 130, 4937, 241, 2 June 1923, 130, 4953, 925 and 8 September 1923, 131, 4967, 318 respectively
'When Love is Young' and 'To a Lady Friend', *To-day*, December 1922, IX, 52, 42 and September 1923, X, 55, 2 respectively

'Our Longer Life' and 'The Poet's Horse', *Nation and Athenaeum*, 20 January 1923, XXXII, 16, 611 and 17 March 1923, XXXII, 24, 917 respectively
'Secrets' and 'The Two Stars', 'The Rainbow', 'My Garden', 'The Doll' and 'The Cave', *London Mercury*, March 1923, VII, 41, 465, May 1923, VIII, 43, 7, June 1923, VIII, 44, 121, September 1923, VIII, 47, 459 and November 1923, IX, 49, 13 respectively
'The Schemes of Love' and 'Down Underground', *Golden Hind*, April 1923, 3
'The Snowflake' and 'The Two Heavens' and 'Rogues', *New Republic*, 25 July 1923, XXXV, 451, 233 and 5 September 1923, XXXVI, 457, 47 respectively
'Leaves', 'The Fates' (as 'A Dead Man's Song'), 'Love's Payment' and 'Love, Like a Drop of Dew', 'Earth Love' and 'The Rivals', 'The Meadow' and 'The Fear' and 'In Spring-time', *Harper's Magazine*, December 1922, CXLVI, DCCCLXXI, 98, April 1923, CXLVI, DCCCLXXV, 608, October 1923, CXLVII, DCCCXXXI, 585, December 1923, CXLVIII, DCCCLXXXIII, 96 and April 1924, CLVIII, DCCCLXXXVI, 592 respectively
'A Miracle' (as ' A Mystery') and 'The Nature Lover', *New Statesman*, 14 July 1923, XXI, 535, 419 and 19 January 1924, XXII, 561, 423 respectively
'Dust', *RPA Annual*, 1924, 74

text changes from first printings to A24:
Love, Like a Drop of Dew: 3rd stanza last line: 'forever' to 'for ever'
Rogues: 1st stanza last line: 'love' to 'Love'; 2nd stanza line 2: 'tomorrow' to 'to-morrow', line 6: 'How' to 'That'; omitting last 2 lines; 3rd stanza (not in the first printing but utilising the last 2 lines of the original 2nd stanza): 'Tell her that though I kiss so wild and oft/ Her flesh that's like a baby's, white and soft,/ Yet kind consideration, at the back,/ Can fear a kiss will bruise and turn it black:/ Go to her, rogues, and show her all the signs/ Where in my face a foolish angel shines.'
The Rivals: 1st stanza line 2: 'market place' to 'market-place', line 3: 'finger tips' to 'finger-tips'
In Springtime: 1st stanza line 2: 'May' to 'may', last line: 'springtime' to 'Spring-time'; 2nd stanza line 7: 'springtime' to 'Spring-time'; title to 'In Spring-time'

notes: (a) 3 copies at HRHRC are bound as above but with a bordeaux cloth spine, paper label printed in green as above; 1 copy at HRHRC is bound in paper-covered boards with an alternating mustard and dark green pattern in horizontal lines on a cream background, lime green cloth spine with a white paper label 2.2 cms deep printed in green as above. Copies with similar boards and either a mustard or maroon cloth spine have also been identified
(b) the decorations are by Philip Hagreen; they are a selection from a much larger number used in *The Best Poems of 1922 (D27)* selected by Thomas Moult (Jonathan Cape, 1923)
(c) the RV copy is inscribed: 'Good luck/ W. H. Davies.'
(d) the HDB copies are inscribed: 'My book/ W. H. Davies./ 1924.' and 'To my wife "Dinah"/ with love/ from "Bunny" (W. H. Davies.)/ 1924'

A24a   Special edition   Jonathan Cape 1924

as *A24* apart from: (1) blank; (2) limitation: (fleuron) OF THIS EDITION OF *Secrets* HAVE BEEN/ PRINTED 100 COPIES FOR SALE, EACH COPY/ SIGNED BY THE AUTHOR/ COPY NUMBER   signed W. H. Davies.; *binding*: purple marbled paper-covered boards, vellum spine; front cover: blank; spine, lettered in gilt: SEC-/ RETS/ (rule)/ W. H./ DAVIES; back cover: blank; *edges*: top edge gilt; *dust-jacket*: front, at foot: (fleuron) *Signed Copy*; front flap, at foot: *Secrets 9s. net/ Signed Copy*

print run: 110 copies; bound by Nevett; *price*: 9s.

copies seen: NL (no 79); HRHRC (no 56)

A24b   First American edition   Harcourt, Brace & Co 1924

within a decorative border: SECRETS/ *by*/ W. H. DAVIES/ (publisher's monogram)/ NEW YORK/ *Harcourt, Brace and Company*

8vo; (A–C) in eights; 24 leaves: (1–4) 5–6 (7–8) 9–48pp; 19.0 × 12.8 cms variable

as *A24* apart from: (1) half-title: *Secrets*; (2) as *A24* (4); (3) title-page; (4) COPYRIGHT, 1924, BY/ HARCOURT, BRACE AND COMPANY, INC./ at foot: *Printed in the U.S.A.*; 5–6 *Contents*; (7) fly-title: Secrets; (8) blank; *binding*: paper-covered boards with an embossed buff floral on white design, repetitive pattern of four green dots in a diamond shape, network background, grass-green cloth spine; front cover: blank; spine, on a white paper label 2.2 cms deep, in black: (rule)/ Secrets/ *by*/ W. H./ Davies/ (rule); back cover: blank; *dust-jacket*: not seen

price: $1.50

copy seen: HRHRC

reviews: A Poet Who Drinks at the Pierian Spring: HD's "Heliodora" of Crystal Beauty – New Verse from Other Pens, Herbert S. Gorman, *New York Times (Book Review)*, 31 August 1924, 5; Three English Lyrists, John Donelson, *Bookman*, October 1924, LX, 2, 226–227; *Boston Transcript*, 24 December 1924, 5; *Booklist*, December 1924, 21, 103; *The Dial*, January 1925, LXXVIII, 1, 77; Four Poets, Archibald MacLeish, *Yale Review*, April 1925, XIV, 3, 587–592; Mr Davies' Poetry, George H. Dillon, *Poetry*, October 1925, XXVII, 1, 44–47

A25   A POET'S ALPHABET   Jonathan Cape 1925

within a decorative border: A POET'S/ ALPHABET/ (vignette of a tree)/ W. H. DAVIES/ at foot: LONDON: JONATHAN CAPE

8vo; (A)–D in eights; 32 leaves: (1–8) 9–10 (11) 12–63 (1)pp; 19.7 × 12.8 cms variable

(1–2) blank; (3) half-title: A POET'S ALPHABET/ at foot: *With Decorations by*/ DORA M. BATTY; (4) blank; (5) title-page; (6) FIRST PUBLISHED IN MCMXXV/ MADE & PRINTED IN GREAT BRITAIN/ BY BUTLER & TANNER LTD/ FROME AND/ LONDON/ (fleuron); (7) dedication: *to*/ MY WIFE; (8) blank; 9–10 Contents; (11) fly-title: A POET'S ALPHABET; 12 A/ is for Artist/ (decorative wreath); 13–63 text; (64) blank

contents: p13 A for Artist; p15 B for Beauty; p17 C for Child; p19 D for Dog; p21 E for Eyes; p23 F for Fiddles; p25 G for Garden; p27 H for Hedge; p29 I for

Implements; p31 J for Jealousy; p33 K for Kings; p35 L for Light; p37 M for Mother; p39 N for Nature; p41 O for Open; p43 P for Pool; p45 Q for Question; p47 R for Remembrance; p49 S for Swimmer; p51 T for Time; p53 U for Union; p55 V for Venus; p57 W for Will; p59 X for Expecting; p61 Y for Youth; p63 Z for Zany

illustrations: decorations on pp(5), 12, 14, 16, 18, 20, 22, 24, 26, 28, 30, 32, 34, 36, 38, 40, 42, 44, 46, 48, 50, 52, 54, 56, 58, 60 and 62; nine decorations in the text

paper: watermarked: – BASINGWERK PARCHMENT -

endpapers: cream; *edges*: deckle fore edge, top edge trimmed

binding: turquoise paper-covered boards marbled and embossed with mid-blue; upper cover, on a white paper label 6.7 × 3.8 cms, in navy and black: (navy decorative rule)/ A POET'S/ ALPHA-/ BET (in black open outline lettering)/ (vignette of a bird in navy)/ W. H./ DAVIES (in black open outline lettering)/ (navy decorative rule); spine, on a white paper label 12.5 cms deep, vertically downwards: W. H. DAVIES. A POET'S ALPHABET (in navy open outline lettering); rear cover: blank

dust-jacket: mottled cream with an embossed surface, printed in black; front: (decorative double rule)/ A POET'S ALPHABET/ *by*/ W. H. DAVIES/ A (decorative)/ is for Artist/ (decorative wreath)/ With Decorations by Dora M. Batty/ (decorative double rule); spine, vertically downwards: W. H. DAVIES (in open outline lettering) (fleuron) A POET'S ALPHABET (in open outline lettering); back: starts: *Books by W. H. Davies*/ ends: *Jonathan Cape Thirty Bedford Square London*; front flap: starts: A POET'S ALPHABET/ ends: *A Poet's Alphabet 3s. 6d. net*; back flap: blank

date of publication: 25 October 1925

print run: 1500 copies printed on 26 August 1925; bound by Nevett; *price*: 3s.6d.

copies seen: BL (shelf mark: 011645.f.113; accession date: 22 October 1925); SH

reviews: British Books: Autumn, Edwin Muir, *Nation*, 18 November 1925, 121, 3150, 577; Some Light Verse, *TLS*, 26 November 1925, 801; Among New Books, *Calendar of Modern Letters*, December 1925, II, 10, 286; The Later Davies, Thomas Moult, *Now & Then*, Winter 1925, 18, 14; Poetry, John Freeman, *London Mercury*, January 1926, XIII, 75, 311–313; The New Poetry, Edward Shanks, *Quarterly Review*, January 1926, 246, 145; A Poet's Alphabet, C. Henry Warren, *Bookman*, March 1926, LXIX, 414, 318

mss: in WHD's hand on plain paper with a single line at the top and bottom of each page; addressed Tor Leven, East Grinstead and dated 1925; with pencil instructions for proof setting in an unknown hand and the original (proof) decorations stuck to the mss; clipped into white paper wrappers in a white envelope postmarked London, 20 August 1925 (with 4 stamps 2 × 1d, 2 × 1½d); addressed in typescript to: W. H. Davies Esq.,/ Tor Leven/ Cantelupe Road/ East Grinstead.; in WHD's hand: Original ms of/ a Poet's Alphabet./ also Proofs of that book/ and Later Days.; wrapped in brown paper (HDB)

WHD's manuscript corrections:
K for Kings: line 16: 'that' to 'who'
L for Light: 2nd stanza line 1: 'a' to 'the'
V for Venus: 3rd stanza line 3: 'dumb' to 'deaf'

WHD's proof corrections:
F for Fiddles: line 14: 'spring' to 'string'
I for Implements: line 3: ';' added
O for Open: line 1: 'lumps' to 'tumps'

previous printings:
'T for Time' (as 'Timepieces'), 'G for Garden' (as 'Garden Plans') and 'D for Dog' (as
'The Bite'), *London Mercury*, March 1924, IX, 53, 456, May 1925, XII, 67, 10 and
October 1925, XII, 72, 574 respectively
'B for Beauty' (as 'The Ghost') and 'W for Will' (as 'The Will') and 'N for Nature' (as
'New Delights'), *Harper's Magazine*, March 1924, CXLVIII, DCCCLXXXVI, 470
and October 1925, 151, 522 respectively
'L for Light' (as 'Light'), 'I for Implements' (as 'Spade and Sword'), 'V for Venus' (as
'Venus'), 'S for Swimmer' (as 'Swimmer'), 'P for Pool' (as 'The Pool'), 'O for Open'
(as 'Distance'), 'R for Remembrance' (as 'A Memory'), 'X for Expecting' (as 'Come,
Come My Love') and 'K for Kings' (as 'Crowns'), *The Spectator*, 8 March 1924,
132, 4993, 368, 26 April 1924, 132, 5000, 673, 21 June 1924, 132, 5008, 1000, 4
October 1924, 133, 5023, 454, 29 November 1924, 133, 5031, 826, 10 January
1925, 134, 5037, 46, 16 May 1925, 134, 5055, 810 and 15 August 1925, 135,
5068, 268 respectively
'U for Union' (as 'Re-Union'), *The Sphere*, 5 July 1924, XCVIII, 1276, 16
'J for Jealousy' (as 'Love the Jealous'), *Yale Review*, October 1924, XIV, 1, 81
'C for Child' (as 'A Child's Movements') and 'Y for Youth' (as 'Dream-Song'), *New Republic*, 10 December 1924, XLI, 523, 72 and 15 April 1925, XLII, 541, 218 respectively

text changes from first printings to A25:
W for Will: 3rd stanza line 2: 'earth' to 'Earth'
Y for Youth: 2nd stanza line 5: 'earth' to 'Earth'
N for Nature: 2nd stanza last line: 'east to west' to 'East to West'

notes: (a) mss: at the head of each poem the title has been changed from just the
capital letter to the full title in an unknown hand
(b) the proofs are in individual gatherings, stitched (HDB)

A25a   Special edition   Jonathan Cape 1925

as *A25* apart from: (1) blank; (2) limitation: (fleuron) OF this edition of *A Poet's
Alphabet*/ 125 copies have been printed for/ sale, each copy signed and num-/ bered
by the Artist/ (fleuron) COPY number   signed W. H. Davies.; *paper*: Japanese
vellum; *binding*: grass-green calico grain cloth; metallic green vellum spine; front
cover: blank; spine, lettered in gilt: A/ POET'S/ ALPHA-/ BET; back cover: blank;
edges: uncut; top edge gilt; *dust-jacket*: front flap, at foot: A Poet's Alphabet/
Special Edition, signed by the author,/ limited to 125 copies for sale. 9s. *net*

date of publication: November 1925

print run: 140 copies printed on 26 August 1925; bound by Nevett

copies seen: NL (no 41); HRHRC (no 29); SH (no 96)

A25b   Second impression   Jonathan Cape 1926

print run: 1000 copies printed on 18 December 1926; bound by Nevett

A25c   Special edition   Jonathan Cape 1927

print run: 140 copies printed on 10 September 1927; bound by Nevett

A25d   Travellers' Library edition   Jonathan Cape 1927

print run: 4000 copies printed on 25 July 1927 by Manning Pike; bound by Nevett

A25e   Travellers' Library edition: second impression   Jonathan Cape 1931

print run: 2000 copies, 16 March 1931 (printed and bound by Garden City Press, transferred to A. W. Bain)

A25f   Cheap edition   Jonathan Cape 1934

print run: 2000 copies printed on 24 September 1934 by Butler & Tanner; bound by Nevett (transferred to A. W. Bain)

A26 LATER DAYS   Jonathan Cape 1925

(decorative rule)/ *By*/ W. H. DAVIES (in open outline lettering)/ *LATER DAYS*/ (publisher's device)/ at foot: L O N D O N/ (decorative rule)/ JONATHAN CAPE LTD

8vo; (A)–I and K–O in eights; 112 leaves: (1–6) 7 (8–10) 11–29 (30) 31–45 (46) 47–83 (84) 85–109 (110) 111–155 (156) 157–173 (174) 175–207 (208) 209–223 (1)pp; 19.0 × 12.0 cms

(1–2) blank; (3) half-title: L A T E R   D A Y S; (4) starts: BOOKS BY W. H. DAVIES/ ends: etc.; (5) title-page; (6) FIRST PUBLISHED IN MDCCCCXXV/ MADE & PRINTED IN GREAT BRITAIN/ BY BUTLER & TANNER LTD/ FROME AND/ LONDON/ (fleuron); 7 *Contents*; (8) blank; (9) fly-title: L A T E R   D A Y S; (10) blank; 11–223 text; (224) blank

contents: 1 p11 The Camp; 2 p31 Literary Men; 3 p47 Authors of the Sea; 4 p63 The Philosopher; 5 p73 A Poet and His Dog; 6 p85 On the Road; 7 p95 The Journey; 8 p111 In Time of War; 9 p127 Reading for Charity; 10 p141 Politics & Society; 11 p157 Works of Art; 12 p175 Artists All; 13 p197 In & Out of Luck; 14 p209 The End

contains: p11 Love kissed me in a strange, untruthful hour; p31 When I went down past Charing Cross; p47 A lonely coast, where sea-gulls scream for wrecks; p63 Who knows the perfect life on earth?; p73 Still do I claim no man can reach; p85 I have two loves, and one is dark; p95 Shall I have jealous thoughts to nurse; p101 Come away, Death, make no mistake; p111 One night, when I was sleeping all alone; p127 All from his cradle to his grave; p141 This life in London – what a waste; p157 When I went wandering far from home; p175 An artist draws his own strange mind; p197 How sordid is this crowded life, its spite; p209 Here with my treasured Three I sit; p217 This little town's a purer place

endpapers: cream; *edges*: top and fore edge trimmed

binding: mid-blue calico textured cloth, lettered in gilt; front cover: blank; spine: LATER/ DAYS/ (fleuron)/ W.H.DAVIES/ at foot: JONATHAN CAPE; back cover: blind-blocked publisher's device

dust-jacket: cream with an embossed surface, printed in dark turquoise; front, within a decorative border: Later Days/ *by*/ W. H. Davies/ Author of *The Autobiography of a Super-Tramp*/ (publisher's device); spine: Later/ Days/ (fleuron)/ W. H. Davies/ at foot: (publisher's device)/ Jonathan Cape; back: starts: *Books by W. H. Davies*/ ends: *Jonathan Cape Ltd. Thirty Bedford Square London*; front flap: starts: LATER DAYS/ ends: *Later Days 6s. net*; back flap: blank

date of publication: October 1925

print run: 1st printing: 1250 copies on 9 July 1925; 2nd printing: 1250 copies on 22 October 1925; bound by Nevett; *price*: 6s.

copies seen: BL (shelf mark: 010826.f.31; accession date: 9 October 1925); HRHRC; RUL, Finzi; HDB (2 copies); SH (2 copies)

reviews: A Poet's Life, *TLS*, 29 October 1925, 714; *The Spectator*, 24 October 1925, 135, 716; *Saturday Review*, 7 November 1925, 140, 540; The Unchanged Poet, *The Spectator*, 14 November 1925, 135, 5081, 885–886; British Books: Autumn, Edwin Muir, *Nation*, 18 November 1925, 121, 3150, 577; Books Abroad, *Living Age*, 28 November 1925, XL (8th series), 4247, 477 (reprinted from *The Observer*); The Later Davies, Thomas Moult, *Now & Then*, Winter 1925, 18, 14; Self-Portrait of a Poet, C. Henry Warren, *Christmas Number of Bookman*, December 1925, LXIX, 411, 179–180 (portrait by Harold Knight); *New Statesman*, 12 December 1925, 26, supplement xxii; by Chartres Biron, *London Mercury*, January 1926, XIII, 75, 326

WHD's proof corrections:
3 p61 line 13: 'long' to 'longer'
4 p65 lines 11/12: 'that felt' to 'that I felt'; p68 line 11 up: 'done a great part of her own' to 'done everything she could in the matter of getting the book published'
5 p74 line 10 up: 'frogrant' to 'fragrant'; p74 line 8 up: 'one' to 'a'
6 p88 line 10: 'arm' to 'arc'
7 p107 line 2: 'respectfully' to 'respectably'
8 p114 line 3 up: 'neighbours' to 'neighbour'; p124 last line: 'bloody boot' to 'boot'
9 p140 line 4: 'thing is damn bad, the thing is bloody bad' to 'thing is rotten, the thing is damn bad'
12 p182 line 14: 'Ennuhi' to 'Ennui'; p183 lines 6/5 up: 'her' to 'he'

previous printings:
'How Sordid is this Crowded Life' (as 'This Crowded Life'), *London Mercury*, November 1924, XI, 61, 10
'When I went down past Charing Cross' (as 'The Poet'), *Bookman*, July 1924, LXVI, 394, 245 (under the pseudonym 'Gwalia')
'Love kissed me in a strange, untruthful hour' (as 'The Rock'), *New Republic*, 12 August 1925, XLII, 558, 311
'Who knows the perfect life on earth' (as 'Philosophy'), *Harper's Magazine*, January 1925, CL, DCCCXCVI, 175

text change from first printing to A26:
How Sordid is this Crowded Life: line 5: 'or' to 'and'

notes: (a) proof copy: (3) half-title: LATER DAYS/ (rule)/ (decorative star); (4) blank; (5) title-page: (decorative rule)/ W. H. DAVIES/ LATER DAYS/ (publisher's device)/ at foot: L O N D O N/ (decorative rule) JONATHAN CAPE LTD.
(b) the HDB copies are inscribed: 'My book,/ W. H. Davies' and 'To my wife Dinah,/ with the author's love./ W. H. Davies./ 1925'
(c) 'Love kissed me in a strange, untruthful hour', 'When I went down past Charing Cross', 'A lonely coast where, seagulls scream for wrecks', 'Who knows the perfect life on earth', 'I have two loves, and one is dark', 'Shall I have no jealous thoughts to nurse', 'Come away, Death, make no mistake', 'One night, when I was sleeping all alone', 'All from his cradle to his grave', 'This life in London – what a waste', 'When I went wandering far from home', 'How sordid is this crowded life, its spite', and 'Here with my treasured three I sit' titled 'The Rock', 'The Poet', 'A Lonely Coast', 'The Perfect Life', 'The Two Loves', 'No-man's Wood', 'Come Away, Death', 'One Night, when I was Sleeping', 'The Life of Man', 'Traffic', 'The Bust', 'How Sordid is this Crowded Life' and 'The Treasured Three' respectively in *Collected Poems (A33)*
(d) 'Still do I claim no man can reach', 'An artist draws his own strange mind' and 'This little town's a purer place' reprinted for the first time in *W. H. Davies: Selected Poems (A53)*

A26a Special edition   Jonathan Cape 1925

as *A26* apart from: 19.0 × 13.0 cms variable; (ii) limitation: (fleuron) OF this edition of *Later Days* have/ been printed 125 copies for sale,/ signed and numbered by the Author/ (fleuron) COPY number   signed W. H. Davies.; *paper*: Japanese vellum; *binding*: mid-blue calico textured cloth, lettered in gilt; front cover: W. H. Davies. (in facsimile of author's script); spine: (decorative rule)/ LATER/ DAYS/ (fleuron)/ W. H. DAVIES/ at foot: JONATHAN CAPE/ (decorative rule); back cover: blank; *edges*: uncut; top edge gilt; *dust-jacket*: not seen

date of publication: October 1925

print run: 140 copies printed on 9 July 1925; bound by Nevett; *price*: 17s.6d.

copies seen: NL (no 17); HRHRC (nos 94 and 116); SH (no 79)

A26b Second impression   Jonathan Cape 1925

A26c First American edition   George H Doran 1926

(decorative rule)/ *By*/ W. H. DAVIES/ *LATER DAYS*/ (publisher's device)/ at foot: GEORGE H. DORAN COMPANY/ On Murray Hill :: New York/ (decorative rule)

8vo; 15 gatherings of eight; 120 leaves: (i-ii) (1–8) 9–234 (4)pp; 19.0 × 13.0 cms variable (i–ii) blank; (1) half-title: LATER DAYS/ W. H. DAVIES; (2) starts: BOOKS BY W. H. DAVIES/ ends: etc.; (3) title-page; (4) COPYRIGHT, 1926,/ BY GEORGE H. DORAN COMPANY/ (publisher's device)/ at foot: LATER DAYS/ – A –/ PRINTED IN THE UNITED STATES OF AMERICA; (5) *Contents*; (6) blank; (7) fly-title: LATER DAYS; (8) blank; 9–234 text; (235–238) blank

endpapers: cream; *edges*: deckle fore edge, top edge trimmed

binding: olive green calico cloth, lettered in orange; front cover: blind-blocked publisher's device; spine: LATER/ DAYS/ (decoration)/ DAVIES/ (decorative rule)/ at foot: DORAN; back cover: blank; *dust-jacket*: not seen

price: $2

copy seen: HRHRC

reviews: *Boston Transcript*, 23 January 1926, 5; *New York World*, 31 January 1926, 7; Domestication of a Super-Tramp, *New York Times (Book Review)*, 7 March 1926, 6; *Outlook*, 24 March 1926, 142, 463; First Glance, Mark Van Doren, *Nation*, 31 March 1926, CXXII, 3169, 344; *Booklist*, April 1926, 22, 291; Our Own Bookshelf, *Living Age*, 5 June 1926, XLII (8th series), 4274, 555; *The Dial*, July 1926, LXXXXI, 1, 83; by G. F. Whicher, *New York Herald Tribune*, 11 July 1926, 13; *Saturday Review of Literature*, 31 July 1926, 3, 11; *Cleveland Open Shelf*, July 1926, 84; by Ernest Boyd, *The Independent*, 31 July 1926, 117, 134; *Canadian Forum*, August 1926, VI, 71, 352

A26d Travellers' Library edition   Jonathan Cape 1927

LATER DAYS/ by/ W. H. DAVIES/ (publisher's device)/ LONDON/ JONATHAN CAPE 30 BEDFORD SQUARE

16mo; (A)–G in sixteens plus a 12pp publisher's catalogue; 112 leaves: (1–6) 7 (8–10) 11–29 (30) 31–45 (46) 47–83 (84) 85–109 (110) 111–155 (156) 157–173 (174) 175–207 (208) 209–223 (224)pp; 17.2 × 11.8 cms

(1–2) blank; (3) half-title: THE TRAVELLERS' LIBRARY/ (star)/ LATER DAYS; (4) starts: A selection of the volumes included in/ ends: found at the end of this volume; (5) title-page; (6) FIRST PUBLISHED IN 1925/ SECOND IMPRESSION 1925/ FIRST ISSUED IN THE TRAVELLERS' LIBRARY 1927/ at foot: PRINTED IN GREAT BRITAIN; 7 *Contents*; (8) blank; (9) fly-title: LATER DAYS; (10) blank; 11–223 text; (224) at foot: PRINTED BY BUTLER AND TANNER LTD., FROME AND LONDON; 12pp publisher's catalogue: starts: A LIST OF VOLUMES ISSUED IN/ ends: JONATHAN CAPE THIRTY BEDFORD SQUARE LONDON

endpapers: cream; *edges*: trimmed

binding: blue calico grain cloth, decorated and lettered in gilt; front cover: blank; spine: (decorative rule)/ LATER/ DAYS/ (star)/ W. H. DAVIES/ (publisher's device)/ at foot: JONATHAN/ CAPE/ (decorative rule); back cover: blind-blocked publisher's monogram; *dust-jacket*: not seen

date of publication: September 1927

print run: 4000 copies printed on 13 May 1927; bound by Nevett; *price*: 3s.6d.

copy seen: HDB

review: *Now & Then*, Christmas 1927, 26, 36

A26e   Travellers' Library edition: second impression   Jonathan Cape 1929

as *A26d* apart from: (4) starts: (fleuron) A descriptive list of some of the volumes in/ ends: or to the publishers.; (6) REPRINTED 1929; (224) at foot: PRINTED BY THE GARDEN CITY PRESS LTD., LETCHWORTH, HERTS.; *52*pp publisher's catalogue: starts: A LIST OF BOOKS IN/ ends: Made and Printed in Great Britain by The Garden City Press Ltd. Letchworth and London (paged (1) 2–50 (2)); *dust-jacket*: front, lower half within yellow panels: THE TRAVELLERS' LIBRARY/ LATER DAYS/ (blank panel)/ W. H. DAVIES/ (decoration); spine: LATER DAYS/ (black decorative star)/ W. H./ DAVIES/ (ship decoration in black and turquoise)/ (decorative rule)/ THE/ TRAVELLERS'/ LIBRARY/ (yellow rule)/ within two yellow panels: No.48/ (publisher's device)/ JONATHAN/ CAPE; back: starts: *The Travellers' Library* is the most extensive/ ends: JONATHAN CAPE THIRTY BEDFORD SQUARE/ LONDON; front flap: starts: No. 48/ ends: net; back flap: blank

print run: 1000 copies printed on 27 February 1929; bound by Nevett

A26f   American Travellers' Library edition
Jonathan Cape & Harrison Smith 1929

A26g   Travellers' Library edition: third impression   Jonathan Cape 1936

print run: 1000 copies printed on 22 April 1936 by Butler & Tanner; bound by Nevett

A26h   Paperback edition   Oxford University Press 1985

W. H. DAVIES/ LATER DAYS/ (fleuron)/ at foot: Oxford   New York/ OXFORD UNIVERSITY PRESS/ 1985

paperback; (i–vi) 1–141 (13)pp; 19.5 × 12.8 cms

(i) half-title: LATER DAYS; (ii) blank; (iii) title-page; (iv) starts: Oxford University Press, Walton Street, *Oxford* OX2 6DP/ ends: Bungay, *Suffolk*; (v) CONTENTS; (vi) blank; 1–141 text; (142) blank; (143–150) starts: (publisher's device)/ ends: tale of gypsy life.; (151–154) blank; *binding*: paper wrappers printed in full-colour: front cover: over a street scene with a horse-drawn hansom cab and a horse-drawn open carriage: L (in red) ATER (in green underlined in red) D (in red) AYS (in green underlined in red)/ W. H. DAVIES (in black)/ (red rule)/ THE SEQUEL TO (in green) The Autobiography of a Super-tramp (in black)/ (red rule); spine, down-wards: DAVIES   LATER DAYS (cream out of green) at foot: (publisher's device in cream out of green); back, cream background: starts: First published in 1925, Later Days is the long-unavailable/ ends: £2.50 net   in UK   9 780192818645

date of publication: 24 January 1985; *price*: £2.50

copy seen: BL (shelf mark: X. 958/ 28007; accession date: 21 January 1985)

notes: (a) reprinted in February (5000 copies)
(b) price increase 25 March 1988: £3.50
(c) remaindered at £2.00 21 May 1991

A27 **THE AUGUSTAN BOOKS OF
MODERN POETRY** Ernest Benn Ltd (1925)

within a decorative border: THE AUGUSTAN BOOKS OF/ MODERN POETRY/ (rule)/ W. H. DAVIES (in open outline lettering)/ at foot: (rule)/ LONDON: ERNEST BENN LTD./ 8, BOUVERIE STREET, E.C.4

8vo; one gathering of 16 leaves: (1–6) 7–31 (1)pp; stapled; 22.2 × 14.0 cms

(1) front cover: title-page; (2) starts: The Augustan Books of Poetry/ ends: BILLING AND SONS, LTD., GUILDFORD AND ESHER; (3) WILLIAM HENRY DAVIES/ *Born* 1870 [sic]; (4) blank; (5) CONTENTS; (6) blank; 7–30 text; 31 starts: WORKS BY W. H. DAVIES/ ends: LATER DAYS. A pendant to *The Auto-biography of a Super-Tramp*. 6s.; (32) back cover, within a frame: starts: MODERN POETRY/ ends: ERNEST BENN LTD., 8 BOUVERIE STREET., E.C.4; poem titles in italics

contents: p7 The Kingfisher; p8 Leisure; p9 The Rain. The Moon; p10 Kings; p11 A Child's Pet; p12 The Rainbow; p13 Sweet Stay-at-Home; p14 Leaves. Oh, Sweet Content; p15 A Great Time. The Rabbit; p16 Union; p17 On Hearing Mrs Woodhouse Play the Harpsichord; p18 The Villain. The Ways of Time; p19 Raptures; p20 The Hour of Magic. Thunderstorms; p21 A Blind Child; p22 The Poet's Horse; p23 Easter; p24 A Thought. Open; p25 Lovely Dames; p26 The Example; p27 Dreams of the Sea; p28 The White Cascade; p29 Impudence; p30 Truly Great

edges: trimmed; *binding*: title-page is front cover

date of publication: November 1925; *price*: 6d.

copies seen: BL (shelf mark: 11605.cc.12/18; accession date: 9 December 1925); SH

text changes from previous printings to A27:
Kings: title from 'K for Kings'
Open: title from 'O for Open'; line 1: 'tumps' to 'lumps'

A27a Second impression Ernest Benn Ltd 1926

A27b Third impression Ernest Benn Ltd 1928

A27c Fourth impression   Ernest Benn Ltd 1931

A27d Fifth impression   Ernest Benn Ltd 1932

as *A27* apart from: (1) front cover (title-page) within a window of the binding: AUGUSTAN BOOKS OF POETRY/ W. H./ DAVIES (in open outline lettering)/ NO. 16   BENN   6d.; (2) starts: BENN'S AUGUSTAN BOOKS OF POETRY/ ends: 61. JOHN DONNE   116. ARTHUR L. SALMON; 3 WILLIAM HENRY DAVIES/ *Born* 1870 [sic]/ at foot: *First published,* 1925/ *Second impression,* 1926/ *Third impression,* 1928/ *Fourth impression,* 1931/ *Fifth impression,* 1932; 31 at foot: PRINTED IN GREAT BRITAIN BY/ BILLING AND SONS LTD., GUILDFORD AND ESHER; back cover: blank; stitched; *binding*: dark rose calico grain imitation cloth; front and back covers as described

copies seen: RUL, Finzi; SH

A27e Sixth impression   Ernest Benn Ltd 1935

as *A27* apart from: 3 *Sixth impression, November* 1935

copy seen: RUL, Finzi

A28 THE SONG OF LOVE   Jonathan Cape 1926

within a decorative border: *The/* SONG *of* LOVE/ (floral vignette)/ W. H. DAVIES/ at foot: LONDON: JONATHAN CAPE

8vo; (A)–D in eights; 32 leaves: (1–10) 11–61 (3)pp; 19.0 × 13.5 cms variable

(1–2) blank; (3) half-title: (vignette of a bird)/ THE SONG OF LOVE/ at foot: *With Decorations by/* DORA M. BATTY; (4) frontispiece of two people in a fenced garden; (5) title-page; (6) FIRST PUBLISHED IN MCMXXVI/ MADE & PRINTED IN GREAT BRITAIN/ BY BUTLER & TANNER LTD/ FROME AND/ LONDON/ (fleuron); (7) NOTE signed W. H. D.; (8) blank; (9) fly-title: THE SONG OF LOVE; (10) blank; 11–61 text; 61 below text: (tailpiece of a bird); (62–64) blank

illustrations: full-page frontispiece; *decorations*: pp(3), (5), 11 and 61

paper: watermarked: – BASINGWERK PARCHMENT –

endpapers: cream; *edges*: deckle fore edge, top edge trimmed

binding: blue paper-covered boards with rose marbled pattern, embossed; front cover, on a white paper label 7.2 × 4.3 cms, in navy and black: (navy decorative rule)/ THE SONG/ OF/ LOVE (in black open outline lettering)/ (navy vignette of a bird)/ W.H./ DAVIES (in black open outline lettering)/ (navy decorative rule); spine, on a white paper label 13.2 cms deep, in navy open outline lettering, vertically downwards: W. H. DAVIES . THE SONG OF LOVE; back cover: blank *dust-jacket*: cream with an embossed surface, printed in black; front: *By/* W. H. DAVIES/ (vignette of an oak tree)/ THE SONG OF LOVE/ 1/ The oak bears little acorns, yet/ Is big in branch and root:/ My love is like the smaller tree,/ That bears a larger fruit.; spine, vertically downwards: W. H. DAVIES (fleuron) THE SONG OF LOVE; back: starts: *Books by W. H. Davies/* ends: *Jonathan Cape Thirty Bedford Square London*; front flap: starts: THE SONG OF LOVE/ ends: 3s. 6d. net; back flap: blank

date of publication: October 1926

print run: 2000 copies printed on 30 August 1926; bound by Nevett; *price*: 3s.6d.

copies seen: BL (shelf mark: 011645.h.44; accession date: 8 October 1926); HDB (2 copies); SH

reviews: Poetry: The Rubayat of W. H. Davies, Richard Church, *The Spectator*, 30 October 1926, 137, 5131, 756–758; Recent Poetry, Robin Flower, *Country Life*, 20 November 1926, LX, 1557, 797; An Artful Lover, *TLS*, 25 November 1926, 846; Three Poets, Vita Sackville-West, *Nation and Athenaeum*, 18 December 1926, 428; W. H. Davies Makes Concessions and Remains W. H. Davies, Holbrook Jackson, *Now & Then*, Christmas 1926, 8; 'Poetry', JCS, *London Mercury*, March 1927, XV, 89, 544–555; Heart and Head, C. Henry Warren, *Bookman*, March 1927, LXXI, 426, 325

mss: in WHD's hand on paper watermarked: RYMANS/ HERTFORD BANK/ LONDON; addressed Malpas House, Oxted, Surrey and dated 1926; clipped into brown paper wrappers (HDB)

previous printings:
20 'Let's marry soon, and live no more' (as 'Where Shall We Live') and 70 'If our contented hearts are blind' (as 'Contented Hearts'), *Atalanta's Garland* (University Press by T & A Constable 1926) 9

note: the HDB copies are inscribed: 'To Dinah (Helen)/ from/ Bunny (W. H. Davies.)/ 1926.' and 'My book/ W. H. Davies./ 1926.'

A28a Special edition   Jonathan Cape 1926

as *A28* apart from: (2) limitation: (fleuron) OF this edition of *The Song of Love/* 125 copies have been printed for/ sale, each copy signed and num-/bered by the Artist/ (fleuron) COPY number / signed W. H. Davies.; *paper*: watermarked P M/ FABRIANO/ (decorative lion)/ PERUSIA; chain lines 2.9 cms apart and horizontal; *binding*: bright blue paper-covered boards, green-gold vellum spine; front cover: blank; spine, lettered in gilt: THE/ SONG/ OF/ LOVE; back cover: blank; *edges*: deckle fore edge, top edge gilt; *dust-jacket*: not seen

date of publication: November 1926

print run: 125 copies printed on 30 August 1926; bound by Nevett; *price*: 9s.

copy seen: HRHRC ('complimentary' copy)

A29   THE ADVENTURES OF
JOHNNY WALKER, TRAMP   Jonathan Cape 1926

THE ADVENTURES OF/ JOHNNY WALKER (in open outline lettering)/ TRAMP/ *by*/ W. H. DAVIES/ (publisher's device)/ at foot: LONDON/ JONATHAN CAPE 30 BEDFORD SQUARE

8vo; (A)–I in eights, K–Q in eights; 128 leaves: (1–4) 5 (6) 7–9 (10) 11–256pp; 19.0 × 12.2 cms variable

(1) half-title: THE ADVENTURES OF JOHNNY WALKER/ TRAMP; (2) starts: BOOKS BY THE SAME AUTHOR/ ends: etc; (3) title-page; (4) FIRST PUBLISHED IN MCMXXVI/ MADE & PRINTED IN GREAT BRITAIN/ BY BUTLER & TANNER LTD/ FROME AND/ LONDON/ (fleuron); 5 *Contents*; (6) blank; 7–9 *Foreword* signed W. H. D.; (10) blank; 11–256 text

contents: 1 p11 The Soup-Kitchen; 2 p28 Strokes of Genius; 3 p45 Stiffs; 4 p59 In Jail; 5 p72 The Lakes; 6 p82 The Religious Beggar; 7 p96 In Disgrace; 8 p117 House-Calling; 9 p131 Proud Blood; 10 p143 Enemies; 11 p155 Navvies; 12 p163 Jack the Giant-Killer; 13 p177 The Simple Life; 14 p192 Back in London; 15 p222 Queer Characters; 16 p241 Nicknames

endpapers: cream; *edges*: top and fore edge trimmed

binding: mid-blue calico grain cloth, lettered in gilt; front cover: blank; spine: THE/ ADVENTURES/ OF/ JOHNNY/ WALKER,/ TRAMP/ (fleuron)/ W. H. DAVIES/ at foot: JONATHAN CAPE; back cover: blind-blocked publisher's device

dust-jacket: mottled cream with an embossed surface, printed in blue; front, within a decorative border: The Adventures of/ Johnny Walker, Tramp/ *by*/ W. H. Davies/ Author of *The Autobiography of a Super-Tramp*/ (publisher's device); spine: The/ Adventures of/ Johnny Walker/ Tramp/ (fleuron)/ W. H. Davies/ at foot: (publisher's device)/ Jonathan Cape; back: starts: *Books by W. H. Davies*/ ends: *Jonathan Cape Thirty Bedford Square London*; front flap: starts: The Adventures of/ Johnny Walker, Tramp/ ends: 7s. 6d. net; back flap: blank

date of publication: October 1926

print run: 2000 copies printed on 24 August 1926; bound by Nevett; *price*: 7s.6d.

copies seen: BL (shelf mark: 010856.aa.45; accession date: 26 October 1926); HDB (2 copies); HRHRC; SH

reviews: Poetry: The Rubayat of W. H. Davies, Richard Church, *The Spectator*, 30 October 1926, 137, 5131, 756–758; The Poet Among Beggars, *TLS*, 2 December 1926, 878; W. H. Davies Makes Concessions and Remains W. H. Davies, Holbrook Jackson, *Now & Then*, Christmas 1926, 22, 8; *Country Life*, 22 January 1927, LXI, 1566, 142

notes: (a) the HDB copies are inscribed: 'My book,/ W. H. Davies.' and 'To Dinah (Helen)/ from/ Bunny (W. H. Davies.)/ 1926.'
(b) the HRHRC copy is a presentation copy to Richard Church

A29a   Special edition   Jonathan Cape 1926

as *A29* apart from: (i–iii) blank; (iv) limitation: (fleuron) OF this Edition of *Johnny Walker: Tramp* have been printed 125 copies/ for Sale, signed and numbered by/ the Author/ (fleuron) COPY number signed W. H. Davies.; *paper*: hand-made; *binding*: bright blue calico grain cloth, lettered in gilt; front cover: William H. Davies. (in facsimile of author's script); spine: (decorative rule)/ THE/ ADVENTURES/ OF/ JOHNNY/ WALKER,/ TRAMP/ (fleuron)/ W. H. DAVIES/ at foot: JONATHAN CAPE/ (decorative rule); back cover: blank; *edges*: deckle fore edge, top edge gilt; *dust-jacket*: front: at foot: *Limited Edition, signed by the Author*; front flap: at foot: *Limited Edition of one hundred copies for/ sale, printed on handmade paper and/ signed by the Author./ £1 1s. net*; back flap: blank

date of publication: November 1926

print run: 150 copies printed on 24 August 1926; bound by Nevett; *price*: 21s.

copies seen: HRHRC (no 90 and an unsigned presentation copy)

A29b   Travellers' Library edition   Jonathan Cape 1927

review: *Now & Then*, Christmas 1927, 26, 36

A29c   Florin Books edition   Jonathan Cape 1932

THE ADVENTURES OF/ JOHNNY WALKER/ *Tramp*/ *By*/ W. H. DAVIES/ Author of/ *The Autobiography of a Super-Tramp*/ (publisher's device)/ at foot: LONDON/ JONATHAN CAPE 30 BEDFORD SQUARE/ AND AT TORONTO

16mo; (A)–H in sixteens; 128 leaves: (1–4) 5 (6) 7–9 (10–12) 13–256pp plus an 8pp publisher's catalogue; 17.7 × 11.4 cms

(1) half-title: THE ADVENTURES OF JOHNNY WALKER/ *Tramp*/ at foot: *Florin Books*; (2) starts: FLORIN BOOKS/ ends: will be found at the end of the book.; (3) title-page; (4) starts: FIRST PUBLISHED OCTOBER 1926/ ends: PAPER SUPPLIED BY SPALDING AND HODGE LTD.; 5 Contents; (6) blank; 7–9 Foreword signed W. H. D.; (10) blank; (11) half-title: JOHNNY WALKER; (12) blank; 13–256 text; 8pp publisher's catalogue: starts: 'The FLORIN BOOKS are/ ends: Russian character.

endpapers: cream; *edges*: trimmed

binding: cream calico grain cloth embossed with brown, lettered in brown; front cover: THE ADVENTURES OF/ JOHNNY WALKER,/ TRAMP/ W. H. DAVIES; spine: THE/ ADVEN-/ TURES/ OF/ JOHNNY/ WALKER,/ TRAMP/ W. H./ DAVIES/ at foot: JONATHAN/ CAPE; back cover: blank

dust-jacket: white, printed in black and green; front: top third in green, lettered in white: THE ADVENTURES/ OF JOHNNY WALKER,/ TRAMP/ centred in black: W. H./ (thick green rule)/ DAVIES/ (publisher's device in green and black)/ at foot, in black on a green block: florin book   No. 5; spine: (green rule)/ THE/ ADVEN-/

TURES OF/ JOHNNY/ WALKER,/ TRAMP/ (green rule)/ W. H./ DAVIES/ between two green and three black vertical rules: No 5/ at foot: 2s/ net/ JONATHAN/ CAPE; back: starts: (green rule)/ ends: (green rule); front flap: starts: No. 5/ ends: 2s. net; back flap: blank

date of publication: 2 May 1932

print run: 10,000 copies printed on 24 February 1932; *price*: 2s.

copies seen: RUL, Finzi; SH

note: RUL, Finzi copy: catalogue ends: "me". *The Manchester Guardian*

A29d Florin Books edition: second impression   Jonathan Cape 1933

date of publication: May 1933

print run: 2500 copies printed on 11 May 1933

A29e Florin Books edition: third impression   Jonathan Cape 1934

date of publication: March 1934

print run: 2000 copies printed on 24 February 1934

A29f Florin Books edition: fourth impression   Jonathan Cape 1934

date of publication: September 1934

print run: 2000 copies

A29g Florin Books edition: fifth impression   Jonathan Cape 1935

print run: 1st printing: 2000 copies printed on 30 December 1935; 2nd printing: 2000 copies printed on 22 February 1938; *price*: 3s.6d.

A29h New edition   Brown, Watson 1963

date of publication: 31 December 1963; *price*: 3s.6d.

A29i School edition   Howard Baker 1970

THE ADVENTURES OF/ JOHNNY WALKER,/ TRAMP/ W. H. Davies/ at foot: (publisher's device)/ HOWARD BAKER, LONDON/ (thick rule)

16mo; 8 unsigned gatherings of sixteen; 128 leaves: (1–6) 7–256pp; 18.4 × 12.0 cms

(1) half-title: starts: THE ADVENTURES OF JOHNNY WALKER, TRAMP/ ends: existence./ (rule); (2) starts: Other Outstanding/ Non-Fiction Titles/ ends: all Howard Baker Books/ (thick rule); (3) title-page; (4) starts: W. H. Davies/ THE ADVENTURES OF/ JOHNNY WALKER, TRAMP/ ends: J. W. Arrowsmith Limited, Bristol BS3 2NT/ (thick rule); (5) *Contents*; (6) blank; 7–256 text

endpapers: white; *edges*: trimmed

binding: royal blue calico grain cloth, lettered in gilt; front cover: blank; spine, vertically downwards: THE ADVENTURES OF/ JOHNNY WALKER, TRAMP W. H. Davies/ at foot: (publisher's device)/ (rule)/ HOWARD/ BAKER; back cover: blank; *dust-jacket*: not seen

date of publication: August 1970; *price*: £1.50p

copy seen: BL (shelf mark: X 808/6699; accession date: 21 October 1970)

A30 **A POET'S CALENDAR**   Jonathan Cape 1927

within a decorative border: A POET'S/ CALENDAR/ (vignette of a woman's head)/ W. H. DAVIES/ at foot: LONDON: JONATHAN CAPE

8vo; (A)–D in eights; 32 leaves: (1–6) 7–8 (9) 10–12 (13) 14–44 (45) 46–61 (3)pp; 19.0 × 13.0 cms variable

(1–2) blank; (3) half-title: A POET'S CALENDAR; (4) starts: BY THE SAME AUTHOR/ ends: *Etc.*; (5) title-page; (6) FIRST PUBLISHED IN MCMXXVII/ MADE & PRINTED IN GREAT BRITAIN/ BY BUTLER & TANNER LTD/ LONDON/ (fleuron); 7–8 Contents; (9) fly-title: A POET'S CALENDAR; 10 JANUARY (in rustic lettering)/ 1 *to* 14/ (vignette of a ship); 11–61 text; (62–64) blank

contents: p11 The Time of Dreams; p15 Frost; p17 Mad; p19 One by One; p21 Hill and Vale; p23 The White Horse; p25 The Mask; p27 Giants; p29 Advice; p31 The Spoiler; p33 Storms; p35 Property; p37 Sun, Tree and Crow; p39 Shooting Stars; p41 A Dull Spirit; p43 The Dragonfly; p47 Light and Darkness; p49 The Evening Star

illustrations: decorations on pp(5), 10, 14, 16, 18, 20, 22, 24, 26, 28, 30, 32, 34, 36, 38, 40, 42, 46, 48, 50, 52, 54, 56, 58 and 60

paper: watermarked: – BASINGWERK PARCHMENT –

endpapers: cream; *edges*: uncut, top edge trimmed

binding: orange paper-covered boards, with rose marbled pattern, embossed; front cover, on a white paper label 7.1 × 4.4 cms, in orange and black: (orange decorative rule)/ A POET'S/ CALEN-/ DAR (in black open outline lettering)/ (orange vignette of a bird)/ W. H./ DAVIES (in black open outline lettering)/ (orange decorative rule); spine, on a white paper label 13.1 cms deep, in orange open outline lettering, vertically upwards: W. H. DAVIES . A POET'S CALENDAR; back cover: blank

dust-jacket: cream, with an embossed surface, printed in black; front: (decorative rule)/ A POET'S CALENDAR/ *by*/ W. H. DAVIES/ (vignette of a torch)/ With

Decorations by Dora M. Batty/ (decorative rule); spine, vertically downwards: W. H. DAVIES (fleuron) A POET'S CALENDAR; back: starts: *Books by W. H. Davies/* ends: *Jonathan Cape Thirty Bedford Square London*; front flap: starts: A POET'S CALENDAR/ ends: 'While laughter comes, and song.'; back flap: blank

date of publication: October 1927; *price*: 3s. 6d.

copies seen: BL (shelf mark: 011645.i.86; accession date: 20 October 1927); HDB; RUL, Finzi; SH

reviews: Poetry, JCS, *London Mercury*, March 1927, XV, 89, 544–555; Heart and Head, C. Henry Warren, *Bookman*, March 1927, LXXI, 426, 325; Poetic Gold, HM, *The Spectator*, 12 November 1927, 139, 5185, 827–828; Mr W. H. Davies, *TLS*, 24 November 1927, 869; The Vase and the Parterre, *Nation and Athenaeum*, 26 November 1927, XLII, 8, 328; Three Poets, Almey St. John Adcock, *Bookman*, February 1928, LXXIII, 437, 278–279

previous printings:
'The White Horse', *London Mercury*, February 1927, XV, 88, 344
'Storms' and 'The Time of Dreams', *New Republic*, 13 July 1927, LI, 658, 196 and 20 July 1927, LI, 659, 224 respectively
'Light and Darkness', *Country Life*, 23 July 1927, LXII, 1592, 109
'Old and Young' (as 'Old or Young'), *The Dragon*, Lent Term 1927, 19

note: the HDB copy is inscribed: 'My book,/ W. H. Davies./ Oct. 1927.'

A30a Special edition   Jonathan Cape 1927

as *A30* apart from: (4) limitation: (fleuron) OF this Edition of *A Poet's Calendar/* have been printed 125 copies for/ Sale/ (fleuron) COPY number   signed W.H. Davies.; *paper*: watermarked: PM/ FABRIANO/ (decorative lion)/ PERUSIA; chain lines 2.7 cms apart and horizontal; *binding*: bordeaux vellum spine, lettered in gilt, vertically downwards: A POET'S/ CALENDAR; *edges*: deckle fore and lower edge, top edge gilt; uncut; *dust-jacket*: front flap, at foot: (fleuron) *Limited Edition of 125 copies/ signed by the Author/* 10s.6d. *net*

print run: 125 copies; *price*: 10s.6d.

copy seen: HRHRC (no 79)

A30b Cheap edition   Jonathan Cape 1934

date of publication: October 1934; *price*: 2s.6d.

A30c First American edition   1934

A30d New edition   Brown, Watson 1963

date of publication: December 1963

A31 DANCING MAD   Jonathan Cape 1927

DANCING MAD/ A NOVEL/ *By*/ W. H. DAVIES/ (publisher's device)/ at foot: LONDON/ JONATHAN CAPE 30 BEDFORD SQUARE

8vo; (A) in ten, B–I and K–O in eights; 114 leaves: (i–iv) 1 (2) 3–6 (7–8) 9–224pp; 19.0 × 12.0 cms

(i) half-title: DANCING MAD; (ii) starts: BY THE SAME AUTHOR/ ends: *etc.*; (iii) title-page; (iv) FIRST PUBLISHED IN MCMXXVII/ MADE & PRINTED IN GREAT BRITAIN/ BY BUTLER & TANNER LTD/ FROME AND/ LONDON/ (fleuron); 1 *Contents*; (2) blank; 3–6 FOREWORD signed X.; (7) fly-title: DANCING MAD; (8) blank; 9–224 text; 224 below text: THE END

contents: 1 p9 The Beresfords; 2 p20 Marriage; 3 p37 The Dinner; 4 p53 The Quarrel; 5 p66 Breaking a Home; 6 p79 Parted; 7 p88 House-Hunting; 8 p97 The Waterside; 9 p109 Birds of Prey; 10 p126 No-Man's Land; 11 p138 The Doctor Proposes; 12 p150 A Second Marriage; 13 p163 The Return; 14 p180 Doctor Michael Surprised; 15 p192 The Interview; 16 p205 The Wrong Man; 17 p217 The End

endpapers: cream; *edges*: trimmed

binding: mid-blue calico grain cloth, lettered in gilt; front cover: blank; spine: DANCING/ MAD/ (fleuron)/ W. H. DAVIES/ at foot: JONATHAN CAPE; back cover: blind-blocked publisher's device

dust-jacket: cream, with an embossed surface, printed in mid-blue and black; front, in black within an outer black ruled border and an inner blue spotted border: DANCING MAD/ A NOVEL BY/ W. H. DAVIES/ Author of The Autobiography of a/ Super-Tramp, *etc.*/ With a Foreword by X/ at foot: (blue publisher's device)/ LONDON/ JONATHAN CAPE 30 BEDFORD SQUARE; spine: (black rule)/ (blue spotted rule)/ DANCING/MAD/ A Novel/ by/ W. H./ DAVIES (in black)/ at foot: (publisher's device in blue)/ JONATHAN/ CAPE (in black)/ (blue spotted rule)/ (black rule); back, in black: starts: *Books by W. H. Davies*/ ends: *Jonathan Cape Thirty Bedford Square London*; front flap: starts: DANCING MAD/ ends: 6s. *net*; back flap: blank

date of publication: November 1927

print run: 2000 copies printed on 10 September 1927; *price*: 6s.

copies seen: BL (shelf mark: 012641.bb.51; accession date: 27 October 1927); HDB; RUL, Finzi; SH

reviews: Fiction, Edwin Muir, *Nation and Athenaeum*, 19 November 1927, XLII, 7, 284; Mr W. H. Davies, *TLS*, 24 November 1927, 869; Books worth Reading. The Best of New Novels, *John o'London's Weekly*, 3 December 1927, XVIII, 450, 327 (portrait); "Dancing Mad' reviewed by 'X", *Now & Then*, Christmas 1927, 26, 36

note: the HDB copy is inscribed: 'To "Dinah" (Helen)/ from/ "Bunny" (W. H. Davies.)/ Oct. 1927.'

A32 MOSS AND FEATHER   Faber & Gwyer 1928

printed in yellow out of black: Moss and Feather/ W. H. Davies/ (vignette of a kingfisher facing up the page) signed Nicholson one gathering of four leaves; (i–viii)pp; sewn; 18.5 × 12.2 cms

(i) front cover: title-page; (ii) blank; (iii) vignette of a kingfisher, facing down the page, printed in blue, green and orange on a white and black background signed Nicholson; (iv) blank; (v) text (in italics) signed W. H. DAVIES; (vi) starts: THE ARIEL POEMS/ ends: 8. By T. S. Eliot: *Journey of the Magi*/ With Drawings by E. McKnight Kauffer; (vii) blank; (viii) back cover, in black on yellow paper: This is No. 10 of/ THE ARIEL POEMS/ Published by Faber & Gwyer Limited/ at 24 Russell Square, London, W.C.1/ Printed at The Curwen Press, Plaistow

edges: trimmed

dust-jacket: the front and back covers are printed on yellow paper with flaps suggestive of a dust-jacket but covering plain paper; the whole is covered by a glacene jacket

date of publication: September 1928

print run: 5000 copies; *price*: 1s.

copies seen: BL (shelf mark: 401.f.4/10; accession date: 24 September 1928); SH

review: Ariel Poems, *TLS*, 20 December 1928, 1007

note: supplied in a buff envelope printed in black; front, within a decorative panel: MOSS AND FEATHER (in open outline lettering)/ by W. H. DAVIES/ below the panel: *The original first printing of the poem, decorated with drawings/ by* WILLIAM NICHOLSON/ to the right, at the head of the envelope, in a ruled panel: *One/ Shilling/ net/* at foot: *The Ariel Poems No. 10*

A32a Large paper edition   Faber & Gwyer 1928

within a double ruled border: MOSS AND FEATHER/ BY/ W. H. DAVIES (in rustic lettering)/ *Drawings by/* WILLIAM NICHOLSON (in rustic lettering)/ at foot: *London:/* FABER & GWYER LTD. (in rustic lettering)/ 1928

one gathering of six leaves; (i–xii)pp; sewn; 21.2 × 13.5 cms variable

(i) limitation: This large-paper edition, printed/ on English hand-made paper, is/ limited to five hundred copies/ This is number   signed W. H. Davies.; (ii) blank; (iii) as *A32* (i); (iv) blank; (v) title-page; (vi) PRINTED IN ENGLAND; (vii) as *A32* (iii); (viii) blank; (ix) as *A32* (v); (x) blank; (xi) as *A32* (vi); (xii) as *A32* (viii) but not on yellow paper

endpapers: cream; *edges*: deckle fore and lower edge, top edge trimmed

binding: cream paper-covered boards with an embossed surface, lettered in gilt; front cover; W. H. DAVIES/ (three gilt stars in an inverted triangle)/ MOSS AND FEATHER; spine and back cover: blank; *dust-jacket*: not seen

date of publication: November 1928

print run: 500 copies; *price*: 7s.6d.

copies seen: BL (shelf mark: Cup 401.f.410a; accession date: 31 October 1928) (no 25); RUL, Finzi (no 9); SH (no 403)

A33 COLLECTED POEMS 1928   Jonathan Cape 1928

THE/ COLLECTED POEMS/ OF/ W. H. DAVIES/ 1928/ (publisher's device)/ at foot: JONATHAN CAPE/ THIRTY BEDFORD SQUARE/ LONDON

16mo; (A) in ten plus tipped-in frontispiece, B in eight, C–I and K–O in sixteens; first page of gatherings B–O signed D.C.P. on inner margin; 210 leaves: (i–vi) vii–xx (1–2) 3–385 (386) 387–399 (1)pp plus tipped-in frontispiece not included in the pagination; 19.2 × 13.0 cms variable

(i) half-title: COLLECTED POEMS/ 1928; (ii) blank; portrait frontispiece captioned: W. H. DAVIES/ from a bust by Jacob Epstein/ in the Newport (Mon.)/ Art Gallery/ *Copyright*; (iii) title-page; (iv) FIRST PUBLISHED MCMXXVIII/ at foot: PRINTED IN GREAT BRITAIN BY/ BUTLER & TANNER LTD/ FROME; (v) starts: In this one volume are collected all the poems I care/ ends: are his best poems and which are his worst. signed W. H. D.; (vi) blank; vii–xx Contents; (1) fly-title: COLLECTED POEMS/ 1928; (2) blank; 3–385 text; (386) blank; 387–399 Index of First Lines; (400) blank

contents: 1 Autumn; 2 Beauty's Light; 3 Sleep; 4 A Drinking Song; 5 Death; 6 Love Absent; 7 The Prover; 8 Love's Coming; 9 In a Lodging House; 10 Lines to a Sparrow; 11 The Hill-side Park; 12 The Lodging House Fire; 13 Saints and Lodgers; 14 The Soul's Destroyer; 15 Margery; 16 The Ways of Time; 17 The Likeness; 18 Ale; 19 'Scotty' Bill; 20 The Ox; 21 Catharine; 22 The Forsaken Dead; 23 A Blind Child; 24 Wondering Brown; 25 Music; 26 Facts; 27 New-comers; 28 Parted; 29 The Jolly Tramp; 30 The Toothache; 31 Hope Abandoned; 32 The Rain; 33 A Life's Love; 34 Robin Redbreast; 35 The Wind; 36 Jenny; 37 Nature's Friend; 38 A Maiden and Her Hair; 39 Early Morn; 40 The Battle; 41 The Moth; 42 Day's Black Star; 43 A Richer Freight; 44 School's Out; 45 A Happy Life; 46 Joy and Pleasure; 47 Truly Great; 48 The Laughers; 49 Australian Bill; 50 The Boy; 51 A Lovely Woman; 52 Money; 53 Where we Differ; 54 The Daisy; 55 The Sea; 56 Waiting; 57 Farewell to Poesy; 58 The Dark Hour; 59 Jenny Wren; 60 The Idiot and the Child; 61 Rose; 62 The Green Tent; 63 To the Wind at Morn; 64 No Master; 65 The Dumb World; 66 Knitting; 67 Clouds; 68 In the Country; 69 The Kingfisher; 70 An old House in London; 71 Scotty's Luck; 72 Happy Wind; 73 The Sluggard; 74 On Expecting some Books; 75 The Sailor to his Parrot; 76 Angry; 77 The Call of the Sea; 78 Come, Honest Boys; 79 To the New Year; 80 The Philosophical Beggar; 81 Fancy; 82 Songs of Joy; 83 The Example; 84 In May; 85 The Flood; 86 Leisure; 87 Fancy's Home; 88 Sheep; 89 Days that have Been; 90 Days too Short; 91 The Power of Music; 92 Christ, the Man; 93 Ingratitude; 94 The Posts; 95 Rich or Poor; 96 The Harvest Home; 97 Seeking Beauty; 98 The Owl; 99 The East in Gold; 100 Sadness and Joy; 101 To Sparrows Fighting; 102 The Happy Child; 103 The Two Flocks; 104 A Dream; 105 The Elements; 106 The Heap of Rags; 107 The Quarrel; 108 Fairies, Take Care; 109 The Doubtful One; 110 The Little Ones; 111 Shopping; 112 The Sleepers; 113 The Bed-sitting-room; 114 The Child and the Mariner; 115 Thunderstorms; 116 Strong Moments; 117 A Greeting; 118 Sweet Stay-at-Home; 119 The Starved; 120 A May Morning; 121 The Lonely Dreamer; 122 Christmas; 123 Laughing Rose; 124 Seeking Joy; 125 The Old Oak Tree; 126 Poor Kings; 127 Love and the Muse; 128 My Youth; 129 Smiles; 130 Mad Poll; 131 Joy Supreme; 132 Francis Thompson; 133 The Bird-Man; 134 Winter's Beauty; 135 The Church Organ; 136 Night Wanderers; 137 Young Beauty; 138 The Two Lives; 139 Hidden

96   A *Books and pamphlets*

Love; 140 Life is Jolly; 141 The Fog; 142 A Woman's Charms; 143 Dreams of the Sea; 144 The Wonder-Maker; 145 An Early Love; 146 Dream Tragedies; 147 Children at Play; 148 Return to Nature; 149 A Strange City; 150 When I am Old; 151 From France; 152 Starers; 153 The Best Friend; 154 Heaven; 155 Sweet Night; 156 Early Spring; 157 The Mind's Liberty; 158 When on a Summer's Morn; 159 Again I Sing; 160 The Dumb World; 161 The Weeping Child; 162 The Den; 163 This World; 164 A Fleeting Passion; 165 Plants and Men; 166 A Midsummer's Night's Storm; 167 The Dreaming Boy; 168 The Hawk; 169 The Signs; 170 The Moon; 171 A Great Time; 172 Her Absence; 173 The Wanderer; 174 The Black Cloud; 175 When I in Praise; 176 Sweet Child; 177 The Life Divine; 178 Love's Youth; 179 Rich Days; 180 Near a Quiet Stream; 181 The Hermit; 182 In the End; 183 On the Mountain; 184 Infancy; 185 Nell Barnes; 186 The Bird of Paradise; 187 The Inexpressible; 188 This Night; 189 The Visitor; 190 April's Charms; 191 Kitty and I; 192 Thou Comest, May; 193 The Hospital Waiting-Room; 194 The White Cascade; 195 The One Singer; 196 The Inquest; 197 The Two Children; 198 Come, thou Sweet Wonder; 199 Charms; 200 Friends; 201 The Power of Silence; 202 A Mother to her Sick Child; 203 The White Monster; 204 Child Lovers; 205 Body and Spirit; 206 Raptures; 207 The Voice; 208 Confession; 209 Easter; 210 My Love could Walk; 211 My Old Acquaintance; 212 A Winter's Night; 213 Birds; 214 Jove Warns Us; 215 The Excuse; 216 In the Snow; 217 Molly; 218 Killed in Action (Edward Thomas); 219 Lovely Dames; 220 Cowslips and Larks; 221 Forgiveness; 222 That Day She Seized; 223 The Bell; 224 A Strange Meeting; 225 When Yon Full Moon; 226 Till I Went Out; 227 The Soul's Companions; 228 The Holly on the Wall; 229 Exalted Flower; 230 What Thoughts are Mine; 231 Angel and Mystery; 232 They're Taxing Ale again; 233 In Time of War; 234 England; 235 Come, let us Find; 236 The Birds of Steel; 237 Rags and Bones; 238 The Dancer; 239 On hearing Mrs Woodhouse play the Harpsichord; 240 Late Singers; 241 The Start; 242 Old Sailors; 243 The Lost Sex; 244 In Neath Valley; 245 The Blind Boxer; 246 Old Acquaintance; 247 I am the Poet Davies, William; 248 The Moon and a Cloud; 249 The Hunt; 250 No Idle Gold; 251 Oh, Sweet Content!; 252 The Villain; 253 Love Speechless; 254 The Dog; 255 The Rat; 256 The Cat; 257 To-day; 258 How Kind is Sleep; 259 The Force of Love; 260 When Leaves Begin; 261 Passion's Hounds; 262 Love Impeached; 263 The Truth; 264 The Coming of Peace; 265 April's Lambs; 266 The Coming of Spring; 267 A Song; 268 Love's Caution; 269 Trees; 270 What County?; 271 A Child's Pet; 272 The Flirt; 273 The Captive Lion; 274 The Clock; 275 A Bird's Anger; 276 Bird and Brook; 277 One Thing Wanting; 278 The Mint; 279 Worm-Proof; 280 Comfort; 281 Her Mouth and Mine; 282 Let Me Confess; 283 Love's Silent Hour; 284 Now That She Gives; 285 You Interfering Ladies; 286 The Song of Life; 287 I Could not Love Him More; 288 See how the Glow-worm's Light; 289 A Chant; 290 Beggar's Song; 291 On What Sweet Banks; 292 Drinking Song; 293 Aroung that Waist; 294 Her Body's a Fine House; 295 Oh for a Glass of Wine!; 296 The Woods and Banks; 297 Without Contentment, what is Life?; 298 When Autumn's Fruit; 299 Now that the Tears; 300 The World May Charge; 301 Where She is Now; 302 Men that have Strength; 303 Night is the only Time I Live; 304 When Diamonds, Nibbling in my Ears; 305 With thy Strong Tide of Beauty; 306 Who Bears in Mind; 307 The Hour of Magic; 308 The Beautiful; 309 Impudence; 310 Wasted Hours; 311 Two Women; 312 Pastures; 313 Her Merriment; 314 Joy; 315 Lamorna Cove; 316 Wild Oats; 317 The Grief of Others; 318 The Portrait; 319 A Thought; 320 Our Sussex Downs; 321 Telling Fortunes; 322 The Collar; 323 To a Fool; 324 Strength; 325 To Bacchus; 326 A Woman's History; 327 The Trance; 328 The Poet's Horse; 329 The Rainbow; 330 Love, Like a Drop of Dew; 331 The Nature Lover; 332 One Token; 333 Rogues; 334 Leaves; 335 At Night; 336 The Pond; 337 See Where Young Love; 338 A Miracle; 339 The Rivals; 340 Earth Love; 341 Love's Payment; 342 In Spring-Time; 343 My Garden; 344 The Schemes of Love; 345 The Meadow; 346 Cant; 347 The Trick; 348 Breath; 349 The Cave; 350 The World Approves; 351 Down Underground; 352 The Fear; 353 The Fates; 354 The Two Stars; 355 The Rabbit; 356 To a Lady Friend; 357 The Two Heavens; 358 The Doll; 359 The Snowflake; 360 Secrets; 361 Our Longer Life; 362 When Love is Young; 363 Dust; 364 Pity; 365 The Joy of Life; 366 Violet and Oak; 367 Evil; 368 A is for Artist; 369 B is for Beauty; 370 C is for Child; 371 D is for Dog; 372 E is for Eyes; 373 F is for Fiddles; 374 G is for Garden; 375 H is for Hedge; 376 I is for Implements; 377 J is for Jealousy; 378 K is for Kings; 379 L is for Light; 380 M is for Mother; 381 N is for Nature; 382 O is for Open; 383 P is for Pool; 384 Q is for Question; 385 R is for Remembrance; 386 S is for Swimmer; 387 T is for Time; 388 U is for Union; 389 V is for Venus; 390 W is for Will; 391 X is for Expecting; 392 Y is for Youth; 393 Z is for Zany; 394 The Rock; 395 The Poet; 396 A Lonely Coast; 397 The Perfect Life; 398 The Two Loves; 399 No-man's Wood; 400 Come Away, Death; 401 One Night, when I was Sleeping; 402 The Life of Man; 403 Traffic; 404 The Bust; 405 How Sordid is this Crowded Life; 406 The Treasured Three; 407 The Song of Love; 408 The Time of Dreams; 409 Frost; 410 Mad; 411 One by One; 412 Hill and Vale; 413 The White Horse; 414 The Mask; 415 Giants; 416 Advice; 417 The Spoiler; 418 Storms; 419 Property; 420 Sun and Crow; 421 Shooting-Stars; 422 A Dull Spirit; 423 The Dragonfly; 424 Light and Darkness; 425 The Evening Star; 426 Old or Young; 427 An Epitaph; 428 Sport; 429 Winter Fire; 430 To a Contemporary; 431 Peace and Goodwill

endpapers: cream; *edges*: uncut, top edge trimmed

binding: bright blue calico cloth, lettered in gilt; front cover: William H. Davies. (in facsimile of author's script); spine: W. H. DAVIES/ (fleuron)/ COLLECTED/ POEMS/ 1928/ at foot: JONATHAN CAPE; back cover: blind-blocked publisher's device

dust-jacket: cream, with an embossed surface, printed in green and black; front, in black within a green triple frame: THE/ COLLECTED POEMS/ of/ W. H. Davies/ 1928/ at foot: (green publisher's device)/ LONDON/ JONATHAN CAPE THIRTY BEDFORD SQUARE; spine: (triple green rule)/ The/ COLLECTED/ POEMS/ of/ W. H. Davies/ 1928 (in black)/ at foot: (green publisher's device)/ JONATHAN CAPE (in black)/ (triple green rule); back, in black: starts: *Other Books by W. H. Davies*/ ends: JONATHAN CAPE 30 BEDFORD SQUARE; front flap: starts: COLLECTED POEMS/ ends: *7s. 6d. net*; back flap: blank

date of publication: October 1928

print run: 1st printing: 2000 copies printed on 8 August 1928; 2nd printing: 2000 copies printed on 17 September 1928; bound by Nevett; *price*: 7s.6d.

copies seen: BL (shelf mark: 011604.g.67; accession date: 4 October 1928); SH; HDB (2 copies)

reviews: More Books of the Week, *The Spectator*, 27 October 1928, 141, 5235, 605–606; Four Poets of Varied Moods. Hardy's reply to his reviewers: the simple things that W. H. Davies loves: Siegfried Sassoon and Wilfrid Gibson, Edward Shanks, *John o'London's Weekly*, 27 October 1928, XX, 497, 103; *Life and Letters*, November 1928, 1, 6, 513; Poetry, Austin Clarke, *Nation and Athenaeum*,

10 November 1928, XLIV, 6, supplement 234; by E. Shanks, *Saturday Review*, 10 November 1928, 146, 610; The Poetry of W. H. Davies, Edward Thompson, *New Statesman*, 17 November 1928, XXII, 812, 194; by Thomas Moult, *Christian Science Monitor*, 28 November 1928, 10; Mr Davies's Poems, H. I'A Fausset, *Christmas Number of Bookman*, December 1928, LXXV, 447, 164–165; Grapes and Vines, Humbert Wolfe, *Country Life*, 15 December 1928, LXIV, 1665, 879; Poetry, E. G. Twitchett, *London Mercury*, February 1929, XIX, 112, 425–427; Mr Davies's Poems, *TLS*, 7 March 1929, 180

text changes from previous printings to A33:
The Lodging House Fire: 2nd stanza line 1: 'chimes' to 'times'
In a Lodging House: line 4: 'to me' to 'me to', line 24: 'me to' to 'to me', line 25: 'To make' to 'And made', line 65: 'they' to 'those'
The Hill-side Park: line 19: 'lips' to 'lip', line 24: 'Though' to 'As'
The Kingfisher: 1st stanza line 4: 'thy' to 'my'
A Dream: one stanza omitted: 'Into my mouth it goes with mine,/ I felt its soft warm waves;/ That fair Enchantress knew full well/ The way to make men slaves.'
The Child and the Mariner: line 1: 'Dear' to 'dear'
Rich Days: 2nd stanza last line: 'loveliest' to 'loneliest'
I am the Poet Davies, William: title from 'To the Woman who will read this Poem to her Husband'
The Moon and a Cloud: title from 'Wasting Time'
England: line 4: 'Their bleeding mouths being froze too hard to move' to 'With bleeding mouths that freeze too hard to move'
A Woman's History: 2nd stanza line 4: 'You come along' to 'You'll come along'
A for . . . to Z for . . .: titles to 'A is for . . .' to 'Z is for . . .'
In Spring-Time: title from 'In Spring-time'
An old House in London: title from 'An Old House in London'
Drinking Song: line 1: 'life' to 'Life'
The Posts: line 1: 'Year's' to 'year's'
The Bed-sitting-room: line 1: from 'scripture' to 'Scripture'
The Sluggard: 1st stanza line 1: 'Jar' to 'jar'
The Song of Life: I line 1: 'Sneeze' to 'sneeze'

notes: (a) p348 line 9: period missing
(b) the HDB copy is inscribed: 'My book, W. H. D./ The Ways of Time/ As butterflies are but winged flowers,/ Half sorry for their change, who fain,/ So still and long they lie on leaves,/ Would be thought flowers again -/ E'en so my thoughts, that should expand,/ And grow to higher themes above,/ Return like butterflies to lie/ On the old things I love./ W. H. Davies./ 1928'

A33a Second impression   Jonathan Cape 1929

print run: 2200 copies printed on 24 January; bound by Nevett

A33b First American edition   Jonathan Cape & Harrison Smith 1929

THE/ COLLECTED POEMS/ OF/ W. H. DAVIES/ 1928/ at foot: NEW YORK:/ JONATHAN CAPE & HARRISON SMITH/ LONDON: JONATHAN CAPE/ 1929

8vo; (A) in ten plus tipped-in frontispiece, B–I, K–U and X–CC in eights; 210 leaves: (i–vi) vii–xx (1–2) 3–385 (386) 387–399 (1)pp plus tipped-in frontispiece not included in the pagination; 18.8 × 12.6 cms; first page of gatherings B–CC signed D.C.P. on inner margin

as *A33* apart from: (iv) PRINTED IN GREAT BRITAIN BY/ BUTLER & TANNER LTD/ FROME; *binding*: bright blue calico grain cloth, lettered in gilt or silver; front cover: William H. Davies. (in facsimile of author's script); spine: W. H. DAVIES/ (fleuron)/ COLLECTED/ POEMS/ 1928/ at foot: JONATHAN CAPE/ HARRISON SMITH; back cover: blank; *edges*: trimmed; *dustjacket*: pale blue with an embossed surface, printed in black; front: COLLECTED/ POEMS/ OF/ W. H. DAVIES/ (decoration in a panel)/ JONATHAN CAPE AND HARRISON SMITH; spine: COLLECTED/ POEMS/ OF/ W. H. DAVIES/ (decoration)/ JONATHAN CAPE/ AND HARRISON SMITH; back: starts: Books by/ ends: HARRISON SMITH, *139 East 46th Street, New York, N.Y.*; front flap: starts: UNTIL this volume appears there/ ends: literature.; back flap: starts: BLUE JUNIATA/ ends: of America.

price: $3

copies seen: HRHRC (2 copies)

reviews: As I Like It, William Lyon Phelps, *Scribner's Magazine*, November 1929, LXXXVI, 50, 575; by Margaret Wallace, *New York Evening Post*, 13 July 1929, 7; by William Stanley Braithwaite, *Boston Evening Transcript*, 27 July 1929, 3; Simple Sincerity in Davies's Collected Poems, *New York Times (Book Review)*, 4 August 1929, 2; by F. A. Doggett, *New York Herald Tribune*, 18 August 1929, LX, 768, 25; *Booklist*, November 1929, 26, 62; by HK, *Springfield Republican*, 5 January 1930, 7

note: p56 line 20: period missing; p94 line 13: period missing

A34   FORTY-NINE POEMS   Medici Society 1928

Forty-Nine Poems/ by/ W. H. Davies/ (full-colour vignette of a centaur)/ *Selected and Illustrated by/ Jacynth Parsons/* at foot: *LONDON/ THE MEDICI SOCIETY/ MCMXXVIII*

4to; (A) in six, (B) in four, (C) in six, (D–F) in twos, (G) in six, (H) in four, (I) in two; 34 leaves: (i–iv) v–viii (1–2) 3–58 (2)pp; 21.9 × 14.3 cms variable

(i) half-title: *Forty-Nine Poems/ by/ W. H. Davies*; (ii) coloured frontispiece of a youth with a book beneath a tree, beside a stream, and a kingfisher captioned: "*The Kingfisher*"; (iii) title-page; (iv) at foot: *The Medici Society Ltd.,/ London, Liverpool, Bournemouth,/ Harrogate and Torquay/ Printed in England*; v–vi PREFACE BY W. H. DAVIES signed *August, 1928* W. H. DAVIES.; vii–viii CONTENTS (poem titles in italics); (1–2) blank; 3–58 text; (59–60) blank; text throughout in italics

contents: p3 Days too Short; p4 The Kingfisher; p5 Rich Days; p6 Winter Fire; p7 The White Cascade; p8 The Example; p9 My Love could Walk; p10 Jenny Wren; p11 Robin Redbreast; p12 The Temper of a Maid; p13 The Rain; p14 In May; p15 Autumn; p16 Raptures; p17 Easter; p18 Charms; p19 The One Singer; p20 The

Forty-Nine Poems

by

W. H. Davies

Selected and Illustrated by
Jacynth Parsons

LONDON
THE MEDICI SOCIETY
MCMXXVIII

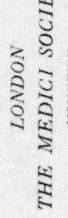

"The Kingfisher"

Hour of Magic; p21 Oh, Sweet Content; p22 Angry; p25 April's Boys and Girls; p26 The Ox; p28 Seeking Joy; p29 The Rainbow; p30 The Sluggard; p31 The Moon; p32 The Villain; p33 Young Beauty; p34 Love's Caution; p36 The Captive Lion; p37 The Mask; p38 The Happy Child; p39 Leisure; p40 A Blind Child; p42 Sweet Youth; p43 Advice; p44 The Owl; p45 The Cat; p46 In Days Gone; p48 A Great Time; p49 The Rat; p50 The Hermit; p51 Impudence; p52 Winter's Beauty; p53 In The Snow; p55 A Life's Love; p56 A Swallow that Flew into the Room; p57 A Winter's Night; p58 Rags and Bones

illustrations: full-page full-colour on pp(ii) and 24; full-colour integrated with text on title-page and pp3, 13, 29, 32, 37 and 48; two-tone integrated with text on pp5, 8, 9, 12, 15, 18, 19, 22, 39, 42, 46; full page black and white on pp35, 41 and 53; black and white integrated with text on pp6, 7, 10, 11, 14, 16, 17, 20, 21, 23, 26, 27, 28, 30, 31, 33, 36, 38, 43, 44, 45, 47, 49, 50, 51, 54, 55, 56, 57 and 58

endpapers: cream; *edges*: uncut, top edge gilt

binding: mushroom calico textured cloth, lettered in gilt; front cover: *Forty Nine Poems/ by/ W. H. Davies/ Illustrated by/ Jacynth Parsons*; spine: (double rule)/ *Forty/ Nine/ Poems/ W.H./ Davies/* at foot: MEDICI/SOCIETY/ (double rule); back cover: blank

dust-jacket: cream, printed in full-colour; front: *Forty-Nine Poems/ by/ W. H. Davies* (in black)/ (full-colour vignette identical to title-page)/ *Selected and Illustrated by/ Jacynth Parsons* (in black)/ *With preface by the Author* (in blue)/ at foot: LONDON/ THE MEDICI SOCIETY (in black); spine: *Forty/ Nine/ Poems/* (fleuron)/ *W. H./ Davies/ Selected/ &/ Illustrated/ by/Jacynth/ Parsons* (in black)/ at foot: *Medici/ Society* (in black); back, within a panel, in black: starts: *Also Illustrated by JACYNTH PARSONS/* ends: *7 GRAFTON STREET, LONDON, W.1*; front flap: starts: JACYNTH PARSONS'/ ends: *8/6 net*; back flap: starts: TWO/ ends: and exquisite prose.

date of publication: November 1928

print run: 3000 copies; *price*: 8s.6d.

copies seen: BL (shelf mark: 11643.l.28; accession date: 23 November 1928); HDB (2 copies); HRHRC; SH (2 copies)

reviews: The Promise of May, EB, *Nation and Athenaeum*, 12 January 1929, XLIV, 15, 528; The Bookman's Table, *Bookman*, January 1929, LXXV, 448, 255; Poetry, E. G. Twitchett, *London Mercury*, February 1929, XIX, 112, 425–427; Mr Davies's Poems, *TLS*, 7 March 1929, 180

notes: (a) WHD had known Jacynth Parsons since she was a child
(b) on p30 she depicts him lying on grass under a tree, smoking his pipe and reading, with a squirrel on his legs and a mug of beer by his side
(c) The Cat: line 1: 'that' misprinted 'this'
(d) second issue binding: mushroom calico grain cloth, lettered in red; front cover: blank; spine: (double rule)/ *Forty/ Nine/ Poems/ W. H./ Davies/* at foot: MEDICI/ SOCIETY/ (double rule); back cover: blank; top edge plain; *dust-jacket*: beige, printed in navy: front: *Forty Nine Poems/ by/ W. H. Davies/ Illustrated by/ Jacynth Parsons*; spine: (double rule)/ *Forty/ Nine/Poems/ W. H./ Davies/* at foot: MEDICI/ SOCIETY/ (double rule); back and both flaps: blank
(e) the HDB copies are inscribed: 'My book,/ W. H. Davies./ 1928.' and 'To "Dinah" (Helen)/ from/ "Bunny" (W. H. Davies)/ 1928.'

A34a   Special edition   Medici Society 1928

as *A34* apart from: 36 leaves; (1–3) blank; (4) limitation: *Of this special edition* 110 *copies have/ been printed of which* 100 *are for sale./ This is number* .... signed Jacynth Parsons./ W. H. Davies.; white ribbon marker; *paper*: Japanese vellum; *binding*: white buckram, lettered in gilt; *edges*: uncut; top edge gilt; *dust-jacket*: front flap, at foot: *Price/ 25/- net*

print run: 110 copies; *price*: 25s.

copies seen: BL (shelf mark: Cup 407.g.49; accession date: 28 February 1978) (no 79); HDB (2 copies: nos 104 and 105); HRHRC (no 34); JG (no 52); RV (no 16)

note: the HDB copies are inscribed 'The White Cascade/ What happy mortal sees that mountain now,/ The white cascade that's shining on its brow;/ The white cascade that's both a bird and star,/ That has a ten mile voice and shines as far?/ Though I may never leave this land again,/ Yet every spring my mind must cross the main/ To hear and see that water bird and star/ That on the mountain sings and shines so far./ W. H. Davies.' (no 105) and 'The Rain/ I hear leaves drinking Rain;/ I hear rich leaves on top/ Giving the poor beneath/ Drop after drop;/ 'Tis a sweet noise to hear/ These green leaves drinking near./ And when the Sun comes out,/ After this Rain shall stop,/ A wondrous Light will fill/ Each dark, round drop;/ I hope the Sun shines bright;/ 'Twill be a lovely sight./ W. H. Davies.' (no 104) beneath the limitation: 'To Dinah, (in WHD's hand)/ Jacynth Parsons./ W. H. Davies.'

A34b   First American edition   Jonathan Cape & Harrison Smith 1929

Forty-Nine Poems/ by/ W. H. Davies/ (vignette as A34)/ New York/ Jonathan Cape and Harrison Smith

8vo; (A–C) in eight, (D) in ten; 34 leaves: (1–2) (i–iv) v–viii 1–56 (2)pp; 22.0 × 14.0 cms

as *A34* apart from: (1) half-title: *Forty-Nine Poems*; (2) *Jonathan Cape and Harrison Smith, Incorporated,/ 139 East 46th Street, New York, N.Y. and 77 Wellington/ Street West, Toronto, Canada; Jonathan Cape, Ltd.,/ 30 Bedford Square, London, W.C.1, England*; (i) blank; (ii) frontispiece; (iii) title-page; (iv) at foot: Printed and Bound in the U.S.A./ By the Plimpton Press at Norwood, Mass.; v–vi *PREFACE BY W. H. DAVIES*; vii–viii *CONTENTS*; 1–56 text; (57–58) blank; *binding*: grass-green calico grain cloth, lettered in gilt; front cover: *Forty-Nine Poems/ by/ W. H. Davies/ Illustrated by/ Jacynth Parsons/ New York/ Jonathan Cape & Harrison Smith*; spine, vertically downwards: FORTY-NINE POEMS – Davies; back cover: blank; *edges*: trimmed; *dust-jacket*: front, at foot: *New York/ Jonathan Cape and Harrison Smith*; spine, vertically downwards: FORTY-NINE POEMS – Davies; back: starts: FOR THE POETRY LOVER/ ends: 139 EAST 46TH STREET NEW YORK, N.Y.; front flap: starts: *By/* ends: beauty." – *Country Life.*; back flap: starts: *By /* ends: $3.00; stamped on front flap: price: $2.50

price: $2.50

copies seen: HRHRC; HDB

review: Ten New Books of Poetry, Percy Hutchison, *New York Times (Book Review)*, 17 August 1930, 16

note: the HDB copy is inscribed: 'To "Dinah" (Helen)/ from/ "Bunny" (W. H. Davies)/ 1929.'

A35 SELECTED POEMS   Gregynog Press 1928

SELECTED POEMS/ of W. H. DAVIES/ ARRANGED BY EDWARD GARNETT/ WITH A FOREWORD BY/ THE AUTHOR/ (publisher's device in black and mustard)/ THE GREGYNOG PRESS/ MCMXXVIII

4to; * in four, (a)–i and k–m in fours, (n) in two, (o) in four (the endpapers and pastedowns are part of the first and final gatherings); 54 leaves omitting endpapers: (1–4) (i–iv) v–vii (viii) 1–91 (5)pp; 23.0 × 15.5 cms variable

omitting endpapers: (1–2) blank; (3) half-title: SELECTED POEMS *of* W. H. DAVIES; (4) blank; (i) blank; (ii) portrait frontispiece protected by a tissue guard and captioned: Engraved by R. A. Maynard from the portrait by Augustus E. John, A.R.A.; (iii) title-page; (iv) blank; v FOREWORD signed *W. H. Davies*; vi–vii THE CONTENTS (poem titles in italics within ruled orange panel); vii below text: *The Selection has been made by the permission/ of Messrs. Jonathan Cape Ltd.,/ the publishers of Mr. W. H. Davies' Works*; (viii) blank; 1–91 text; (92) limitation: PRINTED BY ROBERT ASHWIN MAYNARD AT/ THE GREGYNOG PRESS, NEAR NEWTOWN, IN MONTGOMERYSHIRE, AND COMPLETED ON THE/ TWENTY-FIFTH DAY OF OCTOBER, MCMXXVIII./ ASSISTANTS: HORACE WALTER BRAY, IDRIS/ VAUGHAN JONES (COMPOSITOR), & HERBERT/ JOHN HODGSON (PRESSMAN). THE EDITION IS/ LIMITED TO THREE HUNDRED & TEN COPIES./ No. ; (93–96) blank; throughout the text the poems are within orange ruled panel

contents: p1 Days that have been; p2 The Bed-Sitting Room; p3 The Sleepers; p4 To a Rich Lady; p5 Sweet Stay-at-Home; p6 A Maiden and Her Hair; p7 The Inquest; p8 The Kingfisher; p9 Money; p10 The Call of the Sea; p12 The Lodging House Fire; p15 Body and Spirit; p16 Joy; p17 Night Wanderers; p18 The Bird of Paradise; p19 Christmas; p21 Killed in Action (Edward Thomas); p22 A Child's Pet; p23 The Weeping Child; p24 Facts; p25 Strong Moments; p26 The Long Sleep; p27 The Collier's Wife; p28 Come, Let Me Close; p29 Songs of Joy; p30 The Blind Boxer; p31 This World; p32 Nell Barnes; p33 Joy and Pleasure; p34 In the End; p35 Earth Love; p36 The Sea; p38 The Hermit; p39 The Child and the Mariner; p44 Let Me Confess; p45 Robin Redbreast; p46 My Old Acquaintance; p47 Oh, Sweet Content; p48 Cant; p49 Thunderstorms; p50 The Beautiful; p51 Leisure; p52 In the Snow; p53 The Truth; p54 The Elements; p55 A Winter's Night; p56 Two Women; p57 Infancy; p58 The Rain; p59 Early Morn; p60 Farewell to Poesy; p61 Dreams of the Sea; p62 Strength; p63 School's Out; p64 Birds; p65 Ale; p66 Autumn; p67 To Sparrows Fighting; p68 City and Country; p69 The Villain; p70 On the Death of a Little Child; p71 The Happy Child; p72 Dead Born; p73 Children at Play; p74 Child Lovers; p75 A Blind Child; p76 Fairies, Take Care; p77 The Battle; p78 Her Merriment; p79 Wild Oats; p80 Laughing Rose; p81 Pastures; p82 Joy Supreme; p83 Young Beauty; p84 The Laughers; p85 Impudence; p86 To a Flirt; p87 Kitty and I; p88 Angry; p89 Sound and Grace; p90 Jealousy; p91 The Lonely Dreamer

paper: Japanese vellum

endpapers: vellum and part of the first and final gatherings; *edges*: uncut, top edge trimmed

binding: Cockerell marbled paper-covered boards in black and mustard, black buckram spine and fore edges; front cover: blank; spine, lettered in gilt, vertically upwards: <u>SELECTED POEMS/</u> *By* W. H. DAVIES; back cover: blank; *dust-jacket*: not seen

date of publication: 9 November 1928

print run: 285 copies; *price*: 31s.6d.

copies seen: NL (no 215); HDB (nos 87, 90, 91 and 229); SH (no 292)

reviews: Finely Printed Books, *TLS*, 22 November 1928, 882; Two Gregynog Books, B. H. Newdigate, *London Mercury*, February 1929, XIX, 112, 415–417; Mr Davies's Poems, *TLS*, 7 March 1929, 180

notes: (a) the HDB copies are inscribed: 'My book,/ W. H. Davies./ 1928' (no 90) and '"To Dinah" (Helen)/ from/ "Bunny" (W. H. Davies)./ 1928.' (no 87)
(b) advertised (with 'Penillion Omar Kayam' and 'The Misfortunes of Elphin') in a prospectus on hand-made paper (*A History of the Gregynog Press* by Dorothy A. Harrop *(F359)*)

A35a   Special edition   Gregynog Press 1928

as *A35* apart from: 22.0 × 15.0 cms; * in four (one a stub), (a)–i and k–m in fours, n in two, (o) in four (one a stub); 52 leaves plus two stubs; *binding*: sage green full morocco, polished, decorated and lettered in gilt, bevelled boards; front cover: (three large foliate devices enclosed in two bands of seven lines which continue across the spine); spine: five raised bands, the first and fifth of which are outlined in blind, the second and fourth outlined by bands of gilt lines, lettered: POEMS/ OF/ W. H./ DAVIES; back cover: as front cover; inner dentelles decorated with gilt lines continuing from the covers, signed in gilt on back dentelle: R. ASHWIN MAYNARD   GREGYNOG PRESS BINDERY   GEORGE FISHER; stitched with gold silk; hand sewn headbands

print run: 25 copies; *price*: £12 16s.

copies seen: BL (shelf mark: C 99.h.26; accession date: 14 June 1930) (no 12); HDB (no 11)

note: the HDB copy is inscribed: 'My book,/ W. H. Davies.'

A36 **AMBITION**   Jonathan Cape 1929

within a decorative double rule running vertically down each side of the page: AMBITION/ and Other Poems/ (vignette of a bird flying over flowers)/ W. H. DAVIES/ LONDON: JONATHAN CAPE

8vo; (A)–B in eights; 16 leaves: (1–4) 5 (6) 7–32pp; 19.0 × 13.0 cms variable

POEMS
OF
W.H.
DAVIES

A35a

(1) half-title: AMBITION/ and Other Poems; (2) starts: BY THE SAME AUTHOR/ ends: *Etc.*; (3) title-page; (4) FIRST PUBLISHED MCMXXIX/ at foot: PRINTED IN GREAT BRITAIN BY/ BUTLER & TANNER LTD/ FROME; 5 Contents; (6) blank; 7–32 text; 32 below text: THE END

contents: p7 Friends Unborn; p8 The Richest Stones. This Bantam Star; p9 If Love Survives; p10 Hand or Mouth; p11 Ambition; p12 For Sale; p13 Birthdays; p14 Uncertainty; p15 Charity; p16 A Dream of Winter; p17 A Child's Fancy; p18 Wild Blossoms; p19 A Silver Wonder. Peace and Rest; p20 Moss and Feather; p21 Pot and Kettle; p22 Eyes and Ears; p23 The Blest; p24 The Idiot; p25 Letters; p26 Day or Night; p27 Hunting Joy; p28 A Young Thrush; p29 Born of Tears; p30 Heaven and Earth; p31 In Winter; p32 My Life's Example

paper: watermarked: – BASINGWERK PARCHMENT –

endpapers: cream; *edges*: deckle fore edge, top edge trimmed

binding: olive green calico cloth embossed in orange; front cover: blank; spine, vertically downwards, on a white paper label 7.4 cms deep, in black: AMBITION (fleuron) W. H. DAVIES; back cover: blank

dust-jacket: cream with an embossed surface printed in black; front, within a decorative double rule running vertically down each side: AMBITION/ and other poems/ (vignette of a tree, fields and birds)/ by/ W. H. DAVIES/ author of/ The Autobiography of a Super-Tramp/ etc; spine, vertically downwards: W. H. DAVIES (fleuron) AMBITION; back: starts: *Books by W. H. Davies*/ ends: *Jonathan Cape Thirty Bedford Square London*; front flap: starts: AMBITION/ ends: 3*s*.6*d. net*; back flap: blank

date of publication: 28 October 1929

print run: 2000 copies printed on 30 August 1929; bound by Nevett; *price*: 3s.6d.

copies seen: BL (shelf mark: 011644.f.89; accession date: 23 October 1929); SH (2 copies); HRHRC; HDB

reviews: by William Plomer, *Nation and Athenaeum*, 7 December 1929, supplement 380; Mr Chesterton and Mr Davies, *TLS*, 19 December 1929, 1079; Ambition, Frank Kendon, *Bookman*, January 1930, LXXVII, 460, 260–261; Some Poetry and Verse, V. H. Friedlander, *Country Life*, 8 February 1930, LXVII, 1725, 193; Poetry, E. G. Twitchett, *London Mercury*, June 1930, XXII, 122, 176–178

mss: in WHD's hand addressed Shenstone, Nailsworth, Glos. and dated 1929 (HDB)

previous printings:
'Born of Tears', *New Statesman*, 14 January 1928, XXX, 768, 434
'The Blest', 'Friends Unborn' and 'A Young Thrush', *The Spectator*, 12 January 1929, 5246, 52, 25 May 1929, 5265, 825 and 6 July 1929, 5271, 13 respectively
'Moss and Feather', *Ariel Poem* (A32)
'Charity' and 'Hunting Joy', *Now & Then*, Autumn 1929, 33, 39
'A Dream of Winter' and 'Heaven and Earth', *Country Life*, 24 December 1927, LXII, 1614, 942 and 14 January 1928, LXIII, 1617, 35 respectively
'If Love Survives' and 'Hand or Mouth', *New Republic*, 9 January 1929, LVII, 736, 215 and 23 January 1929, LVII, 738, 270 respectively
'Peace and Rest', *Time and Tide*, 31 May 1929, 10, 22, 659

text changes from first printings to A36:
Moss and Feather: 3rd stanza last line: 'moon' to 'Moon'
If Love Survives: 1st stanza last line: 'last.' to 'last?'

notes: (a) 'In Winter' published separately as a Christmas card: an A3 sheet folded
into four and uncut, printed in black; (i) front cover: (vignette of a robin perched);
(ii–iii) blank; (iv) text: signed *W. H. Davies*; (v) full-page black and white
illustration of a thrush captioned: *Wood-engravings by Eric Daglish*; (vi–vii) blank;
(viii) THE CHRISTMAS CARDS IN THIS SERIES/ are designed by artists of today
and the verses are/ composed by poets of our time. They were/ printed by the Favil
Press, 152 Church Street,/ Kensington, London, W.8 and published, in/ collabor-
ation with the printers, by/ The Poetry Bookshop, 38 Great/ Russell St., London,
W.C.1/ This card is known as/ NUMBER SIX/ in the series./ (short double rule)/
(fleuron); *edges*: deckle lower edge, others trimmed; *paper*: watermarked: –
BASINGWERK PARCHMENT –
(b) the HDB copy is inscribed: 'To Dinah (Helen)/ with love from/ Bunny (W. H.
Davies) Oct 28th 1929.'
(c) 'For Sale' was used by the BBC in a recorded anthology programme of poems
produced by the London Transcription Service in 1944

A36a Special edition   Jonathan Cape 1929

as *A36* apart from: (2) limitation: (fleuron) Of this special author's/ edition of
Ambition and/ Other Poems have been/ issued 210 copies only,/ each copy
numbered and/ signed by the author/ (fleuron) Copy number   signed W. H.
Davies.; *paper*: watermarked: Van Zonda; chain lines 4.0 cms apart and vertical;
binding: quarter green leather over gold and brown mottled paper-covered boards;
front cover: blank; spine, lettered in gilt, vertically downwards: AMBITION
(decorative rule) W. H. DAVIES; back cover: blank; *edges*: deckle fore edge, top edge
gilt; *dust-jacket*: front flap, at foot: *Special Edition, signed by the author,/ limited to
200 copies for sale./ 9s. net*

print run: 140 copies printed on 30 August 1929; bound by Nevett; *price*: 9s.

copies seen: HRHRC (no 163); SH (no 52)

A37 IN WINTER   privately printed 1931

IN WINTER. W. H. DAVIES/ (vignette of a man looking across country-
side)/ PRIVATELY PRINTED IN LONDON/ 1931

4to; one gathering of six leaves including pastedowns and with endpapers tipped-in;
23.1 × 15.0 cms; stitched

(1) title-page; (2) blank; (3) limitation: Of this poem 290 numbered copies, printed
on/ Basingwerk Parchment, have been issued, all signed/ by the author, 250 copies
for sale only. There is/ also an edition of 15 copies, lettered A-O, printed/ on old style
hand-made paper, 10 copies for sale only/ Copy   signed W. H. Davies.; (4) blank;
(5) text; (6) blank; (7) Here ends In Winter, a poem by W. H. Davies,/ the fourth and
last season celebrated in/ a privately printed edition for/ Terence Fytton Armstrong/

18 Dean Street/ London/ W.1; (8) Made and printed in Great Britain by Charles Mitchell Limited

illustrations: black and white decorations on title-page and in text

paper: watermarked: – BASINGWERK PARCHMENT –

endpapers: cream; *edges*: trimmed

binding: mottled orange paper-covered boards, printed in black; front cover, within a double ruled panel: IN WINTER/ W. H. DAVIES; spine and back cover: blank; *dust-jacket*: plain glacene

date of publication: December 1931

print run: 290 copies; *price*: 6s.

copies seen: HRHRC (2 copies: nos 52 and 207); HDB (out of series 'extra'); RUL, Finzi (no 58); SH (no 247)

notes: (a) a completely different poem to that published in *Ambition and Other Poems (A36)* under the same title
(b) one copy at HRHRC is stapled in paper wrappers and has the following limitation: Of this poem 290 numbered copies, printed on old style/ hand-made paper, have been issued, all signed by the/ author, 250 copies for sale only. There is also an/ edition of 15 copies, lettered A–O, 10 copies for sale only/ Copy   ; under the limitation: M. P. S./ an/ Advance/ proof Copy from/ the publishers/ Fytton [all in Fytton's hand apart from Copy which is printed] (M P Shiel 1865–1947)
(c) reprinted in *Poems 1930–1931 (A38)* under the title 'The World Dictates'
(d) nos 52 and 58 do not have endpapers

A37a   De luxe edition   privately printed 1931

as *A37* apart from: 23.5 × 14.7 cms; (1) title-page has a hand-coloured outlined frontispiece; *paper*: hand-made; chain lines 2.7 cms apart and horizontal; *endpapers*: front tipped-in, no rear endpaper; *binding*: front cover printed in blue within a double ruled panel, on a white paper label 6.1 × 9.2 cms: IN WINTER/ W. H. DAVIES; *edges*: deckle fore and lower edges

price: 21s.

copies seen: BL (shelf mark: 11642.eee.56; accession date: 14 March 1932); HRHRC

note: the HRHRC copy (letter M) is signed by WHD and Edward Carrick (the illustrator); the BL copy is also signed by both WHD and Edward Carrick, is unlettered, not outlined in colour and has no endpapers tipped-in

A38 POEMS 1930–1931   Jonathan Cape 1932

Poems 1930–31/ *by*/ W. H. DAVIES/ (vignette of three pigs)/ LONDON: JONATHAN CAPE

8vo; (A)–C in eights; 24 leaves: (1–4) 5–6 (7–8) 9–48pp; 19.0 × 12.5 cms variable

(1) half-title: Poems 1930–31; (2) starts: BY THE SAME AUTHOR/ ends: *Etc.*; (3) title-page; (4) starts: FIRST PUBLISHED 1932/ ends: BOUND BY A. W. BAIN & CO., LTD; 5–6 Contents; (7) fly-title: Poems 1930–31/ (vignette of a floral bouquet); (8) full-page illustration of a young man kneeling under a tree playing a wind instrument; 9–48 text

contents: p9 When and Where; p10 Silver Hours; p11 Here am I; p12 Flowers; p13 Mangers; p14 Ships and Stars; p15 Starlings; p16 Poison; p17 A Prayer; p18 Old Friends; p19 Wonderful Places; p20 What Light?; p21 Old Autumn; p22 Trails; p23 The Poor; p24 No Careless Mind; p25 A Fleeting Wonder; p26 Kiss and Blow; p27 The Visitor; p28 The Chase; p29 Age and Youth; p30 The Prayer of Daft Harry; p31 A Sweeter Life; p32 Epitaph on John Keats; p33 Epitaph on a Child; p34 Come, Melancholy; p35 Jewels; p36 The Legacy; p37 Clocks; p38 A Child's Mint; p39 The World Dictates; p40 The Enemy; p41 The Lady of Light; p42 Playmates; p43 Sick Minds; p44 Bird and Cloud; p45 Ourselves; p46 The Mourner; p47 Loyalty; p48 No Place or Time

illustrations: full-page: p(8); decorations: pp(3), (7), 10, 11, 13, 14, 15, 18, 23, 24, 26, 29, 32, 33, 35, 37, 39, 41, 42, 45 and 47

paper: watermarked: – BASINGWERK PARCHMENT –

endpapers: cream; *edges*: deckle fore edge, top edge trimmed

binding: white cloth with a blue design of birds and scarecrows, blue cloth spine; front cover: blank; spine, on a white paper label 7.2 cms deep, vertically downwards in black: POEMS 1930–31 (fleuron) W. H. DAVIES; back cover: blank

dust-jacket: cream, with an embossed surface, printed in green and black; front, in black: W. H. DAVIES/ Poems/ (vignette of a tree in green)/ 1930=1931/ With decorations by Elizabeth Montgomery; spine: P/O/E/M/S/ 1930/ to/ 1931/ W./ H./ D/A/V/I/E/S/ at foot: *Jonathan*/ CAPE; back: blank; front flap: starts: POEMS 1930=1931/ ends: 3s. 6d. *net*; back flap: blank

date of publication: 10 October 1932

print run: 1500 copies printed on 10 August 1932 by Alden Press; *price*: 3s.6d.

copies seen: BL (shelf mark: 011644.eee.158; accession date: 29 September 1932); HDB; SH

reviews: Poetry of Today, Gerald Bullett, *New Statesman and Nation*, 22 October 1932, IV, 87 (new series), 486; Poetry, *TLS*, 27 October 1932, 794; Poetry, Alan Pryce-Jones, *London Mercury*, November 1932, XXVII, 157, 75–77; by Austin Clarke, *Life and Letters*, December 1932, VIII, 47, 488; Mr Davies' New Lyrics, Edmund Blunden, *The Spectator*, 9 December 1932, 149, 840

previous printings:
'Ships and Stars', *New Statesman*, 24 August 1929, XXXIII, 852, 600
'Old Autumn', *The Spectator*, 9 November 1929, 143, 5289, 662
'Clocks', *The Listener*, 4 March 1931, V, 112, 377
'Come Melancholy' and 'Age and Youth', 'No Place or Time' and 'What Light?', *New Statesman and Nation*, 16 January 1932, III, 47, 65, 2 April 1932, III, 58, 419 and 29 October 1932, IV, 88, 513 respectively
'No Careless Mind', 'Wonderful Places' and 'The Lady of Light', *Argosy*, July 1931, X, 62, 129, September 1931, X, 64, viii and November 1931, X, 66, viii (illustrated by Arthur Wragg) respectively

'Mangers', *The Observer* (not seen)
'The World Dictates' as *In Winter* (*A37*)

text change from first printing to A38:
Wonderful Places: line 4 up: 'off his' to 'off a'

mss: in WHD's hand addressed Nailsworth; undated; clipped into brown paper wrappers (HDB)

notes: (a) BL copy: spine label printed upwards
(b) the HDB copy is inscribed: 'To Dinah (Helen Davies)/ from/ Bunny (W. H. Davies.)/ 1932.'
(c) 1000 copies of a 2nd impression were printed which I have been unable to trace

A38a   Special edition   Jonathan Cape 1932

as *A38* apart from: (1) limitation: (fleuron) This Signed Edition is limited/ to One Hundred and Fifty/ Copies for Sale/ (fleuron) This is Number   signed W. H. Davies.; (4) starts: FIRST PUBLISHED 1932/ ends: BOUND BY A. W. BAIN & CO., LTD; *paper*: chain lines 2.7 cms apart and horizontal; *binding*: mid-blue calico grain cloth, blue vellum spine, lettered in gilt; front cover: blank; spine: POEMS/ 1930–31/ (fleuron)/W. H./ DAVIES; *edges*: deckle fore edge; uncut; top edge gilt; *dust-jacket*: plain glacene

date of publication: 10 October 1932; *print run*: 150 copies printed by Alden Press

copies seen: HRHRC (nos 26 and 27)

A38b   First American edition   Jonathan Cape & Harrison Smith 1932

price: $1.50

reviews: by V. Knowles, *Bookman*, March 1933, LXXXIII, 498, 514; *Booklist*, May 1933, 29, 262

A39 **MY BIRDS**   Jonathan Cape 1933

MY BIRDS/ W. H. DAVIES/ (vignette of a bird feeding)/ *LONDON*/ JONATHAN CAPE 30 BEDFORD SQUARE

8vo; (A)–H in eights; 64 leaves: (1–8) 9 (10–12) 13–127 (1)pp; 19.0 × 12.5 cms variable

(1–2) blank; (3) half-title: MY BIRDS by W. H. DAVIES; (4) starts: OTHER BOOKS BY/ ends: *ETC*.; (5) blank; (6) frontispiece of four birds feeding; (7) title-page; (8) starts: FIRST PUBLISHED 1933/ ends: BOUND BY A. W. BAIN AND CO. LTD.; 9 CONTENTS; (10) blank; (11) fly-title: MY BIRDS; (12) (vignette of a bird on a branch); 13–(128) text *contents*: I p13 The Garden; II p23 Birds of the Past; III p33 Courting; IV p42 Bird-Nesting; V p53 Birds in Trouble; VI p62 Feeding the Birds; VII p71 Saucy Sparrows; VIII p80 The Robin; IX p91 A Summer's Day; X p100 Worms and Crumbs; XI p113 This Changing Life; XII p121 At Night

contains: p13 Dreamers; p23 Wild Creatures; p31 Aye; p33 Magpies; p37 'One Crow – sorrow'; p42 A Dog's Grave; p50 We are but Mortal, and We have our Sting. Dogs; p53 On finding a Dead Bird under My Window; p62 Crumbs and Guineas; p69 Voices of Scorn; p71 One Poet visits Another; p78 My Rockery; p80 To Play Alone; p91 Flying Blossoms; p98 A Bright Day; p100 Breast to Breast; p113 The Cuckoo; p121 Owls; p(128) Old and Crazy

paper: watermarked: – BASINGWERK PARCHMENT –

endpapers: cream; *edges*: deckle fore edge, top edge trimmed

binding: grass green calico grain cloth, blocked in yellow; front cover: blank; spine: vertically upwards: MY BIRDS // W. H. DAVIES; back cover: publisher's device

dust-jacket: cream with an embossed surface printed in red and black; front: (triple red rule)/ MY BIRDS (in black)/ (multiple red rule)/(vignette of a bird feeding)/ by/ (triple red rule)/ W. H. DAVIES (in black)/ (multiple red rule)/; spine: (multiple red rule)/ MY/ BIRDS/ by/ W. H./ DAVIES/ DECORATED/ by/ HILDA M./ QUICK (in black)/(multiple red rule)/ (publisher's device in black)/JONATHAN/ CAPE/ (multiple red rule); back: blank; front flap: starts: MY BIRDS/ ends: HILDA M. QUICK; back flap: blank

date of publication: 20 March 1933

print run: 1500 copies printed on 6 February 1933 by Gray; *price*: 3s.6d.

copies seen: BL: (shelf mark: 7286.aa.26; accession date: 7 March 1933); HDB; CH; HRHRC (3 copies); RUL, Finzi

reviews: Natural History, *TLS*, 20 April 1933, 279; "All a Matter of Love", H. E. Bates, *New Statesman and Nation*, 6 May 1933, V, 115, 576; by Rev T. W. Griffiths, *Monmouthshire Review*, July 1933, I, 3, 310

mss: originally titled My Garden of Birds; in WHD's hand on lined paper addressed The Croft, Nailsworth, Glos and undated; 50pp of microscopic script which can only be read with the aid of a magnifying glass and is frequently illegible (probably the reason for so many changes to first printing); pasted on to another manuscript (possibly an early draft of *Young Emma*); clipped into brown paper wrappers (HDB)

WHD's manuscript corrections:
1 Dreamers: line 7: 'And even I would meet my' to 'I too have my ambitious'; page 13 line 5: 'for writing it is' to 'is'; p14 line 7: 'too' to 'even'; p15 line 14: 'bird half [illegible]' to 'bird huddled under the hedge. In fact my first thought was that it was a stone.'; p16 line 11: 'recognised' to 'remembered', line 2 up: 'poet or a pork butcher' to 'poet, a pork-butcher, or both'; p18 line 4: 'cover' to 'mass'; p19 line 9: 'small Teddy Bear, where he sat' to 'Porcelain Man, where he stood', line 8 up: 'Teddy Bear' to 'Porcelain Man'; p20 line 5: 'impressed me' to 'has had a very strong impression on my mind', last line: 'the day' to 'my journey'; p21 line 11: 'brush the weeds with' to 'heave the weeds on'
2 p24 line 8 up: 'But' to 'So'; p24 lines 4 and 2 up: 'bitch' to 'devil'; p25 line 11: 'bird' to 'parrot'; p28 line 9: 'but' to 'as'; p29 line 2: 'strange language' to 'language', line 9 up: 'man' to 'lover'

4 p43 line 11: 'and I' to 'until'; p43 line 4 up: 'my' to 'this'; p44 line 6 up: 'considering' to 'thinking of'; p48 line 4 up: 'old birds' to 'parents'; p50 line 9: 'having trodden on a wasp, was stung in the foot' to 'was stung'; p52 line 3 up: 'was the gift of a child and' to 'was'

5 p58 line 14: 'now almost' to 'had miraculously '; p60 line 10 up: 'of my chimney top' to 'of a precipice?'

6 p62 line 2 up: 'always' to 'usually'; p63 line 2: 'driven' to 'forced'; p64 line 4: 'the first day' to 'a few hours'

7 p74 line 11: 'was certainly the case' to 'it certainly did'; p76 line 8: 'solution' to 'explanation'; p77 line 5 up: 'heap of rubbish' to 'heap'; p78 line 12: 'a lifelong joy' to 'the joy of a lifetime'

8 p82 line 4: 'by threatening' to 'to intimidate'; p83 line 9: 'to use them – it only means' to 'in offence – but that he is able'; p85 line 3: 'shovel' to 'trowel'

9 p95 line 2 up: 'Unfortunately for the Thrush, and luckily for the worm' to 'Unfortunately for the Thrush'

10 p102 line 12: 'of the same strange taste' to 'called William Blake'

text changes from manuscript to A39 (references are to *A39* not mss):
1 p15 line 14: 'In fact my first thought was that it was' to 'as motionless as'; p19 line 4: 'squirt' to 'throw', line 7: 'Yet dreams are worth having, even for their own sake, however remote they are from being fulfilled' omitted; p20 line 5: 'had a very' to 'made a', line 2 up: 'millions I had met' to 'thousands I had seen'

2 p24 line 9: 'with' to 'language with', line 11: 'bad language' to 'vile words', last line: 'amazed and astonished' to 'amazed'; p26 line 7: 'at once' to 'immediately', line 13: 'Polly' to 'Polly, Polly', last line: 'had died' to 'died'; p28 line 1: 'hour of its' to 'moments of her', line 11: 'afford' to 'well afford'; p29 line 6 up: 'from a bird' to 'so clearly from the throat of a bird', line 2 up: 'man when his words were meant for the woman' to 'woman when his words were meant for the man'; p30 line 3 up: 'looks themselves' to 'looks, which were quite enough'; p31 line 13: 'this' to 'this experience', line 16: 'I am giving this poem the title of 'Aye', according to the refrain' omitted; p32 line 8: 'I have still another strange bird belonging to the past, but as it has been mentioned elsewhere, I will [illegible] no more.' omitted

3 p34 line 9: 'black Spanish' to 'Spanish, black', line 8 up: 'secretly' to 'in secret'; p36 line 4: 'You are not going to laugh at me?' omitted; p37 line 1: 'standing' to 'perching'; p38 line 4: 'black Crow' to 'Crow', line 9 up: 'good' to 'good and faultless', line 2 up: 'from the above verse' to 'poem at the beginning of this chapter'; p39 line 13: 'lady friend' to 'lady near', last line: 'But' to 'However'; p40 line 7: 'carriage' to 'coach', line 8 up: 'her' to 'the', last line: 'any woman' to 'anyone'; p41 line 7: 'house' to 'house in winter', line 4 up: 'See' to 'Let', last line: 'looks for more' to 'makes up his mind to come again'

4 p44 line 11 up: 'grumble' to 'grumble much', line 5 up: 'But I am no philosopher, as my critics, who know nothing, have told me often.' omitted, line 3 up: 'Betty's second nest was in' to 'which was in'; p45 line 9 up: 'certain pleasure' to 'pleasure occasionally'; p46 line 1: 'closer' to 'close', line 13: 'apple and' to 'apple, as fast as it came to earth, and', line 7 up: 'orchard' to 'garden'; p47 line 13: 'However' to 'But'; p48 line 6 up: 'tits' to 'Blue Tits'; p49 line 2: 'young' to 'young ones', line 11: 'big' to 'bigger'; p50 line 13: 'damn the wasp' to 'not a wasp', line 10 up: 'mss' to 'work'; p51 line 2 up: 'But Pharoah' to 'Pharoah'; pp51/52, last/first lines: 'and most glossy black skin in the world' to 'the most glossy black skin in the whole world'; p52 line 8: 'its pretty little' to 'its own innocent little face!'

5 p53 line 6 up: 'with no' to 'without'; p55 line 2: 'or my' to 'or against my'; p56 line 4 up: 'furiously' to 'loudly'; p57 line 3: 'and my firm belief is' to 'It is now my firm belief'; p61 line 5: 'distant' to 'their story to distant'

6 p64 line 5: 'almost as' to 'twice as'; p66/67 line 2 up/first line: 'stood apart on the different trees as though to guard it' to 'divided themselves among the different trees, as though to guard the whole place'; p67 line 6 up: 'secures it' to 'takes possession'; p68 line 2 up: 'Rooks' to 'birds'; p69 line 9: 'ball, or bread' to 'ball of bread'; p69 line 6 up: 'Here's a poem called 'Voices of Scorn'' omitted

7 p72 line 5: 'we' to 'If we', line 6: 'let us remind' to 'shall we not tell'; p72 line 9 up: 'speaking metaphorically' to 'metaphorically speaking'; p73 line 4 up: 'perhaps both, and no one knows which' to 'and no one knew which'; p74 line 4: 'owing to' to 'through', line 14: 'appeared' to 'looked'; p76 line 3: 'the body' to 'it'; p77 line 12 up: 'admire' to 'admit', line 3 up: 'about and dig' to 'and dig'; p78 line 6 up: 'poem' to 'little poem'

8 p80 line 12 up: 'spent and wasted' to 'all spent'; p81 line 3: 'alone' to 'all alone', line 14: 'minutes' to 'seconds', line 7 up: 'sat on a' to 'been sitting on a', line 5 up: 'would fly down for their meal' to 'were allowed to come down for their share'; p82 line 5 up: 'Starlings and quarrelsome Sparrows' to 'Sparrows and quarrelsome Starlings'; p83 line 9 up: 'crumb' to 'crumb for himself'; p84 line 3: 'same irritable spirit as a Robin' to 'Robin's irritable spirit', line 4: 'hide' to 'would rather hide'; p87 line 8: 'Xmas' to 'Christmas'; p89 line 6: 'favourite Robin who was asleep' to 'Robin, my favourite, who was always', line 10: 'black beetle' to 'beetle', line 10 up: 'not of course one thought of my Robin, at that time' to 'of course forgotten my Robin'; p90 line 1: 'its' to 'his'

9 p92 line 1: 'like a' to 'low and deep, like a'; p93 line 5 up: 'single break' to 'break'; p94 line 11: 'spheres' to 'spheres with his naked ears, and without the help of any kind of instrument', last line: 'entirely due' to 'due'; p96 line 10: 'Be quick! Be quick! Be quick!' to 'Be quick! Be quick!'; p97 line 4: 'loud voice, with a voice normally like a duck's' to 'loud voice', line 11: 'unlike man, yet' to 'yet'; p98, line 2: 'beat them to the earth and stun them' to 'sent them to the earth stunned and perhaps dead', line 6: 'to such' to 'or eyesore to such', line 12: 'Here is a poem called' omitted

10 p100 line 4 up: 'tugging a fat worm out of the earth, which is a common sight with the thrush' to 'in the act of tugging a fat worm out of the earth, which is such a common sight with the Thrush'; p101 line 13: 'the consumption of snails' to 'a good feast of snails taken daily', line 3 up: 'foundation' to 'basis'; p102 line 3: 'more' to 'far more', line 11: 'correct – that this strange man had been eating snails alive. The trouble was not ended here for, in thinking of this glass-blower, always led me to think of another man of the same strange taste' to 'Thinking of this glass-blower always led me to think of another strange man whom I had known in the past', line 6 up: 'homes' to 'houses to live in'; p103 line 11 up: 'just left the neighbourhood' to 'only lately left it'; p107 line 3: 'than ever' to 'still', line 3 up: 'seducer' to 'abductor'; p107/108 last 2 lines/first 4 lines: 'If you are a lady, Mrs. Berry, and reasonable, you will give me one chance – I ask no more – to get at that man's dirty-ivory looking skin. Who is this maggotty-looking man that occupies one of your back rooms?'' added; p108 line 13: 'knocked again, as an irritated lady, in the name of Mrs. Higgins' to 'as an irritated lady, knocked again', line 3 up: 'his room' to 'his back room', last line: 'quietly' to 'very quietly'; p109 line 5: 'he' to 'her lodger', line 5 up: 'five' to 'three'; p110 line 1: 'which did not take' to 'This investigation did not take very'; p111 line 11: 'out of the house' to 'into the gutter', line 6 up: 'only been wasted' to 'been only waste of'; p112 line 6: 'dog's soap' to 'dog-soap'

11 p115 line 4: 'born' to 'hatched'; p116 line 8 up: 'move' to 'make the least move', 7 lines up: 'All' to 'But all'; p117 line 9: 'teeth' to 'sharp teeth'; p118 line 4: 'forcibly' to 'roughly and forcibly'; p120 line 2: 'How I arrived at this conclusion was owing to' to 'I arrived at this conclusion by'

12 p121 line 6 up: 'a little' to 'rather'; p122 line 9: 'their wonder' to 'all their wonder', line 3 up: 'about' to 'on', line 2 up: 'member, who was a curate, read' to 'member read'; p123 line 2: 'curate and two other members' to 'reader of Keats and two others', line 9: 'answer the curate said' to 'make an answer, the admirer of Keats said', line 6 up: 'not only bears profusely but is also beautiful in shape. It is apparently in the prime of life, without having lost a single bough' to 'that is not only rich in bearing fruit, but is also full of grace and beauty. Up to the present it has not lost a single bough, and there is no sign of decay in any part of it.'; p124 line 4: 'near' to 'about', line 2 up: 'whole mystery' to 'mystery'; p125 line 7: 'they could do no more' to 'their strength was gone altogether', line 9 up: 'to do' to 'to do next', line 5 up: 'their despondent state' to 'that state of depression'; p126 last line: 'my rent' to 'for my lodgings'; p127 line 2: 'are all dirty liars' to 'are liars and only fit for burning in hell', line 11 up: 'others' to 'other human beings'; p(128) line 9: 'Here's my poem called Old and Crazy' to 'OLD AND CRAZY'; p(128) last line: 'The End' omitted

previous printing:
'On Finding a Dead Bird Under My Window', *Argosy*, February 1933, XIII, 81, 1 (illustrated)

notes: (a) p41 poorly registered as '4' in some copies
(b) the HDB copy is inscribed: 'To Dinah (Helen) with love./ from/ Bunny (W. H. Davies.)/ 1933.'

A39a   Second impression   Jonathan Cape 1933

as *A39* apart from: (8) FIRST PUBLISHED 1933/ REPRINTED APRIL 1933/ JONATHAN CAPE LTD., 30 BEDFORD SQUARE, LONDON/ AND 91 WELLINGTON STREET WEST, TORONTO/ at foot: PRINTED IN GREAT BRITAIN BY J. AND J. GRAY, EDINBURGH/ PAPER SUPPLIED BY GROSVENOR, CHATER AND CO. LTD./ BOUND BY A. W. BAIN AND CO. LTD.

date of publication: April 1933

print run: 1000 copies printed on 18 April 1933

A39b   Third impression   Jonathan Cape 1933

date of publication: December 1933

print run: 1000 copies printed on 15 December 1933

A40 MY GARDEN   Jonathan Cape 1933

MY GARDEN/ W. H. DAVIES/ (floral vignette)/ WITH ILLUSTRATIONS
BY/ HILDA QUICK/ at foot: *LONDON*/ JONATHAN CAPE 30
BEDFORD SQUARE

8vo; (A)–H in eights; 64 leaves: (1–12) 13–126 (2)pp; 18.8 × 12.6 cms variable

(1–2) blank; (3) half-title: MY GARDEN by W. H. DAVIES; (4) starts: OTHER
BOOKS BY/ ends: *ETC.*; (5) blank; (6) frontispiece of a dandelion; (7) title-page; (8)
starts: FIRST PUBLISHED 1933/ ends: BOUND BY A. W. BAIN AND CO. LTD.;
(9) CONTENTS; (10) blank; (11) fly-title: MY GARDEN; (12) (vignette of a flower
in bud); 13–(127) text; (127) at foot: (clover tailpiece); (128) blank

contents: I p13 Flowers; II p22 Strange Visitors; III p32 In Times of Frost; IV p42
Superstition; V p52 In Spring; VI p61 Titbits; VII p71 Strangers; VIII p81 Cherries;
chapter IX p93 Trust; X p105 The Master Blackbird; XI p112 Care of My Garden;
XII p119. Last Remarks

contains: p13 Little Flower; p21 Drink; p22 Eyes; p32 On a Cold Day; p42 The
Dead; p51 The River Severn; p52 The Bee Lover; p60 A Lovely Day; p61 Bells; p71
Beggar's Luck; p79 The Vagabond; p81 Sound and Light; p93 The Man of Moods;
p105 Logic; p112 Compensation; p119 Bewitched

illustrations: frontispiece, titlepage, p(12) and tailpiece p(127)

paper: watermarked: – BASINGWERK PARCHMENT –

endpapers: cream; *edges*: deckle fore edge, top edge trimmed

binding: grass green calico grain cloth, blocked and printed in yellow; front cover:
blank; spine: vertically upwards: MY GARDEN // W.H.DAVIES; back cover:
publisher's device

dust-jacket: cream with an embossed surface, printed in black and green; front:
(triple green rule)/ MY GARDEN (in black)/ (multiple green rule)/ (vignette of a
dandelion in black)/ (triple green rule)/ By W. H. DAVIES (in black)/ (multiple green
rule); spine, in black: MY/ GARDEN/ by/ W. H./ DAVIES/ author/ of/ 'MY BIRDS'/
DECORATED/ by/ HILDA M./ QUICK/ (publisher's device)/ at foot: JONATHAN/
CAPE; back, in black: starts: MY BIRDS (vignette of a tit feeding)/ ends: by (in
black) W. H. DAVIES (in green); front flap, in black: starts: MY GARDEN/ ends:
3s. 6d. net; back flap: blank

date of publication: 18 September 1933

print run: 2000 copies printed on 14 July 1933 by Gray; *price*: 3s.6d.

copies seen: BL (shelf mark: 07028.cc.14; accession date: 30 August 1933); HDB (2
copies); RUL, Finzi

reviews: Literary, *TLS*, 21 September 1933, 634; Thoughts in a Garden, Richard
Church, *The Spectator*, 22 September 1933, 151, 5491, 378–379; *Bookman*,
October 1933, LXXXV, 505, Autumn supplement 91; *Country Life*, 7 October
1933, LXXIV, 1916, 369; Our Local Authors, TWG, *Monmouthshire Review*,
January 1934, II, 1, 84–87

mss: in WHD's hand on lined paper addressed The Croft, Nailsworth, Glos and undated; 58pp of microscopic script with the same problem of legibility as *My Birds* *(A39)*; clipped into brown paper wrappers (HDB)

WHD's manuscript corrections:

1 p16 line 9 up: 'the word piddle' to 'a certain word'; p20 line 11: 'like' to 'dislike', line 6 up: 'flower garden' to 'flower-beds'; p21 line 4: 'for' to 'in', line 11: 'Here it is, and I hope my readers will like it'

2 p23 line 1: 'very seriously' to 'seriously'; p25 line 11: 'bark' to 'voice'; p26 line 6 up: 'or velvety' to 'for velvety'; p27 line 5 up: 'intelligence' to 'despair and agony'; p29 line 11: 'fierce' to 'determined'; p30 line 5: 'where something like a' to 'near which about a'; line 5 up: 'the little' to 'the'

3 p34 line 10 up: 'nothing was' to 'only the bones were'; p36 line 3 up: 'does' to 'can do'; p38 line 10 up: 'would still shrink to their hollows, like leaking bladders again' to 'like leaking bladders, would still shrink back to their hollows again'

4 p45 line 12 and lines 2 and 9 up/p46 lines 6 and 7 up/p47 line 14/p48 lines 8 and 12 up: 'Mrs. Drinkwater' to 'Mrs. Waterlove'; p49 line 9 up: 'the girl's' to 'her'

5 p54 line 2: 'third' to 'unwelcome third', line 6 up: 'find?' to 'see?'; p57 line 7 up: 'being miserable' to 'indulging in misery'

6 p61 Titbits: line 2: 'Millions' to 'Thousands'; p62 line 4 up/p63 line 6: 'Mrs. Littlejohn' to 'Mrs. Littleworth'; p63 line 4: 'preferred England' to 'preferred to stay in her own country', line 10: 'had been told by Mrs. Littlejohn' to 'this lady had invented', line 11: 'this lady' to 'she'; p65 line 6 up: 'and not' to 'than'; p66 line 7: 'an employer' to 'the master'; p67 line 7: 'rare beauty' to 'beauty'; p68 line 9: 'uncommon' to 'unusual'; p69 line 11 up: 'possession' to 'occupation'; p70, lines 3 and 3 up: 'never' to 'seldom'

7 p71 line 5 up: "He saw" to "I see"; p72 line 1: 'lot of' to 'some', line 11: 'came' to 'won my affections'; p73 line 9: 'sedately like men, foot after foot' to 'foot after foot, like men', line 2 up: 'cat' to 'creature'; p74 line 10: 'So this makes' to 'It was rather'; p75 line 5 up: 'false words' to 'lies'

8 chapter heading: 'The Cherry Tree' to 'CHERRIES'; p83 line 2 up: 'look' to 'more'; p84 line 3 up: 'doubtful' to 'likely'; p87 line 2 up: 'touches something suddenly' to 'touches this cotton, which it has not seen'; p90 line 12: "Haw, Haw' again" to 'another 'Haw, Haw!', line 13: 'and a little louder' to 'and again, and louder'; p91 line 7 up: 'to hell with' to 'damn'

9 p93 line 4 up: 'The' to 'One'; p94 line 5 up: 'although I know' to 'But I knew'; p97 line 7: 'much less' to 'certainly not'; p101 line 3 up: 'with his two huge paws hanging down, and with his mouth' to 'and with his mouth'; p102 line 4: 'bear still sat up straight' to 'still sat'

10 p106 line 9 up: 'child, who was now about fourteen years of age' to 'child'; p109 line 11: 'this bird' to 'he'

11 p113 line 7 up: 'no matter' to 'though it'; p114 line 14: 'didn't know' to 'never knew', line 7 up: 'dead or alive' to 'whether I live or die'; p115 line 1: 'that should be necessary' to 'necessary'; pp115/116 last line/first line: 'kept under' to 'cut down?'

12 p125 line 13: 'house' to 'inn'; p126 line 13: 'on the floor' to 'under the table', line 9 up: 'fell over it' to 'fallen on it', line 7 up: 'in our own house' to 'at home and in my own bed', last line: 'limb' to 'bone'; p(127) last line: 'The End' omitted

text changes from manuscript to A40 (references are to A40 not mss):

1 p14 line 4: 'no admiration at all' to 'very little admiration', line 10 up: from 'its only purpose' to 'its best purpose'; p16 line 9 up: 'a certain word' to 'one particular word'; p19 line 7: 'the sweetest' to 'now the sweetest', line 12 up: 'For

instance, why should I' to 'There is no reason at all why I should', line 8 up: 'no more than a' to 'a'; p20 line 13: 'trees, like children's Christmas trees, in every border' to 'bushes in every border, like children's Christmas trees'; p21 line 1: 'weakness' to 'greater weakness'

2 p24 line 1: 'local thief' to 'thief', line 8: 'Well, let the' to '– let the', line 2 up: 'which sometimes kicks' to 'will sometimes kick'; p25 last line: 'answered' to 'said'; p27 line 2 up: 'He had nice large eyes; oh, you should have seen his eyes!' to 'Oh, you should have seen his eyes!'; p29 line 5 up: 'half an hour' to 'half-hour'; p30 line 8 up: 'gardener' to 'poor gardener'; p31 line 6 up: 'the bully, who knew the fighting power of' to 'the big bully, who knew the fighting qualities of'; p38 line 4: 'my bread' to 'my', line 9: 'reach' to 'search', line 10: 'silly thrush' to 'Thrush'

3 p33 9 lines up: 'home stood' to 'house stands'; p34 line 4 up: 'changed considerably' to 'considerably changed'; p36 line 2: 'developed' to 'as developed', line 8 up: 'bread, while right' to 'dry bread right'; p39 line 5: 'masticating' to 'swallowing', line 3 up: 'proved' to 'proved against them', last line: 'load of wood at' to 'wood, the full load, at'; p40 line 6: 'clothes, or' to 'clothes, rags, bones or bottles, or'

4 p44 line 5: 'quite friendly' to 'friendly'; p45 line 1: 'over' to 'over, though more with surprise than fear', line 5: 'happened to be very superstitious' to 'was superstitious'; p46 line 6: 'the window' to 'her window'; p48 line 4 up: 'in suspecting' to 'of suspecting'; p50 line 6: 'at the last extremity, after looking in every other place' to 'in the last extremity', line 5 up: 'near Newport' to 'in Monmouthshire'

5 p54 line 6 up: 'I shall see a nest' to 'A nest'; p55 line 7 up: 'two or three' to 'a few', line 6 up: 'period' to 'time'; p56 line 11 up: 'table' to 'bread-table'; p57 line 8: 'feed him' to 'feed him without forgetfulness'; p58 line 10 up: 'and Daffodils' to 'Daffodils and others'

6 p62 last line: 'make' to 'do'; p63 line 3: 'country' to 'country, as a patriot'; p66 line 10: 'blackbird's' to 'its'; p67 line 8: 'them sing' to 'their voices'; p68 line 5: 'many charms' to 'charms'

7 p75 line 7 up: "God bless you" to "God bless you, sir"

8 p83 line 3: 'song and honey' to 'honey and song'; p85 line 2: 'the bell' to 'it'; p86 line 2 up: 'whole and clean' to 'clean and whole'; p87 line 2 up: 'touches' to 'touch'; p92 line 7: 'wanted really' to 'really wanted'

9 p93 The Man of Moods: line 5: 'life' to 'birth'; p94 line 2: 'several times a day, to and from school' to 'to and from school, and several times a day'; p95 line 7 up: 'is a rat's most unpleasant feature, when it is kept straight' to 'when it is kept straight, is a rat's most unpleasant feature'; p96 line 9: 'away his wits' to 'his wits away', line 11 up: 'presence of a real friend?' to 'real friend and had nothing to fear?'; p98 line 7: 'in one or even two ears' to 'in one ear, or even both', last line: 'small' to 'little'; p102 line 1: 'cried the' to 'said this'

10 p105 Logic: line 1: 'counted' to 'numbered', line 7: 'love' to 'live'; p106 line 5: 'this child' to 'she'; p108 last line: 'on' to 'still on'; p109 line 9 up: 'as long as you have a happy heart' to 'so long as the heart is happy'; p110 line 5: 'literary and artisitic' to 'literary'

11 p112 poem title: 'The Compensation' to 'COMPENSATION'; p113 line 5 up: 'gives us a tremendous interest' to 'becomes important to us'; p114 line 5: from 'greater excitement' to 'my excitement'

12 p120 line 9: 'experienced' to 'experienced since'

previous printings:
'The River Severn', *Monmouthshire Review*, April 1933, I, 2, 107

'The Dead', *The Spectator*, 19 May 1933, 150, 5473, 709
'Logic', *Now & Then*, Winter 1933, 46, 43
'Beggar's Luck' and 'Compensation' (as 'The Compensation'), *Time and Tide*, 24
June 1933, XIV, 25, 765 and 28 October 1933, XIV, 43, 1282 respectively

note: the HDB copies are inscribed: 'With love/ To Dinah (Helen)/ from/ Bunny
(W. H. Davies.)/ August 31st. 1933.' and 'My book,/ W. H. Davies./ August 30th.
1933./ Little Flower/ Little Flower, I hold you here,/ Between my finger-tips;/ Can I do
more for your sweet smell/ Than kiss you with my lips?/ Little Flower,/ I am an old
man -/ But a child could do no more./ W. H. D.'

A40a Second impression   Jonathan Cape 1933

as *A40* apart from: (8) starts: FIRST PUBLISHED 1933/ ends: BY MORTON
SUNDOUR FABRICS LTD.; *dust-jacket*: spine, at foot: 2nd/ Impression; front flap,
at foot: 2nd Impression/ 3s.6d. net

date of publication: December 1933

print run: 1000 copies printed on 15 December 1933; *price*: 3s.6d.

note: transferred to *My Garden and My Birds (A46)*

A41 THE LOVERS' SONG-BOOK   Gregynog Press 1933

THE/ LOVERS' SONG-BOOK/ BY/ W. H. DAVIES/ (publisher's device in
turquoise and black)/ THE GREGYNOG PRESS/ MCMXXXIII

4to; * in four, (a) in two, b–e and (f) in fours (the endpapers and pastedowns are
part of the first and final gatherings); 22 leaves omitting endpapers: (1–4) (i–iv) v
(vi) 1–30 (4)pp; 23.0 × 5.5 cms

omitting endpapers: (1–4) blank; (i) half-title: THE LOVERS' SONG-BOOK; (ii)
blank; (iii) title-page; (iv) blank; v *The Contents* (poem titles in italics within a ruled
turquoise panel); (vi) blank; 1–30 text; (31) limitation: PRINTED AT THE
GREGYNOG PRESS, NEAR/ NEWTOWN, IN MONTGOMERYSHIRE, AND/
COMPLETED ON THE ELEVENTH DAY OF/ NOVEMBER, MCMXXXIII. THE
EDITION IS/ LIMITED TO TWO HUNDRED AND FIFTY COPIES./ No   ; (32–
34) blank; poem titles in italics; throughout the text the poems are within ruled
turquoise panel with the initial letters in turquoise

contents: p1 Where We Agree; p2 Beauty and Song; p3 The Shadow; p4 Past and
Present; p5 To-Morrow; p6 To-Night; p7 Light and Darkness; p8 Married Couples;
p9 Brother Gods; p10 Alone; p11 The Supper; p12 When We Forget; p13 Faults;
p14 Fortunes; p15 Stings; p16 This Old Green Orchard; p17 Pecking; p18 The
Peacemaker; p19 Marvellous Ears; p20 The Laws of Beauty; p21 A Foolish Tongue;
p22 Good and Evil; p23 Regret; p24 Three Score and Ten; p25 A Lullaby of Rest;
p26 Last Thoughts; p27 Love's Rivals; p28 True or Fickle; p29 Love and Money;
p30 The Great Lovers

paper: Japanese vellum

endpapers: Japanese vellum and part of the first and final gatherings; *edges*: trimmed

binding: Cockerell marbled paper-covered boards in blue, beige and lime green, mid-blue buckram spine; front cover: blank; spine, lettered in gilt, vertically upwards: THE LOVERS' SONG-BOOK/ – *By* W. H. DAVIES -; back cover: blank; *dust-jacket*: not seen

date of publication: 1 December 1933

print run: 231 copies completed on 11 November 1933; *price*: 21s.

copies seen: HRHRC (nos 90 and 174); NL (no 62); HDB (no 22); CH (no 156)

reviews: The Lovers' Song-Book, *TLS*, 21 December 1933, 906; Our Local Authors, TWG, *Monmouthshire Review*, January 1934, II, 1, 84–87; The Lovers' Song-Book, B. H. Newdigate, *London Mercury*, January 1934, XXIX, 171, 258

previous printing:
'Faults', *New Statesman*, 8 February 1930, XXXIV, 876, 569

notes: (a) copies 62, 90, and 174 are printed in emerald green (variant) where turquoise is used above and are bound in buff, green, black and beige Cockerell marbled paper-covered boards with a green buckram spine; both the CH copy (turquoise) and the BL copy (emerald green) have the mistake in 'Love and Money' which is corrected in WHD's hand in the HDB copy (turquoise): 1st stanza, line 4: from 'but' to 'buy'
(b) the HDB copy is inscribed: 'My book,/ W. H. Davies./ Dec. 1st. 1933./ Where We Agree/ Give her her ribbon, belt or scarf -/ To match my rainbow in the sky;/ Let her prefer her looking-glass,/ When dewdrops meet me, eye to eye./ Give her her pretty flowers or stars,/ Embossed in silk and figured lace;/ While I prefer their living forms,/ Set in a green or azure place./ Give her her choice, and give me mine,/ Remembering still Love's greater worth -/ That she and I prefer each other/ To any thing in Heaven or Earth./ W. H. D.'
(c) 3 years earlier in 1931 a trial design with sepia wood engraved initials and tailpiece by Blair Hughes-Stanton was rejected by the Gregynog Press board (one of 9 copies, printed on Japanese vellum, was offered for sale at the 1991 ABA London Bookfair by Wilsey Rare Books, New York)
(d) advertised in two different single-leaf prospecti on Japanese vellum, one ruled in green (*A History of the Gregynog Press* by Dorothy A. Harrop *(F359)*)

A41a *Special edition* Gregynog Press 1933

as *A41* apart from: 24 leaves omitting endpapers (f in six); *binding*: full grass-green levant morocco, polished, tooled in gilt: front cover: (decorative design of eleven foliate sprays rising vertically from a double line of lozenges); spine: two raised bands outlined in blind, lettered upwards: THE LOVERS' SONG-BOOK/ BY W. H. DAVIES/ at foot: (foliate sprays rising from lozenges); back cover: as front cover; inner dentelles: (double line of lozenges along the tail, single leaf spray rising up the fore edge); back inner dentelle, signed at foot: GREGYNOG PRESS BINDERY GEORGE FISHER; hand-sewn yellow silk headbands; *edges*: top edge gilt

print run: 19 copies; (nos 1–15, 143, 202, 226 and 227); *price*: 6 guineas

copy seen: BL (shelf mark: C 69.ee.13; accession date: 8 May 1937) (no 14)

A41a

A42 THE POEMS OF W. H. DAVIES   Jonathan Cape 1934

THE POEMS/ *of*/ W. H. DAVIES/ (publisher's device)/ at foot:
JONATHAN CAPE/ THIRTY BEDFORD SQUARE/ LONDON

8vo; (A)–I, K–U and X–GG in eights; 240 leaves: (1–4) 5 (6) 7–20 (21–22) 23–456
(457–458) 459–475 (5)pp; 19.0 × 13.0 cms variable

(1) half-title: THE/ POEMS OF W. H. DAVIES; (2) blank; (3) title-page; (4) starts:
FIRST PUBLISHED 1934/ ends: MADE BY MORTON SUNDOUR FABRICS
LTD.; 5 PUBLISHER'S NOTE; (6) blank; 7–20 Contents; (21) fly-title: POEMS OF
W. H. DAVIES; (22) blank; 23–456 text; (457) fly-title: INDEX OF FIRST LINES;
(458) blank; 459–475 Index of First Lines; (476–500) blank

contents: as A33 with the following additional poems: 432 Friends Unborn; 433
The Richest Stones; 434 This Bantam Star; 435 If Love Survives; 436 Hand or
Mouth; 437 Ambition; 438 For Sale; 439 Birthdays; 440 Uncertainty; 441 Charity;
442 A Dream of Winter; 443 A Child's Fancy; 444 Wild Blossoms; 445 A Silver
Wonder; 446 Peace and Rest; 447 Moss and Feather; 448 Pot and Kettle; 449 Eyes
and Ears; 450 The Blest; 451 The Idiot; 452 Letters; 453 Day or Night; 454
Hunting Joy; 455 A Young Thrush; 456 Born of Tears; 457 Heaven and Earth; 458
In Winter; 459 My Life's Example; 460 When and Where; 461 Silver Hours; 462
Here Am I; 463 Flowers; 464 Mangers; 465 Ships and Stars; 466 Starlings; 467
Poison; 468 A Prayer; 469 Old Friends; 470 Wonderful Places; 471 What Light?;
472 Old Autumn; 473 Trails; 474 The Poor; 475 No Careless Mind; 476 A Fleeting
Wonder; 477 Kiss and Blow; 478 The Visitor; 479 The Chase; 480 Age and Youth;
481 The Prayer of Daft Harry; 482 A Sweeter Life; 483 Epitaph on John Keats; 484
Epitaph on a Child; 485 Come, Melancholy; 486 Jewels; 487 The Legacy; 488
Clocks; 489 A Child's Mint; 490 The World Dictates; 491 The Enemy; 492 The
Lady of Light; 493 Playmates; 494 Sick Minds; 495 Bird and Cloud; 496 Ourselves;
497 The Mourner; 498 Loyalty; 499 No Place or Time; 500 Dreamers; 501 Wild
Creatures; 502 Aye; 503 Magpies; 504 A Dog's Grave; 505 Dogs; 506 On Finding a
Dead Bird Under My Window; 507 Crumbs and Guineas; 508 Voices of Scorn; 509
One Poet Visits Another; 510 My Rockery; 511 To Play Alone; 512 Flying
Blossoms; 513 A Bright Day; 514 Breast to Breast; 515 The Cuckoo; 516 Owls; 517
Old and Crazy; 518 Little Flower; 519 Drink; 520 Eyes; 521 On a Cold Day; 522
The Dead; 523 The River Severn; 524 The Bee Lover; 525 A Lovely Day; 526 Bells;
527 Beggar's Luck; 528 The Vagabond; 529 Sound and Light; 530 The Man of
Moods; 531 Logic; 532 Compensation; 533 Bewitched

endpapers: cream; *edges*: uncut, top edge trimmed

binding: grass-green calico grain cloth, lettered in gilt; front cover: blank; spine:
THE POEMS/ OF/ W. H. DAVIES/ at foot: JONATHAN/ CAPE; back cover: blank

dust-jacket: cream with an embossed surface, divided into five sections; front: first
section, cream out of blue: the/ poems of/ W. H. Davies/ second section, cream,
printed in black: starts: How strange that anyone could think our English tradition/
ends: it is to be found! BASIL DE SELINCOURT in the OBSERVER/ third section:
blue and blank, fourth section, black on cream: starts: When the fashionable poets
of to-day are as out of date as/ ends: SIR JOHN SQUIRE in the DAILY
TELEGRAPH/ fifth section, cream out of blue: W. H. DAVIES; spine, first section,
cream out of blue: *the/ poems/ of/ W. H./ Davies/* second section, black on cream:

533 poems/ third section as front cover/ fourth section, black on cream: (publisher's device)/ JONATHAN CAPE/ fifth section, cream out of blue: W. H./ DAVIES; back: blank; front flap, black on cream: starts: the poems of W. H. Davies/ ends: 7s.6d. net; back flap: blank

date of publication: 24 September 1934

print run: 4000 copies printed on 24 August 1934 by Alden Press; *price*: 7s.6d.

copies seen: BL (shelf mark: 2292.d.36; accession date: 20 September 1934); HDB (2 copies); RUL, Finzi; SH

reviews: *TLS*, 4 October 1934, 679; *The Listener*, 10 October 1934, XII, 300, supplement XV; Songs of Innocence: Mr W. H. Davies Collected Poems to date, Frank Kendon, *John o'London's Weekly*, 27 October 1934, XXXII, 811, 150; W. H. Davies: Poet, Wilfrid Gibson, *Bookman*, November 1934, LXXXVII, 518, 130; Divine Content, Richard Church, *New Statesman and Nation*, 8 December 1934, VIII (new series), 198, 855

text changes from previous printings to A42:
Starlings: 1st stanza line 3: 'greed' to 'green'
The Rain: 1st stanza line 1: 'Rain' to 'rain'; 2nd stanza line 2: 'Rain' to 'rain', line 3: 'Light' to 'light'
The Inexpressible: originally printed in three stanzas
Charms: 7th stanza line 2: 'halfway' to 'half-way'
The Lonely Dreamer: 3rd stanza last line: 'to' to 'in'
The Happy Child: 2nd stanza line 1: 'packhounds' to 'pack-hounds'
The White Cascade: 2nd stanza line 2: 'ten mile' to 'ten-mile'
Christ the Man: 1st stanza line 2 and 2nd stanza line 3: 'Thy' to 'thy'
Early Morn: 1st stanza line 5: 'a' omitted
Robin Redbreast: 1st stanza line 4: 'withered' to 'poor dead'
The Laughers: 2nd stanza line 2: 'he shrieks' to 'shrieketh'
When I am Old: 2nd stanza line 1: time' to 'Time'
Joy and Pleasure: 3rd stanza line 2: 'its' to 'his'
Seeking Beauty: 1st stanza line 3: 'earth' to 'Earth; 4th stanza line 2: 'swallows' to 'Swallows'
The Call of the Sea: line 18: 'when they' to 'who did', line 6 up: 'will' to 'do', line 4 up: 'ships' to 'Ships'
Her Absence: 1st stanza line 6: 'ash' to 'dirt', line 9: 'blest' to 'sweet'; 2nd stanza line 9: 'sweet' to 'dear'
The Power of Music 1st stanza line 2: 'thick-walled' to 'thick walled'
The Daisy: 4th stanza line 2: 'And gone from' to 'Out of all'
The Bird of Paradise: 4th stanza line 4 and 7th stanza last line: 'bed-post' to 'bedpost'
The Lodging House Fire: 2nd stanza line 1: 'Eight bells and then I woke' to 'I woke eight times and rose'
Love's Coming: 2nd stanza lines 1/2: 'entered there,/ He cocked his head with care' to 'entered,/ He tilted then his head'; 5th stanza line 1: 'Is not my say' to 'I do not know'
The Little Ones: 1st stanza line 4: 'Christmas-eve' to 'Christmas eve'; 4th stanza line 4: 'alas' to 'Alas'
The Sea: 2nd stanza last line: 'leap-frog' to 'leapfrog'
A Life's Love: 3rd stanza line 4: 'birds' to 'Birds'

The Hour of Magic: line 3: 'stone still' to 'stone-still'
The Rat: 3rd stanza line 2: 'cheekbones' to 'cheek-bones'
Her Merriment: 3rd stanza line 3: 'gayly' to 'gaily'
No Idle Gold: title from 'A Plain Life'
The Child and the Mariner: originally printed in six stanzas; line 48: 'heartbroken' to 'heart-broken', line 57: 'sometime' to 'some time', line 60: 'grown' to 'rose', line 80: 'Jane' to '*Jane*', line 95: 'slaughterhouse' to 'slaughter-house', line 101: 'fishing smacks' to 'fishing-smacks', line 112: 'stone dead' to 'stone-dead'
A Strange Meeting: 5th stanza line 3: '"Good night"' to "Good-night"
The Wonder-Maker: title from 'The Wonder Maker'
The Forsaken Dead: six additional lines between 'To make them sick with dread of things unseen' and 'Had they no dreamer here who might remain'
The Portrait: four additional lines between 'Strong love of mine, half bite, half kiss?' and 'Now, when I rest awhile from kissing'
The Two Lives: 3rd stanza line 4: 'wine-drops' to 'winedrops'
The Truth: 1st stanza line 1: 'half-away' to 'half away'
The Perfect Life: title from 'Philosophy'
The Song of Life: I, line 1: 'Sneeze' to 'sneeze'; LI, line 2: '"Tritonia"' to '*Tritonia*'
The Kingfisher: 1st stanza line 4: 'thy' to 'my'; 2nd stanza line 4: 'mark' to 'marks'
The Dreaming Boy: line 15: 'castles in the air' to 'castles-in-the-air', line 16: 'tenant keeps' to 'tenants keep'
Wild Oats: line 8: '*one*' to 'one'
The Fates: title from 'A Dead Man's Song'; one stanza shorter omitting last stanza: 'Straight up in bed I sat and smiled,/ And heard them whisper, "See, he smiles,/ We dare not strike that man again;/ Another blow and he will laugh,/ Our Master, in his scorn of pain."'
Without Contentment, what is Life?: title from 'Without contentment, what is life?'
The Posts: 1st stanza line 1: 'Year's' to 'year's'
The Bed-sitting-room: line 1: 'scripture' to 'Scripture'
The Inquest: 1st stanza line 1: 'enquire' to 'inquire'
When Yon Full Moon: title from 'When yon Full Moon'
A Bird's Anger: line 1: 'Summer's' to 'summer's'
Here am I: title from 'Here Am I'
The Cuckoo: line 1: 'by' to 'near'

note: the HDB copies are inscribed: 'My book, W. H. Davies./ 1934./ A Thought/ When I look into a glass,/ Myself's my only care;/ But I look into a pool/ For all the wonders there./ When I look into a glass I see a fool:/ But I see a wise man/ When I look into a pool./ W. H. D.' and 'To my wife Helen,/ with love/ from/ "Bunny" (W. H. Davies.) 1934.'

A42a First American edition   Oxford University Press 1935

price: $3

reviews: *Springfield Republican*, 23 June 1935, 5; An Evaluation of the Poetry of W. H. Davies, Louis Kronenberger, *New York Times (Book Review)*, 21 July 1935, 2; *Nation*, 4 September 1935, CXLI, 3661, 280; *Booklist*, October 1935, 32, 37; About Poets and Poetry, Helen Neville, *New Republic*, 8 January 1936, LXXXV, 1101, 263

A43 LOVE POEMS   Jonathan Cape 1935

Love Poems/ by/ W. H. Davies/ (vignette of a winged star)/ at foot: Jonathan
Cape/ Thirty Bedford Square, London

8vo; (A–B) and C–D in eights; 32 leaves: (1–6) 7–8 (9–10) 11–60 (4) pp; 19.0 ×
13.0 cms variable

(1–2) blank; (3) half-title: Love Poems; (4) starts: *By the same author/* ends: ETC.;
(5) title-page; (6) starts: FIRST PUBLISHED 1935/ ends: PAPER BY GROSVENOR,
CHATER & CO. LTD.; 7–8 Contents; (9) fly-title: Love Poems; (10) blank; 11–60
text; (61) (floral vignette); (62–64) blank

contents: p11 Seed and Flower; p12 The Little Devil; p13 When We Forget; p14
Love and Money; p15 Where We Agree; p16 Brother Gods; p17 Spirits and Bodies;
p18 Regret; p19 To-Morrow; p20 To-Night; p21 Married Couples; p22 The Laws
of Beauty; p23 This Green Orchard; p24 Love Lights His Fire; p25 Past and Present;
p26 Love Ten Years Old; p27 True and Fickle; p28 Alone; p29 The Shadow; p30
Love's Rivals; p31 A Foolish Tongue; p32 Faults; p33 Competitors; p34 Fortunes;
p35 Great Lovers; p36 Let Love Live On; p37 The Ghost; p38 Pecking; p39 Words
and Kisses; p40 Good and Evil; p41 The Peacemaker; p42 The Supper; p43
Marvellous Ears; p44 Beauty and Song; p45 Three Score and Ten; p46 Let Us Lie
Close; p47 Light and Darkness; p48 Stings; p49 Last Thoughts; p50 A Lullaby of
Rest; p51 Beauty and Brain; p52 The Tyrants; p53 Three Loves; p54 His Throne;
p55 Flirting; p56 The Jealous Lover; p57 Love Me No More; p58 The Faithful One;
p59 Eardrops; p60 The Players

illustrations: decorations on title-page and pp11, 14, 15, 16, 17, 18, 19, 24, 32, 36,
40, 54, 60 and (61)

paper: watermarked: – BASINGWERK PARCHMENT –

endpapers: cream; *edges*: deckle fore edge, uncut, top edge trimmed

binding: bright blue calico grain cloth, blocked and lettered in silver; front cover:
(floral decoration); spine, vertically upwards: LOVE POEMS // W. H. DAVIES/ at
foot: (publisher's device); back cover: blank

dust-jacket: cream, with an embossed surface, printed in black and red; front: LOVE
POEMS (in black open outline lettering)/ (vignette of a heart in flames in red)/ W. H.
DAVIES (in black open outline lettering); spine: (red publisher's device)/ vertically
upwards: LOVE POEMS (in black open outline lettering) by W. H. DAVIES (in
black open outline lettering)/ at foot: (red publisher's device); back, in black: starts:
THE POEMS OF W. H. DAVIES/ ends: 533 poems. 7s. 6d. net (in red); front flap:
starts: decorated by/ ELIZABETH/ MONTGOMERY (in black)/ ends: 3s.6d. net (in
black)/ inside margin, vertically upwards: LOVE POEMS (in red open outline
lettering) by W. H. DAVIES (in red open outline lettering); back flap, in black:
starts: 'Mr. Davies was born in 1871 at/ ends: DAILY TELEGRAPH

date of publication: 1 April 1935

print run: 2000 copies printed on 22 February 1935 by Alden Press; bound by A. W.
Bain; *price*: 3s.6d.

copies seen: BL (shelf mark: 11655.aa.60; accession date: 20 March 1935); HDB (2
copies); RUL, Finzi; SH

reviews: However – by Edward Shanks, *John o'London's Weekly*, 6 April 1935, XXXIII, 834, 24; Love Poems, *TLS*, 9 May 1935, 298; Conventional Poems, Michael Roberts, *The Spectator*, 31 May 1935, 154, 5579, 928–930; The Affectionate Muse, Laurence Whistler, *New Statesman and Nation*, 13 July 1935, X, 229 (new series), 69

previous printings:
'Seed and Flower', *Monmouthshire Review*, April 1934, II, 2, 131
'Faults', *New Statesman*, 8 February 1930, XXXIV, 876, 569
'The Little Devil' and 'Love Lights His Fire', *London Mercury*, December 1930, XXIII, 134, 105
'Let Love Live On', 'The Ghost' and 'The Jealous Lover', *New Statesman and Nation*, 10 November 1934, VIII, 194, 669
'A Lullaby of Rest', *The Spectator*, 4 October 1930, 145, 5336, 450
'Flirting' and 'The Faithful One', *The Programme*, February 1935, 2, 12, 1–2

text changes from first printings to A43:
This Old Green Orchard: title to 'This Green Orchard'; 1st stanza line 4: 'apple-trees' to 'apple trees'
A Foolish Tongue: 1st stanza line 1: 'was' to 'is', 'pain' to 'Pain'
Alone: 1st stanza line 2: 'Sun' to 'sun', line 4: 'to' to 'in'
Beauty and Song: 1st stanza line 1: 'fine feathered' to 'fine-feathered'
Brother Gods: 2nd stanza line 4: 'play' to 'pay'
Fortunes: lines 1 and 4: 'eight hundred' to 'a thousand'
Good and Evil: 1st stanza line 1: 'Winter-time' to 'Winter time'; 2nd stanza line 1: 'bumble-bee' to 'Bumble-bee', line 5: 'bee' to 'Bee'
The Great Lovers: title to: 'Great Lovers', 2nd stanza last line: 'Lady' to 'lady'
Last Thoughts: line 5: 'Love' to love'
The Laws of Beauty: line 8: 'please no cramping' to 'never please'
Love and Money: 1st stanza, last line: 'but' to 'buy'
Love's Rivals: line 2: 'cities' to 'Cities'
Past and Present: originally printed in one stanza
Three Score and Ten: line 3 up: 'ninety five' to 'ninety-five'
To-Morrow: title to: 'To-morrow', line 4: 'sparrow' to 'Sparrow', line 2 up: 'bumble-bee' to 'bumble bee'

notes: (a) with the exception of 'Seed and Flower', 'The Little Devil', 'Spirits and Bodies', 'Love Lights His Fire', 'Love Ten Years Old', 'Competitors', 'Let Love Live On', 'The Ghost', 'Words and Kisses', 'Let Us Lie Close', 'Beauty and Brain', 'The Tyrants', 'Three Loves', 'His Throne', 'Flirting', 'The Jealous Lover', 'Love Me No More', 'The Faithful One', 'Eardrops' and 'The Players' the poems were all previously published in *The Lovers' Song-Book (A41)*
(b) a variant dust-jacket has been identified with publisher's device in red at foot of front flap
(c) the HDB copies are inscribed: 'To my wife Helen,/ from/ "Bunny" (W. H. Davies.)/ March, 1935.' and 'My book,/ W. H. Davies./ March, 1935./ Love Lights His Fire/ Love lights his fire to burn my Past -/ There goes the house where I was born!/ And even Friendship – Love declares -/ Must feed his precious flames and burn./ I stuffed my life with odds and ends,/ But how much joy can Knowledge give?/ The World my guide, I lived to learn -/ From Love, alone, I learn to live./ W. H. D.'

A43a First American edition   Oxford University Press 1935

Love Poems/ by/ W. H. Davies/ (decorative star with wings)/ at foot: New York/ Oxford University Press

as *A43* apart from: 18.6 × 12.5 cms; (4) *By the same author*/ THE POEMS OF W. H. DAVIES/ (Complete Edition 1934); (5) title-page; (6) starts: FIRST PUBLISHED 1935/ ends: PRINTED IN THE UNITED STATES OF AMERICA; *binding*: bright blue calico grain textured cloth, lettered and decorated in gilt; front cover: (floral decoration); spine, vertically upwards: LOVE POEMS – W. H. DAVIES; back cover: blank; *edges*: trimmed; *dust-jacket*: not seen

price: $1.25

copy seen: HRHRC

reviews: *Boston Transcript*, 26 June 1935, 2; *New York Herald Tribune (Books)*, 14 July 1935, 8; An Evaluation of the Poetry of W. H. Davies, Louis Kronenberger, *New York Times (Book Review)*, 21 July 1935, 2; by IF, *Christian Science Monitor*, 24 July 1935, 12; *Nation*, 4 September 1935, CXLI, 3661, 280; by Helen Neville, *New Republic*, 8 January 1936, LXXXV, 1101, 263; The Simplicity of Wonder, Stanley J. Kunitz, *Poetry*, July 1936, XLVIII, 4, 232–234

A44 THE BIRTH OF SONG   Jonathan Cape 1936

The/ Birth of Song/ Poems, 1935–36/ by/ W. H. Davies/ (vignette of a lute)/ Jonathan Cape/ Thirty Bedford Square, London

8vo; (A)–B in eights; 16 leaves: (1–8) 9–32pp; 19.0 × 13.0 cms variable

(1–2) blank; (3) half-title: *The Birth of Song*; (4) starts: *By the same author*/ ends: MY BIRDS; (5) title-page; (6) starts: FIRST PUBLISHED 1936/ ends: BOUND BY A. W. BAIN & CO. LTD.; (7) Contents; (8) (decoration); 9–32 text

contents: p9 The Birth of Song; p10 Man; p11 This is a Joy; p12 All's Well; p13 A New World; p14 Street Criers; p15 Scandal; p16 Love in Trouble; p17 Tell me, World, and Tell me, Nature; p18 The Conquerors; p19 Catching the Devil; p20 Named; p21 The Witness; p22 The Age of Gold; p23 The Mongrel; p24 The Lily of our Valley; p25 Combing; p26 Song of the Miners; p27 Father and Son; p28 Good Friends; p29 To W. S. – On his Wonderful Toys; p30 Broken Hearts; p31 Success; p32 Rich Companions

illustrations: decorations on title-page and pp(8), 9, 10, 12, 15, 18, 19, 21, 25, 26 and 31

paper: watermarked: – BASINGWERK PARCHMENT –

endpapers: cream; *edges*: uncut, top edge trimmed

binding: pale grey calico grain cloth embossed with mid-blue and navy, bright blue cloth spine, lettered in gilt; front cover: blank; spine, vertically upwards: THE BIRTH OF SONG ..... W. H. DAVIES; back cover: blank

dust-jacket: mainly cream with an embossed surface; front, mottled bright blue and lettered in cream: THE/ BIRTH/ OF/ SONG/ W. H. DAVIES/ POEMS/ 1935–36; spine, blue and lettered vertically upwards in cream: W. H. DAVIES The Birth of Song   Poems 1935–36; back: blank; front flap: starts: THE BIRTH OF SONG/ ends: speak of./ at foot: 5s. net.; back flap: blank

date of publication: 2 October 1936

print run: 1500 copies printed on 25 August 1936 by Alden Press; *price*: 5s.

copies seen: BL (shelf mark: 11655.bbb.24; accession date: 28 September 1936); RUL, Finzi; SH

reviews: Poetry, *TLS*, 10 October 1936, 817; The Lyrical Impulse, A. C. Boyd, *London Mercury and Bookman*, November 1936, XXXV, 205, 86–87; Two Kinds of Poetry, Michael Roberts, *The Spectator*, 8 January 1937, 158, 5663, 58

previous printing:
'Success', *Argosy*, June 1936, XIX, 121, 28

A44a First American edition   Oxford University Press 1936

The/ Birth of Song/ Poems, 1935–36/ by/ W. H. Davies/ (vignette of a lute)/ New York/ Oxford University Press/ 1936

as *A44* apart from: (5) title-page; (6) COPYRIGHT, 1936, BY/ OXFORD UNIVERSITY PRESS, NEW YORK, INC./ FIRST EDITION/ at foot: PRINTED IN THE UNITED STATES OF AMERICA; *binding*: bright blue calico grain cloth, decorated and lettered in gilt; front cover: (floral spray); spine, vertically upwards: THE BIRTH OF SONG – W. H. DAVIES; back cover: blank; *dust-jacket*: not seen

price: $1

copy seen: HRHRC

review: The Phoenix Nest: Contemporary Poetry, William Rose Benet, *Saturday Review of Literature*, 31 July 1937, XVI, 14, 17

A45 THE LONELIEST MOUNTAIN   Jonathan Cape 1939

The/ Loneliest Mountain/ and Other Poems/ by/ W. H. Davies/ at foot: Jonathan Cape/ Thirty Bedford Square, London

8vo; (A)–B in eights; 16 leaves: (1–8) 9–32pp; 18.8 × 13.0 cms variable

(1) half-title: *The Loneliest Mountain/ and Other Poems*; (2) starts: *By the same author/* ends: AN ANTHOLOGY OF SHORT POEMS; (3) title-page; (4) starts: FIRST PUBLISHED 1939/ ends: BOUND BY A. W. BAIN & CO. LTD.; (5) Contents; (6) blank; (7) Note signed W. H. D.; (8) blank; 9–32 text

contents: p9 The Loneliest Mountain. Pride and Humility; p10 The Load of Pearls. Taking Stock; p11 Worms; p12 Silent Eyes; p13 The Deed; p14 A Cat's Example. Trust; p15 Common Joys; p16 Speed; p17 Armed for War; p18 The Tugged Hand; p19 Days and Years; p20 Following a Bee; p21 Woman; p22 The Last Years; p23

All in June; p24 Men that Think; p25 The Dead Tree; p26 Music's Tragedy; p27 The Worm's Contempt. Life; p28 Nailsworth Hill. A Change of Voice; p29 Slippers; p30 Looks; p31 The Mind Speaks; p32 That Golden Time

paper: watermarked: – BASINGWERK PARCHMENT –

endpapers: cream; *edges*: uncut, top edge trimmed

binding: pale grey calico grain cloth embossed with red, green, yellow, brown and two shades of blue, bright blue cloth spine, lettered in gilt; front cover: blank; spine, vertically upwards: THE LONELIEST MOUNTAIN ..... W. H. DAVIES; back cover: blank

dust-jacket: mainly cream with an embossed surface; front, mottled maroon and lettered in cream: *The/ Loneliest Mountain/ and other poems/ by/ W. H. DAVIES/* at foot: *1939*; spine, maroon and lettered vertically upwards in cream: *The Loneliest Mountain and other poems by W. H. Davies*; back: blank; front flap: starts: THE LONELIEST MOUNTAIN/ ends: sought for in vain.; back flap: blank

date of publication: 8 October 1939

print run: 1500 copies printed on 4 August 1939 by Alden Press; *price*: 3s.6d.

copies seen: BL (shelf mark: 11657.b.33; accession date: 2 October 1939); HDB; RUL, Finzi

reviews: A Bookman's Diary: A Poet's Farewell, Colophon, *John o'London's Weekly*, 8 September 1939, XLI, 1065, 776; A Dream Child Every Day: Mr W. H. Davies bids Farewell, *TLS*, 14 October 1939, 590; by G. Jones, *Welsh Review*, November 1939, II, 4, 232–234; What I Hear, Audax, *John o'London's Weekly*, 17 November 1939, XLII, 1075, 178 (portrait); Recent Verse, Desmond Hawkins, *The Spectator*, 22 December 1939, 163, 5817, 901; *The Listener*, 11 January 1940, XXIII, 574, 88

previous printings:
'The Loneliest Mountain' (as 'The Dreamer'), 'Pride and Humility', 'Life', 'The Worm's Contempt' and 'The Load of Pearls', 'Armed for War', 'Speed' and 'Men that Think', 'Silent Eyes', 'The Deed' and 'Days and Years', *London Mercury and Bookman*, February 1937, XXXV, 208, 360–361, September 1937, XXXVI, 215, 418–419 and June 1938, XXXVIII, 224, 106–107 respectively
'Common Joys', *British Annual of Literature*, 1938, 1, 25
'The Last Years' and 'Worms', *Welsh Review*, February 1939, I, 1, 16
'A Cat's Example' and 'The Tugged Hand', *Time and Tide*, 12 March 1938, XIX, 11, 337 and 14 May 1938, XIX, 20, 670

notes: (a) the HDB copy is inscribed: 'My book,/ W. H. Davies./ Oct 1939./ The loneliest mountain, with no house or tree,/ Still has its little flower so sweet and wild;/ While I, a dreamer, strange and but half known,/ Can find no equal till I meet a child./ W. H. D.'
(b) 'Nailsworth Hill' was published separately on a postcard beneath a photograph of WHD's cottage at Nailsworth

A45a Second impression   Jonathan Cape 1940

print run: 1000 copies printed on 23 February 1940

note: price increase: 30 August 1943 5s.

A46 MY GARDEN AND MY BIRDS   Jonathan Cape 1939

MY GARDEN/ AND/ MY BIRDS/ W. H. DAVIES/ WITH
ILLUSTRATIONS BY/ HILDA M. QUICK/ at foot: *LONDON/*
JONATHAN CAPE 30 BEDFORD SQUARE

8vo; (A)–H in eights, (A) in four, B–H in eights; 124 leaves: (1–12) 13–128 (9–12)
13–127 (1)pp; 19.0 × 12.5 cms variable

(1) half-title: MY GARDEN AND MY BIRDS; (2) starts: *By the same author/* ends:
AN ANTHOLOGY OF SHORT POEMS; (3) blank; (4) frontispiece as *A39*; (5)
title-page; (6) starts: *MY BIRDS/* ends: BOUND BY A. W. BAIN AND CO. LTD.;
7–8 INTRODUCTION signed W. H. D.; (9) fly-title: MY BIRDS/ (vignette of a bird
feeding); (10) (vignette of a bird on a branch); 11 CONTENTS; (12) repeat of
frontispiece; 13-(128) text; (9) fly-title: MY GARDEN/ (floral decoration); (10)
(floral decoration); (11) CONTENTS; (12) (floral decoration); 13-(127) text; (127)
at foot: (floral tailpiece); (128) blank

binding: grass-green calico grain cloth, blocked and lettered in gilt; front cover:
blank; spine: MY GARDEN/ &/ MY BIRDS/ (decorative rule)/ W. H. DAVIES/ at
foot: (publisher's device); back cover: blank

dust-jacket: cream with an embossed surface, printed in black and red; front: My
Garden/ and my Birds (in black)/ (vignette of a dandelion in black)/ W. H. DAVIES
(in red); spine: My/ Garden/ and/ My/ Birds/ by/ W. H./ DAVIES (in black)/ at foot:
(red publisher's device)/ JONATHAN/ CAPE; back cover: blank; front flap: starts:
MY GARDEN AND MY BIRDS/ ends: 5s. net; back flap: blank

date of publication: November 1939

print run: made up from sheets of *A39* and *A40*, 800 24pp cancels printed on 3
November 1939; *price*: 5s.

copy seen: SH

A47 THE POEMS OF
       W. H. DAVIES 1940   Jonathan Cape 1940

THE POEMS/ *of/* W. H. DAVIES/ 1940/ (publisher's device)/ at foot:
JONATHAN CAPE/ THIRTY BEDFORD SQUARE/ LONDON

8vo; (A) in eight plus tipped-in frontispiece, B–I, K–U, X–II and KK in eights; 264
leaves: (i–ii) (1–2) 3 (4) 5–20 (21–22) 23–525 (1)pp plus frontispiece not included in
the pagination; 19.2 × 13.0 cms variable

(i) half-title: THE/ POEMS OF W. H. DAVIES/ 1940; (ii) blank; portrait frontispiece captioned: W. H. DAVIES/ from a portrait by Laura Knight; (1) title-page; (2)
starts: FIRST PUBLISHED 1940/ ends: BOUND BY A. W. BAIN & CO. LTD.; 3
PUBLISHER'S NOTE; (4) blank; 5–20 Contents; (21) fly-title: POEMS OF W. H.
DAVIES/ 1940; (22) blank; 23–507 text; (508) blank; 509–525 Index of First Lines;
(526) blank

contents: as *A42* with the following additional poems: 534 Seed and Flower; 535

The Little Devil; 536 When We Forget; 537 Love and Money; 538 Where We Agree; 539 Brother Gods; 540 Spirits and Bodies; 541 Regret; 542 To-morrow; 543 To-night; 544 Married Couples; 545 The Laws of Beauty; 546 This Green Orchard; 547 Love Lights His Fire; 548 Past and Present; 549 Love Ten Years Old; 550 True or Fickle; 551 Alone; 552 The Shadow; 553 Love's Rivals; 554 A Foolish Tongue; 555 Faults; 556 Competitors; 557 Fortunes; 558 Great Lovers; 559 Let Love Live On; 560 The Ghost; 561 Pecking; 562 Words and Kisses; 563 Good and Evil; 564 The Peacemaker; 565 The Supper; 566 Marvellous Ears; 567 Beauty and Song; 568 Three Score and Ten; 569 Let Us Lie Close; 570 Light and Darkness (ii); 571 Stings; 572 Last Thoughts; 573 A Lullaby of Rest; 574 Beauty and Brain; 575 The Tyrants; 576 Three Loves; 577 His Throne; 578 Flirting; 579 The Jealous Lover; 580 Love Me No More; 581 The Faithful One; 582 Eardrops; 583 The Players; 584 The Birth of Song; 585 Man; 586 This is a Joy; 587 All's Well; 588 A New World; 589 Street Criers; 590 Scandal; 591 Love in Trouble; 592 Tell Me, World, and Tell Me, Nature; 593 The Conquerors; 594 Catching the Devil; 595 Named; 596 The Witness; 597 The Age of Gold; 598 The Mongrel; 599 The Lily of Our Valley; 600 Combing; 601 Song of the Miners; 602 Father and Son; 603 Good Friends; 604 To W.S.- On his Wonderful Toys; 605 Broken Hearts; 606 Success; 607 Rich Companions; 608 The Loneliest Mountain; 609 Pride and Humility; 610 The Load of Pearls; 611 Taking Stock; 612 Worms; 613 Silent Eyes; 614 The Deed; 615 A Cat's Example; 616 Trust; 617 Common Joys; 618 Speed; 619 Armed for War; 620 The Tugged Hand; 621 Days and Years; 622 Following a Bee; 623 Woman; 624 The Last Years; 625 All in June; 626 Men that Think; 627 The Dead Tree; 628 Music's Tragedy; 629 The Worms' Contempt; 630 Life; 631 Nailsworth Hill; 632 A Change of Voice; 633 Slippers; 634 Looks; 635 The Mind Speaks; 636 That Golden Time

endpapers: cream; *edges*: uncut, top edge trimmed

binding: bright blue calico grain cloth, blocked and lettered in gilt; front cover: blank; spine: THE POEMS/ OF/ W. H. DAVIES/ at foot: (publisher's device); back cover: blank

dust-jacket: mainly cream with an embossed surface; front: top half, mottled blue, lettered in cream: The POEMS of/ W. H./ DAVIES/ 1940/ lower half, cream, printed double column in black and blue: starts: 'When (in blue) the fashionable poets of to-/ 'How (in blue) strange that anyone could/ ends: DAILY TELEGRAPH/ OBSERVER/ *The last edition of Mr. Davies's collected poems (1934) is now out of print,/ and the publishers are taking the opportunity of bringing the new edition/ right up to date. Besides the whole contents of the 1934 edition,/ this new volume will include Mr. Davies's three subsequent volumes:/ 'Love Poems' (1935), 'The Birth of Song' (1936), and 'The Loneliest/ Mountain' (1939).*; spine: top half, mottled blue, lettered in cream: THE/ POEMS/ OF/ W. H./ DAVIES/ 1940/ lower half, cream, printed in black and blue: *636/ poems/* at foot: (blue publisher's device)/ JONATHAN CAPE'; back: blank; front flap: starts: THE POEMS OF W. H. DAVIES/ ends: 7s. 6d. net; back flap: blank

date of publication: 26 April 1940

print run: 4000 copies printed on 19 February 1940 by Alden Press; *price*: 7s.6d.

copies seen: BL (shelf mark: 2290.g.18; accession date: 19 April 1940); SH; HDB (3 copies); RUL, Finzi *reviews*: A Bookman's Diary, Colophon, *John o'London's Weekly*, 19 April 1940, XLIII, 1097, 86; Franciscan Riches, *Punch*, 8 May 1940, CXCVIII, 5172, 524; Poetry in War-Time: Can the Young Writer avoid Self-Consciousness, R. L. Megroz, *John o'London's Weekly*, 24 May 1940, XLIII, 1102, 235; *The Listener*, 15 August 1940, XXIV, 605, 246; Proverbial Wisdom: Mr Davies's Promptings, *TLS*, 31 August 1940, 424

text changes from previous printings to A47:
Following a Bee: title from 'April's Boys and Girls'
Tell Me World, and Tell, Me Nature: title from 'Tell me World, and Tell me, Nature'
The Lily of Our Valley: title from 'The Lily of our Valley'
Love and Money: title from 'Love or Money'

note: not one of the HDB copies has a frontispiece; this is possibly because it was attributed to the wrong artist (Laura Knight instead of Harold Knight) and removed by the publishers, therefore copies without frontispieces may be second issues

A48 COMMON JOYS · Faber & Faber 1941

COMMON JOYS/ and other poems/ by/ W. H. DAVIES/ at foot: Faber and Faber/ 24 Russell Square/ London

8vo; (A)–E in eights; 40 leaves: (1–4) 5–7 (8) 9–80pp; 18.7 × 12.2 cms

(1) half-title: COMMON JOYS/ AND OTHER POEMS; (2) blank; (3) title-page; (4) starts: FIRST PUBLISHED IN JUNE MCMXLI/ ends: ALL RIGHTS RESERVED; 5–7 CONTENTS; 7 below contents: ACKNOWLEDGEMENTS/ These poems are reprinted by kind permission/ of Messrs. Jonathan Cape Limited; 8 SELECT BIBLIOGRAPHY; 9–80 text

contents: 1 The Hill-side Park; 2 'Scotty' Bill; 3 Facts; 4 New-comers; 5 The Rain; 6 A Maiden and Her Hair; 7 Joy and Pleasure; 8 Clouds; 9 An Old House in London; 10 The Flood; 11 Leisure; 12 Days that have been; 13 To Sparrows Fighting; 14 Shopping; 15 The Old Oak Tree; 16 A Great Time; 17 Charms; 18 Easter; 19 The Blind Boxer; 20 The Villain; 21 A Chant; 22 When Autumn's Fruit; 23 Now that the Tears; 24 Lamorna Cove; 25 Sweet Stay-at-Home; 26 Rogues; 27 Leaves; 28 At Night; 29 Earth Love; 30 Love's Payment; 31 The Rabbit; 32 The Two Heavens; 33 The Doll; 34 When Love is Young; 35 Pity; 36 B is for Beauty; 37 Y is for Youth; 38 The Rock; 39 The Spoiler; 40 Sun, Tree and Crow; 41 Shooting-Stars; 42 Sport; 43 Winter Fire; 44 For Sale; 45 Charity; 46 A Child's Fancy; 47 Eyes and Ears; 48 Silver Hours; 49 Flowers; 50 Ships and Stars; 51 No Careless Mind; 52 My Rockery; 53 Past and Present; 54 Fortunes; 55 The Ghost; 56 Good and Evil; 57 Marvellous Ears; 58 Street Criers; 59 The Mongrel; 60 Worms; 61 Common Joys; 62 The Dead Tree

paper: watermarked: (crown)/ Abbey Mills/ Greenfield; chain lines 2.4 cms apart and vertical

endpapers: cream; *edges*: trimmed

binding: bright yellow paper-covered boards, mottled with orange and printed in dark green; front cover: *Common Joys/ and other poems/* (decorative star)/ *W. H./ Davies*; spine, vertically downwards: COMMON JOYS & OTHER POEMS BY W. H. DAVIES   FABER; back cover: blank

dust-jacket: pale pink with a ribbed surface, printed in dark green; front, within decorative border: Common Joys/ and/ Other Poems/ *by/* W. H./ DAVIES; spine, vertically downwards: COMMON JOYS & OTHER POEMS BY W. H. DAVIES FABER; back: starts: SESAME BOOKS/ ends: 24 RUSSELL SQUARE, LONDON W C 1 (20 titles listed); front flap: starts: COMMON JOYS/ ends: net; back flap: starts: *By W. H. Davies/* ends: COLLECTED POEMS

date of publication: June 1941; *price*: 2s.6d.

copies seen: BL (shelf mark: 11656.l.73; accession date: 11 July 1941); HDB (2 copies); SH

note: printed by Western Printing Services

A48a Second impression   Faber & Faber 1941

date of publication: August 1941

A48b Third impression   Faber & Faber 1942

as *A48* apart from: (4) SECOND IMPRESSION AUGUST MCMXLI/ THIRD IMPRESSION JULY MCMXLII; *binding*: yellow card wrappers printed as *A48*; *dust-jacket*: yellow, printed in dark green as *A48* apart from back cover which lists 27 titles and ends: Faber & Faber Ltd., 24 Russell Square, London, W.C.1 and back flap which lists 9 titles in 13 lines instead of 11

date of publication: July 1942

copy seen: SH

A48c Fourth impression   Faber & Faber 1943

date of publication: July 1943

A48d Fifth impression   Faber & Faber 1944

as *A48* apart from: (4) FOURTH IMPRESSION JULY MCMXLIII/ FIFTH IMPRESSION AUGUST MCMXLIV; *binding*: cream paper-covered boards, printed in bordeaux as *A48*; *dust-jacket*: not seen

date of publication: August 1944

copy seen: SH

A49   COLLECTED POEMS OF
   W. H. DAVIES   Jonathan Cape 1942

contains: as *A47*

print run: 3788 copies printed on 12 May 1942

notes: (a) price increase: 1 May 1942 8s.6d.
(b) although I have been unable to trace a copy I understand from the Jonathan Cape archives, RUL that this is actually the 2nd impression of *A47* with a new title-page
(c) there is conflicting information regarding the various impressions of this book which I have been unable to clarify and which can lead to confusion. In each case I have recorded all available information

A49a   Third impression   Jonathan Cape 1943

COLLECTED POEMS/ *of*/ W. H. DAVIES/ (publisher's device)/
Introduction by/ OSBERT SITWELL/ at foot: JONATHAN CAPE/
THIRTY BEDFORD SQUARE/ LONDON

8vo; (A) in eight plus tipped-in frontispiece, B–I, K–U, X–II and KK in eights, LL in four; 268 leaves plus portrait frontispiece not included in the pagination: (i–iv) v–xxviii (xxix–xxx) 23–507 (508) 509–525 (3)pp; 19.0 × 13.0 cms

as *A47* apart from: (i) half-title: COLLECTED POEMS/ OF W. H. DAVIES; (ii) starts: OTHER BOOKS BY/ ends: AN ANTHOLOGY OF SHORT POEMS; portrait frontispiece captioned: W. H. DAVIES/ from a portrait by Harold Knight; (iii) title-page; (iv) starts: COLLECTED POEMS: FIRST SERIES/ ends: BOUND BY A. W. BAIN & CO. LTD.; v–xx Contents; xxi–xxviii INTRODUCTION/ by OSBERT SITWELL; (xxix) fly-title: COLLECTED POEMS/ OF W. H. DAVIES; (xxx) blank; *binding*: bright blue calico grain cloth, lettered and decorated in silver; front cover: blank; spine: COLLECTED/ POEMS OF/ W. H. DAVIES/ at foot: publisher's device; back cover: blank; *dust-jacket*: mottled blue, printed in black and lettered in white; front: (black decorative rule)/ COLLECTED (in white)/ POEMS (in white)/ *of* (in white)/ W. H. DAVIES (in white)/ INTRODUCTION BY (in black)/ OSBERT SITWELL (in black); spine, in white: Collected/ Poems/ of/ W. H./ Davies/ *636*/ *poems*/ at foot: publisher's device; back, in black: starts: Collected Poems of/ ends: INTRODUCTION BY OSBERT SITWELL; front flap, in black: starts: COLLECTED POEMS OF W. H. DAVIES/ ends: OSBERT SITWELL/ at foot, slanted: 10s. 6d. net; back flap: blank

print run: 4073 copies printed on 19 August 1943 by Alden Press; *price*: 10s.6d.

copies seen: BL (shelf mark: 11612.dd.22; accession date: 8 December 1943); SH (2 copies)

reviews: W. H. Davies, *Punch*, 22 December 1943, 205, 534; Portrait of My Friend, Richard Church, *John o'London's Weekly*, 31 December 1943, L, 1223, 125; *TLS*, 29 January 1944, 58 (portrait)

notes: (a) new introduction by Osbert Sitwell
(b) the dust-jacket seen was also printed on the verso – probably a result of wartime economy

A49b Fourth Impression   Jonathan Cape 1945

as *A49* apart from: final leaf: a stub pasted to rear endpaper; (iv) THIRD
IMPRESSION APRIL 1945; *dust-jacket*: cream background, printed in grey and
orange; front: (vignette of a bird in flight)/ THE/ COLLECTED/ POEMS/ OF (in
grey)/ W. H. DAVIES (in orange, outlined in grey)/ Introduction by Osbert Sitwell
(in grey); spine: THE/ COLLECTED/ POEMS/ OF/ W. H. DAVIES (in grey on
white)/ (vignette of birds in flight)/ (vignette of a bird on a branch of a tree)/ (vignette
of a bird in flight)/ (grey publisher's device); back: blank; front flap: starts:
COLLECTED POEMS OF/ ends: 10s.6d.; back flap: blank

print run: 3249 copies printed on 22 February 1945 by Alden Press; *price*: 10s.6d.

copy seen: SH

A49c Fifth impression   Jonathan Cape 1946

as *A49b* apart from the following: (iv) FOURTH IMPRESSION DECEMBER 1946

print run: 5009 copies printed on 21 June 1946

copy seen: HDB

A49d Sixth impression   Jonathan Cape 1948

print run: 3000 copies printed on 27 May 1948

note: 15s. overprinted on dust-jacket (not seen); 536pp

A49e Seventh impression   Jonathan Cape 1951

print run: 1972 copies printed on 4 June 1952

note: identified as the 6th impression in the Jonathan Cape archives, RUL

A49f Eighth impression   Jonathan Cape 1955

print run: 2928 copies printed on 14 January 1955

notes: (a) price increase: 1 April 1961 18s.
(b) price increases overall: 7s.6d., 8s.6d., 10s.6d., 15s., 16s. and 18s.
(c) identified as the 7th impression in the Jonathan Cape archives, RUL

A50 THE ESSENTIAL W. H. DAVIES   Jonathan Cape 1951

THE ESSENTIAL/ W. H. DAVIES/ Selected, with an Introduction by/
BRIAN WATERS/ (publisher's device)/ JONATHAN CAPE/ THIRTY
BEDFORD SQUARE/ LONDON

8vo; (A)–I and K–U in eights, X in eight; 168 leaves: (1–4) 5–29 (30) 31–247 (248) 249–283 (284) 285–299 (300) 301–333 (3)pp; 19.8 × 13.2 cms; each gathering apart from (A) is signed E.W.H.D on inner margin

(1) half-title: THE ESSENTIAL W. H. DAVIES; (2) starts: *By the same author/* ends: *etc.*; (3) title-page; (4) starts: *The Autobiography of a Super-Tramp/* ends: BOUND BY A. W. BAIN & CO. LTD. LONDON; 5–8 CONTENTS; 9–20 INTRODUCTION – W. H. DAVIES, MAN AND POET signed BRIAN WATERS; 21–333 text; (334–336) blank

contents: p9 INTRODUCTION – W. H. DAVIES, MAN AND POET; p21 SONGS OF GWENT; p31 THE AUTOBIOGRAPHY OF A SUPER-TRAMP; p153 LONDON POEMS; p177 THE SPORT OF FAME (from *Beggars*); p181 INTRODUCTION TO JEWELS OF SONG; p183 NATURE POEMS; p195 A POET'S PILGRIMAGE; p249 LOVE POEMS; p261 LATER DAYS; p285 SWEET-STAY-AT-HOME; p287 MY BIRDS; p301 MY GARDEN; p315 POEMS OF FANCY

contains: p21 Days that have Been; p22 Old Acquaintance. Love Absent. The Mind's Liberty; p23 R is for Remembrance. M is for Mother; p24 The Richest Stones. The Child and the Mariner; p29 In May; p31 The Autobiography of a Super-Tramp; p153 Beggar's Song. The Lodging-House Fire; p155 Saints and Lodgers; p158 Facts. Australian Bill; p159 The Idiot and the Child; p160 An old house in London; p161 Scotty's luck; p162 The Sailor to His Parrot; p163 The Little Ones. The Sleepers; p164 The Bed-Sitting Room; p165 Strong Moments; p166 Dreams of the Sea. Nell Barnes; p167 The Bird of Paradise; p168 The Hospital Waiting-Room; p169 The Inquest; p170 My Old Acquaintance; p171 They're Taxing Ale Again. The Dog; p172 The Cat. One Thing Wanting; p173 Two Women. Telling Fortunes; p174 A Woman's History; p175 The Poet. Traffic; p176 The Two Loves; p177 The Sport of Fame (from *Beggars*); p183 Thunderstorms. A Great Time; p184 The Hermit. The Rain; p185 The Kingfisher. Happy Wind; p186 The Dumb World. The Example; p187 Sheep. From France; p188 The Hawk. Rich Days; p189 April's Charms. Raptures; p190 Easter. In the Snow. Killed in Action; p191 Cowslips and Larks. England; p192 The Villain. The Captive Lion; p193 Lamorna Cove. Our Sussex Downs; p194 The Rabbit. Songs of Joy; p195 A Poet's Pilgrimage; p249 Where She is Now. A Fleeting Passion; p250 Rich or Poor. The Doubtful One; p251 A Woman's Charms; p252 When I in Praise. The Visitor; p253 Jove Warns Us. Molly; p254 Lovely Dames. That Day she Seized; p255 When Yon Full Moon. What thoughts are mine; p256 Love's Caution. The Flirt; p257 Now that she gives. Impudence; p258 Her Merriment. The Trick; p259 To a Lady Friend. Y is for Youth; p261 Later Days; p285 Sweet Stay-at-Home; p287 My Birds; p301 My Garden; p315 Fancy's Home. Confession. Late Singers; p316 Christ, the Man. Poor Kings; p317 Heaven. The Signs; p318 Near a Quiet Stream. The Two Children; p319 A Winter's night. The Bell; p320 A Strange Meeting; p321 On Hearing Mrs Woodhouse play the Harpsichord. The Start; p322 The Lost Sex. Bird and Brook; p323 Let me Confess; p324 Wild Oats. A Thought. To Bacchus; p325 The Poet's Horse. A Miracle; p326 The Rivals. Earth Love; p327 The Fear. S is for Swimmer; p328 A Lonely Coast. The Life of Man; p329 The Treasured Three. Property. Old or Young; p330 This Bantam Star. Ambition; p331 The Poor. Taking Stock. Armed for War; p332 Nailsworth Hill. The Sluggard; p333 Leisure

endpapers: cream; *edges*: trimmed, top edge red

binding: red calico grain cloth, lettered in gilt; front cover: blank; spine: THE/ ESSENTIAL/ W. H./ DAVIES/ at foot: publisher's device; back cover: blank

dust-jacket: buff and cream background, printed in navy; front, on buff, lettering shadowed in white: *The/ ESSENTIAL/ W. H./ DAVIES/* signed, in white at foot: DURNDELL; spine, on buff: *The/ ESSENTIAL* (in white)/ *W. H./ DAVIES* (in navy)/ at foot: (navy publisher's device); back, on cream, in a double decorative panel: starts: *The* ESSENTIAL *Series*/ ends: 10s.6d. net; front flap, on cream: starts: THE ESSENTIAL W. H. DAVIES/ ends: 12s.6d. net; back flap: blank

date of publication: 2 July 1951

print run: 2500 copies printed on 16 April 1951 by Alden Press; *price*: 12s.6d.

copies seen: BL (shelf mark: 11605.c.35; accession date: 18 June 1951); HDB

review: A Dedicated Poet, *TLS*, 10 August 1951, 500

note: variant dust-jacket: printed in black as above but without the signature on front cover

A51   COMPLETE POEMS   Jonathan Cape 1963

THE/ COMPLETE POEMS OF/ W. H. DAVIES/ (publisher's device)/ *With an Introduction by/* OSBERT SITWELL/ *and a Foreword by/* DANIEL GEORGE/ at foot: JONATHAN CAPE/ THIRTY BEDFORD SQUARE/ LONDON

16mo; (A)–I and K–T in sixteens, U in twelve; 316 leaves: (i–iv) v–xxiii (xxiv) xxv–xxxiv (xxxv–xxxvi) 23–595 (596) 597–616 (2)pp; 19.6 × 13.0 cms

(i) half-title: THE COMPLETE POEMS/ OF W. H. DAVIES; (ii) starts: OTHER BOOKS BY/ ends: AN ANTHOLOGY OF SHORT POEMS; (iii) title-page; (iv) starts: COLLECTED POEMS: FIRST SERIES/ ends: BOUND BY A. W. BAIN & CO. LTD. LONDON; v–xxiii Contents; (xxiv) blank; xxv–xxvi FOREWORD/ by DANIEL GEORGE signed DANIEL GEORGE; xxvii–xxxiv INTRODUCTION/ by OSBERT SITWELL; (xxxv) fly-title: THE COMPLETE POEMS/ OF W. H. DAVIES; (xxxvi) blank; 23–595 text; (596) blank; 597–616 Index of First Lines; (617–618) blank

contents: as A47 with the following additional poems: 637 The Muse; 638 Tyrants; 639 To a Butterfly; 640 The Milkmaid's Call; 641 The Milkmaid's Song; 642 Beauty's Danger; 643 City and Country; 644 A Summer's Noon; 645 A Swallow that Flew into the Room; 646 Now; 647 The Poppy; 648 March; 649 The House Builder; 650 A Luckless Pair; 651 The Change; 652 Selfish Hearts; 653 Old Ragan; 654 A Beggar's Life; 655 A Vagrant's Life; 656 Death's Game; 657 The One Real Gem; 658 A Merry Hour; 659 Love's Birth; 660 To a Flirt; 661 Nature's Moods; 662 A Familiar Voice; 663 The Cheat; 664 When I Returned; 665 The Thieves; 666 Sweet Music; 667 Sweet Youth; 668 Time's Justice; 669 Solitude; 670 The Trickster; 671 Vain Beauty; 672 A Month Ago; 673 The Trusting Young; 674 Childhood's Hours; 675 In Days Gone; 676 Go, Angry One; 677 Dead Born; 678 The Sweetest Dream; 679 On the Death of a little Child; 680 Love's Power; 681 War; 682 Self-Love; 683 In the Wood; 684 Love and Immortality; 685 To a

Working Man; 686 Treasures; 687 Beauty's Revenge; 688 Dreaming of Death; 689 The Stars at Work; 690 The Temper of a Maid; 691 The Grey-haired Child; 692 The Winged Flower; 693 The Little Man; 694 Sound and Grace; 695 A Mother's Science; 696 Man; 697 Love's Happiness; 698 Circumstance; 699 Slum Children; 700 To a Rich Lady; 701 A Woman's Glory; 702 Beauty's Bait; 703 O Happy Blackbird; 704 To a Bore; 705 Captives; 706 The Two Spirits; 707 The Long Sleep; 708 The Child and the Man; 709 In a Garden; 710 The Child Chatters; 711 The Emigrant; 712 The Collier's Wife; 713 Stars; 714 Come, Let Me Close; 715 In Silent Groves; 716 The Rev Ebenezer Paul; 717 The Shameless One; 718 We Aim to Fight; 719 My Lady Comes; 720 To my Thoughts; 721 How Late; 722 Brothers; 723 The Girl is Mad; 724 Passion's Greed; 725 A Safe Estate; 726 The Distinction; 727 The Lament of Age; 728 Heigh Ho, the Rain; 729 Love's Inspiration; 730 Whom I Know; 731 Sweet Birds, I Come; 732 The Helpless; 733 When the Cuckoo Sings; 734 The City's Ways; 735 The Dying; 736 Time's Rule; 737 A Familiar Face; 738 The Calm; 739 Strange People; 740 The Happiest Life; 741 The Primrose; 742 The Homeless Man; 743 Violet to the Bee; 744 In June; 745 The End of Summer; 746 One we Love; 747 Saturday Night in the Slums; 748 April; 749 Whiskey

endpapers: cream; *edges*: trimmed, top edge orange

binding: green paper-covered boards, embossed with darker green, lettered and decorated in gilt; front cover: blank; spine: THE/ COMPLETE/ POEMS/ OF/ W. H./ DAVIES/ at foot: publisher's device; back cover: blank

dust-jacket: mainly cream, printed in black; front, orange with a portrait of WHD, lettered in cream: Complete Poems/ W. H. DAVIES/ *Introduction by Osbert Sitwell/ Foreword by Daniel George*; spine, brown, lettered in orange and cream, vertically upwards: The Complete Poems of (in orange)/ W. H. DAVIES (in cream)/ at foot: (orange publisher's device); back, cream, in black: starts: W. H. DAVIES/ ends: (orange publisher's device); front flap: starts: THE COMPLETE POEMS/ ends: (orange publisher's device) 25s. net; back flap, at foot: Jacket design by Derrick Holmes/ (C) Jonathan Cape Ltd., 1963

date of publication: 25 March 1963

print run: 5200 copies printed on 30 November 1962 by Alden Press; *price*: 25s.

copies seen: BL (shelf mark: 11596.h.36; accession date: 12 March 1963); SH

reviews: Life and Works of Poet Who was a Tramp, *The Times*, 28 March 1963, 15; A Poet the Hard Way, Earl of Birkenhead, *Daily Telegraph and Morning Post*, 29 March 1963, 18; by Patric Dickinson, *The Listener*, 4 April 1963, LXIX, 1775, 603; The Nature of a Super-Tramp, *TLS*, 12 April 1963, 247; *Punch*, 17 April 1963, 24, 573 (by Peter Dickinson); Super-Tramp, Naomi Lewis, *New Statesman*, 3 May 1963, LXV, 1677, 680–682; Sentimental Gentleman, *The Spectator*, 17 May 1963, 210, 7038, 641 (by Elizabeth Jennings); Two Independents, Geoffrey Johnson, *Poetry Review* (new series), Summer 1963, LIV, 3, 190–191; by R. George Thomas, *Anglo-Welsh Review*, Winter 1963, 13, 32, 84

text changes from previous printings to A51:
My Lady Comes: 2nd stanza last line: 'butterflies' to 'Butterflies'; 3rd stanza line 1: 'Grass' to 'grass'
Death's Game: 3rd stanza last line: 'I live here' to 'I do live'
Passion's Greed: 2nd stanza line 4: 'necks' to 'neck'

A51a   First American edition   Wesleyan University Press 1965

THE COMPLETE POEMS OF/ W. H. DAVIES/ (rule)/ *With an Introduction by/* OSBERT SITWELL/ *and a Foreword by/* DANIEL GEORGE/ at
foot: WESLEYAN UNIVERSITY PRESS/ Middletown, Connecticut

as *A51* apart from: (iii) title-page; (iv) (c) 1963 BY JONATHAN CAPE LIMITED/
FIRST AMERICAN EDITION 1965/ PRINTED IN GREAT BRITAIN; *binding*:
buff calico grain cloth; front cover: blank; spine, on a simulated brown label edged
in gilt with a gilt rule above and below, in gilt: The Complete/ Poems of/ W. H.
DAVIES/ (fleuron)/ WESLEYAN; back cover: blank; *dust-jacket*: cream, printed in
black; front, in a yellow block: *The Complete Poems of/* W. H. DAVIES (in cream
outlined in black)/ INTRODUCTION BY OSBERT SITWELL/ FOREWORD BY
DANIEL GEORGE/ (portrait of WHD)/; spine, in a yellow block, vertically
downwards: *The Complete Poems of/* W. H. DAVIES (in cream outlined in black)/
at foot: (publisher's device)/ *Wesleyan/ University/ Press*; back: starts: *W. H.
Davies: A Critical Biography/* ends: *Wesleyan University Press*, MIDDLETOWN,
CONNECTICUT; front flap: starts: $7.50/ ends: (*continued on back flap*); back
flap: starts: (*continued from front flap*)/ ends: MIDDLETOWN, CONNECTICUT

print run: used the sheets of the English edition; 1600 4pp cancels printed on 9
September 1964; *price*: $7.50

copy seen: HRHRC

reviews: *Booklist*, 1 September 1965, 62, 27; The Vagabond Muse, Louis
Untermeyer, *Saturday Review*, 16 October 1965, 48, 51; by John Fandel,
Commonweal, 29 October 1965, 83, 128; *Choice*, November 1965, 2, 578; Two
British Chronicles, Ralph J. Mills Jr, *Poetry*, March 1966, 107, 6, 406–410; *Virginia
Quarterly Review*, Winter 1966, 42, 1, xviii

note: title-page is a cancel

A51b   New edition   Jonathan Cape 1967

W. H. DAVIES/ The Complete Poems/ at foot: JONATHAN CAPE/
THIRTY BEDFORD SQUARE LONDON

as *A51* apart from: paperback; (i–iv) v–xxiii (xxiv) xxv–xxxiv (xxxv–xxxvi)
23–595 (596) 597–616 (6)pp; 19.2 × 12.3 cms; (i) half-title: (publisher's device)/
JONATHAN CAPE/ PAPERBACK/ JCP 50/ THE COMPLETE POEMS/ OF W. H.
DAVIES; (ii) blank; (iii) title-page; (iv) starts: FIRST PUBLISHED 1963/ ends:
Richard Clay (The Chaucer Press) Ltd, Bungay, Suffolk; (619–621) starts:
JONATHAN CAPE PAPERBACKS/ ends: *ROBERT FROST* JCP 52; (622) blank;
binding: paper wrappers; front cover, white out of a purple and lavender photograph of sheep in a field: The Complete/ Poems of/ W. H. Davies/ top right-hand
corner, in a panel: 18s/ (IN U.K. ONLY)/ JONATHAN/ CAPE/ PAPERBACK/
(publisher's device); back cover, white background, lettered in black: starts: (rule)/
ends: millions./ top right-hand corner, in a panel, lettered white out of violet:
JONATHAN/ CAPE/ PAPERBACK/ (publisher's device); spine: not seen

date of publication: June 1967; *price*: 18s.

copy seen: BL (shelf mark: X 908/11283; accession date: 30 May 1967)

A52 **YOUNG EMMA**   Jonathan Cape 1980

W. H. DAVIES/ (fleuron)/ *Young Emma*/ With a foreword by/ C. V.
Wedgwood/ at foot: (publisher's device)/ JONATHAN CAPE/ THIRTY
BEDFORD SQUARE LONDON

8vo; (A)–I and K in eights; 80 leaves: (1–8) 9–158 (2)pp; 21.5 × 13.5 cms

(1) half-title: *Young Emma*; (2) blank; (3) *by the same author*/ THE
AUTOBIOGRAPHY OF A SUPER-TRAMP/ THE COMPLETE POEMS OF W. H.
DAVIES; (4) blank; (5) title-page; (6) starts: First published 1980/ ends: The Trinity
Press, Worcester, and London; (7) *Contents*; (8) blank; 9–14 *Foreword*/ by C. V.
Wedgwood; (15) fly-title: *Young Emma*; (16) blank; 17–23 Introduction; (24)
blank; 25–154 text; 155 starts: This is the end of my story, told bluntly and
honestly,/ ends: stuffing a fat pig.; (156) blank; 157–158 Appendix signed Faith-
fully/ G. Bernard Shaw/ Jonathan Cape Ltd.,/ 11 Gower Street,/ W.C.1/ at foot: (c)
The Bernard Shaw Texts 1980 The Trustees of The British/ Museum, The Governors
and Guardians of the National Gallery of/ Ireland and Royal Academy of Dramatic
Art; (159–160) blank

contents: p9 Foreword by C. V. Wedgwood; p17 Introduction; I p25 Bella; II p30
The Trick; III p36 The Gentle Louise; IV p45 The Silk Stocking; V p54 Young
Emma; VI p61 The Complaint; VII p69 The Break Down; VIII p77 A Night of
Horror; IX p87 The Pilgrimage; X p95 The Return; XI p103 Future Plans; XII p110
Leaving London; XIII p115 The Green Country; XIV p120 The Quarrel; XV p130
The Fur Coat; XVI p137 The Marriage; XVII p142 Solving the Mystery; XVIII
p151 The End; p157 Letter from George Bernard Shaw

contains: p127 'Storms' from *A Poet's Calendar* (*A30*)

endpapers: buff; *edges*: trimmed

binding: cinnamon paper-covered boards, lettered in gilt; front cover: blank; spine:
W. H./ DAVIES/ (double rule)/ *Young*/ *Emma*/ at foot: publisher's device; back
cover: blank

dust-jacket: emerald green, printed in black and white; front: W. H. DAVIES (in
black)/ *Young*/ *Emma* (in white edged with black)/ (photographic portraits of WHD
and his wife Helen in oval frames)/ with a foreword by/ C. V. Wedgwood (in black);
spine, vertically downwards: *Young Emma* (in white edged with black) W. H.
DAVIES (in black)/ at foot: (black publisher's device); back: (black and white
portrait of WHD smoking a pipe)/ W. H. DAVIES; front flap: starts: At the age of
fifty, towards the end of the/ ends: *continued on back flap*; back flap: starts: With
disarming honesty, not to say/ ends: affords us all./ at foot: ISBN 0 224 01853 I

date of publication: provisionally 6 November (proof copy); actually 10 November
1980

print run: 6000 copies; *price*: £5.95

copies seen: BL (shelf mark: X. 981/ 22616; accession date: 21 October 1980);
HDB; SH

reviews: Secret loves of the Newport Super-tramp, Sybil Hollingdrake, *South Wales
Argus*, 6 November 1980, 4 (illustration); The super love of the Supertramp, Sybil
Hollingdrake, *Western Mail*, 8 November 1980, 9 (photograph); Secret for 60 years:

the moving love story of young Emma and the poet W. H. Davies, Claire Tomalin, *Sunday Times (Weekly Review)*, 9 November 1980, 33 (illustration); Wife or wanton, Naomi Lewis, *Observer (Review)*, 9 November 1980, 29 (photograph); Wooing a wife, Neville Braybrooke, *Sunday Telegraph*, 9 November 1980, 12; Poet kept pick-up wife a secret, Ann Jones, *South Wales Argus*, 10 November 1980, 4 (photograph); Do we intrude?, William Trevor, *The Guardian*, 13 November 1980, 16; The Super-Tramp takes a bride, Arthur Calder-Marshall, *TLS*, 14 November 1980, 1278; Tragic tale of poet and a girl called Emma, John Fowler, *Glasgow Herald*, 17 November 1980, 8; Why Bunnykins went back to the streets, Valerie Grove, *New Standard*, 18 November 1980, 19; Complex matters, Kevin Crossley-Holland, *Times Educational Supplement*, 28 November 1980, 21; Man in search of a mate: How lost masterpiece was rediscovered after 55 years, Sean Carberry, *Sunday Press*, 30 November 1980, 19; Cosmo Reads the New Books, Penny Vincenzi, *Cosmopolitan*, December 1980, 7; Sense and Sensuality, Marghanita Laski, *Country Life*, 18 December 1980, CLXVIII, 4348, 2371–2372; Book Review: Young Emma, Kay Dick, *The Times*, 20 December 1980, 8; Settling Down, Karl Miller, *London Review of Books*, 20 November-4 December 1980, 15–17; Doubtful tale, Patricia Beer, *The Listener*, 1 January 1981, 105, 2693, 20; An amazing document, Magdalen Goffin, *The Tablet*, 24 January 1981, 86; Mad passionless love, S. T. Meravi, *Jerusalem Post Magazine*, 13 February 1981, 17; *Publishers' Weekly*, 13 February 1981, 219, 88; Young Emma, Carole Angier, *British Book News*, February 1981, 114; Young Emma, *Kirkus Reviews* (AM), 1 March 1981, 320–322; *Library Journal*, 1 April 1981, 106, 786; *London Magazine*, April/ May 1981, 126; *Scotsman (Weekend)*, 9 May 1981, 3; With candor from a simple man, David Rowbotham, *Courier Mail (Brisbane) Saturday Magazine*, 4 April 1981, 24; Young Emma laid bare, Suellen O'Grady, *Weekend Australian Magazine*, 9–10 May 1981, 14

text changes from proof copy to A52 (references are to *A52*):
foreword: p10 line 20: '*' added; last two lines: '*The letter from George Bernard Shaw to Jonathan Cape, dated/ November 1924, is published as an appendix to this book.' added; p(14) fly-title: 'Young Emma' added
XIV: p127 last two lines: '*The publishers regret that although effort has been made, they have/ been unable to trace the authorship of this poem.' to '* 'Storms' was in fact written by Davies himself, and appeared in/ *The* [sic] *Poet's Calendar*, published by Cape in 1927.'
appendix: pp157–158 and copyright statement added

notes: (a) WHD sent the mss of *Young Emma* to Jonathan Cape on 4 October 1924 ("It frightens me now, when it is done"); on 5 December 1924 he wrote (again to Jonathan Cape) "I have already begun to make use of some of its material, and you can destroy the two typewritten copies as soon as you like" (both these letters are held at HRHRC)
(b) the dust-jacket on the proof copy has a pale blue background instead of emerald green
(c) serialised in *The Sunday Times* commencing 9 November 1980
(d) serialised on BBC Radio Four as 'Book at Bedtime' *(E66)* commencing 27 May 1991
(e) Mrs Larkins, a most unsuitable housekeeper, was immortalised in a 4pp story written by WHD which is said to have been published in the *Girl Guide's Book*, Christmas 1928 but I have been unable to trace it. The typed mss was sold by Phillips in London in 1981

A52a First American edition George Braziller 1980

price: $5.95

reviews: The Satisfactory Cause, Herbert Mitgang, *New York Times (Book Review)*, 28 December 1980, VII, 23; *Booklist*, 1 March 1981, 77, 911; by Ann Hulbert, *New Republic*, 21 March 1981, 184, 39; *New Yorker*, 27 April 1981, 57, 161

A52b Paperback edition Coronet Books 1983

A52c Paperback edition: second impression Coronet Books 1983

Young Emma/ (rule)/ W. H. Davies/ With a Foreword by C. V. Wedgwood/ at foot: (publisher's device)/ CORONET BOOKS/ Hodder and Stoughton

as *A52* apart from: paperback: (3–8) 9–14 (15–16) 17–155 (156) 157–158 (4)pp; 18.0 × 10.0 cms; (3) half-title: starts: YOUNG EMMA/ ends: given the full recognition it so surely deserves.; (4) blank; (5) title-page; (6) starts: Copyright (c) 1980 The Trustee of the Estate of/ ends: 3DP) by Collins, Glasgow.; (159–162) starts: ANNE EDWARDS/ ends: ....; *binding*: paper wrappers; white background, printed in full-colour; front cover: (red and black publisher's device) From the author of (in red)/ AUTOBIOGRAPHY OF A SUPER-TRAMP (in red)/ W. H. DAVIES (in black)/ YOUNG/ EMMA (in mid-blue)/ (vignette of a young girl in a 1920's blue dress and a man in a three-piece brown suit and bowler hat)/ "An extraordinary memoir destined to become a classic" (in red)/ PUBLISHERS WEEKLY (in red); spine, vertically downwards: YOUNG EMMA (in mid-blue) W. H. DAVIES (in black) (red and black publisher's device); back cover: starts: "YOUNG EMMA is a masterpiece. (in red)/ ends: 780340321157

copy seen: BL (shelf mark: X. 958/ 30112; accession date: 1 July 1985)

A52d New edition Sceptre Books 1987

in maroon: W. H. Davies/ (rule)/ YOUNG EMMA/ With a Foreword by C. V. Wedgwood/ at foot: (publisher's device)

paperback: (1–11) 12–15 (16–17) 18–21 (22–23) 24–26 (27) 28–31 (32–33) 34–39 (40–41) 42–47 (48–49) 50–54 (55) 56–61 (62–63) 64–69 (70–71) 72–78 (79) 80–84 (85) 86–91 (92–93) 94–98 (99) 100–102 (103) 104–107 (108–109) 110–116 (117) 118–122 (123) 124–126 (127) 128–133 (134–135) 136–138 (139) 140 (4)pp; 19.5 × 12.8 cms

(1) half-title: starts: W. H. DAVIES (in maroon)/ ends: He died in 1940/ at foot: (maroon publisher's device); (2) blank; (3) starts: 'An extraordinary memoir, which may become a minor/ ends: *Kirkus Reviews*; (4) blank; (5) title-page; (6) printed double column, starts: Copyright (c) 1980 The Trustee of/ This book is sold subject to the con-/ ends: ISBN 0–340–40515–5/ Edmunds, Suffolk.; (7) CONTENTS; (8) blank; (9) fly-title: YOUNG EMMA; (10) blank; (11)-15 FOREWORD BY C. V. WEDGWOOD; (16) blank; (17)-21 INTRODUCTION; (22)-138 text; (139)-140 APPENDIX; (141–144) within an outline border with the publisher's device at foot: starts: GALINA VISHNEVSKAYA/ ends: BOOKS OF DISTINCTION

binding: paper wrappers; white background; front cover, within double border in black: From the author of/ THE AUTOBIOGRAPHY OF A SUPERTRAMP/ W. H. DAVIES/ (vignette of a girl in a blue dress and hat in an oval frame)/ (double rule)/ YOUNG/ EMMA/ (double rule)/ 'An amazing document'/ George Bernard Shaw/ (publisher's device); spine, vertically downwards: W H Davies YOUNG EMMA/ at foot: publisher's device; back cover, divided into two, the top two-thirds within a black border with the publisher's device at head: starts: YOUNG EMMA/ ends: *Observer*, lower third in a grey block, left-hand-side: SCEPTRE Books/ Non Fiction/ right-hand side, in a white block: ISBN 0–340 40515–5/ (bar code) 90295/ 9 780340405154/ UK £2.95

copy seen: BL (shelf mark: YC.1987.a.4573; accession date: 18 March 1987)

A53 **SELECTED POEMS**   Oxford University Press 1985

within a decorative triple-ruled border: W. H. DAVIES/ SELECTED/ POEMS/ (rule)/ Chosen with an Introduction by/ Jonathan Barker/ (rule)/ (vignette of a tree)/ William H. Davies. (in facsimile of the author's script)/ (rule)/ OXFORD UNIVERSITY PRESS/ 1985

paperback; (i–iv) v–xv (xvi–xviii) xix–xlix (lx) 1–191 (192) 193–206pp; 19.5 × 12.8 cms

(i) half-title: starts: W. H. DAVIES/ ends: London.; (ii) blank; (iii) title-page; (iv) starts: *Oxford University Press, Walton Street, Oxford OX2 6DP*/ ends: *Guernsey, Channel Islands*; v–xiv CONTENTS; xv ACKNOWLEDGEMENTS; xvi blank; (xvii) starts: I could not help thinking on this fine morning how little is/ ends: *A Poet's Pilgrimage*, 1918; (xviii) blank; xix–xxxii INTRODUCTION; xxxiii–xlvi A CHRONOLOGY OF W. H. DAVIES' LIFE AND WORK; xlvii–xlix A NOTE ON THE SELECTION; (lx) blank; 1–191 text; (192) blank; 193–206 INDEX OF TITLES AND FIRST LINES

contents: pxv Acknowledgements; pxix Introduction; pxxxiii A Chronology of W. H. Davies's Life and Work; pxlvii A Note on the Selection; p1 from *The Soul's Destroyer and Other Poems* (Of the Author, Farmhouse, Marshalsea Road, S.E., 1905; second edition Alston Rivers, 1907); p14 from *New Poems* (Elkin Mathews, 1907); p23 from *Nature Poems and Others* (Fifield, 1908); p38 from *Farewell to Poesy and Other Pieces* (Fifield, 1910); p50 from *Songs of Joy and Others* (Fifield, 1911); p73 from *Foliage: Various Poems* (Elkin Mathews, 1913); p85 from *The Bird of Paradise and Other Poems* (Methuen, 1914); p96 from *Child Lovers and Other Poems* (Fifield, 1916); p103 from *A Poet's Pilgrimage* (Melrose, 1918); p107 from *Forty New Poems* (Fifield, 1918); p117 from *The Song of Life and Other Poems* (Fifield, 1920); p126 from *The Hour of Magic and Other Poems* (Cape, 1922); p132 from the Foreword to *The Autobiography of a Super-Tramp* (1908, 1923 reprint); p133 from *True Travellers: A Tramp's Opera in Three Acts* (Cape, 1923); p136 from *Secrets* (Cape, 1924); p143 from *Later Days* (Cape, 1923); p147 from *A Poet's Alphabet* (Cape, 1925); p153 from *The Song of Love* (Cape, 1927); p158 from *Ambition and Other Poems* (Cape, 1929); p162 from *Poems 1930–31* (Cape, 1932); p168 from *My Birds* (Cape, 1933); p172 from *My Garden* (Cape, 1933); p174 from *Love Poems* (Cape, 1935); p181 from *The Birth of Song: Poems*

1935–36 (Cape, 1936); p184 from *The Loneliest Mountain and Other Poems* (Cape, 1939); p193 Index of Titles and First Lines

contains: p1 The Soul's Destroyer; p4 The Rill; p5 In a Lodging House; p8 Autumn. A Poet's Epitaph; p9 The Cuckoo; p10 Love Absent. The Lodging House Fire; p13 The Hill-side Park; p14 The Ways of Time. The Likeness. The Distinction; p15 Catharine; p16 A Blind Child; p17 The Calm; p18 The Happiest Life; p19 Facts. New-comers; p20 The End of Summer; p21 Saturday Night in the Slums; p22 Whiskey; p23 The Rain. Robin Redbreast; p24 The Wind; p25 Jenny; p26 Nature's Friend; p27 A Maiden and Her Hair; p28 Early Morn. A Beggar's Life; p29 School's Out; p30 A Happy Life; p31 City and Country. A Merry Hour; p32 Truly Great; p33 The Laughers; p34 Australian Bill. A Lovely Woman; p35 Money; p36 Where We Differ; p37 The Sea; p38 The Dark Hour; p39 Jenny Wren; p40 The Idiot and the Child. Now; p41 Rose; p42 The Green Tent; p43 Selfish Hearts; p44 No Master; p45 On the Death of a Little Child. Clouds; p46 In the Country; p47 The Kingfisher; p48 The Sluggard. Old Ragan; p49 The Call of the Sea; p50 The Example; p51 Leisure; p52 Fancy's Home. Sheep; p53 Days that have Been; p54 To a Working Man. Treasures; p57 Beauty's Revenge; p58 Days too Short. The Temper of a Maid; p59 Christ, the Man. The Grey-haired Child. A Mother's Science; p60 The East in Gold. Circumstance; p61 Slum Children; p62 To Sparrows Fighting. The Two Flocks; p63 A Dream; p64 The Heap of Rags; p65 Fairies, Take Care; p66 Captives. The Little Ones; p67 The Sleepers; p68 The Bed-sitting-room; p69 The Child and the Mariner; p73 Thunderstorms; p74 Strong Moments. A Greeting; p75 Sweet Stay-at-Home; p76 Christmas; p77 The Old Oak Tree; p78 Poor Kings; p79 My Youth. Mad Poll; p80 Francis Thompson; p81 Heigh Ho, the Rain. Night Wanderers; p82 The Two Lives; p83 The Fog; p84 Dreams of the Sea; p85 The Best Friend. Heaven; p86 The Mind's Liberty. The Weeping Child; p87 A Fleeting Passion; p88 The Hawk. The Moon; p89 A Great Time. The Black Cloud; p90 Rich Days. The Child Chatters; p91 The Hermit. The Collier's Wife; p92 Stars; p93 Come, Let Me Close. On the Mountain; p94 The Rev Ebenezer Paul. Nell Barnes; p95 The Bird of Paradise; p96 This Night; p97 Kitty and I; p98 Thou Comest, May. The Hospital Waiting-Room; p99 The White Cascade. The Inquest; p100 The Two Children; p101 Come, thou Sweet Wonder. Charms; p102 Friends; p103 The Power of Silence; p103 In Neath Valley; p104 The Blind Boxer; p105 I am the Poet Davies, William; p106 The Moon and a Cloud. The Hunt; p107 Confession. Easter; p108 My Old Acquaintance; p109 A Winter's Night. The Excuse. In the Snow; p110 Molly. Killed in Action (Edward Thomas); p111 Cowslips and Larks; p112 Forgiveness. Till I Went Out. The Girl is Mad; p113 In Time of War. England; p114 Come, let us Find; p115 The Birds of Steel. The Dancer; p116 On Hearing Mrs Woodhouse Play the Harpsichord; p117 Passion's Greed; p117 Oh, Sweet Content!; p118 The Villain. The Rat; p119 The Cat. To-day. When Leaves Begin; p120 Passion's Hounds; p121 The Truth. Love's Caution; p122 A Child's Pet; p123 One Thing Wanting. Her Mouth and Mine; p124 from *The Song of Life* (XIV, XX–XXX); p126 The Hour of Magic; p127 The Beautiful. Two Women; p128 Pastures. Wild Oats; p129 A Thought. Strength. To Bacchus; p130 A Woman's History; p131 from *The Trance*; p132 (This man has talent . . .); p133 A Chant. Beggar's Song; p134 Around that Waist. Her Body's a Fine House. Oh for a Glass of Wine!; p135 Without Contentment, what is Life? Night is the only Time I Live; p136 Who Bears in Mind; p136 The Rainbow; p137 Love, Like a Drop of Dew. Leaves; p138 The Pond. The Meadow. Cant. Breath; p139 Down Underground; p140 The Rabbit. To a Lady Friend; p141 The Two Heavens. The Doll; p142 Violet and Oak; p143 Evil.

The Poet; p144 A Lonely Coast. (Still do I claim . . .) The Two Loves; p145 No Man's Wood. The Life of Man; p146 The Bust; p147 (An artist draws . . .) The Treasured Three. (This little town's a purer place). J is for Jealousy; p148 N is for Nature; p149 O is for Open. P is for Pool; p150 R is for Remembrance. S is for Swimmer; p151 U is for Union. W is for Will; p152 X is for Expecting; p153 Z is for Zany. from *The Song of Love* LXXX–LXXXVIII; p155 Hill and Vale. Storms; p156 Old or Young. Sport; p157 Winter Fire. Peace and Goodwill; p158 Ambition. For Sale; p159 Uncertainty. Charity; p160 A Child's Fancy. A Silver Wonder; p161 Moss and Feather. Day or Night; p162 In Winter. Silver Hours; p163 Mangers. Starlings; p164 Wonderful Places. Trails; p165 The Poor. A Fleeting Wonder; p166 The Visitor. Age and Youth; p167 Jewels. The World Dictates; p168 Ourselves. Dreamers. Wild Creatures; p169 Magpies. On Finding a Dead Bird Under My Window; p170 Voices of Scorn. One Poet Visits Another; p171 My Rockery. To Play Alone. Flying Blossoms; p172 A Bright Day. Breast to Breast. Eyes; p173 The River Severn. Bells; p174 The Man of Moods. Love and Money. To-night; p175 Married Couples. Love Lights His Fire; p176 Past and Present. Competitors; p177 The Ghost. Pecking; p178 Good and Evil. Let Us Lie Close; p179 Stings. A Lullaby of Rest. Beauty and Brain; p180 The Tyrants. His Throne; p181 The Faithful One. The Birth of Song; p182 Man. All's Well. Street Criers; p183 The Conquerors. Named; p184 Song of the Miners. Good Friends. The Loneliest Mountain; p185 The Load of Pearls. Taking Stock. Worms; p186 A Cat's Example. Trust; p187 Common Joys. Speed; p188 Armed for War. The Tugged Hand; p189 All in June. The Worm's Contempt; p190 Looks. Nailsworth Hill; p191 That Golden Time

binding: paper wrappers, printed in colour: front cover, an outer beige border with an inner brown panel divided into four sections: top panel, turquoise: W. H. DAVIES (in pale blue)/ SELECTED POEMS (in white)/ (beige fleuron) Chosen by Jonathan Barker (in white) (beige fleuron)/ middle panel (of three): portrait of WHD signed at foot: To W. H. Davies/ from/ Augustus John/ Nov. 1918/ side panels, turquoise and blank; spine, beige, lettered downwards: W. H. DAVIES (in brown) SELECTED POEMS (in turquoise) (brown publisher's device); back cover, white, printed in black: starts: In writing these verses I am attempting to make poetry/ ends: constitutes an overdue critical re-evaluation of his work./ at foot: Cover illustration: *W. H. Davies* by Augustus/ ISBN 0-19-281432-X/ John, 1918. National Portrait Gallery, London./ (bar code)/ (publisher's device in bold)/ Oxford Paperbacks/ Oxford University Press/ £3.95 net in UK   9 780192814326

date of publication: 24 January 1985

print run: 4000 copies printed in 1984; *price*: £3.95

copies seen: BL (shelf mark: X.958/ 28008; accession date: 21 January 1985); HDB; CH

reviews: *TLS*, 25 January 1985, 79 (by J. Bayley); by Lawrence Normand, *Poetry Wales*, 1985, 21, 1, 133–136; Paperback Choice, *The Observer*, 3 February 1985, 51; One-legged super-tramp, Peter Quennell, *The Spectator*, 23 February 1985, 254, 8172, 21; *British Book News*, April 1985, 197; *Times Educational Supplement*, 14 June 1985, 28; by WH, *Critical Quarterly*, Summer 1985, 2, 93; Rediscovering W. H. Davies, Michael Cullup, *PN Review 47*, 1985, 12, 3, 36–38; by W. S. Milne, *Agenda*, Spring 1986, 19, 1, 50

note: price increases: 25 March 1988 £4.95; 28 February 1991 £6.95

A53a Oxford Poets edition   Oxford University Press 1992

as *A53* apart from: 21.5 × 13.5 cms; (i) half-title: starts: W. H. DAVIES/
SELECTED POEMS/ ends: Council.; (iii) title-page undated; (iv) starts: *Oxford
University Press, Walton Street, Oxford* OX2 6DP/ ends: *J. W. Arrowsmith Ltd.,
Bristol*; *binding*: paper wrappers: cream background, printed in full-colour: front
cover, within a deep cream border, divided horizontally into three blocks: breaking
the top of the border: OXFORD/ POETS/ breaking the lower border: publisher's
device/ first block, lettered cream out of olive-green: W. H. DAVIES/ Selected
Poems/ (black rule)/ second block, lettered cream out of maroon: CHOSEN BY
JONATHAN BARKER/ third and main block: hills, trees, a house, a train and a
tunnel signed Ethelbert White; spine, in black: W. H. DAVIES SELECTED POEMS/
at foot: OXFORD POETS monogram; rear cover, in black: starts: (OXFORD/
POETS monogram) (portrait of WHD)/ ends: Lawrence Normand, *Poetry Wales*/ at
foot: Cover illustration: *The Tunnel*, 1919, by Ethelbert White./ ISBN 0-19-281432-
X/ Private collection./ (bar code)/ Oxford Paperbacks/ Oxford University Press/
(publisher's device)/ £7.99 net in UK/ 9 780192 814326

date of publication: 29 February 1992

print run: 1750 copies; *price*: £7.99

copy seen: SH

B Works edited or compiled by WHD

B1 FORM (new series) Morland Press 1921

eds A. O. Spare and W. H. Davies

vol 1, no 1, October 1921: p5. editorial by WHD; p6. When I look into a glass. When I had met Fee Fie the twentieth time

de luxe edition limited to 50 copies, specially printed on hand-made paper and signed by the editors, open to subscription; *price*: £1.1.0d. per copy (not seen)

subscription rate: £2.14.0d. per annum; single copies 4s.6d. by post or 3-monthly numbers 14s.0d. (1 vol); 1st and 2nd nos issued free to previous subscribers of new format (issued as a quarterly in 1916 and 1917 then halted by war)

vol 1, no 2, November and December 1921: p40. drawing by William Nicholson captioned: 'R G to W H D "I don't really dislike the Moon Bill!" '; p41. editorial by WHD; p42. The Portrait

vol 1, no 3, January 1922: p79. editorial by WHD; p80. A Woman's History (by Ebenezer Winkle)

folio, printed in colours with woodcuts, etc, in orange wrappers printed in black

copies seen: NL; HRHRC

reviews: New and Recent Periodicals, *London Mercury*, November 1921, V, 25, 5; *The Spectator*, 5 November 1921, 127, 4871, 603

B2 SHORTER LYRICS Poetry Bookshop 1922

SHORTER LYRICS/ *OF THE*/ TWENTIETH CENTURY/ 1900–1922/ SELECTED,/ WITH A *FOREWORD*, BY/ W. H. DAVIES/ (publisher's device)/ at foot: THE POETRY BOOKSHOP/ 35 DEVONSHIRE STREET, LONDON, W.C.1

8vo; (A)–* and J–L in eights; 96 leaves: (1–6) 7–192pp; 17.0 × 10.7 cms variable

(1–2) blank; (3) half-title: SHORTER LYRICS/ *OF THE*/ TWENTIETH CENTURY; (4) blank; (5) title-page; (6) PUBLISHED OCTOBER, 1922/ at foot: THE WESTMINSTER PRESS/ 411A HARROW ROAD/ LONDON, W.9; 7–10 A Foreword signed W. H. DAVIES; 11–16 Index; 17–187 text; 188–190 Acknowledgements; 191–192 Index of Authors

contains: p128. The Kingfisher

paper: watermarked: (crown)/ Abbey Mills/ Greenfield; chain lines 2.3 cms apart and vertical *endpapers*: cream; *edges*: uncut, top edge trimmed and yellow in colour

binding: rose paper-covered boards, decorated and lettered in black; front cover, within a decorative border: SHORTER LYRICS/ *of the* TWENTIETH/ CENTURY, 1900–1922/ (publisher's device)/ SELECTED, WITH A/ FOREWORD, BY/ W. H. DAVIES/ (publisher's device)/ The Poetry Bookshop; spine: (publisher's device)/ SHORTER/ LYRICS/ 1900/ to/ 1922/ Selected/ by/ W. H./ DAVIES/ at foot: THE/ POETRY/ BOOKSHOP/ (publisher's device); back cover, within a decorative border: diamond-shaped decoration incorporating publisher's device; *dust-jacket*: not seen

date of publication: October 1922; *price*: 5s.

copies seen: BL (shelf mark: 011604.ee.31; accession date: 24 October 1922); HRHRC; SH

reviews: Two Anthologies, *Country Life*, 2 December 1922, LII, 1352, 739–740; *English Review*, December 1922, XXXV, 580; *To-day*, December 1922, IX, 52, 76; *Nation and Athenaeum*, 13 January 1923, XXXII, 15, 585–586; Poetry, JCS, *London Mercury*, February 1923, VII, 40, 431–432

note: 5th thousand published the same year bound in orange paper-covered boards with a black mosaic pattern, orange-brown cloth spine; front cover: blank; spine, lettered in brown: (rule)/ SHORTER/ LYRICS/ 1900/ TO/ 1922/ Selected/ by/ W. H./ DAVIES/ at foot: THE/ POETRY/ BOOKSHOP/ (rule); top edge brown; *dust-jacket*: not seen

B2a   Special edition   Poetry Bookshop 1922

as *B2* apart from: 19.0 × 12.5 cms variable; (1) half-title as *B2* (3); (2) blank; (3) limitation: Two Hundred Copies of/ this Edition have been/ printed on Large Paper/ No. ; *paper*: watermarked: HOLBEIN; *endpapers*: cream; *edges*: uncut, deckle fore and lower edge; *binding*: mottled cream paper-covered boards, black cloth spine; front cover, on a white paper label 4.2 × 5.8 cms, in black within a double ruled panel: Shorter Lyrics/ of the Twentieth Century/ 1900–1922/ (fleuron)/ *Selected, With a Foreword,/ by* W. H. *Davies*; spine, lettered in gilt: Shorter/ Lyrics/ of the/ Twentieth/ Century/ (fleuron)/ at foot: *The Poetry/ Bookshop*; *dust-jacket*: cream with an embossed surface, printed in black; front: Shorter Lyrics/ of the Twentieth Century/ 1900–1922/ *Selected, With a Foreword,/ by* W. H. *Davies*/ at foot: *Limited Large Paper Edition*; spine: *Shorter/ Lyrics/ of the/ Twentieth/ Century/* (fleuron)/ at foot: *The Poetry/ Bookshop*; back and both flaps: blank

date of publication: December 1922

print run: 200 copies; *price*: 15s.

copy seen: HRHRC (no 31, Richard Church's copy)

B3   JEWELS OF SONG   Jonathan Cape 1930

JEWELS OF SONG/ AN ANTHOLOGY OF SHORT POEMS/ COMPILED BY/ W. H. DAVIES/ Author of/ *The Autobiography of a Super-Tramp, etc./* (publisher's device)/ at foot: JONATHAN CAPE/ THIRTY BEDFORD SQUARE/ LONDON

8vo; * in ten, A–I and K–P in eights, Q in six; 136 leaves: (i–iv) v–xx 1–250pp; 19.2 × 12.5 cms variable

(i) half-title: JEWELS OF SONG/ An Anthology of Short Poems; (ii) blank; (iii) title-page; (iv) FIRST PUBLISHED 1930/ JONATHAN CAPE, 30 BEDFORD SQUARE, LONDON/ AND 91 WELLINGTON STREET WEST, TORONTO/ JONATHAN CAPE & HARRISON SMITH/ 139 EAST 46TH STREET, NEW YORK/ at foot: PRINTED IN GREAT BRITAIN BY J. AND J. GRAY/ EDINBURGH; v–xviii Contents; xix–xx Introduction signed W. H. DAVIES./ SHENSTONE,/ NAILSWORTH, GLOS./ 26th October 1929.; 1–240 text; 241–250 Index of First Lines; (251–252) blank

contains: p88. The Kingfisher. Leisure

endpapers: cream; *edges*: top and fore edge trimmed

binding: white, blue and grey calico textured cloth with an angular design, mid-blue cloth spine; front cover: blank; spine, lettered in gilt: JEWELS/ OF SONG/ (fleuron)/ W. H./ DAVIES/ at foot: JONATHAN CAPE; back cover: blind-blocked publisher's device; *dust-jacket*: not seen

date of publication: 22 September 1930

print run: 2000 copies printed on 18 July 1930; bound by A. W. Bain; *price*: 6s.

copies seen: BL (shelf mark: 11607.c.33; accession date: 10 September 1930); HDB (2 copies); SH

reviews: TLS, 27 November 1930, 1009; Two Anthologies, AA, *Bookman*, November 1930, LXXIX, 470, 142

notes: (a) the HDB copies are inscribed: 'My Book,/ W. H. Davies.' and 'To Dinah (Helen)/ from/ Bunny (W. H. Davies)/ 1930'
(b) 3s.6d. edition published 10 September 1934
(c) re-issued as *An Anthology of Short Poems (B4)* with new preface

B4 AN ANTHOLOGY OF SHORT POEMS   Jonathan Cape 1938

AN ANTHOLOGY/ OF/ SHORT POEMS/ Compiled by/ W. H. DAVIES/ (publisher's device)/ at foot: JONATHAN CAPE/ THIRTY BEDFORD SQUARE/ LONDON

8vo; * in twelve, A–I and K–P in eights, Q in six; 138 leaves: (1–2) (i–iv) v–xxii 1–250 (2)pp; 19.0 × 12.5 cms

(1–2) blank; (i) half-title: AN ANTHOLOGY OF SHORT POEMS; (ii) blank; (iii) title-page; (iv) starts: FIRST PUBLISHED AS JEWELS OF SONG 1930/ ends: BOUND BY A. W. BAIN & CO. LTD.; v–xviii Contents; xix-xx Preface to the New Edition (1938) signed W. H. DAVIES./ YEWDALES,/ NAILSWORTH,/ GLOS.; xxi–xxii Introduction signed W. H. DAVIES./ SHENSTONE,/ NAILSWORTH,/ GLOS./ 26th October 1929; 1–240 text; 241–250 Index of First Lines; (251–252) blank

endpapers: cream; *edges*: trimmed

binding: turquoise calico grain cloth, embossed, lettered in gilt; front cover: blank; spine: AN/ ANTHOLOGY/ OF/ SHORT POEMS/ (decorative rule)/ W. H. DAVIES/ at foot: (publisher's device); back cover: blank

dust-jacket: mainly canary yellow, printed in black; front: An Anthology/ of/ Short Poems/ compiled by/ W. H. DAVIES/ (publisher's device); spine: An/ Anthology/ of/ SHORT/ POEMS/ compiled/ by/ W. H. DAVIES/ at foot: (publisher's device); back, in purple on a white background: starts: POETRY/ ends: 3s.6d. *net*; in a yellow panel on the outer edge of the back cover, vertically upwards in black: THE WORKS OF W. H. DAVIES; front flap, on white: starts: AN ANTHOLOGY OF/ ends: 3s.6d. net; back flap: blank

date of publication: May 1938; *price*: 3s.6d.

copy seen: SH

B4a Second impression   Jonathan Cape 1938

print run: 2000 copies printed on 3 May 1938 by Alden Press; bound by A. W. Bain

B4b Third impression   Jonathan Cape 1943

as *B4* apart from: (A) in eight (one a stub), B–I and K–R in eights; 136 leaves including a stub: (i–iv) v–xxii 1–250pp; (iv) RE-ISSUED UNDER THE PRESENT TITLE 1938; *binding*: turquoise calico grain cloth; front cover: blank; spine, lettered vertically upwards in gilt: AN ANTHOLOGY OF SHORT POEMS (triple rule) W. H. DAVIES; back cover: blank

date of publication: 8 April 1943

print run: 1000 copies printed on 21 October 1942; *price*: 3s.6d.

copy seen: SH

B4c Fourth impression   Jonathan Cape 1944

print run: 2000 copies printed on 21 January 1944

BI Introductions and epilogues by WHD

BI 1 REFLECTIONS – A SECOND SERIES
OF DRAWINGS by Edmond X. Kapp   Jonathan Cape 1922

REFLECTIONS/ A SECOND SERIES OF DRAWINGS/ WITH
INTRODUCTORY COMMENTS BY/ LAURENCE BINYON AND W. H.
DAVIES/ EDMOND X. KAPP/ (publisher's device)/ at foot: JONATHAN
CAPE/ ELEVEN GOWER STREET, LONDON

contains: 'A lonely coast, where sea-gulls scream' from *Later Days* (*A26*)

copy seen: CH

notes: (a) 6 lines of 'A Lovely Woman' are quoted as the dedication which is signed
WHD
(b) introduction dated November 1922

BI 2 MOLL FLANDERS
         Simpkin, Marshall, Hamilton, Kent & Co Ltd 1924

MOLL/ FLANDERS/ *By*/ DANIEL DEFOE/ *With Biographical Note and
Special/ Introduction by*/ W. H. Davies/ at foot: London:/ Simpkin,
Marshall, Hamilton, Kent & Co. Ld.

copy seen: BL (shelf mark: 11825.bb.36; accession date: 30 October 1924)

note: introduction ppvii–xi

BI 3 MOLL FLANDERS
         Simpkin, Marshall, Hamilton, Kent & Co Ltd 1924

within a decorative panel, at head: THE/ Abbey Classics/ centrally, within a
pictorial border: MOLL/ FLANDERS/ *By*/ DANIEL DEFOE/ *With
Biographical Note and Special/ Introduction by* W. H. DAVIES/
Ornamented by Martin Travers/ beneath main border, within a panel:
Simpkin, Marshall, Hamilton, Kent & Co. Ltd. E.C.4

copy seen: BL (shelf mark: 012201.b.1/21; accession date: 30 January 1925)

notes: (a) introduction ppix–xiii
(b) reprinted 1929 by John Lane/ Bodley Head with illustrations by John Austen

BI 4 BURNS' POETICAL WORKS   Collins (?1925)

within a decorative panel, with a cherub on either side, supported by a
cupid: BURNS'/ POETICAL/ WORKS/ With Introduction by/ W. *J*.[sic]

Davies/ at foot: London and Glasgow/ COLLINS' CLEAR-TYPE PRESS/ signed on the right-hand-side at foot: GARTH/ JONES/ NORFOLK

copy seen: BL (shelf mark: 11612.dd.20; accession date: 11 July 1943)

notes: (a) title-page: 'W. H. Davies' misprinted 'W. J. Davies'
(b) introduction ppvii–xiii
(c) Second edition: BURNS'/ POETICAL/ WORKS/ (fleuron)/ With an Introduction by/ W. H. Davies/ at foot: LONDON & GLASGOW/ COLLINS CLEAR-TYPE PRESS; *copy seen*: BL (shelf mark: 11612.k.5; accession date: 27 May 1942)

BI 5   ADVENTURES OF A SCHOLAR
TRAMP   by Glen H. Mullin   Jonathan Cape 1925

ADVENTURES OF A/ SCHOLAR TRAMP/ *By*/ GLEN H. MULLIN/ *With an Introduction by*/ W. H. DAVIES/ (publisher's device)/ at foot: JONATHAN CAPE LIMITED/ THIRTY BEDFORD SQUARE LONDON

copies seen: BL (shelf mark: 12709.aa.6; accession date: 22 October 1925); SH (review copy)

mss of introduction: in part typescript, part WHD's script (Jonathan Cape archives, RUL)

text changes from manuscript to BI 5 (reference is to *BI 5* not mss):
p10, line 20: from 'great Falls' to 'Falls'

notes: (a) 'Mullin' misprinted 'Mullen' on spine
(b) introduction pp9–12
(c) introduction omitted in American edition

BI 6   A GREENE FOREST   Hesperides Press 1930

A GREENE FOREST (in green)/ or a naturall Historie, Wherein may bee seene first the most/ sufferaigne Vertues in all the whole kinde of Stones & Mettals:/ next of Plants, as of Herbes, Trees, and Shrubs, Lastly of Brute/ Beastes, Foules, Fishes, creeping wormes, and Serpents, and that/ Alphabetically: so that a Table shall not neede/ Compiled by JOHN MAPLET, M. of Arte (in green)/ and student in Cambridge: extending hereby that God might/ especially be glorified: and the people furdered/ (double rule)/ *Reprinted from the Edition of 1567/* (rule)/ With an Introduction by/ W. H. DAVIES/ (double rule)/ THE HESPERIDES PRESS (in green)/ 2, Little Essex Street, W. C. 2/ LONDON/ 1930

copies seen: BL (shelf mark: Cup.510.cef.1; accession date: 31 January 1930) (out of series); HDB (out of series); NL

note: introduction ppv–(ix)

BI 6a   Special edition   Hesperides Press 1930

copies seen: NL (no 10); HDB (out of series)

note: also 6 copies on special hand-made vellum

BI 7   THE ROMANCE OF THE ECHOING
WOOD   Newport 1937

within a decorative border: THE – ROMANCE/ OF – THE/ ECHOING –
WOOD/ (decoration)/ BY/ W – J – T – COLLINS/ WITH/ INTRODUCTION
– BY/ ARTHUR – MACHEN/ EPILOGUE – BY/ WILLIAM – HENRY –
DAVIES/ DECORATIONS – BY – E – F – POWELL – A . R . C . A – LOND.

contains: p43. 'Will no one stop that Blackbird now' from *The Loneliest Mountain*
(*A45*)

copies seen: NL (nos 63, 64 and 75); HRHRC (no 202)

note: epilogue pp41–43

BI 7a   Special edition   Newport 1937

copies seen: BL (shelf mark: 12612.k.2; accession date: 31 December 1937) (author's
presentation copy); NL (no 13); HRHRC (no 34)

C Contributions to periodicals

(poems except where shown)

C1 A Stormscape (published anonymously), *Monmouthshire Merlin and South Wales Advertiser*, 25 February 1887, 7 (*note*: never reprinted)

C2 letter signed W. H. Davies, *Renfrew Mercury*, Ontario, Canada, 1 May 1899

C3 Nature's Moods, *Nation*, 2 May 1908, III, 5, 159

C4 Love's Birth, *Nation*, 11 July 1908, III, 15, 526

C5 Joy and Pleasure, *Nation*, 8 August 1908, III, 19, 676

C6 The Pleasant Life, *Nation*, 14 November 1908, IV, 7, 256; *Literary Digest*, 5 December 1908, 37, 23 (9270), 856

C7 Political and Diplomatic II: How It Feels to be Out of Work, article, *English Review*, 1 December 1908, I, 168–171

C8 The Dark Hour, *Nation*, 9 January 1909, IV, 15, 580

C9 The Milkmaid's Song, *Nation*, 6 February 1909, IV, 19, 717

C10 On Expecting Some Books, *Nation*, 6 March 1909, IV, 23, 862

C11 Clouds, *Nation*, 22 May 1909, V, 8, 284

C12 In the Country, *Country Life*, 29 May 1909, XXV, 647, 766

C13 Roses and Lilies, *Country Life*, 5 June 1909, XXV, 648, 825

C14 Knitting, *Nation*, 19 June 1909, V, 12, 426

C15 A Sweet Day, *Country Life*, 26 June 1909, XXV, 651, 927

C16 A Case of Pearls, *Country Life*, 17 July 1909, XXVI, 654, 76

C17 Jenny Wren, *Country Life*, 31 July 1909, XXVI, 656, 147

C18 Now, *Nation*, 14 August 1909, V, 20, 720

C19 An Old House, *Nation*, 18 September 1909, V, 25, 888

C20 Rose, *Westminster Gazette*, 4 January 1910, 2

C21 Angry. The Kingfisher. Man, *Nation*, 8 January 1910, VI, 15, 612; Angry, *Living Age*, 26 March 1910, XLVI (7th series), 3429, 770; The Kingfisher, *Living Age*, 3 May 1913, LIX (7th series), 3591, 258

C22 The Finder, story, *Nation*, 26 February 1910, VI, 22, 842–843

C23 The House-Builder, *The Tramp*, March 1910, I, 178

C24 Song of the Purbeck Marblers, *Westminster Gazette*, 15 March 1910, 2

C25 To Sparrows Fighting, *Odd Volume*, 1910, 14

C26 The Voice of the Sluggard, article, *The Tramp*, March 1910, I, 56–59 (1 illustration by Arthur Watts)

C27 The Sluggard, *The Tramp*, June 1910, I, 191

C28 A Month Ago, *The Tramp*, June 1910, I, 223

C29 In Spring. In May. O Happy Blackbird, *English Review*, June 1910, V, 385–386; In May, *Living Age*, 31 May 1913, LIX (7th series), 3595, 514

C30 Love's Power, *Westminster Gazette*, 13 June 1910, 2

C31 Shopping, *Westminster Gazette*, 16 June 1910, 2

C32 The Career of Hurdy Gurdy Joe, article, *The Tramp*, September 1910, I, 337–340 (2 illustrations by Joseph Simpson)

C33   The Power of Music, *Nation*, 22 October 1910, VIII, 4, 163; *Living Age*, 26 November 1910, XLIX (7th series), 3464, 514

C34   Songs of Joy, *Vineyard*, November 1910, I, 2, 123; *Living Age*, 25 January 1913, LVIII (7th series), 3577, 194

C35   The Flood, *Westminster Gazette*, 16 November 1910, 2

C36   Seeking Beauty, *Westminster Gazette*, 28 November 1910, 2

C37   Sadness and Joy, *Vineyard*, January 1911, I, 4, 313

C38   Beauty's Revenge, *Westminster Gazette*, 6 January 1911, 2

C39   The Sleepers, *Nation*, 28 January 1911, VIII, 18, 723; *Living Age*, 20 May 1911, LI (7th series), 3489, 450

C40   Days That Have Been, *Nation*, 11 March 1911, VIII, 24, 969

C41   My Lady Comes, *Country Life*, 1 April 1911, XXIX, 743, 435

C42   Leisure, *Vineyard*, May 1911, I, 8, 541; *Girl Guide Gazette*, February 1925, XII, 134, 34; *Argosy*, July 1926, 1, 2, 89, *The Listener* (extract), 10 September 1930, IV, 87, 393 (photograph by Edgar Ward); *This England*, Spring 1983, 4–11 (illustrated)

C43   Fairies, Take Care, *English Review*, May 1911, VIII, 186

C44   The Heap of Rags, *Nation*, 20 May 1911, IX, 8, 294

C45   The Quarrel, *Westminster Gazette*, 27 June 1911, 2

C46   The Example. The Temper of a Maid, *Open Window*, July, 1911, II, 201–202; The Temper of a Maid, *Living Age*, 18 January 1913, LVIII (7th series), 3576, 130

C47   The Winged Flower, *Westminster Gazette*, 4 July 1911, 2

C48   letter: The "English Review" and the "Spectator", with WHD as one of the signatories, *Academy and Literature*, 22 July 1911, LXXXI, 2046, 125

C49   letter re: The Letter (a poem), *Notes and Queries*, 29 July 1911, 11S, IV, 83, 88

C50   The East in Gold, *Vineyard*, August 1911, I, 11, 741

C51   Days Too Short, *English Review*, September 1911, IX, 186; *Living Age*, 27 January 1912, LIV (7th series), 3525, 194; 10 August 1912, LVI (7th series), 3553, 322 and 10 May 1913, LIX (7th series), 3592, 322

C52   In the Wood, *Westminster Gazette*, 5 September 1911, 2; *Living Age*, 2 December 1911, LIII (7th series), 3517, 514

C53   Fancy's Home, *Westminster Gazette*, 8 September 1911, 2; *Living Age*, 6 January 1912, LIV (7th series), 3522, 2

C54   The Elements, *Nation*, 16 September 1911, IX, 25, 878

C55   When the Cuckoo Sings, *Nash's Magazine*, October 1911, V, 1, 125

C56   Children at Play, *Vineyard*, November 1911, 2nd year, 2, 131

C57   A Happy Wind, *Great Thoughts*, 1911, I (7th series), 274

C58   Hidden Love, *Nash's Magazine*, November 1911, V, 2, 231

C59   Dream Tragedies, *Nash's Magazine*, January 1912, V, 4, 491

C60   Joy Supreme. A Woman's Charms, *English Review*, January 1912, X, 204–205

C61   Strong Moments, *Nation*, 17 February 1912, X, 20, 819; *New Republic*, 10 November 1920, XXIV, 310, 273

C62   Winter's Beauty, *Westminster Gazette*, 23 February 1912, 2

C63   In Knole Park, *Nation*, 27 April 1912, XI, 4, 130

C64   The Owl, *Living Age*, 11 May 1912, LV (7th series), 3540, 322

C65   Young Beauty, *Rhythm*, June 1912, II, V, 20

C66   The Wonder-Maker, *Westminster Gazette*, 25 June 1912, 2

C67 Mad Poll, *Nation*, 29 June 1912, XI, 13, 477

C68 A Greeting, *Westminster Gazette*, 2 July 1912, 2; *Literary Digest*, 11 January 1913, 46, 2 (1186), 104; under 'Extracts from Recent Poetry', *Poetry and Drama*, March 1914, 5, 81–82

C69 Sheep, *Living Age*, 27 July 1912, LVI (7th series), 3551, 194

C70 The Two Lives, *Rhythm*, August 1912, II, VII, 84

C71 Eldorado's Gold, *English Review*, August 1912, XII, 1–2

C72 Smiles, *Rhythm*, September 1912, II, VIII, 135

C73 The Lonely Dreamer, *Westminster Gazette*, 9 October 1912, 2

C74 Dreams of the Sea, *Nation*, 19 October 1912, XII, 3, 142

C75 Christmas, *English Review*, December 1912, XIII, 1

C76 Night Wanderers, *Nation*, 28 December 1912, XII, 13, 571

C77 The Best Friend, *Odd Volume*, 1913, 40

C78 Love and the Muse, *Nation*, 1 February 1913, XII, 18, 748; *Literary Digest*, 5 April 1913, 46, 14 (1198), 793–794

C79 Love's Inspiration, *Nash's Magazine*, March 1913, VII, 6, 803

C80 Francis Thompson, *Nation*, 8 March 1913, XII, 23, 928; *Literary Digest*, 19 April 1913, 46, 16 (1200), 911

C81 The Strange City, *English Review*, April 1913, XIV, 1–12; part as 'The Fog', *Literary Digest*, 3 May 1913, 46, 18 (1202), 1032; part as 'Heigh Ho! The Rain', *Living Age*, 10 January 1914, LXII (7th series), 3627, 66; part as 'Poor Kings', *Living Age*, 25 July 1914, LXIV (7th series), 3655, 194; part as 'My Youth', *Living Age*, 1 August 1914, LXIV (7th series), 3656, 258

C82 Laughing Rose, *Nash's Magazine*, April 1913, VIII, 1, 84

C83 Thunderstorms, *New Statesman*, 12 April 1913, I, 1, 17; *Living Age*, 4 July 1914, LXIV (7th series), 3652, 2

C84 The Beggar's Hunt, article, *Blue Review*, May 1913, 1, 1, 24–27 (includes 'The Hunt')

C85 The Blind Boxer, *Nation*, 24 May 1913, XIII, 8, 314

C86 The Signs, *New Statesman*, 28 June 1913, I, 12, 370

C87 In a Garden, *Nation*, 19 July 1913, XIII, 16, 608

C88 Love's Youth, *Blue Review*, July 1913, 1, 3, 151

C89 A Great Time, *New Statesman*, 23 August 1913, I, 20, 626

C90 The Hawk, *Nation*, 30 August 1913, XIII, 22, 814; *Living Age*, 13 December 1913, LXI (7th series), 3623, 642

C91 This World, *New Statesman*, 4 October 1913, I, 26, 819

C92 The Mind's Liberty, *New Statesman*, 1 November 1913, II, 30, 115

C93 The Hermit, *Nation*, 8 November 1913, XIV, 6, 256

C94 In Silent Groves, *Nation*, 22 November 1913, XIV, 8, 361

C95 Infancy, *Westminster Gazette*, 28 November 1913, 2

C96 The Bird of Paradise, *Poetry and Drama*, December 1913, I, 4, 421

C97 The Dumb World, *New Statesman*, 20 December 1913, II, 37, 338

C98 Sweet Stay-at-Home, *Living Age*, 20 December 1913, LXI (7th series), 3624, 706

C99 The Collier's Wife, *Nation*, 10 January 1914, XIV, 15, 642

C100 Heaven, *New Statesman*, 17 January 1914, II, 41, 467; as 'The Welshman's Heaven', *Wales*, March 1914, 6, 39

C101 Near a Quiet Stream, *Westminster Gazette*, 5 February 1914, 2

C102 A Greeting. A May Morning. Dream Tragedies, (under 'Extracts from

Recent Poetry') *Poetry and Drama*, March 1914, 5, 81–82; A May Morning, *Millgate*, May 1940, part II, 416 (portrait)

C103   The Wanderer, *New Statesman*, 28 March 1914, II, 51, 787

C104   Early Spring. Her Absence, *New Weekly*, 28 March 1914, I, 2, 44; Early Spring, *Literary Digest*, 2 May 1914, 47, 18 (1254), 1055; *Poetry and Drama*, December 1914, II, 8, 425 under 'Extracts from Recent Poetry'

C105   Two Spring Songs: From France and Starers, *Westminster Gazette*, 8 April 1914, 2

C106   A Midsummer Night's Storm, *Nation*, 30 May 1914, XV, 9, 341; *Living Age*, 10 October 1914, LXV (7th series), 3666, 66

C107   Plants and Men, *Nation*, 11 July 1914, XV, 15, 567

C108   Seeking Joy, *Living Age*, 18 July 1914, LXIV (7th series), 3654, 130

C109   Body and Spirit, *Poetry and Drama*, December 1914, II, 8, 350

C110   This Night, *Nation*, 26 December 1914, XVI, 13, 416

C111   The One Singer, *New Statesman*, 23 January 1915, IV, 94, 391

C112   April's Charms, *Nation*, 17 April 1915, XVII, 3, 85

C113   Thou Comest, May, *Nation*, 29 May 1915, XVII, 9, 289

C114   Friends, *Nation*, 19 June 1915, XVII, 12, 388

C115   The Hospital Waiting-Room, *Nation*, 17 July 1915, XVII, 16, 513

C116   The White Monster, *Nation*, 18 September 1915, XVII, 25, 804

C117   The Power of Silence. Kitty and I. The Inquest, *English Review*, October 1915, XXI, 233–235

C118   Child Lovers, *Nation*, 9 October 1915, XVIII, 2, 53

C119   The Two Children, *Nation*, 27 November 1915, XVIII, 9, 328

C120   Come, Thou Sweet Wonder, *Nation*, 29 January 1916, XVIII, 18, 641

C121   The White Cascade, *Nation*, 4 March 1916, XVIII, 23, 793

C122   The Visitor, *Form*, eds A. O. Spare and Francis Marsden, April 1916, I, 1, 45

C123   Charms, *Form*, April 1916, I, 1, 48

C124   Shakespeare Works, *A Book of Homage to Shakespeare: To Commemorate the Three Hundredth Anniversary of Shakespeare's Death* MCMXVI, Humphrey Milford/ Oxford University Press 1916, 105 (*note*: limited to 250 copies)

C125   Birds, *Nation*, 3 June 1916, XIX, 10, 289

C126   Lovely Dames, *Nation*, 23 September 1916, XIX, 26, 791

C127   Cowslips and Larks, *New Statesman*, 23 September 1916, VII, 181, 591

C128   Come, Let Us Find, *Nation*, 4 November 1916, XX, 5, 179

C129   A Strange Meeting, *New Statesman*, 18 November 1916, VIII, 189, 160

C130   In the Snow, *New Statesman*, 9 December 1916, VIII, 192, 232; *Living Age*, 23 December 1916, IV (8th series), 3781, 706 and 7 April 1917, VI (8th series), 3796, 2

C131   My Love Could Walk. My Old Acquaintance, *Nation*, 30 December 1916, XX, 13, 472; My Love Could Walk, *Living Age*, 5 May 1917, VI (8th series), 3800, 258

C132   Till I Went Out, *New Statesman*, 6 January 1917, VIII, 196, 327

C133   The Dancer, *Nation*, 10 February 1917, XX, 19, 653

C134   Raptures, *To-day*, March 1917, I, 1, 26

C135   What Thoughts are Mine. Confession, *Form*, April 1917, 1, 2, 18

C136   Easter, *Nation*, 5 April 1917, XXI, 1, 14

C137 Killed in Action (Edward Thomas), *Nation*, 21 April 1917, XXI, 3, 70; as 'To Edward Thomas', *Living Age*, 8 February 1919, XIII (8th series), 3892, 329

C138 Rags and Bones, *Nation*, 2 June 1917, XXI, 9, 223

C139 To My Thoughts, *New Statesman*, 9 June 1917, IX, 218, 231

C140 When Yon Full Moon, *Nation*, 28 July 1917, XXI, 17, 432; *Welsh Poets*, collated by A. G. Prys Jones (Erskine Macdonald 1917) 30

C141 Late Singers, *Nation*, 15 September 1917, XXI, 24, 612

C142 In Time of War, *Nation*, 17 November 1917, XXII, 7, 243

C143 The Holly on the Wall, *Nation*, 29 December 1917, XXII, 13, 440

C144 Molly, *To-day*, January 1918, II, 11, 172

C145 April's Lambs, *To-day*, April 1918, III, 14, 42

C146 When Leaves Begin. The Truth, *Nation*, 6 April 1918, XXIII, 1, 14

C147 The Soul's Companions, *Nation*, 20 April 1918, XXIII, 3, 64

C148 On Hearing Mrs Woodhouse Play the Harpsichord, *Nation*, 18 May 1918, XXIII, 7, 171; *Life and Letters To-Day continuing London Mercury and Bookman*, September 1942, XXXIV, 61, 166

C149 The Birds of Steel, *Nation*, 10 August 1918, XXIII, 19, 499

C150 The Force of Love, *To-day*, December 1918, IV, 22, 144

C151 The Coming of Peace, *New Statesman*, 21 December 1918, XII, 298, 241; *Living Age*, 8 February 1919, XIII (8th series), 3892, 384

C152 Passion's Hounds, *Nation*, 8 March 1919, XXIV, 23, 672

C153 Her Mouth and Mine, *To-day*, April 1919, V, 26, 62

C154 The Dog. A Child's Pet, *Nation*, 10 May 1919, XXV, 6, 170

C155 Love Impeached, *The Owl*, May 1919, I, 12; *Living Age*, 18 October 1919, XVI (8th series), 3928, 163

C156 The Rat, *The Chapbook*, Poetry Bookshop, July 1919, 1, 30

C157 The Cat, *New Statesman*, 12 July 1919, XIII, 327, 371; *Living Age*, 30 August 1919, XV (8th series), 3921, 571

C158 Worm-Proof. Comfort, *Voices in Poetry and Prose*, August 1919, II, 2, 45

C159 What County?, *Nation*, 9 August 1919, XXV, 19, 562

C160 The Flirt, *To-day*, September 1919, VI, 34, 15

C161 Love's Caution, *London Mercury*, November 1919, I, 1, 13

C162 How Kind is Sleep, *To-day*, December 1919, VI, 34, 122; *Living Age*, 17 January 1920, XVII (8th series), 3941, 173

C163 The Song of Life, *English Review*, January 1920, XXX, 1–9

C164 Love's Silent Hour, *Nation*, 10 April 1920, XXVII, 2, 45

C165 Let Me Confess, *To-day*, May 1920, VII, 39, 87; *Living Age*, 3 July 1920, XIX (8th series), 3965, 62

C166 Now That She Gives, *To-day*, June 1920, VII, 40, 131

C167 Lamorna Cove, *Nation*, 21 August 1920, XXVII, 21, 642; *Now & Then*, October 1922, 27

C168 My Memory of Edward Thomas, article, *Voices in Poetry and Prose*, October 1920, IV, 4, 118–22; as 'Memories', *School*, November 1933, I, 3, 19–20

note: mss held at HRHRC with the following corrections: (in WHD's hand): p120 line 3: 'general' to 'every', line 7 up: 'met' to 'known'; (in an unknown hand): title: 'Edward Thomas' to 'My Memory of Edward Thomas'; p120 line 19: 'the *Nation*' to 'this journal', line 20: 'the *Times Literary Supple-*

ment' to 'that journal' and 'the *Athenaeum*' to 'a third', last line: 'two' to 'three'; p121 line 3: 'Delamare' to 'Walter de la Mare' and 'and others' to 'among them', line 17: 'Mr Delamare's' to 'Mr de la Mare's', line 4 up: 'My condition was not very firm and steady at that time' to 'I was suffering from great nervous fatigue on that occasion'; p122 line 2: 'Rd' to 'Road', line 7: 'How quickly these editors have changed their minds' added; (nb: pp nos relate to the *Voices* article)

C169   To Bacchus, *To-day*, December 1920, VIII, 44, 57; *Living Age*, 16 April 1921, XXII (8th series), 4006, 62

C170   Margery, *New Republic*, 1 December 1920, XXV, 313, 18

C171   When Autumn's Fruit. Now that the Tears, *The Chapbook*, January 1921, 19, 3–4

C172   When Autumn's Fruit, *New Republic*, 26 January 1921, XXV, 321, 251

C173   A Second Innocence, *Nation and Athenaeum*, 26 February 1921, XXVIII, 22, 739

C174   Without Contentment, *To-day*, June 1921, VIII, 46, 149; *Living Age*, 6 August 1921, XXIII (8th series), 4022, 368

C175   Where She is Now, *New Republic*, 15 June 1921, XXVII, 341, 80

C176   On What Sweet Banks, *New Republic*, 13 July 1921, XXVII, 345, 196

C177   The Happy Man, *Now & Then*, September 1921, 16; *New Republic*, 4 January 1922, XXIX, 370, 151

C178   When I look into a glass. When I had met Fee Fie the twentieth time, *Form* (new series), October 1921, 1, 1, 6; 'When I look into a glass' as 'A Thought', *Living Age*, 30 June 1923, XXX (8th series), 4121, 793

C179   The Portrait, *Form*, November/ December 1921, 1, 2, 42

C180   Joy, *To-day*, December 1921, VIII, 48, 218; *Living Age*, 28 January 1922, XXV (8th series), 4047, 244

C181   A Woman's History, *Form*, January 1922, 1, 3, 80

C182   The Woods and Banks, *New Republic*, 4 January 1922, XXIX, 370, 155; *Now & Then*, July 1922, 13

C183   The Collar. Strength, *The Chapbook*, February 1922, 25, 5

C184   Impudence. Telling Fortunes. Two Women. The Hour of Magic. How Many Buds, *Harper's Magazine*, March 1922, CXLIV, DCCCCLXII, 488–489; 'How Many Buds' as 'Wasted Hours', *Living Age*, 24 February 1923, XXIX (8th series), 4103, 486

C185   Wild Oats, *Youth*, March 1922, 1, 2, 56; *Now & Then*, October 1922, 7

C186   Our Sussex Downs, *Nation and Athenaeum*, 23 September 1922, XXXI, 26, 821; *Living Age*, 2 December 1922, XXVIII (8th series), 4091, 505

C187   When Love is Young, *To-day*, December 1922, IX, 52, 42

C188   Leaves. Love's Payment. Love, Like a Drop of Dew, *Harper's Magazine*, December 1922, CXLVI, DCCCLXXI, 98; Leaves, *The Spectator*, 8 September 1923, 131, 4967, 318

C189   Our Longer Life, *Nation and Athenaeum*, 20 January 1923, XXXII, 16, 611; *Living Age*, 7 April 1923, XXX (8th series), 4109, 45

C190   At Night. Violet and Oak, *The Spectator*, 10 February 1923, 130, 4937, 241; At Night, *New Republic*, 5 September 1923, XXXVI, 457, 47

C191   The Poet's Horse, *Nation and Athenaeum*, 17 March 1923, XXXII, 24, 917; *Harper's Magazine*, December 1923, CXLVIII, DCCCLXXIII, 96

C192 Secrets. The Two Stars, *London Mercury*, March 1923, VII, 41, 465; The
      Two Stars, *New Republic*, 21 November 1921, XXXVI, 468, 327
C193 The Schemes of Love. Down Underground, *Golden Hind*, April 1923, 3
C194 A Dead Man's Song, *Harper's Magazine*, April 1923, CXLVI, DCCCLXXV,
      608
C195 The Rainbow, *London Mercury*, May 1923, VIII, 43, 7; *Living Age*, 28
      June 1924, XXXIV (8th series), 4173, 1256
C196 See Where Young Love, *The Spectator*, 2 June 1923, 130, 4953, 925
C197 My Garden, *London Mercury*, June 1923, VIII, 44, 121
C198 What I Gained and Lost by Not Staying at School, article, *Teachers World*,
      13 June 1923, XXIX, 970, 543
C199 Moll Flanders, review of *Moll Flanders (BI 3)* by Daniel Defoe, *New
      Statesman*, 23 June 1923, XXI, 532, 330 ('One by One' quoted)
C200 A Mystery, *New Statesman*, 14 July 1923, XXI, 535, 419
C201 The Snowflake. The Two Heavens, *New Republic*, 25 July 1923, XXXV,
      451, 233
C202 At Night. Rogues, *New Republic*, 5 September 1923, XXXVI, 457, 47;
      Rogues, *Winter Owl*, eds Robert Graves and William Nicholson, 1923, 4
C203 Leaves. One Token, *The Spectator*, 8 September 1923, 131, 4967, 318
C204 The Doll, *London Mercury*, September 1923, VIII, 47, 459
C205 To a Lady Friend, *To-day*, September 1923, X, 55, 2
C206 Poets and Critics, article, *New Statesman*, 8 September 1923, XXI, 543, 619
      ('The Time of Dreams' quoted)
C207 Earth Love. The Rivals, *Harper's Magazine*, October 1923, CXLVII,
      DCCCLXXXI, 585
C208 The Cave, *London Mercury*, November 1923, IX, 49, 13
C209 review of *Songs of Childhood* (Longmans Green & Co 1923) and *Come
      Hither* (Constable 1923) by Walter de la Mare, *New Statesman*, 8 December
      1923, XXII, 556, 272
C210 The Meadow. The Fear. The Poet's Horse, *Harper's Magazine*, December
      1923, CXLVIII, DCCCLXXXIII, 96

C211 On the King's Highway, article, *Green-Kirtled Spring*, note by N. Graham
      Smith (Elkin Mathews 1924) unpaginated (review: PAG, *Country Life*, 3
      May 1924, LV, 1426, 706–707)
C212 The Nature Lover, *New Statesman*, 19 January 1924, XXII, 561, 423
C213 Timepieces, *London Mercury*, March 1924, IX, 53, 456
C214 The Ghost. The Will, *Harper's Magazine*, March 1924, CXLVIII,
      DCCCLXXXVI, 470; The Ghost, *New Statesman and Nation*, 10
      November 1934, VIII, 194, 669
C215 Light, *The Spectator*, 8 March 1924, 132, 4993, 368; *Yale Review*, July
      1926, XV, 4, 671
C216 In Springtime, *Harper's Magazine*, April 1924, CLVIII, DCCCLXXXVI,
      592; *Sunday Graphic and Sunday News*, 26 May 1940, 1312, 19
C217 Spade and Sword, *The Spectator*, 26 April 1924, 132, 5000, 673
C218 Venus, *The Spectator*, 21 June 1924, 132, 5008, 1000
C219 The Poet, *Bookman*, July 1924, LXVI, 394, 245 (under the pseudonym
      "Gwalia")
C220 Re-Union, *The Sphere*, 5 July 1924, XCVIII, 1276, 16
C221 The Swimmer, *The Spectator*, 30 August 1924, 133, 5018, 292
C222 Love the Jealous, *Yale Review*, October 1924, XIV, 1, 81

C223   The Pool, *The Spectator*, 4 October 1924, 133, 5023, 454; *Living Age*, 15
       November 1924, XXXVI (8th series), 4193, 398
C224   This Crowded Life, *London Mercury*, November 1924, XI, 61, 10; *New
       Republic*, 28 January 1925, XLI, 530, 255
C225   Distance, *The Spectator*, 29 November 1924, 133, 5031, 826
C226   A Child's Movements, *New Republic*, 10 December 1924, XLI, 523, 72
C227   Dust, *RPA Annual*, 1924, 74

C228   A Memory, *The Spectator*, 10 January 1925, 134, 5037, 46; *Living Age*, 28
       March 1925, XXXVII (8th series), 4212, 714
C229   Philosophy, *Harper's Magazine*, January 1925, CL, DCCCXCVI, 175
C230   Dream-Song, *New Republic*, 15 April 1925, XLII, 541, 218
C231   Garden Plans, *London Mercury*, May 1925, XII, 67, 10
C232   Come, Come My Love, *The Spectator*, 16 May 1925, 134, 5055, 810
C233   The Rock, *New Republic*, 12 August 1925, XLII, 558, 311
C234   Crowns, *The Spectator*, 15 August 1925, 135, 5068, 268
C235   The Bite, *London Mercury*, October 1925, XII, 72, 574
C236   New Delights, *Harper's Magazine*, October 1925, 151, 522

C237   Love's Plans, *The Spectator*, 27 March 1926, 136, 5100, 587; *Living Age*,
       24 April 1926, XLII (8th series), 4268, 187; *Bookman*, December 1926,
       LXIV, 4, 419
C238   Space, *The Spectator*, 22 May 1926, 136, 5108, 866
C239   Where Shall We Live. Contented Hearts, *Atalanta's Garland: Being the
       Book of the Edinburgh University Women's Union* (University Press by T &
       A Constable 1926) 9; Contented Hearts, *Bookman*, April 1928, LXVII, 2,
       140

C240   The White Horse, *London Mercury*, February 1927, XV, 88, 344
C241   An Epitaph, *Living Age*, 1 April 1927, 332, 4303, 599
C242   Storms, *New Republic*, 13 July 1927, LI, 658, 196; *Literary Digest*, 6
       August 1927, 94, 6 (1946), 35
C243   The Time of Dreams, *New Republic*, 20 July 1927, LI, 659, 224
C244   Light and Darkness, *Country Life*, 23 July 1927, LXII, 1592, 109
C245   Old or Young, *The Dragon*, Lent Term 1927, 19; *Literary Digest*, 18
       February 1928, 96, 7 (1974), 32; *Harper's Magazine*, February 1928, 156, 320
C246   A Dream of Winter, *Country Life*, 24 December 1927, LXII, 1614, 942

C247   To A Contemporary, *Harper's Magazine*, January 1928, 156, 242
C248   Born of Tears, *New Statesman*, 14 January 1928, XXX, 768, 434
C249   Heaven and Earth, *Country Life*, 14 January 1928, LXIII, 1617, 35
C250   The Skylark, *New Republic*, 7 March 1928, LIV, 692, 98

C251   If Love Survives, *New Republic*, 9 January 1929, LVII, 736, 215
C252   The Blest, *The Spectator*, 12 January 1929, 142, 5246, 52
C253   Hand or Mouth, *New Republic*, 23 January 1929, LVII, 738, 270
C254   Friends Unborn, *The Spectator*, 25 May 1929, 142, 5265, 825
C255   Peace and Rest, *Time and Tide*, 31 May 1929, 10, 22, 659
C256   A Young Thrush, *The Spectator*, 6 July 1929, 143, 5271, 13
C257   Ships and Stars, *New Statesman*, 24 August 1929, XXXIII, 852, 600
C258   Charity. Hunting Joy, *Now & Then*, Autumn 1929, 33, 39
C259   Old Autumn, *The Spectator*, 9 November 1929, 143, 5289, 662; *Living
       Age*, 15 December 1929, 337, 4352, 504; *Everybody's*, 11 October 1930, 6

C260   The [sic] Bantam Star, *New Republic*, 27 November 1929, LXI, 782, 14

C261   Faults, *New Statesman*, 8 February 1930, XXXIV, 876, 569

C262   A Lullaby of Rest, *The Spectator*, 4 October 1930, 145, 5336, 450

C263   "Jewels of Song", letter to the Editor, address: Nailsworth, Glos, *New Statesman*, 22 November 1930, XXXVI, 917, 204

C264   The Little Devil. Love Lights His Fire, *London Mercury*, December 1930, XXIII, 134, 105

C265   Clocks, *The Listener*, 4 March 1931, V, 112, 377

C266   No Careless Mind, *Argosy*, July 1931, X, 62, 129

C267   Wonderful Places, *Argosy*, September 1931, X, 64, viii

C268   The Lady of Light, *Argosy*, November 1931, X, 66, viii (illustrated by Arthur Wragg)

C269   Come Melancholy. Age and Youth, *New Statesman and Nation*, 16 January 1932, III, 47, 65

C270   No Place or Time, *New Statesman and Nation*, 2 April 1932, III, 58, 419

C271   Cotswold Country, review of *Wold without End* by H. J. Massingham (Cobden-Sanderson 1932), *The Listener*, 4 May 1932, VII, 173, Late Spring Book Supplement, VIII

C272   Rungs of the Ladder – II, article, *The Listener*, 18 May 1932, VII, 175, 724–725

C273   What Light, *New Statesman and Nation*, 29 October 1932, IV, 88, 513

C274   On Finding a Dead Bird Under my Window, *Argosy*, February 1933, XIII, 81, 1 (illustrated)

C275   Confessions of a Down and Out, review of *Down and Out in Paris and London* by George Orwell (Victor Gollancz 1933), *New Statesman and Nation*, 18 March 1933, V, 108, 338–339

C276   The River Severn, *Monmouthshire Review*, April 1933, I, 2, 107

C277   The Dead, *The Spectator*, 19 May 1933, 150, 5473, 709

C278   Beggar's Luck, *Time and Tide*, 24 June 1933, XIV, 25, 765

C279   The Compensation, *Time and Tide*, 28 October 1933, XIV, 43, 1282

C280   Logic, *Now & Then*, Winter 1933, 46, 43

C281   Seed and Flower, *Monmouthshire Review*, April 1934, II, 2, 131

C282   Let Love Live On. The Ghost. The Jealous Lover, *New Statesman and Nation*, 10 November 1934, VIII, 194, 669

C283   A Cotswold Village, article in *English Country: Fifteen Essays by Various Authors*, edited with an introduction by H. J. Massingham (Wishart & Co 1934) 97–110

C284   England, *Daily Express*, 24 December 1934, 10802, 8

C285   Flirting. The Faithful One, *The Programme*, February 1935, 2, 12, 1–2; Flirting, (under 'A Page of Poetry'), *Books of To-Day*, August 1935, 20

C286   Reluctant Sorrow. Flirting. Brother Gods, *Books of To-Day: A Monthly Journal for General Readers*, August 1935, 20 (under 'A Page of Poetry')

C287   Success, *Argosy*, June 1936, XIX, 121, 28

C288   The Dreamer. Pride and Humility. Life. The Worm's Contempt. The Load of Pearls, *London Mercury and Bookman*, February 1937, XXXV, 208, 360–361

C289   Armed for War. Speed. Men that Think, *London Mercury and Bookman*, September 1937, XXXVI, 215, 418–419

C290   Common Joys, *British Annual of Literature*, 1938, 1, 25
C291   A Cat's Example, *Time and Tide*, 12 March 1938, XIX, 11, 337
C292   The Tugged Hand, *Time and Tide*, 14 May 1938, XIX, 20, 670
C293   Silent Eyes. The Deed. Days and Years, *London Mercury and Bookman*, June 1938, XXXVIII, 224, 106–107

C294   The Last Years. Worms, *Welsh Review*, February 1939, 1, 1, 16

C295   In Winter, *Literary Digest*, October 1946, I, 3, 19 (as 'Poems of this Century: 1')

C296   March, *This England*, Spring 1983, 25
C297   extract from *The Autobiography of a Super-Tramp (A3)*, *This England*, Spring 1983, 28 and 35

C298   No man lives life so well, (photocopy of an undated signed mss held at NL)

D Prose and poems appearing in anthologies

D1   **The Pocket Book of Poems and Songs for the Open Air**   E Grant Richards 1907
compiled by Edward Thomas; p197 A Drinking Song; p249 Lines from *The Soul's Destroyer (A1)*

D2   **Georgian Poetry 1911–1912**   Poetry Bookshop 1913
ed E. H. Marsh; p55 The Child and the Mariner; p60 Days too Short; p61 In May; p62 The Heap of Rags; p63 The Kingfisher

D3   **The Winged Anthology**   John Richmond Ltd 1914
selected and arranged by Irene Osgood and Horace Wyndham; p277 Robin-Redbreast; p339 To a Butterfly; p352 The Moth

D4   **The Children's Cameos of Poetry and Prose for Use in Schools: Book III**   George Philip (1914)
p44 The Rain

D5   **The Country Life Anthology of Verse**   Offices of *Country Life* 1915
ed P. Anderson Graham; p104 My Lady Comes

D6   **Poems of Today**   Sidgwick & Jackson 1915
p60 Days that have been; p67 Early Morn; p101 Leisure

D7   **Georgian Poetry 1913–1915**   Poetry Bookshop 1916
ed as *D2*; p65 Thunderstorms; p66 The Mind's Liberty; p67 The Moon; p68 When on a Summer's Morn; p69 A Great Time; p70 The Hawk; p71 Sweet Stay-at-Home; p72 A Fleeting Passion; p73 The Bird of Paradise

D8   **The Flowers I Love**   T C & E C Jack Ltd (1916)
a series of twenty-four drawings in colour by Katharine Cameron; with an anthology of flower poems selected by Edward Thomas; p44 The Primrose; p55 The Daisy; p72 The End of Summer

D9   **An Annual of New Poetry**   Constable & Co 1917
p19 Brothers; p20 The Bell; p21 In England; p22 Jove Warns Us; p23 Angel and Mystery

D10 **A Book of the Sea**   Clarendon Press 1918
selected and arranged by Lady Sybil Scott; p103 Dreams of the Sea; p104 The Sea

D11 **Twelve Poets**   Selwyn & Blount 1918
p21 Love Speechless; p22 When Leaves Begin; p23 The Captive Lion; p24 One Thing Wanting

D12 **Georgian Poetry 1916–1917**   Poetry Bookshop 1918
ed as *D2*; p159 The White Cascade; p160 Easter; p161 Raptures; p162 Cowslips and Larks

D13 **New Paths: Verse. Prose. Pictures 1917–1918**   C W Beaumont 1918
eds C. W. Beaumont and M. T. H. Sadler; decorated by Anne Estelle Rice; p12 Birds; p13 That Day She Seized

D14 **Georgian Poetry 1918–1919**   Poetry Bookshop 1919
ed as *D2*; p29 Lovely Dames; p30 When Yon Full Moon; p31 On Hearing

Mrs Woodhouse Play the Harpsichord; p32 Birds; p33 Oh, Sweet Content!; p34 A Child's Pet; p35 England; p36 The Bell

D15   **A Miscellany of Poetry – 1919 –**   Cecil Palmer & Hayward 1919
ed W. Kean Seymour; decorations by Doris Palmer; p38 The Villain; p39 Bird and Brook; p40 Passion's Hounds; p41 The Truth; p42 The Force of Love; p43 April's Lambs

D16   **Air Pie: The Royal Air Force Annual**   Cecil Palmer & Hayward 1919
eds Private W. Kean Seymour and Cadet Cecil Palmer of the RAF; p47 A Song

D17   **The Years at the Spring**   Harrap & Co Ltd 1920
compiled by L. D'O. Walters; introduction by Harold Monro; illustrated by Harry Clarke; p85 The Kingfisher; p86 Sheep

D18   **The Way of Poetry**   Collins (1920)
ed John Drinkwater; p35 Raptures; p84 Leisure; p212 The Moon

D19   **An Anthology of Modern Verse**   Methuen & Co Ltd 1921
chosen by A. Methuen; introduction by Robert Lynd; p52 Where She is Now; p53 Leisure. The Kingfisher; p54 Rich Days; p55 A Great Time. Early Spring; p56 The Moon

D20   **Selections from Modern Poets**   Martin Secker 1921
made by J. C. Squire; p135 Days too Short; p136 The Example; p137 The East in Gold; p138 The Happy Child; p139 A Great Time; p140 The White Cascade; p141 In May; p142 Thunderstorms; p143 Sweet Stay-at-Home

D21   **Georgian Poetry 1920–1922**   Poetry Bookshop 1922
ed as D2; p37 The Captive Lion; p38 A Bird's Anger; p39 The Villain; p40 Love's Caution; p41 Wasted Hours; p42 The Truth

D22   **A Miscellany of Poetry 1920–1922**   John G Wilson 1922
ed William Kean Seymour; p49 Our Sussex Downs

D23   **Poems about Birds from the Middle Ages to the Present Day**   T Fisher Unwin Ltd 1922
chosen and edited with an introduction and notes by H. J. Massingham; preface by J. C. Squire; p351 Day's Black Star

D24   **The Poet's Year**   Cambridge University Press 1922
compiled by Ada Sharpley; 8 January. Robin Redbreast; 8 May. Early Morn; 9 July. The Green Tent

D25   **Modern American and British Poetry**   Harcourt, Brace & Co 1923
ed Louis Untermeyer; with suggestions for study by Olive Ely Hart; p277 Days too Short; p278 The Moon. The Example; p279 A Greeting

D26   **Come Hither**   Constable 1923
made by Walter de la Mare; 7 Early Morn; 44 Sweet Stay-at-Home; 96 A Child's Pet; 151 Leisure; 267 Oh, Sweet Content; 399 The Child and the Mariner

D27   **The Best Poems of 1922**   Jonathan Cape 1923
selected by Thomas Moult; decorated by Philip Hagreen; p109 Our Sussex Downs

D28   **Childhood in Verse and Prose**   Oxford University Press 1923
chosen by Susan Miles; p57 The Inquest; p58 Infancy

D29   **The Golden Book of Modern English Poetry 1870–1920**   J M Dent 1923
selected and arranged by Thomas Caldwell; introduction by Lord Dunsany; p219 Truly Great; p220 The Kingfisher; p221 The Moon. Lovely Dames; p222 Leisure

D30   **An Anthology of English Verse**   Collins (1924)
ed John Drinkwater; p100 The Moon

D31   **A Book of English Poems Graded for Use in Schools:**
Part Two   University of London Press 1924
ed J. H. Jagger; illustrated by Gladys M. Rees; p70 Rich Days

D32   **The Best Poems of 1923**   Jonathan Cape 1924
selected and decorated as D27; p56 The Rainbow; p77 See Where Young
Love

D33   **The Best Poems of 1924**   Small, Maynard & Co 1924
ed L. A. G. Strong; p58 Rogues

D34   **The Golden Treasury of Modern Lyrics**   Macmillan 1924
arranged by Laurence Binyon; p200 Thunderstorms; p214 The Example;
p311 The Hawk; p314 A Thought

D35   **The Chilswell Book of English Poetry**   Longmans Green & Co 1924
compiled and annotated for the use of schools by Robert Bridges; 163 The
Kingfisher

D36   **The Poetry of Flight**   Heath Granton Ltd 1925
ed Stella Wolfe Murray; foreword by Sir Samuel J. T. Hoare, Secretary of
State for Air; p55 The Birds of Steel

D37   **A Treasury of Verse**   George G. Harrap/D. Taraporevala, Bombay 1925
selected by Madalen Edgar, revised (1947) and arranged by Dorothy
Margaret Stuart; p145 Early Spring; p303 Leisure

D38   **The Best Poems of 1924**   Jonathan Cape 1925
selected and decorated as D27; p69 Venus; p70 Re-Union; p90 The Poet

D39   **The Bookman Treasury of Living Poets**   Hodder & Stoughton (1925)
ed A. St. John Adcock; p72 April's Charms; p73 The Kingfisher. Sweet Stay-
at-Home; p74 The Likeness

D40   **Robin Redbreast**   Chelsea Publishing Co 1925
chosen by Florence B. Hyett; p26 Robin Redbreast

D41   **Pattern Poetry: Part II.**   Thomas Nelson & Sons 1926
compiled by Richard Wilson; p38 Leisure

D42   **The Poetry of Toil**   Faber & Gwyer 1926
compiled by Dorothy Wooldridge; p132 Leisure; p133 A Great Time

D43   **By What Sweet Name?**   Faber & Gwyer 1926
ed Stephen Langton; p172 Margery

D44   **A Book of Modern Verse**   Clarendon Press 1926
compiled by J. C. Smith; p16 Leisure

D45   **The Mercury Book**   Williams & Norgate Ltd 1926
made by HCM; p52 Love's Caution; p86 portrait of WHD by E. Powys
Evans

D46   **Fifty London Rhymes for Children**   Basil Blackwell (1926)
chosen by Florence B. Hyett; p46 The Sleepers

D47   **The Book of English Verse for School and Home**   Harrap & Co Ltd 1926
selected by M. G. Edgar and Eric Chilman; p223 Early Spring; p487
Leisure

D48   **A Book of Verse for Boys and Girls: Part II**   Clarendon Press 1927
new edition with many modern poems; compiled by J. C. Smith; p98 Leisure

D49   **The Best Poems of 1926**   Jonathan Cape 1927
selected by Thomas Moult; decorated by John Austen; p54 Love's Plans

D50   **The Best Poems of 1927**   Jonathan Cape 1927
selected and decorated as D49; p47 Frost

D51 **A Poetry Book for Boys and Girls: Part 1**   Cambridge University Press 1927
compiled by A. Watson Bain; p89 Raptures

D52 **The Tramp's Anthology**   Peter Davies 1928
ed Stephen Graham; pp133–136 Davies loses his leg (extract from *The Autobiography of a Super-Tramp (A3)*)

D53 **Models and Values**   Oxford University Press 1928
selected by Walter C. Phillips, William G. Crane and Frank R. Byers; pp16–17 Unwritten Law (extract from *The Autobiography of a Super-Tramp (A3)*)

D54 **The Best Poems of 1928**   Jonathan Cape 1928
selected and decorated as *D49*; p1 The Time of Dreams; p61 Heaven and Earth

D55 **The Golden Staircase**   Thomas Nelson & Sons Ltd (1928)
chosen by Louey Chisholm with pictures by C. E. Brock and H. M. Brock; p122 A Happy Wind; p250 A Child's Pet; p319 Leisure; p324 Sheep; p379 A Great Time; p468 Peace and Goodwill

D56 **An Anthology of World Poetry**   Cassell & Co Ltd 1929
edited by Mark Van Doren; p1123 Leisure

D57 **The Best Poems of 1929**   Jonathan Cape 1929
selected and decorated as *D49*; p5 For Sale

D58 **Chief Modern Poets of England and America**   Macmillan Company 1929
selected and edited by Gerald DeWitt Sanders and John Herbert Nelson; p132 Leisure. The Rain; p133 The Example. The Sleepers; p134 In the Country; p135 Christ the Man. Truly Great; p136 Jenny Wren; p137 Fancy's Home. Sheep; p138 The Little Ones. The Ways of Time; p139 Raptures. A Child's Pet; p140 The Bell. Birds; p141 The Captive Lion; p142 Winter's Beauty. Strong Moments; p143 My Love Could Walk. Rags and Bones; p144 Forgiveness. Telling Fortunes; p145 The Ox. The Rainbow; p146 Love, Like a Drop of Dew. One Token; p147 The Rivals. The Two Stars; p148 The Joy of Life

D59 **Twentieth Century Poetry**   Chatto & Windus 1929
chosen by Harold Monro; p20 Sweet Stay-at-Home; p110 The Inquest; p171 The Villain. To Sparrows Fighting; p194 Dreams of the Sea

D60 **The Legion Book**   Cassell & Co Ltd 1929
ed Captain H. Cotton Minchin; p151 This Bantam Star
note: the HDB copy (privately printed in London 1929) is inscribed: 'To Dinah (Helen)/ from/ Bunny (W. H. Davies)/ This Bantam Star/ Is this the Blackbird's richest song -/ Is this his greatest hour?/ And still the Bee stands on his head/ To suck his sweetest flower;/ While I, a poet with my pen,/ Make music only known to men./ How merrily this bantam world/ Can clap his wings and crow!/ Is there a merrier world than this?/ 'No,' says the Blackbird – 'No!/ No other worlds, though bigger far,/ Can match this little bantam star!/ W. H. Davies./ 1929'.
In this copy 'This Bantam Star' is on p154

D61 **The Best Poems of 1930**   Jonathan Cape 1930
selected by Thomas Moult; decorated by Elizabeth Montgomery; p39 Old Autumn

D62 **Longer English Poems from Spenser to Alfred Noyes**   Harrap & Co Ltd 1930
ed Benn R. Gibbs; p229 The Child and the Mariner

D63 **The Land of Poetry: Transition**   James Nisbet & Co Ltd 1930
eds Wentworth Hill and H. G. Wood; p90 Cowslips and Larks

D64 **The Mercury Book of Verse**   Macmillan & Co 1931
introduction by Sir Henry Newbolt; p90 Timepieces. Love's Caution

D65 **The Best Poems of 1931**   Jonathan Cape 1931
selected and decorated as *D61*; p48 Love Lights the [sic] Fire

D66 **New English Poems**   Victor Gollancz 1931
collection made by Lascelles Abercrombie; p160 Bird and Cloud

D67 **Anthology of Modern English Poetry**   Tauchnitz 1931
vol 5000; selected by Levin L. Schucking; p78 Dreams of the Sea; p80 Early
Morn

D68 **The Week-End Book**   Nonesuch Press 1931
decorated by T. L. Poulton; p130 Leisure. The Likeness; p131 The Two
Children. A Great Time; p231 The Kingfisher; p232 Jenny Wren

D69 **The Cambridge Book of Poetry for Children** Cambridge University Press 1932
new edition; ed Kenneth Grahame; p122 The East in Gold

D70 **A First Book of Modern Poetry**   Macmillan & Co Ltd 1932
selected and arranged by H. A. Treble MA; p25 The Kingfisher; p27 Jenny
Wren; p28 Days Too Short

D71 **The Silver Ship**   Putnam 1932
collected by Lady Cynthia Asquith; p81 The Cuckoo; p130 Owls

D72 **Known Signatures**   Rich & Cowan Ltd 1932
edited with an introduction by John Gawsworth; p31 Come, Melancholy;
p32 Age and Youth; p33 In Winter

D73 **The Best Poems of 1932**   Jonathan Cape 1932
selected and decorated as *D61*; p126 No Place or Time

D74 **Tom Tiddler's Ground**   Collins (1932)
chosen by Walter de la Mare; decorated with oldworld woodcuts; p223 The
Rain

D75 **The Pocket Trivet**   *Morning Post* 1932
p23 People are not to be blamed for their doubts, but that they make no
effort to arrive at the truth

D76 **The Golden Staircase**   Thomas Nelson & Sons Ltd (1933)
poems for 10–16 year olds; chosen by Louey Chisholm; with colour
frontispiece by M. D. Spooner; drawings in text by C. E. Brock and H. M.
Brock; p64 A Child's Pet; p133 Leisure; p138 Sheep; p193 A Great
Time

D77 **The Golden Staircase**   Thomas Nelson & Sons Ltd (1933)
poems for 4–10 year olds; chosen and illustrated as *D76*; p122 Happy Wind

D78 **The Out-of-Doors Book**   J M Dent 1933
selected and arranged by Arthur Stanley; p95 An Encounter in Savernake
(from *A Poet's Pilgrimage (A15)*); p277 The Rain

D79 **The Albatross Book of Living Verse**   Collins (1933)
ed Louis Untermeyer; p524 Leisure. The Hermit; p525 A Great Time

D80 **The Poetry of Nature: Vol IV**   Davis & Moughton Ltd 1934
garnered by William J. Moughton; illustrated in colour by K. Nixon; p26
Clouds; p32 The East in Gold; p54 Sheep

D81 **Modern Poetry 1922–1934**   Macmillan & Co Ltd 1934
compiled by Maurice Wollman; p33 Winter's Beauty; p124 Age and Youth

D82 **Talk of Many Things**   Thomas Nelson & Sons Ltd (1935)
compiled by Richard Wilson; p160 Raptures

D83 **The Princess Elizabeth Gift Book**   Hodder & Stoughton (1935)
p128 The Street Criers (illustrated by Sylvia Salisbury)

D84 **These Things the Poets Said**   Pear Tree Press 1935
foreword by Robert P. Eckert Jr; p5 Killed in Action (Edward Thomas)

D85 **The Year's Poetry 1935**   John Lane the Bodley Head 1935
compiled by Denys Kilham Roberts, Gerald Gould and John Lehmann; p23
The Ghost; p24 Love Lights his Fire

D86 **Then and Now**   Jonathan Cape 1935
p26 Logic; p58 The Woods and Banks; p111 Lamorna Cove; p126 Charity;
p140 Hunting Joy; p209 Wild Oats; facing p58 illustration of the Epstein
bust of WHD

D87 **Oxford Book of Modern Verse 1892–1935**   Clarendon Press 1936
chosen by W. B. Yeats; 116 Joy and Pleasure; 117 Truly Great; 118
Money; 119 Leisure; 120 The Sluggard; 121 The Best Friend; 122 School's
Out

D88 **A Treasury of Modern Poetry**   Sir Isaac Pitman & Sons 1936
ed R. L. Megroz; p66 In Winter. Nell Barnes; p67 Impudence. Lamorna
Cove; p68 Thunderstorms

D89 **Life and Literature To-day: Part Two**   James Nisbet & Co Ltd 1937
compiled by Andrew Scotland MA PhD; p220 The Kingfisher

D90 **The Garden Book**   Herbert Jenkins Ltd 1937
collected by Anne Lamplugh; p52 I have very little admiration (from *My
Garden (A40)*); p221 But even this strong weed poison (from *My Garden
(A40)*)

D91 **A Book of Birds**   Victor Gollancz 1937
ed Mary Priestley; wood engravings by C. F. Tunnicliffe; p43 Oft have I
seen in fields the little birds (from 'Birds'); p114 To Sparrows Fighting;
p118 When I did wake this morn from sleep (from 'Early Morn'); p119
Somehow this world is wonderful ('The East in Gold'); p121 The Mother
Bird

D92 **The Best Poems of 1937**   Jonathan Cape 1937
selected by Thomas Moult; decorated by Mary M. Kessell; p82 Life

D93 **The Bird-Lovers' Book of Verse**   H F & G Witherby Ltd 1937
collected by Christina Chapin; illustrated with lino-cuts by Raphael Nelson
FRSA; foreword by Arthur Waugh; p43 Robin Redbreast; p52 The
Kingfisher; p116 To Sparrows Fighting

D94 **Fifty Years of Modern Verse**   Martin Secker 1938
selected by John Gawsworth; p50 Come, Melancholy. In Winter; p51 Age
and Youth

D95 **Poems of Today: Third Series**   Macmillan & Co 1938
published for the English Association; p44 The Mongrel; p45 Frost. The
Poet

D96 **The Century's Poetry 1837–1937: Vol 2**   Penguin Books Ltd 1938
compiled by Denys Kilham Roberts; p354 The Truth; p355 Dreams of the
Sea

D97 **The Best Poems of 1938**   Jonathan Cape 1938
selected by Thomas Moult; drawings by Hans Aufseeser; p29 Armed for
War

D98 **Poems of Twenty Years**   Macmillan & Co 1938
compiled by Maurice Wollman; p145 Love lights his Fire; p162 The
Players; p119 The Time of Dreams

D99 **The Music of Poetry: Poetry Section**   Thomas Nelson & Sons Ltd (1939)
by Alfred H. Body; p1 School's Out; p48 School's Out (set to music)

D100   **Modern Poetry**   Thomas Nelson & Sons Ltd 1939
chosen by Robert Lynd; p75 Birds; p76 The White Cascade. Thunderstorms. Leisure; p77 A Great Time

D101   **Selections from Modern Poets**   Macmillan & Co 1939
selected and edited by Maurice Wollman MA; p16 Age and Youth

D102   **The Oxford Book of English Verse 1250–1918**   Clarendon Press (1940)
new edition; chosen and edited by Sir Arthur Quiller-Couch; 926 The Kingfisher; 927 Money; 928 Leisure

D103   **Modern Verse 1900–1940**   World's Classics, Oxford University Press 1940
p59 Joy and Pleasure; p60 Leisure; p61 School's Out. Days that have Been

D104   **The House of Tranquillity [sic] – An Anthology for Today**
                                                Eyre & Spottiswoode 1941
chosen by Arthur Stanley; p161 Seeking Beauty

D105   **Adventures into Poetry for Primary Schools:**
Junior Book 1   Macmillan & Co 1941
selected and arranged by Mary Daunt; p32 School's Out

D106   **A New Anthology of Modern Verse 1920–1940**   Methuen & Co 1941
chosen with an introduction by C. Day Lewis and L. A. G. Strong; p55 Light. Rogues

D107   **An Anthology of Nature Poetry**   Jonathan Cape 1941
made by Viola Meynell; p44 England; p91 The Likeness; p111 A Great Time; p167 The Kingfisher; p200 Day's Black Star; p223 The Villain; p293 Days too Short; p300 The Evening Star; p342 Robin Redbreast; p371 Venus; p395 The Voice; p409 Leisure

D108   **Wings**   Faber & Faber 1942
ed H. G. Bryden; p109 The White Monster

D109   **The Book of a Thousand Poems for the Young and**
Very Young   Evans Brothers 1942
p39 Sheep; p203 Rich Days; p248 Leisure; p258 The Rain

D110   **Modern British Poetry**   Harcourt, Brace & Co 1942
5th revised edition; ed Louis Untermeyer; p186 The Hour of Magic. A Greeting. The Moon. Days too Short. The Villain; p187 The Example. Jenny Wren. The Two Stars. Ambition. The Dog. The Hermit; p188 When Yon Full Moon. Sheep; p189 The Mind's Liberty. Leaves. A Great Time. Songs of Joy. The Elements; p190 To a Lady Friend. Leisure

D111   **Love**   Faber & Faber 1943
by Walter de la Mare; p243 My Love could Walk

D112   **Country Scrap-Book for Boys and Girls**   Gramol Publications 1944
ed Malcolm Saville; p7 Leisure

D113   **Other Men's Flowers**   Jonathan Cape 1944
selected and annotated by Field-Marshal A. P. Wavell; p62 Leisure

D114   **Poems of Our Time 1900–1942**   J M Dent 1945
chosen by Richard Church and Mildred Bozman; p34 The Happy Child; p46 Days too Short; p53 Sweet Stay-at-Home; p63 The Example; p65 Thunderstorms; p66 The Kingfisher. The Rain; p68 School's Out; p79 In the Snow; p86 The Moon. A Great Time; p119 A Thought; p125 The Villain; p137 The Beautiful; p250 The Mourner

D115   **These Also**   Cambridge University Press 1945
selected and arranged by M. M. Johnson; introduction by Walter de la Mare; p141 A Child's Pet; p213 The Rabbit; p217 The Unattained (extract from *The Autobiography of a Super-Tramp (A3)*); p225 Sport; p239 The Captive Lion

D116   **Vintage Verse**   Hollis & Carter 1945
compiled with commentary by Clifford Bax; p296 To Sparrows Fighting;
p297 Sheep

D117   **The Good Life**   Eyre & Spottiswoode 1946
ed C. Henry Warren; illustrated by Alexander Walker; pp12–13 from
Foliage (A10)

D118   **Lords of Life**   Rich & Cowan (1946)
chosen and edited, with introduction by Derek Gilpin Barnes; illustrated by
Kathleen Gardiner; p44 The Ox; p59 Sheep; p66 The Captive Lion; p101
Birds; p105 The East in Gold; p118 The Truth; p125 The Kingfisher; p144
Jenny Wren

D119   **The Writer's Way**   Christophers 1948
chosen and edited by James Reeves; p107. Beggars in America (from *The
Adventures of Johnny Walker, Tramp (A29)*)

D120   **The Poet's World**   William Heinemann Ltd 1948
chosen and edited as *D119*; p238 In the Country; p239 The Heap of Rags;
p240 The Villain

D121   **The Oxford Book of Victorian Verse**   Oxford University Press 1948
compiled by Arthur Quiller-Couch; p970 Songs of Joy; p971 Truly Great;
p972 Money. In May; p973 Leisure; p974 The Elements

D122   **The Oxford Book of English Verse 1250–1918** Oxford University Press 1948
compiled by Arthur Quiller-Couch; p1100 The Kingfisher; p1101 Leisure.
Money

D123   **Orpheus: Book One**   William Heinemann Ltd 1949
chosen and edited as *D119*; p135 A Strange Meeting; p136 The Cat. My
Garden; p137 The Rabbit

D124   **Monmouthshire Poetry**   R H Johns (1949)
compiled and edited by Lawrence W. Hockey; p21 Days that have been;
p27 Alone; p31 Truly Great; p37 A Great Time; p55 The Kingfisher; p63
The Mind's Liberty; p67 Life; p71 The Rainbow; p84 Leisure; p91 Christ,
the Man; p97 The Battle; p113 The Little Ones; p119 Songs of Joy; p122
Slippers; p130 Money; p139 The Villain

D125   **Orpheus: Book Two**   William Heinemann Ltd 1950
chosen and edited as *D123*; p139 A Child's Pet; p140 The Sailor to His Parrot

D126   **River Diary**   Allan Wingate 1950
ed Dorothea Eastwood; p45 When I reached the Clytha Arms (from *A
Poet's Pilgrimage (A15)*); p247 Light and Darkness

D127   **Poems of Yesterday and Today: Book III**   Cassell & Co Ltd 1951
compiled by Andrew Scotland MA PHD; p107 The Kingfisher

D128   **The Children's Treasury: Book 2**   Cassell & Co Ltd 1953
compiled by Andrew Scotland MA PHD; illustrations by Harry Baines; p64
Nature's Friend

D129   **A Book of Wales**   Collins 1953
eds D. M. and E. M. Lloyd; p341 Days that have Been

D130   **The Faber Book of Twentieth Century Verse**   Faber & Faber 1953
eds John Heath-Stubbs and David Wright; p124 One Poet visits another.
The Truth; p125 A Lovely Woman

D131   **Heinemann's Junior Poetry Books: Book IV**   William Heinemann Ltd 1954
chosen by James Reeves; with illustrations by John Mackay; p7 The Cat;
p32 In Spring-time; p48 My Garden; p49 Nailsworth Hill; p72 Sheep; p111
The Woods and Banks

D132 **A Book of Delights** Hulton Press 1954
compiled by John Hadfield; p24 First Joys ('Infancy'); p32 When on a Summer's Morn

D133 **The Merry-go-round** William Heinemann Ltd 1955
chosen and illustrated as *D131*; p257 The Cat; p282 In Spring-time; p298 My Garden; p299 Nailsworth Hill; p322 Sheep; p361 The Woods and Banks

D134 **Modern Verse 1900–1950** Oxford University Press 1955
compiled by Phyllis M. Jones; p63 Joy and Pleasure; p64 Leisure; p65 School's Out. Days that have been

D135 **The Chatto Book of Modern Poetry 1915–1955** Chatto & Windus 1956
eds C. Day Lewis and John Lehmann; p40 An Epitaph; p41 The Pond. The Trick. Love's Caution

D136 **Time & Tide Anthology** Andre Deutsch Ltd 1956
introduction by Lady Rhondda; ed Anthony Lejeune; p141 The Compensation

D137 **The Modern Poet's World** William Heinemann 1957
edited with an introduction by James Reeves; p17 I am the Poet Davies, William; p18 The Bust. The Tugged Hand

D138 **Enjoying Poetry 1: Silver and Gold** Longmans, Green & Co Ltd 1957
chosen by E. W. Parker; decorations by Kiddell-Monroe; p17 A Child's Pet

D139 **The Oxford Books of Verse for Juniors: 4** Oxford University Press 1957
chosen by James Britton; p68 Silver Hours

D140 **An Anthology of Verse for Children** Oxford University Press 1957
as *D139*

D141 **English Love Poems** Faber & Faber 1957
eds John Betjeman and Geoffrey Taylor; 163 The Flirt; p164 Her Merriment

D142 **On Wings of Verse: Book One** Blackie & Son Ltd 1957
compiled by W. G. Humphreys and J. P. Parry; illustrated by J. S. Goodall; p17 Rich Days; p86 The Fog

D143 **On Wings of Verse: Book Two** Blackie & Son Ltd 1957
compiled as *D142*; illustrated by I. A. McIntosh; p1 Mangers; p17 Rich Days; p22 A Happy Life

D144 **The Batsford Book of Children's Verse** B T Batsford Ltd 1958
ed Elizabeth Jennings; p55 Street Criers

D145 **Modern Verse in English** Eyre & Spottiswoode 1958
eds David Cecil and Allen Tate; p155 The Moon. A Great Time. The Bird of Paradise; p156 The Kingfisher

D146 **The Rhyming River: Book One** William Heinemann Ltd 1959
chosen by James Reeves; illustrations by Peter Dunbar; p34 My Garden; p42 Sheep; p43 photograph of Augustus John portrait (1918)

D147 **On Wings of Verse: Book Three** Blackie & Son Ltd 1959
compiled and illustrated as *D142*; p61 The Truth; p73 Winter's Beauty; p104 Sheep

D148 **On Wings of Verse: Book Four** Blackie & Son Ltd 1959
compiled and illustrated as *D142*; p84 A Blind Child

D149 **The Atlantic Book of British and American Poetry** Victor Gollancz 1959
ed Dame Edith Sitwell; (vol II) p817 Fancy's Home. The Happy Child; p818 The Bird of Paradise; p819 Body and Spirit

D150 **Presenting Welsh Poetry** Faber 1959
ed G. Williams; p104 Sheep; p105 Days that have Been

D151   **The Harrap Book of Sea Verse**   published by Harrap & Co in co-operation
with the Seafarer's Education Services 1960
ed Ronald Hope; p49 Dreams of the Sea; p192 The Sea

D152   **A Tale that is Told**   Barrie & Rockliff 1960
compiled by Arthur B. Allen; p159 The Example. Nature's Friend

D153   **The Golden Road to English Literature: Book 1**   Longmans 1960
eds W. J. Ball and G. C. Thornley; p56 The Truth

D154   **Country Book**   George Newnes 1961
ed Macdonald Hastings; p178 extract from 'Leisure'

D155   **Poetry One**   Chatto & Windus 1961
chosen by Raymond O'Malley and Denys Thompson; illustrated by
Geraldine Spence; p76 April's Charms

D156   **Poetry and Life: Junior Two**   Schofield & Sims Ltd 1961
compiled by Nora Grisenthwaite; p14 School's Out

D157   **Poetry and Life: Book Three**   Schofield & Sims Ltd 1961
compiled as *D156*; p78 Sheep; p79 A Child's Pet

D158   **Poetry and Life: Book Four**   Schofield & Sims Ltd 1961
compiled as *D156*; p28 The Fog

D159   **Love for Life**   Book Society (1961)
compiled by John Hadfield for members of Book Society; p29 First Joys
(from 'Infancy')

D160   **Pegasus: Book One**   Schofield & Sims Ltd 1962
compiled by N. Grisenthwaite; p45 Sheep; p102 A Strange Meeting; p103
The Fog

D161   **A Book of Joy**   Vista Books 1962
compiled by John Hadfield; p76 Skylark ('Day's Black Star')

D162   **Birds, Beasts and Fishes**   Oxford University Press 1962
compiled by Ruth Manning-Sanders; p23. Dogs; p112 On a Cold Day

D163   **Georgian Poetry**   Penguin Books 1962
selected and introduced by James Reeves; p33 A Dream; p34 Sweet-Stay-at-
Home; p35 Heaven; p36 The Hospital Waiting-Room; p37 The Inquest;
p38 The Two Children. The Power of Silence; p39 Confession. My Old
Acquaintance; p40 I am the Poet Davies, William. The Villain; p41 One
Thing Wanting. Beggar's Song; p42 A Child's Fancy. Love Lights His Fire;
p43 Competitors. The Ghost; p44 Beauty and Brain. The Faithful One; p45
The Birth of Song. The Tugged Hand; p46 All in June

D164   **Vigorous Verse**   Macmillan & Co Ltd/ St Martin's Press 1963
ed W. R. S. McIntyre; illustrated by Gilbert Dunlop; p2 Lost in the Fog; p65
The Captive Lion

D165   **The Wheel of Poetry: 2**   University of London/ Athlone Press 1963
compiled by Jerome Hanratty; p136 Clocks

D166   **The Railway Lover's Companion**   Eyre & Spottiswoode 1963
ed Bryan Martin; p415 Hobo's Train (from *The Autobiography of a Super-
Tramp (A3)*)

D167   **The Pattern of Poetry**   Burke Publishing Co 1963
Poetry Society Verse-Speaking Anthology; p190 For Sale

D168   **Oxford Book of Poetry for Children**   Oxford University Press 1963
compiled by Edward Blishen; illustrations by Brian Wildsmith; p148 A
Strange Meeting

D169   **The Colour of Saying: An Anthology of Verse spoken by
Dylan Thomas**   J M Dent 1963

eds R. N. Maud and A. T. Davies; p50 The Inquest; p51 One Poet Visits Another; p52 The Poet

D170 **The Little Kingdom: A Kentish Collection**   Hutchinson of London 1964
ed Richard Church; illustrated by John Ward; p100 The Sluggard; p101 In May

D171 **The Golden Treasury**   Oxford University Press 1964
ed F. T. Palgrave; 5th edition with new fifth book ed John Press; p435 The Inquest

D172 **The Cassell Book of English Poetry**   Cassell & Co Ltd 1965
compiled by John Reeves; p959 The Hospital Waiting-Room; p960 I am the Poet Davies, William; p961 The Inquest

D173 **Fresh Flights: Book 4**   Johnston & Bacon Ltd 1965
ed A. Elliott-Cannon; illustrated by W. Browning White; p47 Leisure

D174 **By Heart**   Nonesuch Press Cygnet 1965
chosen by Francis Meynell; p220 A Great Time. The Likeness

D175 **The Poetry of Nature**   Rupert Hart-Davis 1965
selected by Leonard Clark; p108 In May

D176 **The Merry Minstrel Book 2: Music and Mime**   Blackie & Son Ltd 1967
new edition; compiled by Haydn Perry; p33 The Rain

D177 **The Poet's Choice**   Evans Bros 1967
compiled by Patric Dickinson and Sheila Shannon; p364 The Sleepers; p365 The Two Heavens; p366 To Sparrows Fighting

D178 **Music and Sweet Poetry**   John Baker 1968
compiled by John Bishop; drawings by Edmond X. Kapp; p13 On Hearing Mrs Woodhouse Play the Harpsichord; p25 Music's Tragedy; p31 F is for Fiddler [sic]

D179 **Passport to Poetry**   Cassell & Co Ltd 1968
eds E. L. Black and D. S. Davies; illustrations by J. Lathey; p37 School's Out

D180 **Flutes and Cymbals**   The Bodley Head 1968
selected by Leonard Clark; illustrated by Shirley Hughes; p68 Sheep

D181 **A Map of Modern English Verse**   Oxford University Press 1969
ed John Press; p123 The Inquest; p124 The Cat; p125 Earth Love

D182 **Unrespectable Verse**   Allen Lane/ Penguin Press 1971
ed Geoffrey Grigson; p139 The Inquest

D183 **My Kind of Rhymes**   Burke Books 1972
compiled by John Smith; illustrated by Beryl Sanders; p51 School's Out

D184 **Say It Aloud**   Hutchinson Educational Ltd 1972
edited for Poetry Society by Norman Hidden; p56 Leisure

D185 **The Oxford Book of Twentieth Century English Verse** Clarendon Press 1973
chosen by Philip Larkin; p106 The Rain; p107 The Dumb World; p108 The Inquest; p109 The Villain; p110 The Rat; p111 The White Horse

D186 **The Faber Book of Love Poems**   Faber & Faber 1973
edited with introduction by Geoffrey Grigson; p220 The Visitor

D187 **The Garden Lover's Companion**   Eyre Methuen 1974
ed Peter Hunt; p50 Personal Opinions; p53 Drink (from *My Garden (A40)*); p168 Care of a Garden (from *My Garden (A40)*)

D188 **Fancy Free**   Evans Bros Ltd 1974
selected by Dennis Saunders; photographs by Terry Williams; p12 The Cat

D189 **Library Looking Glass**   Constable 1975
ed David Cecil; p38 Sweet Chance, that led my steps abroad (12 lines from 'A Great Time')

D190   **Round About Nine**   Frederick Warne 1976
       selected by Geoffrey Palmer and Noel Lloyd; illustrations by Denis Wrigley;
       p25 The East in Gold
D191   **Country Verse**   Chancellor Press 1979
       ed Samuel Carr; p28 The Woods and Banks; p34 The Rain; p94 Cowslips
       and Larks
D192   **Round About Ten**   Frederick Warne 1979
       selected and illustrated as *D190*; p45 A Dream of Winter
D193   **The Macmillan Treasury of Relevant Quotations**   Macmillan Press Ltd 1979
       ed Edward Murphy; lines from 'Leisure'
D194   **A Country Calendar of Rural Rhymes**   Eyre Methuen 1980
       chosen by Robin Holmes; p22 April's Charms; p38 Jenny Wren; p46
       Lamorna Cove; p57 A Dream of Winter; p62 Winter's Beauty
D195   **Fellow Mortals**   Macdonald & Evans 1981
       chosen by Roy Fuller; original illustrations by David Koster; p239 Eyes. The
       Last Years; p240 To a Butterfly
D196   **Anglo-Welsh Poetry 1480–1980**   Poetry Wales Press 1984
       edited and introduced by Raymond Garlick and Roland Mathias; p126 The
       Kingfisher; p127 Days That Have Been; p128 Leisure. A Great Time. The
       Inquest; p129 The Villain
D197   **Poems for Over Ten Year-Olds**   Viking Kestrel 1984
       chosen by Kit Wright; p49. Sheep
D198   **The Extended Circle: A Dictionary of Humane Thought**   Centaur Press 1985
       compiled by Jon Wynne-Tyson; p63 A Child's Pet; p64 The Rabbit. Sport.
       10 lines from *The Autobiography of a Super-Tramp (A3)*; p65 4 lines from
       'Sheep'
D199   **Voices in the Gallery**   Tate Gallery 1986
       chosen by Dannie and Joan Abse; p153 The Bird of Paradise
D200   **Favourite Love Poems**   Michael O'Mara Books 1988
       chosen by Charles Osborne; illustrations by Robert Anning Bell; p187 The
       Visitor
D201   **Food for a Future**   Thorsons 1988
       revised edition; by Jon Wynne-Tyson; p138 They sniffed, poor things, for
       their green fields (from 'Sheep')
D202   **The Coloured Counties**   J M Dent 1988
       selected with introduction by John Arlott; p9 The Sleepers
D203   **Common Ground**   Carcanet 1989
       selected by Marghanita Laski; p108 Leisure; p131 A Child's Pet
D204   **A New Treasury of Poetry**   Blackie & Co 1990
       selected and introduced by Neil Philip; illustrated by John Lawrence; p109
       Sheep; p142 Leisure; p158 The Beautiful
D205   **The Chatto Book of Love Poetry**   Chatto & Windus 1990
       edited, with introduction by John Fuller; 110 A Dream; 183 Her Mouth and
       Mine; 215 Kitty and I; 280 When I in Praise
D206   **English Poetry of the First World War**   Harvester Wheatsheaf 1990
       ed George Parfitt; p11 The Bird of Paradise
D207   **Shades of Green**   Julia MacRae Books 1991
       chosen by Anne Harvey; illustrated by John Lawrence; p146 The Example;
       p155 The Kingfisher

E Broadcasting

(The first part of this section covers broadcasts by WHD, the second programmes about WHD and the third programmes using his material; the sections are numbered in sequence and arranged by programme title, then contributors and finally the prose or poems used. All timings are GMT.)

BBC Broadcasts by WHD

E1	3 September 1924	London 21.40	W. H. Davies in a Recital of His Own Poems The Poet; Re-Union; The Moon; Sweet Stay-at-Home; The Kingfisher; Dreams of the Sea; A Blind Child; Raptures; When Yon Full Moon; Lovely Dames; Days that have Been; The Sluggard; Secrets; Down Underground; Pity
E2	3 December 1925	London 21.26	Discussion: The Reading of Poetry WHD, Miles Malleson and Harold Monro, with illustrations
E3	16 May 1932	National 21.20	The Rungs of the Ladder II WHD (portrait in *Radio Times*)
E4	1 December 1933	London 20.35	A Poetry Reading: W. H. Davies Where We Agree; Love's Rivals; Success; Three Loves; Seed and Flower; The Laws of Beauty; The Little Devil; The Kingfisher; Robin Redbreast; Raptures; Dreams of the Sea; Sweet Stay-at-Home; Impudence; Days that have Been; The Moon
E5	20 September 1937	Wales 21.20	"The Poets": A Reading by W. H. Davies The Mind's Liberty; Sweet Stay-at-Home; Days that have been; Sheep; Dreams of the Sea; Street Criers; The Lily of Our Valley; Scotty's Luck; The Life of Man; Raptures; The Laws of Beauty; Youth; The Little Devil; Seed and Flower; On finding a dead bird under my window; Old and crazy; Bells; The Kingfisher; The Best Friend; The Moon
E6	22 September 1937	National 12.25	"The Poets" (repeat of *E5*)
E7	5 February 1938	Regional 20.00	W. H. Davies reading his Poems Love's Caution; Youth; Love in Trouble; Pity; A Child's Pet; Wondering Brown; The Sluggard; On a Cold Day; Bells; A Change of Voice; A Maiden and Her Hair; Catharine

175

E8	2 May 1938	Midland 17.40	W. H. Davies: Time turns Back. The Trial of William Shakespeare for Deer-stealing
E9	16 October– 20 November 1938	Midland 17.50	*The Autobiography of a Super-Tramp* (serialisation of *A3* read by WHD)
E10	18 October– 22 November 1938	Regional 16.00	*The Autobiography of a Super-Tramp* (repeat of *E9*)
E11	7 January 1939	National 22.45	Love Poetry by Dead Masters: Poetry Reading by W. H. Davies
E12	2 February 1939	London 16.00	W. H. Davies: Time turns Back. The Trial of William Shakespeare for Deer-stealing (repeat of *E8*)
E13	2 October 1940	Home 18.45	The World Goes By by F. H. Grisewood WHD reading a selection of his poems: A Winter's Night; Who bears in Mind; Money; The Sluggard; Dreamers (recording: WHD died on 26 September 1940)
E14	3 October 1940	Forces 12.30	The World Goes By (repeat of *E13*)

BBC Broadcasts about WHD

E15	16 October– 20 November 1938	Midland 17.40	*The Autobiography of a Super-Tramp* (serialisation of *A3* read by WHD)
E16	18 October– 22 November 1938	Regional 16.00	*The Autobiography of a Super-Tramp* (repeat of *E15*)
E17	27 April 1941	Overseas 22.00	Super-Tramp The Moon; A Great Time; Seeking Beauty; A Happy Life; The Song of Life; The Lodging-House Fire; The Richest Stones; Friends Unborn; Leisure; extract from *The Autobiography of a Super-Tramp (A3)*
E18	22 July 1941	Home 22.35	Super-Tramp (repeat of *E17*)
E19	24 February 1942	Home 14.35	Schools: Senior English II: Dramatic Biography W. H. Davies by S. P. B. Mais: extracts from *The Autobiography of a Super-Tramp (A3)*
E20	19 June 1942	Home 18.30	Books and the Writer: W. H. Davies by Martin Armstrong
E21	17 August 1942		Books and People
E22	4 March 1945	Home 17.20	Children's Hour: The Man who stood and stared. A Portrait by Tudor Watkins: N is for Nature; The Rain; Sheep; The Kingfisher; Smiles; Days too Short; One Token

E23	6 July 1945	Overseas 14.45	The Man who stood and stared (repeat of *E22*)
E24	15 January 1946	Home 14.35	Dramatic Biography: W. H. Davies by Penelope Knox
E25	25 January 1946	Light 10.00	*The Autobiography of a Super-Tramp (A3)* dramatised presentation by Brian Rowland
E26	8 March 1946	Home 23.30	Poetry Promenade II: W. H. Davies selected by Sheila Shannon; produced by Patric Dickinson: The Poet; The Hermit; Confession; The Lodging-House Fire; The Sleepers; The Two Children; Body and Spirit; The Two Heavens; The Villain; Light and Darkness; On the Mountain
E27	31 August 1946	Overseas 15.50	Book of Verse (99): W. H. Davies by Richard Church: No Master; To Sparrows Fighting; Who bears in Mind; The Hour of Magic; School's Out; Truly Great; In the Snow; The Inquest; extract from *The Autobiography of a Super-Tramp (A3)*
E28	25 February 1947	Overseas 15.10	The Written Word. Biographies and Auto-biographies. No 22: W. H. Davies written and narrated by Richard Church; read by Raf de la Torre
E29	9 October 1947	Home 14.00	Woman's Hour: Poetry Programme W. H. Davies read by Barbara MacFadyean
E30	28 December– 3 April 1947	Home 11.00	*The Autobiography of a Super-Tramp (A3)* serialisation read by Dylan Thomas
E31	12 March 1948	European 17.30	W. H. Davies I am the Poet Davies, William; No Master; read by O. Nes
E32	29 October 1949	Light 14.00	New Books and Old *The Autobiography of a Super-Tramp (A3)* reviewed by James Langham; read by Frank Duncan
E33	9 January– 13 February 1950	European 21.45	*The Autobiography of a Super-Tramp (A3)* serialisation read by Basil Jones
E34	13 June 1950	Home 14.35	Schools: Senior English II: A programme about the Life and Poems of a Super-Tramp
E35	20 August 1951	Home 16.45	Mainly for Women: On the Road
E36	22 October 1952	West 22.00	Apollo in the West: October: W. H. Davies reconsidered by Clifford Dyment
E37	17 November 1952	Home 14.20	Schools: Prose and Verse Reading A Night's Ride (extract from *The Auto-biography of a Super-Tramp (A3)*)

E38	22 October 1953	Wales 21.15	Super-Tramp: radio biography of W. H. Davies by P. H. Binton: Leisure; Scotty Bill; The Child and the Mariner; The Treasured Three; Friends Unborn; Speed; Drink
E39	21 May 1954	Third 21.55	The Secret Traveller by Patric Dickinson (portrait in *Radio Times*)
E40	22 May 1954	Third 19.00	The Secret Traveller (repeat of *E39*)
E41	13 June 1954	Home 21.30	Super-Tramp (repeat of *E38*)
E42	27 September 1954	Third 20.10	The Secret Traveller (repeat of *E39*)
E43	15 February 1955	Overseas 19.00	Super-Tramp (repeat of *E38*)
E44	27 March 1955	Third 20.15	The Integrity of the Poet by Robert Graves: The Inquest
E45	30 May 1955	Third 23.10	The Integrity of the Poet (repeat of *E44*)
E46	1 November 1955	Home 14.20	Schools: Senior English II: A bibliographical programme: W. H. Davies' poems arranged by Anthony Brown: The Child and the Mariner; Sheep; A Winter's Night; extract from *The Autobiography of a Super-Tramp (A3)*
E47	2 July 1956	Home 14.40	The Distant Scene Tramps on Vacation (extract from *The Autobiography of a Super-Tramp (A3)*) read by John Glyn Jones
E48	8 February 1960	Home 14.50	Schools: Prose and Verse Reading On the Road in America (extract from *The Autobiography of a Super-Tramp (A3)*)
E49	19 October 1960	Wales 08.15	Hook Up. 20th Anniversary of W. H. Davies' Death by John Parker
E50	26 September 1961		Round Up Anniversary: Spot on W. H. Davies
E51	26 September 1961	BBC. TV 13.04	Heddiw: W. H. Davies: 21st Commemoration of his Death
E52	12 October– 23 November 1961	Home 13.40	*The Autobiography of a Super-Tramp (A3)* serialisation edited by H. Oldfield Box, read by Frederick Treves
E53	11 April 1963	Midland 17.00	Midland Miscellany: Poet and Tramp
E54	18 April 1963	Wales 08.15	Hook Up: W. H. Davies (repeat of *E49*)
E55	25 April 1963	Home 22.30	Horizons: *W. H. Davies: A Critical Biography (F324)* by Richard Stonesifer; reviewed by J. H. B. Peel

E56	6 May 1963	Wales 18.40	Bookmark: *The Complete Poems of W. H. Davies (A51)* and *W. H. Davies: A Critical Biography (F324)* by Richard Stonesifer; reviewed by Ronnie Williams: The Inquest; Scotty Bill; J is for Jealousy; Days that have Been; The Kingfisher
E57	18 May 1963	Home 22.10	The World of Books: *The Complete Poems of W. H. Davies (A51)* and *W. H. Davies: A Critical Biography (F324)* by Richard Stonesifer reviewed
E58	16 March 1964	Home 14.30	Schools: Prose and Verse Reading A Tramp's Summer Vacation (extract from *The Autobiography of a Super-Tramp (A3)*)
E59	15 February 1968	Wales 20.30	Time to Stand and Stare
E60	20 January 1970	Third 19.30	The Georgians No 2: W. H. Davies
E61	12 June– 17 July 1970	Radio Four 16.30	*The Autobiography of a Super-Tramp (A3)* serialisation adapted by Howard Jones; read by David Davis
E62	23 February 1971	Radio Three 22.45	To Feel the Wound: W. H. Davies. The Super-Tramp's Attitude to Suffering by Roger Frith
E63	21 July 1971	Radio Three	To Feel the Wound: W. H. Davies (repeat of E62)
E64	12 November 1981	Radio Four 10.20	Stories and Rhymes: To Stand and Stare: the Poems of W. H. Davies script by Leslie Norris: I am the Poet, Davies William; School's Out; The Green Tent; A Child's Pet; The Fog; In the Snow
E65	22 August 1984	Radio Four 20.15	Folk for the Job. Songs and Stories about People on the Open Road, including the Poet W. H. Davies
E66	27 May– 31 May 1991	Radio Four 22.45	Book at Bedtime: *Young Emma (A52)* read by David Burke; produced by Marilyn Imrie

note: where there are gaps I was unable to trace the programme's transmission although royalties were paid to Mrs Davies by the BBC

Broadcasts using WHD's work

E67	3 November 1927	London/Daventry: Poetry Reading 20.30 The Kingfisher; To Sparrows Fighting; Robin Redbreast; Jenny Wren; read by Evan Morgan
E68	3 February 1928	Daventry Experimental: A Day's Companion 20.25 extract from *The Autobiography of a Super-Tramp (A3)*; read by Vincent Curran

E69	24 February 1928	London 20.45	A Programme of Poetry and Song Leisure; The Example
E70	13 April 1928	Cardiff 19.45	A Spring Idyll composed by Wynford Vaughan Thomas: A Great Time; Days too Short; In May
E71	10 January 1929	London 20.22	Interlude from the Studio Sweet Stay-at-Home; read by Godfrey Winn
E72	14 April 1929	Daventry Experimental: Poetry Reading 17.00 A Great Time
E73	15 May 1929	National 22.45	Poetry Reading Leisure; Oh, Sweet Content; In May; read by Robert Harris
E74	22 September 1929	Daventry Experimental: Poetry Reading: Both Great and Small 15.30 A Child's Pet; read by Ronald Watkins
E75	6 October 1929	Manchester 15.30	Springtime to Harvesttide Early Spring; read by Bay Macpherson
E76	26 July 1930	National 19.00	The Seventh Literary Competition lines from 'The Child and the Mariner'
E77	8 September 1930	National 18.00	Poetry Reading A Great Time; Happy Wind
E78	22 September 1931	National 22.00	Mosaic I lines from 'The Child and the Mariner'
E79	3 November 1931	National 22.20	Mosaic III In May
E80	15 July 1932	London 20.00	Poetry Recital: Summer's Morn Jenny Wren; When on a Summer's Morn; spoken by Margaret Greenwood
E81	18 October 1932	West 18.00	Nocturne: Reading of Verse Days that have Been; The Moon; read by Hedley Goodall
E82	17 March 1933	National 22.45	The Kingfisher; read by Cecil Ramage
E83	18 March 1933	National 22.30	Sweet Stay-at-Home; read by Cecil Ramage
E84	21 April 1933	West 20.00	A Great Time; Early Spring
E85	17 November 1933	National 22.50	Leisure; read by Margaret Greenwood
E86	13 December 1933	National 22.15	Mosaic III extract from 'The Child and the Mariner'
E87	14 January 1934	National 21.06	Pilgrim's Way The Happy Child
E88	18 March 1934	Midland 18.15	Poetry Reading A Happy Life; read by Godfrey Kenton
E89	22 April 1934	North 18.30	April Showers by Kenneth Adam; The Rain
E90	3 June 1934	National 21.05	Pilgrim's Way: A Tale of Everyman's Journey through Life, and of his many Moods: Leisure

E91	11 December 1934	National 23.08	extract from 'The Child and the Mariner'; read by Eithne McNeight
E92	8 February 1935	Midland 18.30	Pastorale Leisure; read by Owen Reed
E93	27 February 1935	National 14.30	Schools: English Literature: Delight in Poetry. Private and Public Poetry by Leila Davies: A Great Time
E94	8 March 1935	Scottish 19.30	Songs My Mother Taught Me The Two Children
E95	20 October 1935	Empire 15.00	The Day's Work devised and presented by William MacLurg: Leisure
E96	3 December 1935	National 22.00	Have You Read This? A Night's Ride from *The Autobiography of a Super-Tramp (A3)*; read by V. C. Clinton-Baddeley
E97	22 January 1936	Midland 17.15	Children's Hour The Kingfisher; read by Doreen Hyde (programme scheduled but cancelled due to the death of King George V)
E98	28 April 1936	National 14.05	Schools Poetry In May
E99	18 August 1936	Empire 11.45	Three Per Cent Cucumber by Stephen Potter; The Rain
E100	5 October 1936	Midland 17.15	Children's Hour Leisure
E101	28 September 1936	West 20.15	Wales Visited by Constance and Ifan Kyrle Fletcher; extract from *A Poet's Pilgrimage (A15)*; Days that have Been
E102	10 December 1936	National 22.20	The Stars. A Mosaic of Words and Music The Evening Star (programme scheduled but cancelled due to the abdication of Edward VIII)
E103	4 March 1938	National 14.55	Schools: Junior English Jenny Wren
E104	2 August 1940	Home 20.30	The Land We Defend. Wales by Gwyn Jones: Days that have Been
E105	18 October 1940	Home 20.10	Literary Anthology: The Poetry of Content arranged and produced by M. H. Allan: A Greeting
E106	30 October 1940		Leisure
E107	12 November 1940	Home 22.45	Sea Coast of Bohemia Wonderful Places; Sweet Stay-at-Home
E108	26 November 1941	Home 18.45	The World Goes By poems read by Wyn Griffith: I am the Poet Davies, William; Money; The Sluggard; Leisure; A Winter's Night; Who bears in mind; Dreamers

E109	6 September 1942	North America 22.30	Britain to America: Wales with L. W. Brockington as narrator: Days that have Been
E110	25 September 1942	Home 20.00	Britain to America: Wales (repeat of E109)
E111	2 March 1943	Home 14.35	Schools: Senior English: Good Writing arranged by Robert Gittings: A Strange Meeting
E112	16 March 1943	Home 19.55	To Start You Talking. . . . about Christianity: "Why should we read the Bible?" A Thought; introduced by Douglas Allan
E113	1 May 1943	Home 14.30	During the Interval: Poetry of Spring presented by Edward Sackville-West: The Likeness
E114	30 May 1943	Home 22.15	What the Poet sees: The World in a Grain of Sand presented by Francis Meynell: The Two Children
E115	23 June 1943	Forces 21.25	The Radio Padre Leisure
E116	28 June 1943		The Shining Land Days that have Been
E117	21 July 1943	Home 23.00	And so to Bed Evening Star
E118	25 July 1943	Home 22.15	What the Poet sees A Lovely Day
E119	21 October 1943	Home 11.00	Schools: Rhythm and Melody School's Out
E120	28 October 1943	Home 11.00	Schools: Rhythm and Melody (repeat of E119)
E121	4 November 1943	Home 18.30	Welsh Half Hour Days that have Been
E122	26 December 1943	Home 19.05	Christmas Field-Fare by Brian Vesey-Fitzgerald: Leisure
E123	24 February 1944	Home 18.30	Welsh Half Hour (repeat of E121)
E124	15 March 1944	Overseas 09.45	Country Calendar The Likeness
E125	2 April 1944	Home 17.20	Children's Hour: Verse for Children on Palm Sunday A Great Time
E126	13 April 1944	Overseas 07.15	Country Calendar A Great Time
E127	16 May 1944	Home 23.10	Personal Choice Miles Malleson chooses some poems by WHD: Leisure; The Likeness; A Great Time
E128	3 August 1944	Overseas 08.15	Country Calendar Leisure
E129	1 February 1945	Overseas 16.15	Chapter and Verse Leisure
E130	10 April 1945	European 10.30	Days too Short; Her absence; Return to Nature; The Coming of Spring

E131	26 August 1945	Overseas 16.15	Chapter and Verse The Kingfisher; Starers; Smiles; The Happy Child; Charms; Body and Spirit; The Two Children; Speed; Leisure
E132	2 November 1945	Overseas 08.30	Country Calendar Robin Redbreast
E133	31 December 1945	Overseas 19.45	New Year's Eve Verse Programme, Poetry, Prose, and Music produced by Noel Iliff Starers; The Happy Child
E134	20 January 1946	Light 19.15	The Richard Tauber Programme The Moon
E135	25 January 1946	Light 10.00	Forces Educational Broadcast by Brian Rowland: Leisure; dramatisation of *The Autobiography of a Super-Tramp (A3)*
E136	12 February 1946	Overseas 14.30	Modern English Poets (3): W. H. Davies and James Stephens; translated and read by Paul Way: The Rain
E137	8 March 1946	Home 23.00	Poetry Parade selected by Sheila Shannon: The Poet; The Hermit; Confession; The Lodging-House Fire; The Sleepers; The Two Heavens; Beggar's Song; The Two Children; Body and Spirit; The Villain; The Rock; Light and Darkness; Oh Sweet Content
E138	21 May 1946	Home 14.10	Senior English II. Poetry The Sleepers
E139	29 May 1946	Home 15.00	Seven to Fourteen Leisure
E140	5 June 1946	Home 15.00	Seven to Fourteen The Happy Child
E141	14 July 1946	Home 13.10	Country Magazine introduced by George Purvis: Days that have Been (set to music by Arwel Hughes)
E142	31 August 1946	Overseas 15.50	Book of Verse: W. H. Davies by Richard Church: No Master; To Sparrows Fighting; Who bears in Mind; The Hour of Magic; School's Out; Truly Great; In the Snow; The Inquest; extract from *The Autobiography of a Super-Tramp (A3)*
E143	13 September 1946	Wales 21.30	Portrait of a Town by P. H. Burton: Days that have Been
E144	16 October 1946	European 05.45	English by Radio Leisure read by A. Brown
E145	15 December 1946	European 05.45	English by Radio Silver Hours
E146	30 January 1947	European 19.30	English Poetry in Danish Translation Dreams of the Sea
E147	12 February 1947	European 05.45	English by Radio The Cat

E148	25 February 1947	Overseas 15.10	The Written Words: Biographies and Autobiographies (no 22): W. H. Davies written and narrated by Richard Church; read by Raf de la Torre: extract from *The Autobiography of a Super-Tramp (A3)*
E149	11 September 1947	Light 10.00	Forces Educational Broadcast: Pleasure from Books Leisure; extract from *The Autobiography of a Super-Tramp (A3)*
E150	5 October 1947	Northern 17.00	Children's Hour Leisure
E151	7 October 1947	European 16.45	When on a Summer's Morn (musical setting by Ernest Relf)
E152	9 October 1947	Light 14.00	Woman's Hour Rich Days; Clouds; The Kingfisher; A Great Time; Near a Quiet Stream; Leisure
E153	29 October 1947	European 06.45 and 07.00	English by Radio The Happy Child
E154	28 November 1947	Home 11.40	Talks for Sixth Forms extract from *The Autobiography of a Super-Tramp (A3)*; The Likeness; Sheep; Autumn
E155	14 December 1947	European 05.45	English by Radio Frost
E156	15 February 1948	Home 22.40	Time for Verse (no 7) produced by Patric Dickinson: Leisure; The Bed-Sitting Room; Body and Spirit
E157	25 April 1948	Home 17.00	Children's Hour: Calendar for April Early Spring; April's Charms
E158	9 October 1948	Overseas 07.15	Book of Verse Nailsworth Hill
E159	17 November 1948	Third 21.40	On the Birth of a Prince. An Anthology compiled by Ormerod Greenwood; The Happy Child
E160	2 December 1948	Light 22.15	John Arlott's Book of Verse A Great Time
E161	3 March 1949	Overseas 10.00	Chapter and Verse The Weather; The Rain
E162	20 July 1949	Light 14.00	Woman's Hour The Kingfisher; The Happy Child
E163	15 August 1949		Leisure
E164	24 November 1949		Leisure
E165	26 February 1950	European 22.00	Anthology of Modern Verse (no 1) The Example
E166	11 March 1950	North 17.35	Children's Hour A Great Time
E167	17 March 1950		The Example

E168	19 March 1950		The Example
E169	13 June 1950	Home 14.35	Schools: Senior English II The Child and the Mariner; Sheep; The Blind Boxer; Return to Nature; A Winter's Night (extract from *The Autobiography of a Super-Tramp (A3)*)
E170	8 November 1950	European 18.30	London Calling Europe Days too Short
E171	1 January 1951	North 17.30	Children's Hour Robin Redbreast
E172	12 January 1951	Light 14.00	Woman's Hour: Poems for a January Day Robin Redbreast
E173	25 February 1951	European 17.30	Life in Great Britain as reflected in Her Literature extract from 'Leisure' (in German)
E174	2 March 1951	European 21.15	Anthology of Modern Verse (no 1) (repeat of *E165*)
E175	18 March 1951	Home 17.00	Children's Hour: When Young Things Thrive chosen and presented by George Henschel and Norman Claridge: Day's Black Star
E176	19 March 1951	Wales 19.00	In Manuscript musical setting of 'A Great Time'
E177	30 March 1951	Light 14.00	Woman's Hour: Poems for a March Day extract from 'Days too Short'
E178	15 April 1951	Home 17.00	Children's Hour: Sally-into-Spring compiled and conducted by Benedict Ellis: School's Out
E179	11 June 1951	Home 14.25	Schools: Senior English I: Tramps and Gypsies extract from *The Autobiography of a Super-Tramp (A3)*
E180	1 August 1951	Overseas 14.45	London Calling Asia The Beautiful
E181	20 August 1951	BBC. TV 21.45	Adventure in Sight extract from 'Leisure'
E182	22 August 1951	Overseas 14.45	London Calling Asia Leisure
E183	23 September 1951	Home 22.30	Time for Verse I produced, compiled and narrated by Patric Dickinson: A Strange Meeting
E184	7 October 1951	Home 22.30	Time for Verse III produced, compiled and narrated by Patric Dickinson: Confession
E185	28 November 1951	Third 20.20	Personal Anthology chosen by Dr Edith Sitwell: Body and Spirit
E186	30 November 1951	Third 22.30	Personal Anthology (repeat of *E185*)
E187	30 July 1952	Light 20.15	Leisure Hour: The Pleasure's Mine Where She is Now; read by Wilfred Pickles
E188	29 August 1952	Third 22.25	Personal Anthology (repeat of *E185*)

E189	14 November 1952	Home 11.40	Schools: Talks for Sixth Forms: (8) Seeing Things Vividly: A Place for Poetry The Villain
E190	17 November 1952	Home 14.20	Schools: Prose and Verse Reading A Night's Ride (extract from *The Autobiography of a Super-Tramp (A3)*); read by Philip Phillips
E191	1 March 1953	Wales 22.30	Dylan Thomas: Anthology arranged by Dylan Thomas: Child Lovers
E192	26 August 1953	Light 14.00	Old Folks' Corner Leisure
E193	20 September 1953	Home 17.30	Children's Hour Welcome to You Rich Autumn Days; Rich Days
E194	19 February 1954	BFEBS 15.15	English by Radio: What Did You Say? written and read by V. M. Huggins: Leisure
E195	26 February 1954	BFEBS 15.15	English by Radio (repeat of *E194*)
E196	4 March 1954	Home 17.15	When Visiting Wales The White Cascade
E197	28 March 1954	Home 18.30	Prelude to Spring A Great Time
E198	4 April 1954	Home 18.30	Prelude to Spring The Likeness
E199	11 April 1954	Home 18.30	Prelude to Spring Love's Caution
E200	23 May 1954	Home 18.30	In Story and Song The Two Lives; Leisure; Impudence
E201	31 May 1954	Light 14.00	Woman's Hour: Outside View Naomi Lewis reviews The Blessings of Old Age My Youth
E202	20 July 1954	Light 14.45	Break for Summer: Old Folks' Corner Leisure
E203	1 August 1954	Home 16.00	Ships and Voyages Dreams of the Sea
E204	11 November 1954	Midland 17.30	Children's Hour: I Saw Old Autumn; When Autumn's Fruit
E205	10 December 1954	BFEBS 15.30	English by Radio: Learn it by Heart (no 8) by T. Walton: Leisure
E206	17 December 1954	BFEBS 15.30	English by Radio: Learn it by Heart (repeat of *E205*)
E207	17 January 1955	Light 14.00	Woman's Hour: Quotation Club Leisure
E208	21 February 1955	Third 20.05	The Poetry Bookshop by Alida Monro: The Moon
E209	22 February 1955	Third 22.10	The Poetry Bookshop (repeat of *E208*)
E210	6 March 1955	Home 15.32	Voices Jenny Wren

E211	18 March	Overseas	Spring Gale
	1955	20.00	Dreams of the Sea
E212	10 April	European	The Tramp in English Literature
	1955	17.15	extract from *The Autobiography of a Super-Tramp (A3)* (in German)
E213	3 May		May Day
	1955		In May; Days too Short
E214	4 August	Third	The Poetry Bookshop (repeat of *E208*)
	1955	20.00	
E215	2 September	Light	Woman's Hour: Quotation Club
	1955	14.00	Dreams of the Sea
E216	4 September	Home	Children's Hour: Verse and Music
	1955	17.00	Venus
E217	25 September	Home	The Poetry Bookshop (repeat of *E208*)
	1955	16.30	
E218	9 October	Wales	In Manuscript
	1955	15.00	A Great Time
E219	17 October	Overseas	London Calling Asia: Lyric Interlude
	1955	13.25	A Great Time; read by Beth Boyd
E220	15 November	Home	Schools: Senior English II
	1955	14.20	Sheep
E221	20 November	Home	Portraits by Poets
	1955	22.25	Sweet Stay-at-Home
E222	11 December	European	English Lessons to German Listeners
	1955	18.15	School's Out; The Happy Child
E223	13 December	Home	Portraits by Poets (repeat of *E221*)
	1955	16.15	
E224	14 December	European	English Lessons to German Listeners
	1955	18.15	(repeat of *E222*)
E225	18 December	European	English Lessons to German Listeners
	1955	18.15	Leisure
E226	21 December	European	English Lessons to German Listeners
	1955	18.15	(repeat of *E225*)
E227	25 December	Overseas	London Calling Asia: Christmas Day Verse
	1955	13.45	The East in Gold; When Leaves Begin
E228	22 January	Overseas	Wild Sang the Evening Birds
	1956	13.15	Venus
E229	28 January	Overseas	Wild Sang the Evening Birds (repeat of *E228*)
	1956	09.45	
E230	18 March	Overseas	Portraits by Poets (repeat of *E221*)
	1956	07.30	
E231	20 March	Overseas	Portraits by Poets (repeat of *E221*)
	1956	12.15	
E232	23 March	Overseas	Portraits by Poets (repeat of *E221*)
	1956	14.30	
E233	25 March	Wales	Welsh Landscape
	1956	21.15	No Place or Time
E234	2 July	Home	The Distant Scene II
	1956	14.40	Tramps on Vacation (extract from *The Autobiography of a Super-Tramp (A3)*); read by John Glyn Jones

E235	26 July 1956	Light 21.30	The Pleasure's Mine (5th series) Leisure
E236	29 July 1956	Home 17.25	Children's Hour: High Welcome on the Hills The Rain
E237	17 September 1956	Overseas 14.25	London Calling Asia: Children in Verse The Two Children
E238	13 December 1956	North 17.30	Children's Hour Robin Redbreast
E239	25 January 1957	Overseas 16.15	The Echoing Air Leisure
E240	1 March 1957	Overseas 00.15	Think on These Things (8) The Moon
E241	3 March 1957	Overseas 23.15	The Pleasure's Mine (repeat of *E235*)
E242	29 March 1957	Overseas 00.15	Think on These Things (12) Sweet Child
E243	19 June 1957	Home 16.45	Indian Summer One Token
E244	16 January 1958	Home 22.45	Personal Choice by J. B. Priestley: The White Cascade
E245	26 January 1958	Overseas 00.30	Treasures of the Kingdom (5) Dreams of the Sea
E246	16 March 1958	Overseas 00.30	Treasures of the Kingdom (12) The Moon
E247	20 March 1958	Overseas 16.45	Treasures of the Kingdom (12) (repeat of *E246*)
E248	6 April 1958	Home 17.30	I got me Flowers Days too Short
E249	13 April 1958	European 19.45	extract from *The Autobiography of a Super-Tramp (A3)*
E250	17 April 1958	Home 17.30	Children's Hour: As I before my Cottage Door (1) by Gordon C. Glover: Jenny Wren
E251	15 July 1958	West 18.45	Sweet Refreshing Rain A Midsummer Night's Storm
E252	19 September 1958	Home 19.00	On Holiday Leisure
E253	30 September 1958	Home 17.25	Children's Hour: Welcome Autumn Rich Days
E254	5 October 1958	Overseas 14.45	Personal Choice (repeat of *E244*)
E255	28 March 1959	Wales 17.15	Children's Hour: Over the Border to Wales. Monmouthshire by Myfanwy Howell Leisure; Days that have Been
E256	1 June 1959	Overseas 20.45	From Strength to Strength (9) The Example
E257	6 June 1959	Overseas 03.45	From Strength to Strength (9) (repeat of *E256*)
E258	15 June 1959	Overseas 20.45	From Strength to Strength The Hour of Magic

E259	20 June 1959	Overseas 03.45	From Strength to Strength (repeat of *E258*)
E260	28 June 1959	West 17.30	Verse and Music My Garden
E261	20 July 1959	Home 17.00	Children's Hour: All Kinds of Creatures The Kingfisher
E262	21 July 1959	Light 14.01	Woman's Hour: Catching Joy as it Flies. Words and Music for July Seeking Joy
E263	2 December 1959	BFEBS 15.45	English by Radio: More about Andrew (7) by Thomas Walton: Leisure
E264	5 December 1959	BFEBS 15.45	English by Radio (repeat of *E263*)
E265	8 February 1960	Home 14.50	Schools: Prose and Verse Readings On the Road in America (extract from *The Autobiography of a Super-Tramp (A3)*) read by Richard Bebb
E266	26 June 1960	BFEBS 15.45	English by Radio: Listen and Teach (4) by F. G. French: Leisure
E267	5 August 1960	Overseas 14.30	Life and Letters by V. C. Clinton-Baddeley: Sheep; read by Peter Duval
E268	7 August 1960	Overseas 03.15	Life and Letters (repeat of *E267*)
E269	27 November 1960	BFEBS 15.45	English by Radio: Listen and Teach (1) by W. R. Lee: The Kingfisher
E270	21 May 1961	Home 17.00	Children's Hour: Come Hither The Moon; Clouds
E271	23 July 1961	Third 21.35	Georgian Poetry 1912–1922 by George MacBeth: A Child's Pet
E272	5 September 1961	Home 13.40	Readings on Record The Kingfisher; read by Carleton Hobbs
E273	20 September 1961	Home 20.42	The River of Life The Happy Child
E274	29 September 1961	TV (Wales) 13.05	Heddiw Leisure
E275	22 October 1961	Scottish 17.50	Poems chosen and read by Mary Riggans The Kingfisher
E276	26 November 1961	Home 17.00	Children's Hour: Come Hither A Strange Meeting
E277	31 January 1962	Light 14.00	Woman's Hour: Village Idiom Leisure
E278	19 August 1962	BBC. TV 22.10	Rhyme or Reason (2) The Inquest
E279	26 August 1962	Home 16.15	The Written Word The Rain; The Moon
E280	26 August 1962	BBC. TV 22.10	Rhyme or Reason (3) Armed for War
E281	29 August 1962	BBC. TV 22.11	Rhyme or Reason (2) Exits and Entrances The Inquest

E282	2 September 1962	BBC. TV 22.12	Rhyme or Reason (4) The Truth
E283	26 September 1962	Overseas 22.30	Welsh Magazine A Great Time
E284	11 November 1962	Home 21.00	Readings on Record by Martin Starkie The Kingfisher
E285	14 March 1963	Home 14.00	Schools: Adventures in English (9) Sheep
E286	22 March 1963	Home 15.30	A World of Sound: A Sort of Agony Derek Parker examines the art of writing
E287	25 June 1963	Light 14.00	Woman's Hour Leisure
E288	29 September 1963	Home 13.10	The Countryside in September The Starers
E289	4 November 1963	Home 10.30	Friends and Contemporaries Leisure
E290	16 March 1964	Home 14.30	Prose and Verse Reading A Tramp's Summer Vacation (extract from *The Autobiography of a Super-Tramp (A3)*)
E291	23 April 1964	Home 14.00	Schools: Adventures in English: There and back again. Strange Places Michael Baldwin introduces 'The Fog'
E292	20 June 1964	Home 23.30	Readings on Record Leisure
E293	13 July 1964	Home 16.45	Home this Afternoon Leisure
E294	8 September 1964	Home 16.15	How to stand still Leisure
E295	4 February 1965	Home 14.00	Schools: Adventures in English Dogs
E296	11 February 1965	Home 14.00	Schools: Adventures in English A Child's Pet
E297	20 February 1965	Home 19.30	Words and Music A Blind Child; The Rain
E298	5 April 1965	Home 11.30	Readings on Record Leisure; Sheep
E299	11 May 1965	Light 14.00	Woman's Hour: Contrasts in Poetry Patric Dickinson contrasts a poem by WHD on trees with another
E300	24 September 1965	Home 14.20	Schools: Bible and Life Sheep
E301	5 October 1965	Light 20.40	Souvenir Leisure; Poor Kings
E302	11 February 1966	Home 14.00	Schools: Stories and Rhymes Charity; The Rain
E303	11 October 1966	Home 07.50	Ten to Eight: By Request Leisure
E304	6 April 1967	Home 07.50	Ten to Eight: Private Collection (WHD recording)

E305	16 June 1967	Home 10.50	Poetry Corner Nailsworth Hill
E306	17 October 1967	Radio 4 07.50	Ten to Eight Leisure
E307	22 May 1968	Radio 4 07.40	Ten to Eight: Other Men's Shoes: The Character of a Happy Life
E308	3 August 1968	Third 18.50	Violet Gordon Woodhouse On Hearing Mrs Woodhouse play the Harpsichord
E309	14 November 1968	Radio 4 14.20	Poetry Corner The Cat
E310	22 January 1970	Third 20.30	The Georgians No 3: Harold Monro 1879–1932
E311	21 May 1970	Radio 4 14.00	Living Language: Near and Far III: Comings and Goings . . . Work A Strange Meeting
E312	12 July 1972	Radio 4 21.40	The Modern British Poems The Sleepers
E313	31 January 1975	Radio 3 20.15	Apprehensions: A Selection of Poems compiled by Patric Dickinson: The Two Children
E314	14 March 1975	Radio 3 21.15	Jack Young: A Personal Anthology The Kingfisher; A Great Time
E315	20 April 1975	Radio 3 21.50	Apprehensions (repeat of E313)
E316	1 June 1977	Radio 3 08.55	Rural Rhymes: Robin Holmes reads from Poets who have loved the English Countryside New-comers
E317	6 June 1977	Radio 3 13.05	Rural Rhymes (repeat of E316)
E318	1 January 1979	Radio 4 12.02	Give us a Kiss To a Sweet Mouthed Girl (clearly identified in the BBC's 'Programme as Broadcast' as WHD's but not in *Complete Poems (A51)*)
E319	1 June 1979	Radio 3 08.55	Rural Rhymes (repeat of E316)
E320	1 July 1979	Radio 3 08.55	Rural Rhymes Jenny Wren
E321	1 September 1979	Radio 3 08.55	Rural Rhymes Lamorna Cove
E322	1 December 1979	Radio 3 08.55	Rural Rhymes Winter's Beauty
E323	28 April 1980	Radio 4 11.50	Poetry Please presented by Charles Tomlinson; The Rain

notes:

(a) where there are gaps I was unable to trace the programme's transmission although royalties were paid to Mrs Davies by the BBC

(b) BFEBS is abbreviation of British Forces Educational Broadcasting Service

F Articles and books about or referring to WHD

F1 Boys stealing from shops, account of WHD and four other boys charged with stealing and given a sentence of birching and one day in prison, *Monmouthshire Merlin and South Wales Advertiser*, 25 January 1884, 8

F2 Lost His Foot, report of WHD's accident and amputation of right (incorrect) foot, *Renfrew Mercury*, Ontario, Canada, 24 March 1899

F3 It was the Writer's Mistake, correction to F2, *Renfrew Mercury*, 31 March 1899

(*note*: although these two articles have not been seen the dates are supported by two totally different sources: *W. H. Davies: A Critical Biography* by Richard Stonesifer (*F324*) and 'From a Doss-House to Parnassus' by Louis Blake Duff (*F190*))

F4 A Cripple Poet: Realistic and Whimsical Word Pictures: Curious Life History, *Daily Mail*, 22 July 1905, 3 (by A. St. John Adcock)

F5 The Crippled Poet, portrait, *Tatler*, 13 September 1905, XVII, 220, 384

F6 Political and Diplomatic I: The Unemployed, *English Review*, December 1908, I, 163

F7 *Nature Poems (A4)*, *TLS*, 22 October 1908, 367

F8 A Newport-Born Poet: Mr Wm H. Davies's Latest Book, *South Wales Argus*, 14 November 1908, (3)

F9 *Beggars (A5)*, *TLS*, 16 September 1909, 339

F10 The Making of a Poet, Stephen Gwynn, *Nineteenth Century and After*, January 1910, 67, 395, 65–78; *Living Age*, 21 May 1910, XLVII (7th series), 3437, 489–492

F11 William H. Davies: A Note, Edward Thomas, *Odd Volume*, 1910, 15–16

F12 'The Sluggard' quoted, *The Feminine Influence on the Poets* by Edward Thomas (Martin Secker 1910) 89

F13 *A Weak Woman (A7)*, *TLS*, 23 February 1911, 79

F14 Pension for Tramp Poet: W. H. Davies to Have £50 a Year – Conrad and Yeats Also Aided, *New York Times*, 7 July 1911, 1

F15 *Songs of Joy (A8)*, Books in Preparation, *Academy and Literature*, 14 October 1911, LXXXI, 2058, 484; Verse, *Academy and Literature*, 2 December 1911, LXXXI, 2065, 715; *Current Literature of the Month*, December 1911, 36 (new series) 218

F16 A Singer in Vagabondia, Milton Bronner, *Bookman*, November 1911, XXXIV, 3, 275–279

F17 The Poetry of William Henry Davies, James Guthrie, *The Elf: A Magazine of Drawing and Writing*, Pear Tree Press, Spring 1912, 37–42

F18 *The True Traveller (A9)*, *TLS*, 28 March 1912, 130

F19   Mr William H. Davies, Darrell Figgis, *Studies and Appreciations* (J M Dent & Sons 1912) 138–147

F20   *Georgian Poetry 1911–1912 (D2),* Georgian Poetry of the Twentieth Century, *Westminster Gazette,* 4 January 1913, 3; Georgian Poetry, Filson Young, *Living Age,* 18 January 1913, LVIII (7th series), 276, 185 (reprinted from *Saturday Review*); Georgian Poetry, *The Spectator,* 18 January 1913, 110, 4412, 107–108; Criticism, Henry Newbolt, *Poetry and Drama,* March 1913, I, 1, 45–52; An Elizabethan Poet and Modern Poetry, Walter de la Mare, *Edinburgh Review,* April 1913, 217, 444, 372–386; The New Poetry, Arthur Waugh, *Quarterly Review,* 1916, 226, 365–386

F21   *Foliage (A10), TLS,* 2 October 1913, 415; *Current Literature of the Month,* November 1913, 59 (new series), 196

F22   A Song to the Poets, poem by Will H. Ogilvie, *Westminster Gazette,* 8 December 1913, 2

F23   'Days that have Been' quoted, *The Country* by Edward Thomas (B T Batsford 1913) 1

F24   *The Literary Year Book,* 1914, 75

F25   Recent English Poetry, Martin D. Armstrong, *Fortnightly Review,* 2 March 1914, 95, DLXVII, 498–512

F26   *Nature (A11), TLS,* 26 March 1914, 155

F27   Two Poets of the Open Air: Norinah Gale and William Davies, V. G. Hartley, *Poetry Review,* May 1914, IV, 5, 253–255

F28   Notes on the Poets of To-day – III, Francis Bickley, *Westminster Gazette,* 6 June 1914, 2

F29   Current Poetry, *Literary Digest,* 19 September 1914, 49, 12 (1274), 517

F30   *The Bird of Paradise (A12), TLS,* 5 November 1914, 495; *Current Literature of the Month,* December 1914, 72, 178

F31   English Poetry, Harold Monro, *Poetry and Drama,* December 1914, II, 8, 375–383

F32   *The Literary Year Book,* 1915, 75

F33   *Georgian Poetry 1913–1915 (D7),* The World of Books, *Nation,* 27 November 1915, XVIII, 9, 329; The Georgians, *Nation,* 11 December 1915, XVIII, 11, 396–398

F34   *Georgian Poetry 1913–1915 (D7),* The Young Poets, Katharine Tynan, *Bookman,* February 1916, XLIX, 293, 164–165; Books: Georgian Poetry 1913–1915, *The Spectator,* 5 February 1916, 116, 4571, 190; The New Poetry, Arthur Waugh, *Quarterly Review,* 1916, 226, 365–386 (reprinted in *Living Age,* 9 December 1916, IV (8th series), 3779, 602–615)

F35   *The Literary Year Book,* 1916, 75

F36   *Child Lovers (A13), TLS,* 8 June 1916, 275; *Current Literature of the Month,* July 1916, 91, 79

F37   *Child Lovers* (2nd edition) *(A13a), Current Literature of the Month,* August 1916, 92, 90

F38   In the Pink, poem by Siegfried Sassoon, *Nation,* 28 October 1916, XX, 4, 146

F39   Some Poets of Today, S. P. B. Mais, *Nineteenth Century and After,* November 1916, 80, 477, 1008–1022

F40   *Collected Poems (A14), TLS,* 23 November 1916, 564; *Current Literature of the Month,* December 1916, 96, 139

F41   William H. Davies, *Studies of Contemporary Poets* by Mary C. Sturgeon (Harrap 1916) 53–71

F42   *The Literary Year Book*, 1917, 77

F43   *Nature Poems (A4), Books and Persons* by Arnold Bennett (Chatto & Windus 1917) 78; 325

F44   Noted English Poet Studies America as a Tramp: William H. Davies Begged His Way, Not to Write His Book About Us, but Because He Really Likes to Live a Tramp's Life, *New York Times (Magazine)*, 18 March 1917, VII, 9 (portrait)

F45   *Nature Poems* (3rd edition) *(A4b)*, *Current Literature of the Month*, February 1917, 98, 15

F46   News in Brief (Epstein bust presented to Newport), *The Times*, 27 February 1917, 3

F47   How They Do It: 2. Mr W. H. Davies I and II, *Tricks of the Trade* by J. C. Squire (Martin Secker 1917) 10–11

F48   Davies, William Henry, *Who's Who 1918* (A & C Black Ltd 1918) 612

F49   Mr W. H. Davies, portrait frontispiece by David Morris, *To-day*, January 1918, II, 11, facing 165

F50   *Georgian Poetry 1916–1917 (D12)*, The Georgians, *Nation*, 19 January 1918, XXII, 16, 518; Feelings and Words, W. H. Chesson, *Bookman*, April 1918, LIV, 319, 22–24; Latest Books of English Poets, Jessie Rittenhouse, *Bookman*, June 1918, XLVII, 4, 444–451; by E. Wm David, *Welsh Outlook*, July 1918, V, 55, 235; Once More the Georgians, John Gould Fletcher, *Poetry*, September 1918, XII, VI, 332–337

F51   Essays in Criticism: A Tramp Poet, W. M. Parkes, *Poetry Review*, 1918, IX, 231

F52   Tramp and Poet, George A. Greenwood, *Great Thoughts*, 20 April 1918, V (8th series), 1308

F53   W. H. Davies, portrait by Walter Sickert, *Art and Letters*, June 1918, I, 4, 129

F54   *Forty New Poems (A17)*, TLS, 3 October 1918, 470; *Current Literature of the Month*, November 1918, 119, 94

F55   Mr W. H. Davies, *Studies in Contemporary Literature* by H. G. Wright (Jarvis & Foster 1918) 29–68

F56   Life and Letters: Mr W. H. Davies, J. C. Squire, *Land & Water*, 3 October 1918, LXXII, 2943, 15

F57   William H. Davies b 1870 [sic], *Modern English Writers: Being a Study of Imaginative Literature 1890–1914* (Sidgwick & Jackson 1918) 129–131

F58   "Integer Vitae": As It Might Have Been Translated by W. H. Davies, Louis Untermeyer, *New Republic*, 21 December 1918, XVII, 216, 224

F59   To W. H. Davies, poem by Louis Golding, *Voices in Poetry and Prose*, April 1919, I, 2, 223

F60   The Chapbook and the Committee, Ezra Dove, *New Witness*, 5 September 1919, XIV, 357, 394

F61   Bibliographies of Modern Authors: W. H. Davies, *London Mercury*, November 1919, I, 1, 122–123

F62   A Modern Lyricist, *Letters to X* by H. J. Massingham (Constable & Co 1919) 278–286

F63   *Georgian Poetry 1918–1919 (D14)*, The Genteel Georgians, *Nation*, 6 December 1919, XXVI, 10, 338–340

F64   *Georgian Poetry 1918–1919 (D14)*, Is Poetry played out?, S. P. B. Mais, *John o'London's Weekly*, 3 January 1920, II, 39, 379; The Georgians at Home, Lola Ridge, *New Republic*, 11 January 1920, XVII, 219, 316; Books: The Georgian Poetry Book, 1918–1919, *The Spectator*, 31 January 1920, 124, 4779, 143; *To-day*, April 1920, VII, 38, 74; Anglo-Saxon Adventures in Verse, MVD, *Nation*, 26 June 1920, CX, 2869, 855a–b

F65   W. H. Davies, *A Bibliography of Modern Poetry With Notes on Some Contemporary Poets* compiled by Recorder, *The Chapbook*, June 1920, II, 12, 12–13

F66   *The Literary Who's Who*, 1920, 67

F67   lunch with WHD, *The First World War 1914–1918: Personal Experiences of Lieut – Col C. A. Court Repington* (Constable & Co 1920) vol I, 188–189

F68   Some Letters of Edward Thomas, Edward Garnett, *Athenaeum*, 16 April 1920, 501–503

F69   William H. Davies, portrait by Laura Knight, *Voices in Poetry and Prose*, June 1920, III, 5–6, facing (170)

F70   Edward Thomas's Letters to W. H. Hudson, James Guthrie, *London Mercury*, August 1920, II, 10, 434

F71   End Papers: Appalling Slaughter of Poets, Bernard Lintot, *To-day*, August 1920, VII, 42, 235–240

F72   Thumb-nail Appreciations: Yeats and W. H. Davies, L. C. Jacks, *Poetry of To-day: The Poetry Review New Verse Supplement*, September-October 1920, II, 5, 312

F73   *The Song of Life (A18)*, TLS, 9 September 1920, 587; *Current Literature of the Month*, October 1920, 142, 158

F74   End Pages: Personnel, *Voices in Poetry and Prose*, October 1920, IV, 4, 163

F75   *The Autobiography of a Super-Tramp* (5th edition) *(A3e)*, TLS, 25 November 1920, 781; *Current Literature of the Month*, December 1920, 144, 190

F76   The Prose of William H. Davies, Thomas Moult, *To-day*, December 1920, VIII, 44, 68–71

F77   *Collected Poems* (2nd impression) *(A14b)*, *Current Literature of the Month*, December 1920, 144, 194

F78   *Some Contemporary Poets (1920)* by Harold Monro (Leonard Parsons 1920) 21; 23; quoted, 70–75

F79   *The Literary Year Book*, 1921, 131

F80   Tramp Poet gets Pension. Britain Puts Davies on Civil List as Recognition of His Work, *New York Times*, 20 July 1921, 15

F81   W. H. Davies, portrait after a painting by Augustus John, *Now & Then*, September 1921, facing 16

F82   *The Londoner*, week ending 8 October 1921, 3

F83   *Farewell to Poesy* (Life & Colour Series) *(A6a)*, TLS, 3 November 1921, 719; *Current Literature of the Month*, November 1921, 155, 181

F84   *Nature Poems* (Life & Colour Series) *(A4c)*, *Current Literature of the Month*, November 1921, 155, 181

F85   William H. Davies, Thomas Moult, *Bookman*, November 1921, LXI, 362, 85–88 (illustrations) (reprinted as 'W. H. Davies, A Tramp Poet', *Living Age*, 24 December 1921, XXIV (8th series), 4042, 798–801)

F86   W. H. Davies: A Loved Poet, Herbert E. Palmer, *John o'London's Weekly*, 3 December 1921, VI, 139, 275 (portrait)

F87   *Songs of Joy* (Life and Colour Series) *(A8a)*, *TLS*, 15 December 1921, 846
F88   No 2: W. H. Davies, *Collected Parodies* by J. C. Squire (Hodder & Stoughton (1921)) 36–37
F89   The Rovers, *Parodies Regained* by "Evoe"; illustrated by Geo Morrow (Methuen & Co 1921) 86–91
F90   cartoon from *Parodies Regained* by "Evoe" captioned: 'Mr Ezra Pound and M [sic]/ W. H. Davies on the/ Underground', *Christmas Number of Bookman*, December 1921, LXI, 363, supplement 100
F91   The Golden Book, Harold Monro, *Christmas Number of Bookman*, December 1921, LXI, 363, 137–140

F92   *The Literary Year Book*, 1922, 769
F93   Wales and English Poetry, A. G. Prys-Jones, *Poetry Review*, 1922, XIII, 76–87
F94   W. H. Davies: A Case of Dual Personality, Theodore Maynard, *Our Best Poets English and American* (Henry Holt & Co 1922) 107–115
F95   A Bibliography of William Henry Davies, George Francis Wilson, *Bookman's Journal and Print Collector*, March 1922, V (new series), 6, 202 (also April, VI, 7, 29 and May VI, 8, 59)
F96   *Songs of Joy* (Life and Colour Series) *(A8a)*, *Current Literature of the Month*, January 1922, 157, 14
F97   *Child Lovers (A13)*, *Current Literature of the Month*, March 1922, 159, 13
F98   Modern Portraits II: W. H. Davies, portrait by E. Powys Evans, *London Mercury*, March 1922, V, 29, 577
F99   *The Soul's Destroyer* (re-issue of 3rd impression) *(A1d)*, *Current Literature of the Month*, March 1922, 159, 13
F100 William Henry Davies, Belle Cooper, *Los Angeles Times (Magazine)*, 2 April 1922, 8
F101 To William Henry Davies, poem by Belle Cooper, *Los Angeles Times (Magazine)*, 2 April 1922, 8
F102 W. H. Davies, *The Chapbook*, Poetry Bookshop, July 1922, 27, 7
F103 *The Hour of Magic (A20)*, *TLS*, 12 October 1922, 651; *Current Literature of the Month*, November 1922, 167, 15
F104 W. H. Davies, frontispiece by William Nicholson (from *The Hour of Magic*), *To-day*, December 1922, IX, 52, facing (41)
F105 The World of Books, HJM, *Nation and Athenaeum*, 9 December 1922, 32, 4832, 419
F106 *Georgian Poetry 1920–1922 (D21)*, Poets and Poetry: Georgian Poetry, A. Williams-Ellis, *The Spectator*, 16 December 1922, 129, 4929, 927

F107 The War and "The Georgians", *Modern American and British Poetry*, ed Louis Untermeyer; with suggestions for study by Olive Ely Hart (Harcourt, Brace & Co 1923) 225 (also: 'William H. Davies', 276–277)
F108 Companions, parody, *These Liberties* by E. V. Knox (Methuen & Co 1923) 129–130
F109 *Georgian Poetry 1920–1922 (D21)*, The Georgians, *Nation and Athenaeum*, 13 January 1923, XXXII, 15 (4837), 585
F110 *Foliage* (new revised edition, Life and Colour Series) *(A10a)*, *Current Literature of the Month*, January 1923, 169, 12
F111 *New Poems* (new edition, Life and Colour Series) *(A2b)*, *Current Literature of the Month*, January 1923, 169, 12
F112 *The Chapbook*, March 1923, 35, 3–4

F113   *Collected Poems: Second Series (A21), Current Literature of the Month*, May 1923, 173, 13

F114   Talks with Famous Writers: XXV – Mr W. H. Davies, R. L. Megroz, *Teachers World*, 9 May 1923, XXIX, 964, 300 and 321 (portrait)

F115   W. H. Davies, *Twenty-Four Portraits* by William Rothenstein (with Critical Appreciations by Various Hands: Second Series) (Chatto & Windus 1923) unpaginated (*note*: edition limited to 1500 copies))

F116   William Henry Davies, *Gods of Modern Grub Street: Impressions of Contemporary Authors etc* by A. St. John Adcock (Sampson Low, Marston & Co (1923)) 63–70 (portrait by E. O. Hoppe)

F117   *True Travellers (A22), Current Literature of the Month*, November 1923, 179, 24

F118   *Collected Poems: First Series (A14e), Current Literature of the Month*, December 1923, 180, 19

F119   *The Autobiography of a Super-Tramp* (reprint 1923) *(A3f)*, TLS, 6 December 1923, 853

F120   *Selected Poems (A23), TLS*, 27 December 1923, 911

F121   *Collected Poems (A21), Current Literature of the Month*, January 1924, 181, 14

F122   *Selected Poems (A23), Current Literature of the Month*, January 1924, 181, 14

F123   The Poems of the Month, selected by Margaret Widdemer, *Bookman*, February 1924, LVIII, 6, 649–651 ('The Two Stars')

F124   *Secrets (A24), Current Literature of the Month*, June 1924, 186, 19

F125   *The Muse in Council* by John Drinkwater (Houghton Mifflin Co 1925) 37; 302

F126   meets WHD, *More Changes, More Chances* by H. W. Nevinson (Nisbet & Co 1925) 178

F127   Old Age of a Georgian, *Babbling April* by Graham Greene (Basil Blackwell 1925) 19

F128   Poets in Revolt, EVL, *Punch*, 18 March 1925, 168, 292–293

F129   Spring in the Poets. Lovely Verses of the Happy Season, Robert Lynd, *John o'London's Weekly*, 21 March 1925, XII, 311, 911

F130   Personalities on Parnassus. Five English Poets of Established Fame, *John o'London's Weekly*, 27 June 1925, XIII, 325, 415 (portrait)

F131   Poetic Refusals (Mr W. H. Davies refuses to spend a night at the Ritz Hotel, London), poem, *Punch*, 19 August 1925, 169, 175

F132   "Wailing Winds and Naked Woods." The Poetry of Autumn in Town and Country, *John o'London's Weekly*, 3 October 1925, XIV, 339, 10 (portrait)

F133   *A Poet's Alphabet (A25), Current Literature of the Month*, November 1925, 203, 22

F134   correspondence re *Later Days (A26)* signed Max Beerbohm, TLS, 26 November 1925, 812

F135   The Innocent Abroad. The Early Adventures of W. H. Davies, Tramp and Poet, *John o'London's Weekly*, 28 November 1925, XIV, 346, 322

F136   Davies, William Henry, *Who's Who 1926* (A & C Black 1926) 740

F137   The New Poetry 1911–1925, Edward Shanks, *Quarterly Review*, January 1926, 246, 145 (reprinted in *Second Essays in Literature* (W Collins Sons & Co 1927) 106–125)

F138   W. H. Davies, *Authors Dead and Living* by F. L. Lucas (Chatto & Windus 1926) 198–204

F139   *The Autobiography of a Super-Tramp* (Travellers' Library) *(A3j)*, *TLS*, 29 April 1926, 326

F140   *The Bird of Paradise* (new edition) *(A12a)*, *TLS*, 29 April 1926, 327

F141   W. H. Davies: His Poetry, J. H. Swann, *Papers of the Manchester Literary Club*, 1926, 52, 54–63

F142   background, *Herman Melville* by John Freeman (Macmillan Co 1926) 87

F143   Songs of Rapture. Modern Poets and the Glories of Spring, *John o'London's Weekly*, 19 March 1927, XVI, 413, 852

F144   *A Poet's Pilgrimage* (Travellers' Library) *(A15a)*, *TLS*, 29 September 1927, 670

F145   *Later Days* (Travellers' Library) *(A26d)*, *TLS*, 29 September 1927, 670

F146   W. H. Davies: His Poetry, D. R. Lock, *Holborn Review*, October 1927, 483–490

F147   Bibliographies of Modern Authors: No III: W. H. Davies Part I, Gwendolen Murphy, *London Mercury*, November 1927, XVII, 97, 76–80 (also January 1928, XVII, 301–304 (Part II) and April, XVII, 684–688 (Part III))

F148   *A Poet's Calendar (A30)*, *Now & Then*, Autumn 1927, 25, 18

F149   *Movements in Modern English Poetry and Prose* by Sherard Vines; introductory note by G. S. Gordon (Oxford University Press 1927) quoted, 28–30; 'The Meadow' quoted, 120; bibliography, 340

F150   *A Survey of Modernist Poetry* by Laura Riding and Robert Graves (William Heinemann 1927) 200–201

F151   An Edward Thomas Revival: A Great Welshman Who Loved Wales: Poet, Essayist and Mystic, Geraint Goodwin, *Welsh Outlook*, November 1927, XIV, 11, 297–298

F152   Davies, William Henry, *Who's Who*, 1928 (A & C Black 1928) 760

F153   Poetry: 6. Nature Poetry, *Twentieth Century Literature 1901–1950* by A. C. Ward (Methuen & Co 1928) IV; 182–186

F154   W. H. Davies, portrait from a drawing by Frank E. Slater, *Christmas Number of Bookman*, December 1928, LXXV, 447, facing 164

F155   *Selected Poems (A35)*, *TLS*, 22 November 1928, 914

F156   Man and Super-Tramp – W. H. Davies: His Life and Work, Samuel J. Looker, *Bookman's Journal . . . Print Collector*, 1928, XVI, 7, 363–370

F157   W. H. Davies: An Appreciation, I. A. Williams, *Now & Then*, Winter 1928, 30, 32–33

F158   W. H. Davies: A Nature Poet, *Five More Famous Living Poets* by Coulson Kernahan (Thornton Butterworth 1928) 20

F159   W. H. Davies, His Later Bibliography, 1922–1928, Samuel J. Looker, *Bookman's Journal . . . Print Collector*, 1929, 17, 10, 123–127

F160   Mr William Henry Davies, MP, *Everyman*, 28 February 1929, 1, 5, 6

F161   Some Poems and Verse, V. H. Friedlander, *Country Life*, 13 April 1929, LXV, 1682, 523–524

F162   *Ambition (A36)*, *Life and Letters*, November 1929, III, 18, 472

F163   Mr W. H. Davies: The Poet Who Abandoned Security to become a Beggar, Robert Lynd, *John o'London's Weekly*, 21 December 1929, XXII, 557, 468 (portrait)

F164   illustration by John Austen from *The Fortunes and Misfortunes of the Famous Moll Flanders* by Daniel Defoe (introduction by WHD), *Special Christmas Number of Bookman*, December 1929, supplement 12 and 13

F165   *Postscript to Adventure* by Ashley Gibson (J M Dent & Sons 1930) 37; and a dog, 49–50

F166   W. H. Davies, *Poetry at Present* by Charles Williams (Clarendon Press 1930) 78–81

F167   W. H. Davies, *Chief Modern Poets of England and America*; selected and edited by Gerald DeWitt Saunders and John Herbert Nelson (Macmillan Company 1930) 129–131

F168   The Poetry of W. H. Davies, Lawrence W. Hockey, *Great Thoughts*, January 1930, VIII, 2406, 183–184 (portrait)

F169   *Jewels of Song (B3)*, TLS, 2 October 1930, 783

F170   The Humble Home of a Wizard with the Pen. Where Newport's Poet was Born, FJH, *South Wales Argus*, 29 October 1930, 3

F171   *The Autobiography of a Super-Tramp* (Life & Letters Series) *(A3t)*, TLS, 30 October 1930, 894

F172   notice of civic luncheon at Newport, *The Times*, 31 October 1930, 16 (at which WHD read his favourite poem: 'Days that have been')

F173   "Sweet is the Smile of Home". The Tramp Poet Comes Back Home. W. H. Davies Feted in Town of His Birth, *South Wales Argus*, 30 October 1930, 1 and 6

F174   Mr W. H. Davies, drawing by Raphael Nelson, *Special Christmas Number of Bookman*, December 1930, LXXIX, 471, 219

F175   Poète-vagabond, Louis Bonnerot, *Revue Anglo-Américaine*, February 1931, 208–220

F176   Davies, William Henry, *Who's Who*, 1932 (A & C Black 1932) 814

F177   *Men and Memories* by William Rothenstein (Faber & Faber 1932) vol II: 1900–1922; 341

F178   The "Georgian Poets," or Twenty Years After, Wilfrid Gibson, *Bookman*, September 1932, LXXXII, 492, 280–281

F179   *Discovery* by John Drinkwater (Ernest Benn 1932) 230

F180   *The Letters of D. H. Lawrence*, ed Aldous Huxley (William Heinemann 1932) autograph for, 127; 130; 135; agrees to visit DHL in Italy, 146; DHL on, 151–152, 164; *Nature Poems (A4)*, 174

F181   *Laughing Torso* by Nina Hamnett (Roy Long & Richard R Smith 1932) 98–99

F182   *The Journals of Arnold Bennett 1911–1912*, ed Newman Flower (Cassell & Co 1932) 251

F183   *Recent Poetry 1923–1933*, edited with an introduction by Alida Monro (Gerald Howe Ltd & Poetry Bookshop 1933) vii

F184   W. H. Davies, *Men of Monmouthshire* by L. Twiston Davies FSA (*Western Mail & Echo* 1933) vol II; 195–201 (photograph of oil painting by Harold Knight)

F185   W. H. Davies: A Monmouthshire Poet, Rev T. W. Griffiths, *Monmouthshire Review*, January 1933, I, 1, 28–42

F186   Some Monmouthshire Characters, John Kyrle Fletcher, *Monmouthshire Review*, April 1933, I, 2, 112–121

F187   illustration by Hilda M. Quick from *My Birds (A39), Bookman*, April 1933, LXXXIV, 499, supplement, 71

F188   *Modern English Poetry, 1882–1932* by R. L. Megroz (Ivor Nicholson & Watson 1933) 179

F189   William H. Davies, *Aspects of Modern Poetry* by Edith Sitwell (Duckworth 1934) 90–98

F190   From a Doss-House to Parnassus, Louis Blake Duff, *Colophon*, 1934, 5, 19, chapter/ article 3

F191   *Modern Writers and Playwrights: W. H. Davies* by Thomas Moult (Thornton Butterworth 1934) (review: 'A Poet Displayed', *TLS*, 23 August 1934, 575)

F192   English Poetry Since Brooke, L. A. G. Strong, *Nineteenth Century and After*, October 1934, 116, 692, 460–468

F193   Davies, William Henry, *Who's Who*, 1934 (A & C Black 1934) 840

F194   Pre-War Poets, *The Georgian Literary Scene* by Frank Swinnerton (Hutchinson & Co 1935) and Georgian Poetry, 265, 267, 285, 287; and Walter de la Mare, 274

F195   The Wheel of Life: Poet's Pub, Colophon, *John o'London's Weekly*, 29 June 1935, XXXIII, 846, 459 (portrait)

F196   *The Birth of Song (A44)*, A Bookman's Diary, Colophon, *John o' London's Weekly*, 26 September 1936, XXXV, 911, 918

F197   *John Freeman's Letters* by John Freeman (Macmillan & Co 1936) 188

F198   W. H. Davies, *Letters from Limbo* by Ernest Rhys (J M Dent & Sons 1936) 216–218

F199   *Life is My Song: The Autobiography of John Gould Fletcher* (Farrar & Rinehart 1937) Georgian poets, 61

F200   Edward Thomas's Letters to W. H. Hudson, *To the Memory of Edward Thomas* by James Guthrie (Pear Tree Press 1937) 21–31

F201   *The Time of Yeats: English Poetry of Today against an American Background* by Cornelius Weygandt (D Appleton-Century Co 1937) and fees, 15; 23; 255; and animals, 330; background and poetry, 344–351; 356; 397; 410

F202   The Life and Works of W. H. Davies, K. J. Rider, read at a meeting of Birmingham and District Branch of Library Association and Midland Division of Association of Assistant Librarians Section, Stafford, 11 March 1937 (10pp typed mss held at NL)

F203   *Edward Thomas: A Biography and a Bibliography* by Robert P. Eckert (J M Dent & Sons/ E P Dutton & Co 1937) his letters to ET offered for sale, xiii; W. H. Hudson's copy of *The Autobiography of a Super-Tramp (A3)* offered for sale, xiv; acknowledgement to, xviii; meets ET, 79; given financial help by ET and friends, 79–80; *The Soul's Destroyer (A1)* reviewed by ET in *Daily Chronicle*, 80; and *The Pocket Book of Poems and Songs for the Open Air (D1)*, 80, 89 and 90; ET and the preparation of *The Autobiography of a Super-Tramp (A3)*, 80; proposal that GBS contribute an introduction, 80–81; GBS consents, 81; W. H. Hudson on *The Autobiography of a Super-Tramp (A3)*, 81; ET on *New Poems (A2)*, 81; and Edward Garnett's lunches, 96; Ashley Gibson and the dog, 97; meets Walter de la Mare, 97; his tribute to ET, 99; *The Autobiography of a Super-Tramp (A3)* reviewed by ET, 110; joins *Literary World* and later, *TP's Weekly*, 120; 'Killed in Action (Edward Thomas)' quoted, 133; critiques ET's poems, 159; and *The Flowers I Love (D8)*, 168; *Child Lovers (A13)*, 174; last meeting with ET, 177

F204   Two Readings, *Radio Times*, 10 September 1937, 90 (portrait)

F205   Author's Parade (3), caricature, *John o'London's Weekly*, 10 June 1938, XXXIX, 1000, front cover (key 350)

F206   Poetry and Otherwise, C. E. Lawrence, *Quarterly Review*, July 1938, 271, 537, 162

F207   The W. H. Davies Plaque: Plans for Newport Unveiling, *South Wales Argus*, 1 September 1938, 7

F208   Tramp Poet of Gwent: To be Honoured by His County, Lawrence W. Hockey, *South Wales Argus*, 21 September 1938, 8 (pen picture)

F209   Where the Walls have Diamond Eyes: Mr W. H. Davies at House where He Was Born: Plaque unveiled in his honour, *South Wales Argus*, 22 September 1938, 1

F210   W. H. Davies Fight: How Poet Won His Fame, Lawrence W. Hockey, *South Wales Argus*, 22 September 1938, 8 (photograph of plaque on wall of Church House, Newport)

F211   *Post Victorian Poetry* by Herbert Palmer (J M Dent & Sons 1938) lyrical, 53; 71; and *Tramp*, 72; and *Rhythm*, 72; *Shorter Lyrics of the Twentieth Century (B2)*, 73; and Georgian poets, 79, 81, 90, 197; 'The Kingfisher', 82–83; 'The Heap of Rags', 93; Gibson and, 136–145; 'The Moon' quoted, 185; 186; parody of, 200; 218; 344

F212   Poet honoured by his birthplace: Poet Laureate's Tribute to W. H. Davies commemorative plaque unveiled at Newport, *The Times*, 23 September 1938, 9

F213   Poets and the Crisis, *The Times*, 26 September 1938, 13

F214   *The Victorians and After 1830–1914* by Edith Batho and Bonamy Dobree (Cresset Press 1938) poetry, 153; Georgians, 221; bibliography, 253

F215   W. H. Davies, sketch by Jack Stark, *Welsh Review*, February 1939, I, 1, 15

F216   *A Number of People: A Book of Reminiscences* by Edward Marsh (William Heinemann/ Hamish Hamilton/ Harper & Bros 1939) 287; tea with, 297; breakfast with, 300; 325; 'The Kingfisher', 345

F217   Davies Fits the Modern Dilemma, Petronius Applejoy, *Catholic World*, September 1939, 673

F218   *The Life and Letters of Edward Thomas* by John Moore (William Heinemann 1939) meets ET, 125; *The Soul's Destroyer (A1)*, 125, 141, 299; broken wooden leg, 133–134; *The Autobiography of a Super-Tramp (A3)*, 140; 148; and the Mont Blanc restaurant, 178; parody, 182; 190; and Poetry Bookshop, 201; 316; 317

F219   *Selections From Modern Poets* selected and edited by Maurice Wollman MA (Macmillan & Co 1939) viii

F220   Georgian Poetry, *Poetry and the Modern World: A Study of Poetry in England Between 1900 and 1939* by David Daiches (University of Chicago Press 1940) 38–60

F221   *New Poets from Old: A Study in Literary Genetics* by Henry W. Wells (Columbia University Press 1940) a lyric poet, 23, 155, and 209; diction in lyrics, 77; poetry of, 238–245; his reading, 238; paraphrases Latin lyricists, 249; relation to Herrick, 241–243; 247; 251; 265

F222   W. H. Davies The Man and His Work, Richard Church, *Fortnightly Review*, January 1940, 147, 80–86 (reprinted in *Eight for Immortality* by Richard Church (J M Dent & Sons 1941) 1–12; dedicated to WHD with a portrait frontispiece of him)

F223   To W. H. Davies on his Collected Poems, poem by G. Rostrever Hamilton, *The Observer*, 28 April 1940, 6

F224   postcard with a photograph of WHD's cottage at Nailsworth, Gloucester-shire and the poem 'Nailsworth Hill' signed 'W H DAVIES'

F225   Bernard Shaw's "Super-Tramp". Noted Newport-Born Poet W. H. Davies Dead. He held a Mirror to Nature, *South Wales Argus*, 26 September 1940, 3 (photograph)

F226   Mr W. H. Davies The "Tramp Poet", *The Times*, 27 September 1940, 7

F227   W. H. Davies 'One of the Immortal Writers', *South Wales Argus*, 27 September 1940, 5

F228   A Tribute by Mr J. Kyrle Fletcher, *South Wales Argus*, 27 September 1940, 5

F229   letter signed Charles A. Watts re publication of *The Soul's Destroyer (A1)*, *The Times*, 2 October 1940, 5

F230   Mr W. H. Davies: A Further Tribute, *The Times*, 3 October 1940, 9

F231   W. H. Davies 1870 [sic]-1940, Richard Church, *The Listener*, 3 October 1940, XXIV, 612, 478

F232   A Bookman's Diary, tribute by Colophon, *John o'London's Weekly*, 4 October 1940, XLIV, 1121, 14

F233   In Memoriam, Desmond MacCarthy, *New Statesman and Nation*, 12 October 1940, XX, 503, 352–353 (includes 7 extracts from WHD's poems)

F234   obituaries: William H. Davies Welsh Hobo Poet: Writer Who Roamed America 'Hopping' Freights Dies in Gloucestershire Home: The Author of 50 Books: His First Volume of Verse Won from G. B. Shaw Favorable Word to Literary Friends, *New York Times*, 27 September 1940, 23; Mr W. H. Davies: "The Tramp Poet", *The Times*, 27 September 1940, 7; *Daily Telegraph*, 27 September 1940, 5; W. H. Davies, E. H. W. Meyerstein, *TLS*, 5 October 1940, 508

F235   Earth-Lover, poem by E. H. W. Meyerstein, *TLS*, 5 October 1940, 508

F236   W. H. Davies: The Tramp Poet, Herbert Palmer, *John o'London's Weekly*, 11 October 1940, XLIV, 1122, 34–36

F237   W. H. Davies, poem by John Gawsworth, *John o'London's Weekly*, 11 October 1940, XLIV, 1122, 35

F238   W. H. Davies, S. P. B. Mais, *Country Life*, 26 October 1940, LXXXVIII, 2284, 373

F239   He tramped the road to Beauty, T. W. Mercer, *Millgate*, November 1940, 103–107 (illustrations, also 'The Rain' and 'The Wind')

F240   Farewell (In Memory of W. H. Davies), poem by Lawrence W. Hockey, *Poetry Review*, November-December 1940, XXXI, 6, 446

F241   *The Best Poems of 1940* selected by Thomas Moult; decorated by Elizabeth Montgomery (Jonathan Cape 1940) dedicated to the memory of WHD

F242   *Wales England Wed* by Ernest Rhys (J M Dent & Son 1940) his accident, 170–171; 'Leisure' quoted, 171

F243   *Pleasures and Speculations* by Walter de la Mare (Faber & Faber 1940) 202; 218

F244   *The Long Week-End* by Robert Graves and Alan Hodge (Faber & Faber 1940) and *Country Life*, 23; Georgian Poetry, 53; 435

F245   Davies, William Henry, *Who Was Who*, 1929–1940 (A & C Black 1941) 338

F246   *Magic Casements* by Eleanor Farjeon (George Allen & Unwin 1941) 42

F247   Homage to W. H. Davies at Rest, poem by Arthur Shirley Cripps, *Poetry Review*, May–June 1941, XXXII, 3, 138

F248   *Common Joys (A48)*, *TLS*, 9 August 1941, 380 and 388

F249   Autolycus Inc, *TLS*, 9 August 1941, 383

F250   W. H. Davies (1870 [sic]-1940), *Modern British Poetry: A Critical Anthology*, ed Louis Untermeyer (Harcourt, Brace & Co 1942 (5th revised edition)) 184–190

F251   W. H. Davies, poem by John Gawsworth, *The Best Poems of 1941* selected by Thomas Moult (Jonathan Cape 1942) 48

F252   W. H. Davies, poem by E. H. W. Meyerstein, *The Best Poems of 1941* (F251) 49

F253   The Simple Philosopher, Martin Armstrong, *The Listener*, 16 July 1942, XXVII, 705, 84–85 (illustrations)

F254   A Character of the Late W. H. Davies, Osbert Sitwell, *Life and Letters Today continuing London Mercury and Bookman*, July 1942, 34, 59, 2–12 (also August, 60, 81–91 and September, 61, 156–171)

F255   W. H. Davies: Cousin of Sir Henry Irving, *South Wales Argus*, 6 August 1942, 4

F256   W. H. Davies and Henry Irving, Lawrence W. Hockey, *South Wales Argus*, 14 August 1942, 4

F257   W. H. Davies: 1871–1940, *British Authors: A Twentieth Century Gallery* by Richard Church (for British Council, Longmans Green & Co 1943) 58–61 (portrait by Dame Laura Knight)

F258   Portrait of My Friend, Richard Church, *John o'London's Weekly*, 31 December 1943, L, 1223, 125

F259   The Diamond Ring, Samuel J. Looker, *American Notes and Queries*, 1943, 2 (on 'The Trance')

F260   background, *A Critical History of English Poetry* by Herbert J. C. Grierson and J. C. Smith (Chatto & Windus 1944) 492

F261   Irving and W. H. Davies, letter signed Lawrence W. Hockey, *TLS*, 5 February 1944, 67

F262   Irving and W. H. Davies, letter signed Osbert Sitwell, *TLS*, 12 February 1944, 79

F263   Men and Women 2: W. H. Davies, Caradoc Evans, *Welsh Review*, September 1944, III, 3, 183–186

F264   "The Soul's Destroyer and Other Poems": The First Book of W. H. Davies, Lawrence W. Hockey, *Poetry Review*, July-August 1945, 36, 3, 143–148

F265   W. H. Davies "The Tramp Poet", *Monmouthshire Writers: A Literary History and Anthology* by W. J. Townsend Collins (R H Johns 1945) 94–98 (with photograph of the Epstein bust) also see 'Lawrence William Hockey', 132–135 (includes 'Farewell (In Memory of W. H. Davies)')

F266   dinner with, *Bookman's Holiday: A Recreation for Booklovers* by Holbrook Jackson (Faber & Faber 1945) 151

F267   Writers I have known V: Darrell Figgis and W. H. Davies, *Confessions of an Un-Common Attorney* by Reginald L. Hine (J M Dent & Sons 1945) 161–164

F268   letter, signed Lawrence W. Hockey, *TLS*, 20 April 1946, 187

F269   W. H. Davies and His Family, Lawrence W. Hockey, *Welsh Review*, Autumn 1946, V, 3, 191–195

F270   Gwent's Greatest Poet: The Background to the Genius W. H. Davies, Lawrence W. Hockey, *South Wales Argus*, 11 October 1946, 3

F271   *The Reading of Books* by Holbrook Jackson (Faber & Faber 1946) 'Leisure', 103; subjective, 162

F272   W. H. Davies's First Book in London, Lawrence W. Hockey, *South Wales Argus*, 23 April 1947, 4

F273   The Tramp Poet's First Volume: Suffered Many Hard Days to Pay Printers, Lawrence W. Hockey, *South Wales Argus*, 7 May 1947, 2

F274   Edward Thomas, Athalie Bushnall, *Poetry Review*, August 1947, XXXVIII, 4, 241–251

F275   W. H. Davies's Manuscript for Newport, Lawrence W. Hockey, *South Wales Argus*, 25 November 1947, 3

F276   *Red Wine of Youth: A Life of Rupert Brooke* by Arthur Stringer (Bobbs-Merrill Co 1948) the Georgians, 118, 121, 128; at Sevenoaks, 186; lectures, 187

F277   W. H. Davies, *Fifty Years 1898–1948* (Gerald Duckworth & Co for private circulation 1948) 21 (13 lines)

F278   Edward Thomas and W. H. Davies, Lawrence W. Hockey, *Welsh Review*, Summer 1948, VII, 2, 81–91

F279   *Kent* by Richard Church (Robert Hale (1948)) *The Soul's Destroyer (A1)*, 83; Edward Thomas and the cottage, 83; 'The Example' quoted, 83

F280   The Georgian Poets, Alan Pryce-Jones, *Penguin New Writing* (Penguin Books 1948) 91–100

F281   W. H. Davies 1871–1940, *A Dictionary of Cat Lovers* compiled by Christabel Aberconway (Michael Joseph 1949) 113–115

F282   *Laughter in the Next Room* by Osbert Sitwell (Macmillan & Co 1949) 56

F283   Great Gloucestrians, *Gloucestershire* by Kenneth Hare (Robert Hale (1949)) 174–182

F284   W. H. Davies put some of his own story in his first novel, Lawrence W. Hockey, *South Wales Argus*, 2 March 1949, 4

F285   W. H. Davies Poem Challenges Record of Smith Brothers: A Ten-Foot Boat Sailed the Atlantic, Lawrence W. Hockey, *South Wales Argus*, 24 August 1949, 4

F286   W. H. Davies and Edward Thomas 1905–1907, Lawrence W. Hockey, *Poetry Review*, October-November 1949, XL, 5, 333–339

F287   W. H. Davies Composes, poem by John Gawsworth dated Nailsworth, December 19, 1931, *Poetry Review*, October-November 1949, XL, 5, 339

F288   To W. H. Davies (On first visiting Liswery), poem by Neville Penry Thomas; To W. H. Davies (In Memory), poem by John Gawsworth; Farewell (In Memory of W. H. Davies), poem by Lawrence W. Hockey, *Monmouthshire Poetry: An Anthology of Poetry Relating to the County or Composed by Writers associated with Monmouthshire* (R H Johns (1949)), 70, 81 and 108 respectively

F289   Davies, William Henry (1871–1940), *Dictionary of National Biography*, 1931–1940 (Oxford University Press 1949) 213–215

F290   W. H. Davies, *Noble Essences or Courteous Revelations* by Osbert Sitwell (Macmillan & Co 1950) 207–244

F291   *The Letters of Ezra Pound*, ed D. D. Paige (Harcourt, Brace & Co 1950) impressed by poetry reading, 81

F292   Pedlar of Poems, poem by Noel Scott, *Sunday Times*, 23 April 1950, 6627, 6

F293   Ten Years Ago Today One of Newport's Greatest Sons Died..., Lawrence W. Hockey, *South Wales Argus*, 26 September 1950, 5 (portrait)

F294   Shaw Could see "a Real Poet" in W. H. Davies, Lawrence W. Hockey, *South Wales Argus*, 25 November 1950, 4

F295   Shaw "Named" the Autobiography for W. H. Davies, Lawrence W. Hockey, *South Wales Argus*, 27 November 1950, 4

F296   *100 Years of English Literature* by Sherard Vines (Duckworth & Co 1950) *The Autobiography of a Super-Tramp (A3)*, 131–132; and Georgian Poetry, 174; 177

F297   W. H. Davies: The Super-Tramp, *Some I knew Well* by Clifford Bax (Phoenix House 1951) 64–68 (photograph of Augustus John portrait)

F298   Early Days of W. H. Davies, Lawrence W. Hockey, *South Wales Argus*, 3 February 1951, 4

F299   Anglo-Welsh Poetry, A. G. Prys-Jones, *Dock Leaves*, May 1951, II, 5, 5–9 (reprinted from *British Weekly*)

F300   *Crisis in English Poetry* by Vivian de Sola Pinto (Hutchinson's University Library 951) 120; *The Soul's Destroyer (A1)*, 128–129; and Georgian Poetry, 130–1; *Collected Poems (A14)*, 213 (review: Margaret Willy, *English*, 1951, IX, 48, 290–291)

F301   The 'Super-tramp' is still remembered by Sevenoaks friends: Stories of a Modest Poet, *Sevenoaks Chronicle*, 7 September 1951, 3 (illustration)

F302   *Autobiography of a Super-Tramp* (school edition) *(A3oo)*. TLS, 21 December 1951, 826

F303   letter signed Richard Stonesifer, *TLS*, 28 December 1951, 837

F304   *The Life and Works of D. H. Lawrence* by Harry T. Moore (George Allen & Unwin 1951) 58

F305   *Chiaroscuro* by Augustus John (Jonathan Cape 1952) AJ on, 151–152

F306   Welsh Poets: W. H. Davies, *Quite Early One Morning* by Dylan Thomas (J M Dent & Sons 1954) 145–147 ('The Inquest' quoted, 145; 'The Bust' quoted, 147)

F307   Friendship's Romancer, Richard Church, *Country Life*, 16 June 1955, CXVII, 3048, 1549 (illustration of Harold Knight portrait)

F308   Nature Poetry, *Twentieth-Century Literature 1901–1950* by A. C. Ward (Methuen & Co 1956) 185

F309   *Edward Thomas: A Critical Study* by H. Coombes (Chatto & Windus 1956) 11

F310   Memories of a Poet's Wife, Mrs Lascelles Abercrombie, *The Listener*, 15 November 1956, LVI, 1442, 793–794 (portrait)

F311   *The Romantic Survival: A Study in Poetic Evolution* by John Bayley (Constable 1957) 202

F312   W. H. Davies, *Famous Men and Women of Wales* by Beryl M. Jones; illustrated by Margaret Blundell (Wrexham, Hughes A'I Fab (1957)) vol II; 5–17

F313   *Edward Thomas: The Last Four Years: Book One of the Memoirs of Eleanor Farjeon* (Oxford University Press 1958) *Foliage (A10)*, 12; lunch with, 38; at Selsfield House, 47; 103; 139; 146; his wooden leg, 175; 199

F314   *Teaching Poetry* by James Reeves (William Heinemann 1958) 'The Rabbit', 65, 82

F315   *Edward Marsh: Patron of the Arts: A Biography* by Christopher Hassall (Longmans 1959) 189, 205–207, 209, 236, 244, 272–273, 286, 'The Kingfisher', 193; meets D. H. Lawrence, 235; Lawrence on, 260; *The Bird of Paradise (A12)*, 267 and 362; quarrel with Gosse, 341; EM and Gosse on, 366–367; criticisms of, 377–378 and 380; on the Brooke Memoir, 446; 'Lovely Dames', 475; benefit from the Brooke Memorial Fund, 461–462; celebration of Brooke's *Collected Poems*, 461; meets Blunden, 492; *The Loneliest Mountain (A45)*, 619; *Nation* on, 687

F316   W. H. Davies, *The Atlantic Book of British and American Poetry* ed Dame Edith Sitwell (Victor Gollancz 1959) vol II; 816–819

F317   *Robert Frost: The Trial by Existence* by Elizabeth Shepley Sergeant (Holt, Rinehart & Winston 1960) 'The Example' quoted, 134; lyricist, 143–144; 297

F318   *Ezra Pound* by Charles Norman (Macmillan & Co 1960) and Georgians, 103

F319   background, *A Short History of English Poetry 1340–1940* by James Reeves (William Heinemann 1961) 211

F320   *The Garnett Family* by Carolyn G. Heilbrun (George Allen & Unwin 1961) *Later Days (A26)* quoted, 85

F321   "Georgians", *Religious Trends in English Poetry: Vol V 1880–1920* by Hoxie Neale Fairchild (Columbia University Press 1962) 345–391 (also: his influence on James Stephens, 274)

F322   The So-Called Georgian Poets, Richard Church, *Poetry Review* (new series), Summer 1962, LIII, 3, 154–157

F323   Georgian Poetry 1912–1922, George MacBeth, *London Magazine* (new series), June 1962, 2, 3, 74–80

F324   *W. H. Davies: A Critical Biography* by Richard Stonesifer (Jonathan Cape 1963)

F325   The Discovery of W. H. Davies, Helen Thomas, *The Times*, 27 March 1963, 12

F326   *Selected Letters of Robert Frost*, ed Lawrence Thompson (Holt, Rinehart & Winston 1964) RF on, 105, 116–117, 122–124, 136, 139, 184

F327   W. H. Davies, Laura Knight, *Cornhill*, Winter 1964/1965, 1042, 282–292 (illustration)

F328   *English Poetry of the First World War: A Study in the Evolution of Lyric and Narrative Form* by John H. Johnston (Princeton University Press 1964) and Georgian Poetry, 4; narrative poetry, 8

F329   *Rupert Brooke: A Biography* by Christopher Hassall (Faber & Faber 1964) RB visits at Sevenoaks, 373; 451

F330   *The Voyage Home* by Richard Church (William Heinemann 1964) *The Autobiography of a Super-Tramp (A3)*, 4–5, 14; Civil List pension, 40; visits RC, 44–47; meets RC, 80; 164; 191; and Edmund Blunden's poem 'Almswomen', 192

F331   *Understanding Poetry* by James Reeves (William Heinemann 1965) 'In the Country' quoted, 166–167

F332   *The Georgian Revolt 1910–1922: The Rise and Fall of a Poetic Ideal* by Robert H. Ross (Southern Illinois University Press 1965) x; 12; 77; and

Georgian Poetry, 100–101, 108, 112–113, 115, 145; 'The Kingfisher', 101, 239; as a nature poet, 116, 228–231; and pre-war vitality, 118, 240; poetic diction of, 124; 'Days too Short' quoted, 124; and *Chapbook*, 169; and *Owl*, 182; parody of, 195; 'Confession' quoted, 229; 'Wasted Time' quoted, 229; 'Down Underground' quoted, 229–230; 'The Truth' quoted, 230

F333   *Robert Frost: Life and Talks-Walking* by Louis Mertins (University of Oklahoma Press 1966) and Little Iddens, 130

F334   *Siegfried Sassoon: A Critical Study* by Michael Thorpe (Universitaire Pers Leiden/ Oxford University Press 1966) *The Mercury Book of Verse (D64)*, 56; 149; 227; 271; 'The Sleepers' quoted, 155

F335   *Harold Monro and The Poetry Bookshop* by Joy Grant (Routledge & Kegan Paul 1967) a lyricist, 29, 208; and *Rhythm*, 34; and *Poetry Review*, 48; and Poetry Bookshop, 63; and poetry readings, 82; and *Chapbook*, 138, 142; and Georgian Poetry, 232, 257; a Georgian poet, 261

F336   *Seeing to the Heart, English and Imagination in the Junior School* by Marie Peel (Chatto & Windus 1967) 'The Cat' quoted, 41; *The Autobiography of a Super-Tramp (A3)*, 235

F337   *The Handsomest Young Man in Britain: Rupert Brooke* by Michael Hastings (Michael Joseph 1967) 'School's Out' quoted, 10; breakfast with, 59

F338   The Tramp Poet and The So-Called Georgian Poets, *Speaking Aloud* by Richard Church (William Heinemann 1968) 120–126 and 127–132 respectively

F339   *Letters from Edward Thomas to Gordon Bottomley*, edited and introduced by R. George Thomas (Oxford University Press 1968) 10, 28, 53, 108, 126, 198; and ET, 11, 24–26, 29, 105, 115, 117, 136, 141, 183, 197, 222, 227; *The Soul's Destroyer (A1)*, 94, 102, 135–136; ET on, 102–103, 130, 179, 209–210, 233; his *New Poems (A2)*, 124, 127–128, 145; and Shaw, 124, 142; *The Autobiography of a Super-Tramp (A3)*, 164; *Nature Poems (A4)*, 179; *Farewell to Poesy (A6)*, 209; *A Weak Woman (A7)*, 209; *The True Traveller (A9)*, 209; a pension for, 210; stays with the Thomases, 218; his biography by Stonesifer, 233; and Hodgson, 243; *Later Days (A26)*, 265; and poetry readings, 266–267

F340   *Commitment to Poetry* by James Reeves (William Heinemann 1969) natural poet, 13

F341   Davies, William Henry, 1871–1940, *A Bibliography of British Literary Bibliographies* by T. Howard Hill (Oxford University Press 1969) 302

F342   The Georgians, *A Map of Modern English Verse* by John Press (Oxford University Press 1969) 4; 111; 114–115; 'The Inquest' quoted, 123; 'The Cat' quoted, 124; 'A Woman's History' quoted, 125; 'Earth Love' quoted, 125; 'Lovely Dames', 146

F343   William Henry Davies 1871–1940, *A Bibliography of Anglo-Welsh Literature, 1900–1965* by Brynmor Jones (Wales and Monmouthshire Branch of Library Association 1970) 22–25

F344   *Edward Thomas: A Critical Biography* by William Cooke (Faber & Faber 1970) ET and, 5–51; and Poetry Bookshop, 64–65; WHD on ET's poetry, 87, 197–198; and Georgian Poetry, 92; 95

F345   W. H. Davies, Lawrence W. Hockey, *Writers of Wales* (University of Wales Press on behalf of Welsh Arts Council 1971) (portrait frontispiece of photograph of a medallic portrait of WHD by Theodore Spicer-Simson)

F346   Centenary of a Super-Tramp, Patrick O'Leary, *The Times*, 4 March 1971, Wales, supplement II (photograph of Epstein bust of WHD and Lawrence Hockey)

F347   Remembering the Tramp Poet, Richard Church, *Country Life*, 24 June 1971, CXLIX, 3863, 1598–1599 (illustration)

F348   Post Office First Day Cover to celebrate the WHD Centenary (1871–1971) 5 July 1971

F349   The Inn Steps of a Super-Tramp, Sybil Hollingdrake, *South Wales Argus*, 5 July 1971, 6

F350   Farewell: In Memory of W. H. Davies, poem by Lawrence W. Hockey, *South Wales Argus*, 5 July 1971, 6

F351   *Robert Frost: The Years of Triumph 1915–1938* by Lawrence Thompson (Jonathan Cape 1971) RF visits, 335–336

F352   W. H. Davies: The Man, Lawrence W. Hockey, *Anglo-Welsh Review*, Spring 1972, 20, 46, 135–138

F353   Farewell (In Memory of W. H. Davies), poem by Lawrence W. Hockey, *Anglo-Welsh Review*, Spring 1972, 20, 46, 139

F354   Tribute to W. H. Davies (1871–1971), Alison J. Bielski, *Anglo-Welsh Review*, Spring 1972, 20, 46, 140–141

F355   The Soul's Destroyer: W. H. Davies's First Book, Lawrence W. Hockey, *Anglo-Welsh Review*, Spring 1973, 22, 49, 58–68

F356   My Memory of W. H. Davies, Helen Thomas (Tregara Press 1973) (*note*: limited to 150 copies, number 71 seen)

F357   Davies (8) William Henry (1871–1940), *Chambers Biographical Dictionary* (W & R Chambers 1974) 359

F358   W. H. Davies, *Helen Thomas: Time and Again: Memoirs and Letters,* ed Myfanwy Thomas (Carcanet 1978) 87–90

F359   *A History of the Gregynog Press* by Dorothy A. Harrop (Private Libraries Association 1980) *Selected Poems (A35)*, 48; *The Lovers' Song Book (A41)*, 82–83, 116, 125, 199–200, 224; *The Lovers' Song Book* prospectus, 232

F360   Atticus note re *Young Emma (A52)*, *Sunday Times*, 26 October 1980, 32

F361   Let's polish up the Name of our Hero, Sybil Hollingdrake, *South Wales Argus*, 10 November 1980, 4

F362   *Young Emma*, PJF, *UKC Library Staff Newsletter*, November 1980, 61, 1–4

F363   *The Super-Tramp in Monmouthshire* by Sybil Hollingdrake (printed by George Selwyn, Aberdare (1981))

F364   Alms and the Supertramp: Nineteen unpublished letters from W. H. Davies to Edward Thomas, William Cooke, *Anglo-Welsh Review*, 1982, 70, 34–39

F365   W. H. Davies: The Tramp who became a Literary Legend, Simon Appleyard, *This England*, Spring 1983, 24–27

F366   *Poetry Wales: W. H. Davies*, ed Cary Archard (Poetry Wales Press 1983) 18, 2 (*contents*: p5 W. H. Davies: a chronology; p7 six poems by W. H. Davies; p15 photos; p25 W. H. Davies: The True Traveller by Sybil Hollingdrake; p46 'Songs of Childhood, Birds and Flowers' by Jonathan Barker; p57 'Immortal Moments': Edward Thomas and W. H. Davies by R. George

Thomas; p67 portraits; p73 W. H. Davies and Contemporary Artists by Fiona Pearson; p80 The Poetry of W. H. Davies; p89 A Bibliography of W. H. Davies; *contains*: p7 The Lodging House Fire; p9 The Kingfisher; p10 The Sea; p11 Body and Spirit; p12 The Heap of Rags; p13 The Inquest)

F367   Freshly Scrubbed Potato, *Required Writing: Miscellaneous Pieces 1955–1982* by Philip Larkin (Faber & Faber 1983) 164–167

F368   Portrait of a Super-Rustic, E. M. Palmer, *Western Mail*, 25 April 1985, 11 (portrait)

F369   'Authentic W. H. Davies', Lawrence Normand, *Poetry Wales*, 1985, 21, 2, 68–77

F370   *Edward Thomas: A Portrait* by R. George Thomas (Clarendon Press 1985) friendship with ET, 126–131, 138–139, 163, 166, 173, 175, 197, 214, 248, 280; *New Poems (A2)* published, 133; financial aid for, 140; ET questions on love poems, 173; Civil List pension, 175; and 'Walking Tom', 213; and ET's foreword to *Cloud Castle*, 295; and ET's 'The Outcast', 300; ET champions, 307–308; *The Autobiography of a Super-Tramp (A3)*, 129, 141, 146

F371   Vagrant Poet: George Bernard Shaw's protégé W. H. Davies, William E. Lee, *Country Quest*, December 1988, 31 and 36

F372   *Elkin Mathews: Publisher to Yeats, Joyce, Pound* by James G. Nelson (University of Wisconsin Press 1989) *New Poems (A2)*, 91; mentioned, 125; origin of title for *Foliage (A10)*, 191; royalties paid on *Foliage*, 191

F373   Poet among Painters, Colin Campbell, *Country Life*, 19 April 1990, CLXXXIV, 16, 180 and 182 (illustration and portraits)

F374   Autobiography for a Change: W. H. Davies's *Autobiography of a Super-Tramp* and *Young Emma*, Lawrence Normand, *New Welsh Review*, Summer 1990, III, 1, 29–33

F375   'To Stand and Stare', Editor's column, *New Welsh Review*, Summer 1990, III, 1, 33 (photograph of new 9-foot bronze statue of W. H. Davies by Paul Bothwell Kincaid for Newport's Commercial Street)

F376   Sculpture honours Poet, *South Wales Argus*, 12 December 1990, 9

F377   Honour for Tramp Poet who crossed a Continent. Wanderer who became a Literary Giant, Mario Basini, *Western Mail*, 14 December 1990, 10 (portrait)

F378   'Challenging' New Landmark, *South Wales Argus,* 15 December 1990, 1 (photograph of Paul Bothwell Kincaid's statue of WHD)

F379   poster produced by Nailsworth Civic Society to celebrate 50th anniversary of the death of WHD at Nailsworth, 26 September 1940 (illustration from *The Hour of Magic (A20)*), advertising a programme to be held on Friday 28 September 1990 with readings by David Goodland, a first performance of settings of poems with music by Michael Hurd and presentation to the town of a new WHD sculpture by David John

F380   poster published by Nailsworth Town Council to celebrate Nailsworth Centenary 1892–1992, using the poem 'Leisure' with a separate caption: '*An artistic impression of Nailsworth from/ Watledge Hill by Terry Thomas/ Poem taken from "The Complete Works* [sic] *of W H Davies"/ published by Jonathan Cape/ W H Davies lived in Nailsworth from 1930 until/ his death in 1940/ Printed by Barry Hathaway Printers Nailsworth*'

F381   official programme, with historical notes, to celebrate Nailsworth Centenary 1892–1992; advertisement for item *F380*, 36

Index of titles and first lines of poems

(titles are shown in italics)

His car was worth a thousand pounds and more, *A39, 42, 47, 51, 53, D130, 169*

His chin went up and down, and chewed at nothing, *A36, 42, 47, 48, 51, 53, D163*

His constant wonder keeps him back *A17, 19, 21, 51, 53*

His Throne A43, 47, 51, 53

Holly on the Wall, The A17, 19, 33, 42, 47, 51, C143

Home A1

Homeless Man, The A2, 51

Hope Abandoned A2, 33, 42, 47, 51

Hospital Waiting-Room, The A13, 33, 42, 47, 50, 51, 53, C115, D163, 172

Hour of Magic, The A20, 21, 23, 27, 33, 34, 42, 47, 51, 53, C184, D110, E27, 142, 258

House Builder, The A6, 51, C23

How bleak and cold the air is now – *A30, 33, 34, 42, 47, 48, 51, 53*

How can she safely walk this earth, *A4, 51*

How I do love to sit and dream *A4, 14, 33, 34, 42, 47, 51*

How I have watched thy coming, Spring, *A18, 19, 21, 33, 42, 47, 51, E130*

How Kind is Sleep A18, 19, 21, 33, 42, 47, 51, C162

How kind is sleep, how merciful: *A18, 19, 21, 33, 42, 47, 51, C162*

How Late A16, 17, 19, 21, 51

How Many Buds C184

How many buds in this warm light *A20, 21, 23, 33, 42, 47, 51, C184, D21*

How many plates of crumbs, my little friend, *A39, 42, 47, 51*

How many years since I, a wandering man, *A39, 42, 47, 51*

How often in my dreams have I beheld *A24, 33, 42, 47, 51, 53*

How rich hath Time become through her, *A12, 14, 33, 42, 47, 51, C104, E130*

How sad a face this Knowledge wears! *A36, 42, 47, 51, C258, D86*

How sad my life had been were't not for her, *A6, 33, 42, 47, 51*

How slowly moves the snail, that builds *A20, 21, 33, 35, 42, 47, 50, 51, 53, C185, D86*

How softly now my Days go by – *A45, 47, 51, C293*

How Sordid is this Crowded Life A33, 42, 47, 51

How sordid is this crowded life, its spite *A26, 33, 42, 47, 51, C224*

How strange is this: I cannot pass this wood *A15*

How strange that Love should be like this *A41, 43, 47, 51*

How sweet is Life, how beautiful, *A24, 33, 42, 47, 51, D58*

How sweet this morning air in spring *A12, 33, 42, 47, 51, C104, D19, 37, 47, E75, 84, 157*

How those wet tombstones in the sun *A24, 33, 42, 47, 51, 53*

Hunt, The A15, 33, 42, 47, 51, 53, C84

Hunters, hunters *A30, 33, 42, 47, 48, 51, 53, D115, 198*

Hunting Joy A36, 42, 47, 51, C258, D86

I am a jolly tramp: I whine to you, *A2, 33, 42, 47, 51*

I am as certain of my song, *A44, 47, 51, 53, D163*

I am haunted by wonderful places – *A38, 42, 47, 51, 53, C267, E107*

I am the Poet Davies, William A33, 42, 47, 51, 53, D137, 163, 172, E31, 64, 108

I am the Poet Davies, William, *A15, 33, 42, 47, 51, 53, D137, 163, 172, E31, 64, 108*

I ask no time when sunrise is *C30*

I ask not of high tide or low, *A8, 51, C30*

I bought my Love some cherries red. *C13*

I brought two friends to share my fire, *A44, 47, 51, 53*

I cannot see the short, white curls *A6, 33, 42, 47, 51*

I climb a tree to bring them down – *A25, 33, 42, 47, 51*

I Could not Love Him More A33, 42, 47, 51

I could not love him more *A22, 33, 42, 47, 51*

I count my pounds as three times two, *A43, 47, 51, 53*

General index

(titles of books, major articles and periodicals are shown in italics)

Richmond, John *D3*
Rickword, Edgell *A23*
Rider, K. J. *F202*
Ridge, Lola *F64*
Riding, Laura *F150*
Riggans, Mary *E275*
Ritchie, A. M. *A23*
Rittenhouse, Jessie B. *A14a, F50*
River Diary D126
RNIB *A3*
Robert Frost: The Trial by Existence F317
Robert Frost: Life and Talks-Walking F333
Robert Frost: The Years of Triumph F351
Roberts, Denys Kilham *D85, 96*
Roberts, Michael *A43, 44*
Robin Redbreast D40
Romance of the Echoing Wood, The BI 7
Romantic Survival, The F311
Ross, Robert H. *F332*
Rothenstein, William *chronology, A14, 14a, F115, 177*
Round About Nine D190
Round About Ten D192
Routledge & Kegan Paul Ltd *F335*
Rowbotham, David *A52*
Rowland, Brian *E25, 135*
RPA Annual C227
Rungs of the Ladder C272
Rupert Brooke F329

Sackville-West, Edward *E113*
Sackville-West, Vita *A24, 28*
Sadler, M. T. H. *D13*
Salisbury, Sylvia *D83*
Sampson Low, Marston & Co *F116*
Sanders, Beryl *D183*
Sangorski, F. *A16*
Sargeant, Elizabeth Shepley *F317*
Sassoon, Siegfried *A20, F38, 334*
Saturday Review A20, 22, 26, 33, 51a, F20
Saturday Review of Literature A8a, 26c, 44a
Saunders, Dennis *D188*
Saville, Malcolm *D112*
Say It Aloud D184
Sceptre Books *A52c*
Schauffer, Robert H. *A19*

Schofield & Sims Ltd *D156, 157, 158, 160*
School C168
Schucking, Levin L. *D67*
Scotland, Andrew *D89, 127, 128*
Scotsman A52
Scott, Lady Sybil *D10*
Scribner's Magazine A33b
Seafarer's Education Services *D151*
Secker, Martin *D20, 94, F12, 47*
Second Essays in Literature F137
Secrets A24, F124
Seed, Rev T. A. *A6*
Seeing to the Heart F336
Selected Letters of Robert Frost F326
Selected Poems (1923) A23, 120, 123
Selected Poems (1928) A35, F155, 359
Selected Poems (1985) introduction, A1, 53
Selections from Modern Poets D20, 101, F219
Selwyn & Blount Ltd *D11*
Selwyn, George *F363*
Sesame Books *A48*
Sevenoaks Chronicle F301
Seymour, W. Kean *D15, 16, 22*
Shades of Green D207
Shakespeare, William *C124, E8, 12*
Shanks, Edward *A25, 33, 43, F137*
Shannon, Sheila *D177, E26, 137*
Sharpley, Ada *D24*
Shaw, George Bernard *chronology, A1, 3, 3c, 3d, 3e, 3i, 3t, 3dd, 3nn, 3qq, 3rr, 3yy, 52, F203, 225, 339, 371*
Shaw, Mrs George Bernard *chronology, A3*
Shiel, M. P. *A37*
Shorter, Clement K. *chronology*
Shorter Lyrics of the Twentieth Century B2, F211
Sickert, Walter *F53*
Sidgwick & Jackson *D6, F57*
Siegfried Sassoon F334
Silver Ship, The D71
Simpkin, Marshall, Hamilton, Kent & Co Ltd *BI 2, 3*
Simpson, Joseph *C32*
Sitwell, Dame Edith *chronology, A20, D149, E185, 186, 188, F189, 316*
Sitwell, Osbert *chronology, A49a, 49b, 51, 51a, F254, 262, 282, 290*
Slater, Frank E. *F154*